THE HOUSE WITH A HUNDRED GATES

The HOUSE with a HUNDRED GATES

Catholic Converts Through the Ages

JOHN BEAUMONT

Foreword by Joseph Pearce

Angelico Press

First published in the USA
by Angelico Press 2022
Copyright © John Beaumont 2022

For information, address:
Angelico Press, Ltd.
169 Monitor St.
Brooklyn, NY 11222
www.angelicopress.com

paper 978-1-62138-891-3
cloth 978-1-62138-892-0

Book and cover design
by Michael Schrauzer

CONTENTS

The House With a Hundred Gates

BY JOSEPH PEARCE

I HAVE KNOWN THE AUTHOR OF THIS BOOK for many years. He is a good friend and trusted colleague. For more years than I care to remember he has been a columnist for the *St. Austin Review*, the Catholic cultural journal of which I am the editor. And yet, we have much more in common than our friendship and working relationship. He and I are both converts to the Faith, though he beat me to the punch, being received into the Church in 1980, nine years earlier than my own reception. As converts, he and I have always been fascinated by other converts, and by their conversion stories. This fascination has inspired us both to write extensively on the subject. I have written a book called *Literary Converts* and penned biographies of some of the great convert writers, such as G.K. Chesterton, Roy Campbell, and Oscar Wilde. Mr. Beaumont's column for the *St. Austin Review* is called "Roads to Rome," which was also the title of his compendious book on notable British and Irish converts to the Faith published in 2010. Four years later, he published a companion volume, *The Mississippi Flows Into the Tiber*, a comprehensive study of notable American converts. There is little doubt that the diligence and extent of his research makes him the leading expert on the history of Catholic converts in the English-speaking world. Clearly, Mr. Beaumont's works are well worth reading and studying!

Roads to Rome and *The Mississippi Flows Into the Tiber* were encyclopedic in scope, offering brief biographical entries, arranged alphabetically by surname, on hundreds of notable converts, many of them unknown to most of us, but all of whom we should know. Imagine a Catholic version of the *Oxford Dictionary of National Biography* or the *Chambers Biographical Dictionary*, and you get the idea. To put the matter plainly, both of Mr. Beaumont's earlier groundbreaking and foundational volumes are priceless reference works that should be an essential part of any reputable scholar's library.

The present volume builds on these earlier works, delving deeper into the stories of some of the better-known converts, while also surprising us with intriguing accounts of interesting converts of whom we might not be aware. In the case of the better-known converts, Mr. Beaumont offers many a provocative and thought-provoking insight. Take for instance the two chapters on Evelyn Waugh: the first recounts Waugh's path to Rome; the second praises his tradition-oriented stance (especially with respect to the liturgy) in the face of the destructive modernist innovations masquerading under the mask of the so-called "spirit of Vatican II." Evelyn Waugh was indeed a fighter, and Mr. Beaumont praises him for his pugilism.

Crossing the Pond, we find ourselves in the company of Ernest Hemingway, a quirkily idiosyncratic American so far removed from the quintessentially English Waugh that it could be said the abyss separating them is wider than the Atlantic itself. Yet they are both converts to the Faith, illustrating that the roads that lead to Rome begin in all sorts of places and in all sorts of psyches. Hemingway was as uncomfortable with life as any of the characters of his novels, and, as it turns out, he was equally uncomfortable with the Faith he had adopted. Mr. Beaumont looks Hemingway in the eye and asks him (and us) whether he was a real Catholic, or not. He weighs up the evidence, revisits it, then passes judgment.

Mr. Beaumont is particularly on form when discussing "deathbed conversions and near misses"—to quote the title of one of his chapters. Especially striking is his discussion of the mystery surrounding the deathbed conversion (or not) of the poet Wallace Stevens. Then comes the deathbed conversion (or, allegedly, not) of Oscar Wilde. As probing and provoking as ever, Mr. Beaumont asks of the enigmatic Wilde whether he was a convert, a revert, or neither.

There is a penetrative depth to many of the essays—to which, in view of the sheer range of converts, is added great breadth as well. The whole spectrum is here. There are actors, poets, novelists, philosophers, historians, communists, journalists, musicians, martyrs, puritans and priests; there is a mother of priests and nuns, and there are members of the Royal Family. There is the man who was converted by Galileo, and two converts whose path to Rome was enlightened by their admiration for Jane Austen—the admirable Miss Austen being that most "catholic" of non-Catholic writers.

One of the high points of the book (a true feather in Mr. Beaumont's cap) is the inclusion of Maurice Baring, whom Mr. Beaumont describes as "the neglected third of three." What an apposite description of this unconscionably underrated genius! The "three" to whom Mr. Beaumont refers are G. K. Chesterton, Hilaire Belloc, and Maurice Baring, who were not only great friends but were immortalized in a famous group portrait by Sir James Gunn. Most educated Catholics, when they see this portrait, will recognize the seated figure of Chesterton; many will recognize Belloc; but few will recognize Baring, "the neglected third of three." He was, however, a highly celebrated and widely read novelist between the two world wars, as well as being a fine poet. His neglect is indeed unwarranted and scandalous.

The same could be said of the neglect of Sir James Gunn, the artist who painted the famous group portrait! A convert to the Faith, he was one of the greatest painters of the last century, who deserves much more renown.

With characteristic candor, the final chapter asks yet another provocative question: *Does the Catholic Church Still Want to Make Converts?* The answer depends on whether the Church wants to move the world, or whether it merely wants to move with it (to paraphrase Chesterton). The converts who form the subject of this important volume were moved by a Church that sought to move the world. And they became in turn the sort of Catholics who moved the world themselves. Mr. Beaumont is himself the sort of Catholic who wants to move the world. In writing this wonderful book, we might hope that he will succeed in doing so.

PREFACE

ON MARCH 5, 1980, I WAS RECEIVED INTO THE
Catholic Church by Father John Twist, SJ. This was the culmination of several years of thinking about whether to take
this particular step. That was a personal matter, but the whole
question of conversion itself and its parameters can be and
should be approached on a general level. It is not surprising that,
as a convert myself, I became very interested in that process.
For example, certain particular issues were important for me in
deciding whether to become Catholic. But were these the same
for all people? As will be seen, a rather roundabout route led to
a life-changing move, enabling me to research these questions
in some detail. This experience acted as yet another example
of the application on a personal level of the old Portuguese
saying, "God writes straight with crooked lines" (*Deus escrive
certo por lignas tortas*).

At school I was always interested in science, but classics and
Western literature and history were always taught better in my
experience. So that was the route I took. It led eventually to the
law and, providentially, a great interest in proof and the law of
evidence, which of course proved useful in assessing such things
as the case for the Resurrection of Christ, but also dangerous in
that the temptation was to believe that one's own devices had
led to the Catholic Church and to ignore the crucial matter of
God's grace.

However, to return to science, many years later I discovered
the writings of the late, great priest-physicist Fr. Stanley Jaki,
OSB. Being rather cheeky, I wrote to him and thus there began
a correspondence between us. This led me to work with him for
five years, until his death in 2009. Fr. Jaki was the most focused
person I have ever met, which in part accounts for his over 50
published books and over 350 published articles. The areas of
his expertise were many and included much more than science.
He was a hard task master, but he taught me many things about
science and the crucial question of the true relationship between

science and religion. In methodology, he also taught me the importance of going back to the original sources.

On the topic of converts, Fr. Jaki believed that the Church seemed to have lost to some extent its zeal for evangelization. He was greatly saddened by this. Hearing that I was a convert myself, he wanted to know all about how I came to the Church. He then immediately pressed upon me the importance of stressing again the importance of the Catholic Church, if she was truly the one ark of salvation, continuing to gain converts to the Faith. He himself had done much work in this field, notably in his writings on one of the greatest of all converts, St John Henry Newman, in particular his *Newman to Converts* (2001), a detailed study of Newman's advice to prospective converts.

Fr. Jaki's encouragement led me to research the history of the conversion process from the period of the Reformation until the present day. The main concern in each case was to explore the reasons given for conversion. As a result of my research I ended up writing three booklets on converts, one on notable twentieth-century converts (2006), one on notable nineteenth-century converts (2007), and one on notable Jewish converts (2007). These were introductory works, but led to much more exhaustive research on the subject, culminating in two very detailed books, both published in the United States: *Roads to Rome* (2010) (together with its supplement published in 2016) and *The Mississippi Flows Into the Tiber* (2014). The first of these books examines notable British and Irish converts, the second notable American converts. There is in preparation a third volume covering other countries of origin. In addition, I have written articles on several notable individual converts, primarily in the *Downside Review*, the *Catholic Herald*, *Culture Wars* magazine, and the *Saint Austin Review*.

The two last-mentioned books were in the nature of encyclopedias of notable converts in the English-speaking world, with an emphasis on apologetics. Some classic works of this kind are still read today, notably of course that of Newman under the appropriate title *Apologia pro Vita Sua*. But many such accounts have been forgotten, and a major goal of both books was to resurrect the genre, a particular mark of which was the presentation of powerful arguments for the Faith, valuable to those considering whether to convert today, even though one must emphasize the role of divine grace in any conversion.

The present book seeks to give a more personal account of a number of notable converts. It is not just the arguments for entering the Church that are important. Equally valuable, and often very moving, are the essentially human stories of lives lived in great adversity and the overcoming of difficult circumstances in order to, as so many converts express it, come home to one's true resting place. These frequently inspire others and lead to more conversions than even well-reasoned arguments.

The book begins with a chapter based on a lecture I gave in New York, investigating the primary reasons generally given by converts for leaving their previous religious beliefs, if any, and cleaving to the Catholic Church. These reasons are many, but I submitted that ten are especially common. These are listed with examples given. Names most likely to be mentioned as influences behind conversion are John Henry Newman, Thomas Aquinas, and perhaps most often and most remarkably of all (since he himself never became a Catholic), C. S. Lewis.

The specific conversion stories that follow encompass a total of thirty-eight chapters, portraying a remarkable variety of accounts of the journey to the house of truth, from every place on earth, proceeding, as the phrase goes, "through hundred gates." These inspiring stories stem from persons from all kinds of backgrounds: novelists, actors, philosophers, priests, historians, communists, scientists, and poets. There is a chapter dealing with royalty and two with deathbed conversions.

Chapter forty, the final chapter of the book, deals with a question of great contemporary importance: whether the Catholic Church still wants to make converts. It contrasts the classic and traditional approach to conversion, illustrated specifically by the experience of Newman, as the acceptance of the Catholic Church as the one true fold of Christ the Redeemer, the one ark of salvation, with a disturbing relaxation of this requirement and its replacement by a much wider criterion. Under this the attempt to convert people has even been spoken of as a sin. The book concludes with a refutation of the latter approach and a restatement of the classic position.

An excellent account of the impact of conversion stories of this more traditional kind was given to me after I had finished writing *Roads to Rome* and the manuscript had been sent off to the publisher. The latter had the book proofed by a very educated and careful proofreader (one Cathy—I never did find out her surname). She found, in the words of the representative of the publisher, "a fair amount of the smallest stuff, and a few things that are easily missed but could be embarrassing (e.g. 'convent' for 'convert')." "But," he went on, "unlike the other jobs she's done for me, she felt constrained to comment on the text, which I'm sending to you herewith." Here is what she wrote:

> Here is the proofed material in *Roads to Rome*. I have to tell you—at the midway point I was simply gob-smacked by these personal stories, and by the consistency of their reasons for moving to Catholicism. Dry historical facts such as the number of priests who were hung, drawn and quartered at Tyburn in Elizabeth's time completely obscure the actual story behind most of them—I had no idea (gaps in my education?) that most of these guys went first to France for seminary/college and then *volunteered* for the "English mission"—returning to England and risking a horrendous death in order to preach and bring the sacraments to recusant Catholics.
>
> One after another, a steady line of incredible faith. It blows me away... so I say: HEY!! Let's get those intercessory prayers going. We have on tap a wealth of saints who have suffered more than we can ever know, in addition to more modern men and women who have fought their own battles with family and society during their journey back home. For me, even from childhood, the Litany of the Saints has felt like a direct connection to all of them, and I always feel transported when praying it. I thought that as a publisher, you might like some feedback on the impact one of your offerings had on at least one person!

As one who has spent some twenty years looking into accounts of conversions, and compiled several hundreds of them—constraints of space enforced a quite strict selection process for both previous books—I can only endorse what she says, and what follows is a detailed examination of the most interesting (for both reasoned analysis and individual personality) of the conversion stories that I have been privileged to come across.

This book is dedicated to St. Margaret Clitherow and to St. Edmund Campion, two great English converts and martyrs.

All errors and omissions in *The House With a Hundred Gates* are down to me and to me alone.

John Beaumont
Yorkshire
England

Feast of the Forty Martyrs of England and Wales

October 25, 2022

The Church is a house with a hundred gates:
    and no two men enter at exactly the same angle.
                                     (G. K. Chesterton)

God's grace! What a mystery!
                       (Archbishop Fulton J. Sheen)

The sages have a hundred maps to give
That trace their crawling cosmos like a tree,
They rattle reason out through many a sieve
That stores the sand and lets the gold go free:
And all these things are less than dust to me
Because my name is Lazarus and I live.
                               (G. K. Chesterton)

Why chuse we then like Bilanders to creep
Along the coast, and land in view to keep,
When safely we may launch into the deep?
In the same vessel which our Saviour bore
Himself the Pilot, let us leave the shoar,
And with a better guide a better world explore.
                                    (John Dryden)

(A bilander is a small boat hugging the English coastline)

CHAPTER ONE
Converts to Rome

WHO ARE THEY AND
HOW DO THEY GET THERE?

WHY DO PEOPLE CONVERT AND BECOME CATH-
olics? Who are they and where do they come from? Well, the
present writer's impression, from having read the conversion
stories of hundreds of people and having met many converts, is
very straightforward. They come in all shapes and sizes, and for
all sorts of reasons. In the words of G. K. Chesterton, one of them
of course, "the Church is a house with one hundred gates and no
two men [or women] enter at exactly the same angle."[1]

TYPES OF CONVERTS

From where do they come? Well, there are high- and low-
church Anglicans, Episcopalians, Methodists and Presbyterians,
Lutherans and Baptists, Jews and atheists. There are the famous,
like Newman and Chesterton, and the infamous, like Guy Fawkes
of the Gunpowder Plot and Baron Corvo. There are saints like
Edmund Campion and sinners like Dutch Schultz. But the majority
of them (which indeed makes them so interesting) are people you

1   *The Catholic Church and Conversion* (1926), 23.

I

have probably never heard of. And some of those who wrote most powerfully in witness of the Catholic faith are the least known. One of the objects of this book is to bring them back into the light.

Even if we just list converts from one country alphabetically, the entries make for some surprising juxtapositions. Take England for example. When we get to the letter "G" we find next to each other "Green" and "Greene." Blessed Hugh Green (1594–1642) was martyred by the Puritans. He worked in England for nearly thirty years. When Charles I ordered all priests to depart the realm within a stated time, Fr. Green admitted to a custom-house officer at the port of Lyme Regis that he was a priest, not realizing that the leaving date had passed. He was committed to Dorchester prison and five months later tried and sentenced to death for being a priest. While in prison he converted two condemned women and went to his own death with holy joy. He was hanged, drawn, and quartered at Dorchester (a hotbed of Puritans, some of whom incidentally played football with his head after his death).

Standing cheek by jowl with Blessed Hugh Green is the novelist Graham Greene (1904–1991), who called himself in turn a "Catholic," a "Catholic-atheist," and finally a "Catholic-agnostic." It's interesting, however, that throughout all he kept a picture of Padre Pio in his wallet—till the very end. Let us hope he saved his soul as well as the picture.

Converts, then, comprise all kinds of people. Some come to be known in other contexts. For example, John von Neumann (1903–1957), the great mathematician, partly inspired the character of Dr. Strangelove in the film of that name, although sadly he himself was not all that devout. In the case of the archaeologist Sylvanus Morley (1883–1948), there is speculation that he may have provided some of the inspiration for the character of Indiana Jones in the Spielberg films! So, we have all sorts here, from kings and courtiers to beggars, bankers, and even lawyers (like the present writer). And all ages. Harold Riley, the New Testament scholar, had been an Anglican minister for 63 years. He then converted, and was ordained a Catholic priest at the age of 91! If we go to the other end of the age range, we find J. R. R. Tolkien (1892–1973), who can be called a convert, although a very young one, having been instructed in the Catholic religion at the age of eight by his recently converted mother—and with the added burden of the loss of this saintly and wonderful mother while he was very young.

Some converts leave it until very late indeed. There are not a few deathbed conversions—for example, King Charles II (1630–1685); probably Oscar Wilde (1854–1900); Sir Kenneth Clark (1903–1983); almost certainly Wallace Stevens (1879–1955), the poet; and perhaps the writer W. H. Mallock (1849–1923). All of these are referred to in later chapters of this book.

Some, of course, just could not make up their minds. Richard Waldo Sibthorp, born in 1792, became a Catholic in 1841, returned to Anglicanism in 1843, and came back to the Catholic Church in 1865. When he died in 1879 he had first a Catholic funeral and then an Anglican one! It reminds one of some words of St Thomas More (1478–1535) to his son-in-law, William Roper (1496–1578), in Robert Bolt's *A Man for all Seasons*: "Listen, Roper. Two years ago you were a passionate Churchman; now you are a passionate Lutheran. We must just pray that when your head's finished turning, your face is to the front again." Happily for Roper it was, and he wrote the first biography of More. Not so simple in Sibthorp's case, however.

A COMMON THEME?

Is there a common theme running through conversion accounts? It is difficult to find one. As we have seen, they come from all sorts of backgrounds, though I'm inclined to say that in many cases there is some sort of journey through adversity to a sense of truth. The convert often admits to a feeling of "coming home." Let us take a simple example. It is one with hardship of a kind, but also a touch of humor in that the coming home here is not at first what it should be. Sir Francis Burnand (1836–1917) was a playwright, famous in his day for humorous burlesques, and also a barrister and editor of *Punch*. He collaborated with Sir Arthur Sullivan at one point. As a young man at university he was influenced, like many, by Newman, in particular his *Essay on the Development of Christian Doctrine* (1845). After term ended he rushed home to his father's house to announce his decision to become a Catholic. Burnand writes at some length about what happened in his delightful memoir, *Records and Reminiscences, Personal and General* (1905), but it is well summarized by Madeleine Beard in her excellent book *Faith and Fortune* (1997):

Burnand faced opposition on all fronts. When his father learned of his decision to become a Catholic he was disinherited. He had suspected there was something wrong when on his arrival home his suitcase was not taken up to his room, but left in the hall. After an interview with his father [one can only begin to imagine what was said there], it was the butler who showed him off the premises with some degree of kindness.[2]

Oh dear! Fortunately, however, things were about to improve. Here is Madeleine Beard again:

He immediately went to see an old Catholic friend from Cambridge. Arriving at his house he found a note to say that dinner had been prepared for two and he would be back after Mass in Farm Street [the church in London run by the Jesuits]. Waiting inside the warm room, so welcoming after the coldness of his father's establishment, Burnand noticed in the corner of the room a statue of the Blessed Virgin Mary in a niche under a canopy. A light flickered at her feet and flowers were placed close by. Suddenly the door opened and in came his host, beaming with delight. Hearing the news of Burnand's decision to become a Catholic he was overcome with joy and heartily shook his hand. He had had a presentiment that this would happen and that it would occur on or about the Feast of the Immaculate Conception. And so it did.[3]

Before we leave Francis Burnand, it is worth narrating another amusing story involving him. He was on one occasion at a dinner given by Cardinal Manning in honor of the famous Jewish convert Fr. Marie-Alphonse Ratisbonne (1814–1884), who in 1842 was miraculously converted to Catholicism in the church of Sant'Andrea delle Fratte in Rome by an apparition of the Blessed Virgin Mary. Burnand and a friend, Walter Richards, reflected on the fact that neither of them had said anything during the occasion on which they were introduced to Ratisbonne:

I call to my mind ... how silent we were for some time after he had left, and how Walter Richards and myself

---

2   *Faith and Fortune* (1997), 184.
3   Ibid. Burnand's own account of this whole event is to be found in his *Records and Reminiscences, Personal and General, Volume I* (1904), 321–25.

sat together without speaking a word, both of us wrapt in thought. However, routine work had to be done, and so we broke up our stance.

"We've been very silent," I observed to Walter Richards, with something of an effort.

"We have," he replied gravely, "but you see, my dear fellow, it isn't every day one meets a man who *has actually seen Our Lady*."[4]

What can one say?! Very little will catch the occasion.

Another who journeyed through difficult times was Thomas Arnold (1823–1900), a literary scholar, teacher, and barrister. He was a son of Dr. Thomas Arnold (1795–1842), a headmaster of Rugby school. He had to put up with something slightly different. He also had been influenced in his decision to convert by Cardinal Newman. However, Arnold's Protestant first wife, Julia, was not best pleased. She wrote to Newman accusing him of persuading her husband "to ignore every social duty and become a pervert." She added, "From the bottom of my heart I curse you for it." She also turned up for her husband's confirmation and smashed the windows of the chapel during the service.[5]

Finally, we come to Lucy Phillips, whose date of birth is unknown, but who died in 1857. She and her three children, having been received into the Catholic Church by Newman, had to escape to Malines in Belgium to prevent her family, who resented her conversion, from seizing the children. Later they returned to live near to Newman's home, the Birmingham Oratory. She gave herself up to works of charity, founding a small hospital with the help of the Oratorians, until her health broke down. After her death an uncle and aunt of her children tried to reclaim them to Protestantism, but after legal action two Catholics were appointed as sole guardians. Lucy's son George E. Phillips (1843–1918) subsequently became a Catholic priest.

Of course, Newman himself knew all about such unfortunate things for another reason. His sister Harriet, who was utterly prejudiced against the Roman faith, felt great bitterness towards

4   Ibid., 338.
5   Later he reverted to Anglicanism, but in 1878 he re-converted to Catholicism, again to the horror of his wife and leading to what was referred to as a "semi-detached" marriage.

Newman leading up to and following his conversion in 1845. She effectively broke off relations with her brother in 1843 and never communicated with him again. Another of Newman's sisters, Jemima, also opposed his conversion in the considerable correspondence that took place between them, but she expressed far greater sympathy and understanding than Harriet, as when in 1844 she assured her brother that "my first wish is that you should see the truth, whatever it is. I hope and trust that I desire this for you above all things." After his conversion they continued to correspond and eventually met up together with Jemima's only daughter, Janie. Finally, Newman's relationship with his youngest sister, Mary, was a very close one, but there was further sadness there, since Mary died in 1828 at the age of nineteen.

BLINDING FLASH CONVERTS

In the classic tradition prospective converts are said to need to take three steps. These consist in acceptance of (a) the existence of One God; (b) the divinity of One Lord Jesus Christ; and (c) the founding of the One Church by Christ, that being the Catholic Church. Together, these claims imply that what the One Church of Christ teaches is God's revealed truth. It may be valuable, in order to set in context the specific cases dealt with in the later chapters of the book, to examine the most significant arguments usually put forward to support these three steps.

But first, it is necessary to emphasize that sometimes, through the grace of God, a person will come to these conclusions without the need for considered thought, through what is sometimes called a "blinding flash" conversion, rather along the lines of St Paul on the road to Damascus. A friend of mine once described her own experience to me in the following words:

> I was born into a family with no particular religion. My father would describe himself as an agnostic and my mother had been brought up in Scotland with Calvinist roots. However, we never went to church. I was never taught to pray and I was quite oblivious to the fact that God existed and still less to the fact that He loved me.
>
> All that changed one day when I was twelve. We were on holiday in Paris and to take shelter from the pouring rain, we went into a church [it was in fact Sacré Coeur

in Paris]. Some sort of service was going on, the church was full of people at prayer and I had never seen anything so beautiful. I walked in as a damp English tourist tagging along with her parents and walked out with my eyes opened to a new reality, another life. From then on, I knew that God was calling me to the Catholic Church and that I would find Truth there.

Equally interesting was the experience of the political commentator Robert Novak (1931–2009):

I came to Syracuse to deliver the annual Flowers Lecture, partially financed by the Conservative Young America Foundation and sponsored by the College Republicans. Standard procedure for college lectures is a pre-speech dinner for the speaker, hosted by the sponsoring student committee. There was one woman on the College Republicans committee, seated across the table from me. She was striking-looking, wearing a gold cross on her neck.

What happened next may be distorted in my memory and shaped by the religious mysteries that I see entwined in this episode. Without mentioning the cross, I was impelled to ask the woman a question that normally I would not consider posing. Was she a Catholic? I thought she answered yes and then asked me whether I was one. "No," I replied, "but my wife and I have been going to Mass every Sunday for about four years." "Do you plan to join the Church?" she asked. I answered: "No, not at the present time."

Then the young woman looked at me and said evenly: "Mr. Novak, life is short, but eternity is for ever." I was so shaken by what she said that I could barely get through the rest of the dinner and my speech that night. Sometime during the short night before rising to catch a seven AM flight back to Washington, I became convinced that the Holy Spirit was speaking through this Syracuse student.[6]

GOD AND REASON

Remarkable perhaps, or in the second case, maybe an extreme coincidence, but then we should expect that on occasions God will give this utterly unmerited but free gift. In most cases, however, I suspect that the three reasoned grounds, traditionally referred to

6   *The Prince of Darkness: 50 Years Reporting in Washington* (2007), 553.

as "God, Christ, the Church," play at least some part and often a major one. It is, then, to these that we must now turn.

Let us begin with the words of Newman: "Private judgment *must* be your guide, till you are in the Church. You do not begin with faith, but with reason, and you *end* with faith. How are you to get into the way of faith, but by history or some other equivalent method of inquiry? You *must* have some *ground* of becoming a Catholic, or you will not make a good one."[7] This is contrary to the approach taken by atheists. As was well put, "Why do atheists always define themselves in terms of what they don't believe? Just for once, it would be nice to hear one of them say, for example, 'I believe that the universe results from the operation of unconscious matter which came into existence spontaneously from nothing, and happened by chance to have properties that allowed it to evolve to the present complex state.' Nothing wrong with that as a statement of belief, but there's no more evidence for it than there is for believing that the primal matter was consciously created."[8]

Thus, the intellectual process of conversion begins, as previously observed, by considering the question "Is there a God?" Of course, these days an inquirer will meet with considerable opposition even at this stage. The atheist may well have read one of the books of the "New Atheists" (whose arguments are nothing new). For example, the late Stephen Hawking said on a number of occasions that there was no need to invoke God to get the universe going. Why? Because, as there is the law of gravity, the universe can and will create itself from nothing. Therefore, spontaneous creation is the reason there is something rather than nothing, why the universe and we exist.

Well, okay, but hang on a minute! Unfortunately for him there is an obvious question, namely, "Where did the law of gravity come from?" In reality Hawking is using cheap trickery and relying on his reputation and hoping to deceive us by sleight of hand. He has not shown that something can come from nothing. He has shown the opposite, in that there must first be a law of physics in the shape of the law of gravity, and that is certainly something, not nothing. One is reminded of the intrepid Dr. Samuel Johnson's

7   Letter to Magdalene Helbert, September 10, 1869, in *The Letters and Diaries of John Henry Newman*, Vol. XXIV, 331.
8   John Bunting, Letter to the editor, *The Spectator*, September 17, 2005, 18.

words about Jean-Jacques Rousseau's argument for the supposed superior happiness of the savage life: "A man who talks nonsense like this must know he is talking nonsense."[9]

What this all emphasizes is the need for an eternal being, which has always existed, and had no beginning. As someone said when asked to prove the existence of God: "Nothing comes from nothing; there is something; therefore, there was never nothing. This something could not bring itself into existence, because to do that, it would have to exist before it existed. Therefore, something else had to bring it into existence. That something is what is called God."[10]

The late Fr. Benedict Ashley brings out the relationship between science and religion in setting out the second and arguably most powerful of St Thomas Aquinas's famous Five Ways of proving God's existence:

> Although modern scientific explanations may be very true, they are never complete. Science can only explain events by the action of some changing entity, but such changing entities exist and act only because they are being actualized by some other changing entity. Such a chain of material causation cannot be circular nor can it be infinite but must have a first cause, since without a first cause an infinite chain of agents and recipients would be merely potential and unable to produce the final observed effect. The First Cause cannot itself be changing and material, since if it were such it would again require another cause to actualize it. Thus the causes of our changing material world always presuppose the existence and action of some unchanging and non-material cause.[11]

St Thomas concludes there must be "one primary being, unchangeable, first cause, necessary and not contingent on anything else, highest (infinite) in positive perfections, and master-mind."[12] Dr. James Higgins brings out the practical implications of all this:

> In a TV interview many years back an aged Pole was quizzed about many things (what Stalin did to Poland, etc....) and mentioned God, which, in view of some of

9 James Boswell, *The Life of Dr. Samuel Johnson, LLD*, Vol. I (1791), 311.
10 E. Michael Jones, *Logos Rising* (2020), 13.
11 Fr. Benedict Ashley, *A Begging Friar's Journey*, vol. 1: *Atheism Bumps Into Reality: A Conversion Story, 1915–1952* (2010), 117.
12 *Summa Theologiae*, I, q. 2, art. 3.

the hard things he'd said, prompted the question, "Oh, you believe that God exists?" And out it came, quite spontaneously: "If he didn't, there wouldn't be anything else."... He was (unwittingly) summarizing [the classic] argument, shorn of every possible digression, an elaboration of the mundane notion of causation. Common sense.[13]

Finally, Professor C. J. F. Williams disposes of the "New Atheist" school's hackneyed response to the argument from a first cause:

Following St. Thomas Aquinas...we affirm the existence of God because we need an explanation of certain facts about the world, the fact of its changeableness, the fact of its contingency, the fact of its limited perfection, the fact of its order. The first of [these] ways starts from the premiss that what is in the process of change must be caused to change by something else.... I start with the present state of the world, and trace that back and back through a vast number of previous states until I reach, perhaps, a big bang. What, I ask, produced the big bang? The only explanation is that the big bang was made by God. Ah, [says the atheist,] but who made God? As though a philosopher as considerable as St. Thomas would have left himself open to the charge that he had used the premiss "Everything has a cause" to obtain the conclusion "There is an uncaused cause." But of course, he did *not* use that premiss. He used the qualified premiss "everything that is in the process of change has a cause," or "Everything that has a beginning of existence has a cause." If we reach a cause which is not itself in process of change, which had no beginning of existence, and whose existence is necessary, the pressure to take the series of *explanantia* further and further back comes to an end.[14]

Objections will continue to be raised, and much more could be (and has been) said concerning the classic arguments for God's existence. Yet certain facts about the world—its changeableness and

13   E-mail to the writer, January 19, 2012.
14   "Not by confounding the persons nor dividing the substance," in A. G. Padgett (ed.), *Reason and the Christian Religion: Essays in Honour of Richard Swinburne* (1994), 227. See also the detailed examination of this issue by W. Norris Clarke, SJ, "A Curious Blind Spot in the Anglo-American Tradition of Antitheistic Argument," in his posthumously published *The Creative Retrieval of St. Thomas Aquinas: Essays in Thomistic Philosophy, New and Old* (2009), 48.

contingency, its fine-tuning and intelligibility, together with the principle that nothing comes from nothing—require an unchanging First Cause, God.[15] These arguments are just as powerful today as when Aquinas formulated them.

OBJECTIONS

Aquinas also notes that there are only two serious arguments for atheism. The first is that the world is self-explanatory; therefore there is no need to postulate the existence of God. The second is that if God exists, He would, being all-powerful and all-good, prevent the suffering we see around us; yet suffering persists; therefore God does not exist.

The first of these arguments today takes the form of saying that science can give such good explanations of the world that the old recourse to gods or a God is unnecessary. But, as Fr. Ashley states, "the kind of explanations that science gives, although true and useful, stop at causes which are still only caused causes, and thus in no way contradict Aquinas's proofs."[16] In addition, a self-explanatory and self-creating universe makes no sense for one very simple reason: in order to bring itself into existence, the universe would have to have existed before it existed. But this is impossible.

Edward Feser summarizes Aquinas's response to the argument from the existence of evil:

> The first premise of the atheist's argument is simply false, or at least unjustifiable—that is to say, there is no reason whatever to think that an all-powerful and all-good God would prevent the suffering we see around us—for it is "part of the infinite goodness of God, that He should allow evil to exist, *and out of it to produce good*" (*Summa Theologiae*, I, q. 2, a. 3, ad 1).... For even the worst evils we suffer are finite.[17]

Elsewhere, Feser writes,

15 See, for example, the following readily available modern texts: Mortimer J. Adler, *How to Think about God* (1980); Brian Davies, OP, *Thinking about God* (1985); Brian Davies and Brian Leftow (ed.), *Thomas Aquinas:* Summa Theologiae, *Questions on God* (2006); Edward Feser, *The Last Superstition* (2008); Thomas V. Morris, *Making Sense of It All* (1992); Robert Spaemann, "Rationality and Faith in God," *Communio*, Winter 2005, 618.
16 *A Begging Friar's Journey*, Vol. 1, 118.
17 Edward Feser, *The Last Superstition*, 161-62.

God is utterly distinct from the natural order of things, creating and sustaining it in being *ex nihilo* while being in no way affected by it in turn. But the "logical problem of evil" implicitly presupposes that God is himself part of the natural order, or at least causally related to it in something like the way that entities within that order are related to one another. Hence, the "problem" rests on a category mistake. So, to expose the mistake is to dissolve the problem.[18]

Two other writers sum up the matter for us:

Morality presupposes a moral community: and a moral community must be of beings with a common language, roughly equal powers, and roughly similar needs, desires and interests. God can no more be part of a moral community with them than he can be part of a political community with them. As Aristotle said, we cannot attribute moral virtues to divinity: the praise would be vulgar. Equally moral blame would be laughable.[19]

A man or a cabbage or an argument is good by measuring up to some standard. God is not good like that; God is good just by being there. Nothing else and nobody else is good that way.[20]

One further line of defense is to argue as follows: Suppose one had very good reason for believing that God exists. One would also have reason for denying that evil makes it unlikely that God exists from the very fact that one already had such good reason to believe in the existence of God.

THE DIVINITY OF CHRIST

Now for the question whether, on the assumption that God exists, He has spoken to us—in other words, the question of the divinity of Christ. It is very important to appreciate that, as stated again by Edward Feser, the case for the resurrection of Christ does not exist in a vacuum. It presupposes that we have

18 Edward Feser, "The Thomistic Dissolution of the Logical Problem of Evil," *Religions*, April 2021, www.mdpi.com/2077-1444/12/4/268/htm. This article gives a detailed account of the issues involved. See also Brian Davies, *The Reality of God and the Problem of Evil* (2006); and Edward Feser, *The Last Superstition*, 154–65 (a shorter summary).
19 Anthony Kenny, *What Is Faith?* (1992), 87.
20 Peter Geach, *Truth and Hope* (2001), 91–92.

already proved by pure reason that there is a God (and also that we have immortal souls, and that there is a natural moral law). Feser explains this as follows:

> Without that background in place, the historical evidence for Christ's resurrection might seem inconclusive at best, since any miracle will obviously seem less likely *a priori* if you don't already know that there is a God who might produce one. But when interpreted *in light of* that background, as it should be, the evidence for Christ's resurrection can be seen to be overwhelming.[21]

There are two arguments here, the first historical. Our chief source of information about Christ's life is the four Gospels. The old idea of a long process of transmission that separated the original eyewitnesses from those who wrote the Gospels is disappearing. The better-supported view today is that the period between Jesus's life on earth and the final composition of the Gospels is spanned by the continuing presence and testimony of those who participated in his story, the eyewitnesses. There is a persuasive case that all four Gospels provide an appropriate and credible means of access to the historical Jesus, since they draw on such testimony. In addition, there is much evidence of great devotion to Jesus from an early stage; and also the heavenly pre-existence of Jesus is presupposed in all the Synoptic Gospels.[22]

However, even if this were not true, and we had no evidence that the Gospels were written by those whose names they bear, or even by eyewitnesses of the events they treat, we reply that, as was asserted by Fr. John Gerard, SJ, "it is unnecessary for the sake of the present argument to examine [these arguments], for the basis which we require is altogether independent of the points they raise. Our contention is that the character of Christ as portrayed to us by the Gospels, whenever and by whomsoever they were written, as also by tradition, is of such a nature that it cannot be a fiction, and can only have been drawn from the life."[23]

21   *The Last Superstition* (2008), 155.
22   See, for example, Richard Bauckham, *Jesus and the Eyewitnesses: The Gospels as Eyewitness Testimony* (2006; extended and updated edition 2017); Larry W. Hurtado, *Lord Jesus Christ: Devotion to Jesus in Earliest Christianity* (2003); Simon Gathercole, *The Pre-Existent Son* (2006).
23   *A Course of Religious Instruction for Catholic Youth* (1901), 38–39.

The case for the resurrection can be summarized as follows.[24] Christ died and was buried. Nobody has ever seriously questioned this. Was the tomb empty? Yes, because if not, the Jewish leaders would have produced the body. What happened to the body? It was not taken by either the Jews or the Romans, as doing so would have been completely contrary to their interests. Did the apostles or other disciples take it? No, because the tomb was guarded by Roman soldiers. Even if the apostles or disciples took the body, this cannot explain their transformation and willingness to die for their belief in a resurrection which they knew was a fraud. Were they simply mistaken? No, they could not be mistaken in thinking Christ walked, talked, and ate with them. And it could not have been a hallucination, since large numbers of people were there. Finally, if there were no resurrection, making Christ a fraud, we could hardly explain the spread and endurance of the Church through great persecution.

In reality, both the reported appearances of Christ to the apostles and the empty tomb itself prove a great deal. The appearances were many and in different circumstances, involving more than a few witnesses. The empty tomb is a further factor of great significance. After all, the tomb was available for a visit in the very place where the events took place. It is powerful evidence that Jesus rose bodily from the dead. Here it is important to appreciate that although it was in the interests of both the Jewish establishment and the Roman authorities to disprove the resurrection, they did not do so. It is a reasonable inference that this was because they were unable to do so. A further factor is that within two months of the resurrection, again in Jerusalem itself, and at a time when many eyewitnesses must have been available, the apostles had made more than five thousand converts.

If, in addition, we accept the point made by Edward Feser, U.S. Supreme Court Justice Antonin Scalia's statement that a refusal to believe in Christ's resurrection might be construed as ridiculous makes sense.

> To deny it implies that everything from the Easter morning to the Ascension had to be made up by the groveling enthusiasts as part of their plan to get themselves martyred.

24 This summary is drawn from the detailed account given by Charles E. Rice in his book *Fifty Questions on the Natural Law* (1993), 176–81. See also the other authorities cited there.

No meeting along the road to Emmaus, no Doubting
Thomas, no fishing trip to Tiberias. If Christ's followers
were indeed fabricators of evidence, why would they make
up these stories, in all their puzzling complexity and, let's
face it, intimacy of scale? By setting out the case in this
way, Justice Scalia invites us to find it much easier to accept
that Jesus rose from the dead than that an elaborate and
unlikely conspiracy was concocted among his disciples.[25]

The other argument is a philosophical one, with a two-thousand-
year tradition: Christ claimed to be the way, the truth, and the life,
i.e., to be God. This is not the claim of one who is merely a good
man or of a great ethical teacher. He must have been bad, mad, or
God. But can anyone believe the Sermon on the Mount and the
Parable of the Prodigal Son are the discourses of an evil or mad
man? Of course not. No one else ever spoke or acted with com-
parable assurance of the things of God. And no one puts this case
better than C. S. Lewis in these memorable words: "You can shut
Him up for a fool, you can spit at Him and kill Him as a demon;
or you can fall at His feet and call Him Lord and God. But let us
not come with any patronizing nonsense about His being a great
human teacher. He has not left that open to us. He did not intend
to."[26] Here is the argument in a short and simple version, that of
St Thomas More: "Surely if he Christ were not God, he would be
no good man either, since he plainly said he was God."[27]

St Thomas Aquinas uses a similar argument. He writes not of
madness or badness if Jesus is not divine, but of pride:

> The man Christ, speaking of himself, says many divine
> and supernatural things, as, "I will raise him up at the last
> day" (John 6:40), "I give them life everlasting" (John 10:28).
> Such language would be the height of pride, if the speaker
> were not himself God, but only had God dwelling in him.
> And still Christ says of himself: "Learn of me, because I
> am meek and humble of heart" (Matthew 9:29).[28]

One final point about the bad, mad, or God argument is that
certain theologians, in particular the late Professor John C. O'Neill

25 See Dennis Sewell, *The Political Gene* (2009), 11.
26 *Mere Christianity* (rev. ed., 1952), 52.
27 *A Dialogue of Comfort against Tribulation* (1534), Book 3, Ch. XIV, 179.
28 *Summa contra Gentiles*, Bk. 4, Ch. 34.

(1930–2003), maintain that under Jewish law at the time of Christ's coming it would be blasphemy for anyone to say he was the Messiah until God the Father had clearly spoken.[29] This would obviously affect our argument if the claim was made by Christ in words, because under this thesis the person making the claim could not be the Messiah. Such theologians argue that passages in the New Testament that make this claim are either scribal additions or revelatory sayings only attributed to Jesus posthumously. They conclude that Jesus neither said in so many words that he was the Messiah, but, importantly, nor did he deny that he was Messiah. The answer to all of this, of course, is that, in the words of O'Neill, "although Jesus did not claim in words to be God, he raised the expectation that that was the issue by his actions: accepting baptism in Jordan, teaching in the desert, feeding the multitude in the desert, choosing twelve disciples, entering Jerusalem on a donkey and so on."[30] So this argument for the divinity of Christ remains intact.

The whole matter of the resurrection and the divinity of Christ is put even more simply by another giant of the Church:

> St. Augustine...argues thus: Either the Resurrection happened or it did not. If it did, then we have all the proof we need. If it did not, then the Apostles preached a lie and the world accepted it. But that would itself be a miracle, that twelve such men should impose the doctrinally difficult and the morally hard principles of Christianity on all sorts of men, in the teeth of their passion and pride, in virtue of a supposed event which men knew could not possibly happen.[31]

Another relevant matter is the question of prophecy. The Bible is the only book in the world to offer specific predictions hundreds of years before they were fulfilled. There are nearly two thousand individual prophecies contained in the Bible, which is about thirty-per-cent prophecy. There are no such fulfilled prophecies in any other major religious book. Also, the Messiah is unique in that his coming was foretold in many specific prophecies, which were

29   See, in particular, the fascinating work of Professor O'Neill in *Who Did Jesus Think He Was?* (1995) and *The Point of It All: Essays on Jesus Christ* (2000), especially 73–96 in the latter.
30   E-mail from John O'Neill to the writer, October 23, 2000.
31   Joseph Faà Di Bruno, *Catholic Belief: A Simple Exposition of Catholic Doctrine* (1957), 3.

fulfilled in the greatest detail in the life, death, and resurrection of Jesus Christ. Pascal spells out the significance of all this:

> If a single man had written a book foretelling the time and manner of Jesus's coming and Jesus had come in conformity with these prophecies, this would carry infinite weight. But there is much more here. There is a succession of men over a period of 4,000 years, coming consistently and invariably one after the other, to foretell the same coming; there is an entire people proclaiming it, existing for 4,000 years to testify in a body to the certainty they feel about it, from which they cannot be deflected by whatever threats and persecutions they may suffer. This is of a quite different order of importance.[32]

In addition, one can only marvel at Christ's uniqueness and uninventibility. As has been well said, "To claim that later Christians just made up the figure of Christ as a ruse to start a new religion, as some skeptics claim, [is] unthinkable: they would have had to be holy themselves to invent such a personality, and if they were holy they would not have lied."[33] This point is further argued by Joseph Sobran:

> If you want to contend that the Gospels are packs of lies and that Jesus never said all those things or performed all those wonders, you should at least admit that Christianity is the most brilliant hoax of all time. Everything fits so well. How could a few unlearned and provincial Jews invent such a supremely memorable character, endow him with the ability to speak immortal words on all occasions, then make virtually all the details of his story cohere so well, tallying even with Old Testament prophecy?[34]

We can add to this Christ's impact on history, influencing even the calendar so that up to the present day, most of our public holidays derive their very existence from his birth, death, and resurrection; the very years being divided into BC and AD—those before Christ, and those called anything from the first to the two-thousand-twenty-second year of our Lord.

32   Blaise Pascal, *Pensées* (1670), no. 332.
33   Ronda Chervin, "In Search of the Savior," in Robert Baram (ed.), *Spiritual Journeys* (1988), 59.
34   *Subtracting Christianity: Essays on American Culture and Society* (2015), 15–16.

Thus can be seen the powerful nature of the argument for the divinity of Christ.[35]

THE CATHOLIC CHURCH

The third and final question is through whom has God spoken to us: in other words, the question of the Church. Msgr George MacGillivray answers it forcefully:

> If Jesus Christ was God, and founded a divine body to be the teacher and source of grace to the world until he comes again, that body must exist today. It is inconceivable that he should allow his purpose to be frustrated. The question, therefore, arises: Where is that body? And to this there is only one possible answer, because there is only one reasonable claimant. There is practically only one body which claims to be, to the exclusion of every other, the Body of Christ, and that is the Holy Catholic Roman Church.[36]

There are also a number of necessary marks, or criteria, through which the Church can always be identified:

> If Christ was the Son of God I did not doubt that the Roman Church was the Church of Christ. The "churches" were all agreed that Christ had founded a church; none ventured to assert that He had founded the present variety of "churches." All were agreed, too, that His church was imperishable, that "the gates of hell" were not to prevail against it. That being so, the "one, holy, Catholic and Apostolic Church," of which the Creed speaks, must be in existence somewhere today, and must have been in existence continuously ever since the times of the Apostles. There seemed to me to be nowhere that this Church could be found save in the obedience to Rome. The very definitions of the Church,

---

35 For a more expansive treatment of arguments for the divinity of Jesus Christ, see, *inter alia*, Arnold Lunn, *The Third Day* (1945); Hugo A. Meynell, *Is Christianity True?* (1994); Gerald O'Collins, SJ, *Interpreting Jesus* (1983); John Redford, *Bad, Mad or God?* (2004); Richard Swinburne, *The Resurrection of God Incarnate* (2003); Richard Swinburne, *Was Jesus God?* (2008); O. R. Vassall-Phillips, *The Mustard Tree* (1923); N. T. Wright, *The Resurrection of the Son of God* (2003).
36 *Through the East to Rome* (1932). For more detail on the arguments for the Catholic Church, see, for example, the classic account by Saint John Henry Newman, *Apologia Pro Vita Sua* (1864), and the analysis of Newman's correspondence with potential converts by Fr Stanley L. Jaki, *Newman to Converts: An Existential Ecclesiology* (2001).

as given by those outside this obedience, are a denial of her unity. She alone is Catholic. And, if she be not apostolic, certainly no other is, for all others can trace their ancestry back to the Apostles only through her. If Christ was God, the Church must exist, and if the Church exists, the Church of Rome cannot but be the true Church.[37]

The American writer Thomas Howard (1935–2020) put forward an argument not based on strict logic but nevertheless very cogent indeed:

> The fundamental question, of course, is whether the Roman claim is true. There are only two possible answers to that. If I say no, then I have Augustine and Bede and Gregory and Aquinas and Erasmus and Thomas More and Ignatius and Bellarmine and Bossuet and Suarez and Newman and Chesterton and Knox against me for starters, and that makes me nervous. But infinitely more serene than that, I have the colossal *securus judicat orbis terrarum* looking passionlessly at me. "The calm judgment of the whole world" is against me. The Roman Church has, as it were, nothing to prove. Everyone else has to do the sleeve-plucking and arm-pawing to validate their cases.[38]

With mention there of Newman, and also that Latin phrase, first used by St Augustine and influential in Newman's conversion to Catholicism, the following text, often quoted to prospective converts, comes to mind: "Few days pass without my having letters from strangers, young and old, men and women, on the subject of the Catholic religion. I answer them that it is the one and only true and safe religion."[39]

THE TEN KEY FACTORS

We have now set out the three steps and arrived at the Catholic Church.[40] What are the main reasons to take this final step and

---

37   Christopher Hollis, "Finding Christ's Church," in John A. O'Brien (ed.), *The Road to Damascus, Volume II* (1950), 151–152.

38   "Lead Kindly Light," in Dan O'Neill, *The New Catholics: Contemporary Converts Tell Their Stories* (1987), 94.

39   John Henry Newman, Letter to Canon Loughnan, in *The Letters and Diaries of John Henry Newman*, Vol. XXX, 165.

40   There is a huge literature on all of the three questions relating to converting to the Catholic faith. See, in particular, Benedict Ashley, OP, *Friar's*

be received into the Catholic Church? The stories that follow will mention many different factors, but it would be well first of all to look at some of the most common—ten, to be precise.

Visibility: The word "church" is used over one hundred times in the New Testament, never in a purely abstract sense. Many converts speak of a concrete, visible institution embodying unity; a city set on a hill, with a visible head, the Pope.

> The invisible church was never heard of until after the Protestants broke away, fifteen hundred years after Christ.[41]

> What, then, led me to take the step? It was a belief in the Visible Church, in the absolute necessity for that Church having a Visible Head, and in the irresistible evidence in favor of the supremacy of the Pope. This is all. All other questions seemed to me to depend entirely upon this one.[42]

Universality: The Church is literally Catholic in this sense. Converts often express a joy of belonging to a really big family, of feeling at home everywhere; black and white, rich and poor, all kneeling at the same altar, side by side.

> Never did I set foot in a Catholic church but that I saw people there at home with Him; First Fridays, novenas, and missions brought the masses thronging in and out of the Catholic churches. They were of all nationalities, of all classes, but most of all they were the poor. The very attacks made against the Church proved her Divinity to me. Nothing but a divine institution could have survived the betrayal of Judas, the denial of Peter, the sins of many

Folly (2010); Kenneth Baker, SJ, *Fundamentals of Catholicism*, three volumes (1982); Hilaire Belloc, *The Question and the Answer* (1938); Robert Hugh Benson, *The Religion of the Plain Man* (1906); Denys Blakelock, *Finding My Way* (1958); G. K. Chesterton, *The Everlasting Man* (1925); Richard Conrad, OP, *The Catholic Faith: A Dominican's Vision* (1994); Thomas Crean, *Letters to a Non-Believer* (2009); W. Devivier and Joseph C. Sasia, *Christian Apologetics*, two volumes (1924); Avery Dulles, *A Testimonial to Grace* (1996); A. N. Gilbey, *We Believe* (1983); Ian Ker, *Mere Catholicism* (2006); Ronald Knox, *The Belief of Catholics* (1927); Ronald Knox, *The Hidden Stream* (1953); Arnold Lunn, *Now I See* (1933); John Henry Newman, *Apologia pro Vita Sua* (1864); John Redford, *Catholicism: Hard Questions* (1997); O. R. Vassall-Phillips, CSsR, *Catholic Christianity* (1920); O. R. Vassall-Phillips, CSsR, *After Fifty Years* (1928); Paul Williams, *The Unexpected Way* (2002).
41 Sheldon Vanauken, "The English Channel," *New Oxford Review*, March 1981, 9.
42 Robert Sadleir Moodie, essay in J. G. F. Raupert (ed.), *Roads to Rome* (1901), 162.

of those who professed her Faith and who were supposed
to minister to her poor.[43]

Continuity: The Catholic Church has been sustained from the
Apostles' time to ours. The early Fathers were clearly Catholic; the
line of popes runs from the start to today. The Church is the same
old seaworthy ship, preserving the treasure of faith intact through
all ages. And Christ promised always to be with his Church.

> From the earliest days of Protestantism, "Where was your
> Church before Luther?" was a deadly question. Equally
> deadly is the question: "If your theory be true as to the
> old Church having become corrupt in her teaching—the
> theory on which, admittedly, alone can your history and
> actions be defended or justified—what has become of the
> promises of Christ?"[44]

If we ask, "Where was the Church of England before Henry
the Eighth?" the only answer that can be given is: "In union with
the Catholic Church."

Also, we have the endurance of the Church through bad circumstances that a false religion could hardly survive:

> It is not the saints that one has to talk about if one is
> to prove the sanctity of the Church. It's bad priests and
> popes. A Church governed by saints continues on, that's
> normal and human. But a Church that can be governed
> by villains and imbeciles, and still continue, that is neither
> normal nor human.[45]

> That such an institution as the Church of Rome—with all
> its human faults—had lasted for nearly 2,000 years, while
> parties and factions and kingdoms had had their day and
> withered, seemed to me to be utterly wonderful. Some
> mysterious power seemed to be preserving it against the
> assaults and erosions of time.[46]

It might be pointed out here that the Latin Mass was a significant example of both universality and continuity. Once, converts

43 Dorothy Day, "From Communism to Christ," in John A. O'Brien (ed.),
The Road to Damascus, Vol. II (1950), 72.
44 Fr. Oliver Vassall-Phillips, CSsR, *After Fifty Years,* 139.
45 Julien Green, *Pamphlet contre les Catholiques de France* (1924).
46 George Mackay Brown, "The Way of Literature," *The Tablet,* June 12,
1982, 584.

would often be impressed by the sameness of the Mass wherever they might go throughout the world. Sadly this is no longer so.

Authority: The claim to be protected from error and to be the pillar and foundation of truth; a necessity if she was to withstand the gates of hell.

> Christ said to St. Peter, "I will build my Church on you, and it shall never fail, I commission you to feed my sheep in my absence." For a lifetime only? No, surely for all posterity. To the Apostles he had said, "I charge you with teaching all nations, baptizing them in the name of the Father, of the Son, and of the Holy Ghost. I will send the Holy Ghost to guide you, so that your teaching may be infallible. The sins which you forgive on earth will be forgiven in heaven."[47]

Beauty: The Church's twofold legacy of aesthetics (art, architecture, and liturgy) and the saints: God's beauty shining through both human beings and human art, as expressed by Dr William Oddie.

> I remember going into [York Minster]...and standing in the middle of the nave, with the majestic Norman arches towering above me, and I simply found myself saying to myself, "Either this is based on the truth, or it's based on a lie. If it's a lie, how come it is so sublime. What's the sublimity of all this mean?"[48]

> The Life of Christ, beginning with the great central fact of Christianity, the Incarnation, with all that radiated from it, fills the art of more than a thousand years, from the Catacombs to the Reformation.[49]

The Mass and the Real Presence: The recognition of this sacrifice as no invention of man, but as God's own act—Christ offering himself to God the Father.

> What is Christian culture? It is essentially the Mass. That is not my or anyone's opinion or theory or wish but the central fact of two thousand years of history. Christendom, what secularists call Western Civilization, is the Mass and the paraphernalia which protect and facilitate it. All architecture, art, political and social forms, economics, the

---

47 Cardinal Avery Dulles, *Testimonial to Grace*, 103-4.
48 See John Beaumont, *Roads to Rome* (2010), 322.
49 Edward Hutton, *The Life of Christ in the Old Italian Masters* (1939), v.

way people live and feel and think, music, literature—all
these things when they are right are ways of fostering
and protecting the Holy Sacrifice of the Mass.[50]

In this context there are many paradoxes inherent in the claim
of some Anglicans to be part of the Catholic Church. One of
these, relating to All Souls College, Oxford, is brought out by
the convert Alfred Verney-Cave, later Lord Braye (1849–1928):

> All Souls was founded on purpose to endow masses for the
> soldiers who fell at Agincourt: the emoluments were for
> that object only. Not a Mass has been said since 1559—on
> the contrary, learned men enjoy the funds, men who are
> bound to aver that the doctrine of Rome is wrong. I now
> saw clearly from what a quagmire of contradictions I had
> escaped. Logic, simple logic, had triumphed.[51]

The Blessed Virgin Mary: Her humanity and answer to cries of
help from people in distress; the devotions to her; the Rosary;
the Memorare; pilgrimages to shrines such as Lourdes and Fatima.

> The great achievements of the Catholic Church lay in
> harmonizing, humanizing, civilizing the deepest impulses
> of ordinary, ignorant people. Take the cult of the Virgin.
> In the early twelfth century the Virgin had been the
> supreme protectress of civilization. She had taught a race
> of tough and ruthless barbarians the virtues of tenderness
> and compassion. The great cathedrals of the Middle Ages
> were her dwelling places upon earth. In the Renaissance,
> while remaining the Queen of Heaven, she became also
> the human mother in whom everyone could recognize
> qualities of warmth and love and approachability.[52]

> Did I ever tell you how Our Lady first came into my life? It
> was by the Memorare.... It took me off my feet at once, for
> it was so daring a statement that I thought it could not have
> lived if it had been a lie, and I said it constantly and clung
> to it as the first definite something that seemed to come
> authentically after my seven years of groping in the dark.[53]

50 John Senior, *The Restoration of Christian Culture* (2008), 17.
51 *Fewness of My Days: A Life in Two Centuries* (1927), 83.
52 Kenneth Clark, *Civilization: A Personal View* (1969), 175.
53 Maude Monaghan, *Life and Letters of Janet Erskine Stuart, Superior General of the Society of the Sacred Heart, 1857–1914* (1934), 24 (letter to a friend written in 1909).

Saints and Christian witness generally: Living examples of holiness, often witnessed firsthand by a convert, such as heroic works over many years, recusancy, or martyrdom.

> Even nonbelievers admire famous saints such as Francis of Assisi, Thomas More, Vincent de Paul, and Thérèse of Lisieux. But every Christian who renounces wealth, enjoyment, and status for a dedicated life of service makes Jesus' kingdom visible in this broken and suffering world (taking and fulfilling the vows of poverty, chastity, and obedience thus is an important sign of the kingdom). And even those who fall short of putting belief into practice can bear witness to the truth of their faith by acknowledging themselves to be the sinners they are.[54]

> The outburst of saints in 1500–1600 after the monstrous corruption seems to me one of the great arguments for Christianity. It is the third marvelous phenomenon in its history; the conversion of the Roman Empire, the reaction under Hildebrand, the resurrection under Ignatius Loyola, Teresa of Avila, Francis de Sales and a host of others. Think of the contrast between Alexander VI and Pius V, think of the Cardinals of the beginning, and then those of the end of the 16th century.[55]

Moral teaching: Many recent converts have seen the Church as a sign of contradiction against the main planks of secular humanism, namely sexual liberation, abortion, and pornography. Also, whereas Catholic dissidents have opposed the Church's moral teachings, complaining that she won't change with the times, many converts have come to the Church precisely because she is an authoritative, unswerving guide on morality. An excellent example was the journalist and broadcaster Malcolm Muggeridge (1903-1990), who stated that it was the Catholic Church's firm stand against contraception and abortion which finally made him decide to become a Catholic. About the encyclical *Humanae Vitae* he wrote:

> I do not doubt that in the history books when our squalid moral decline is recounted, with the final breakdown in law and order that must follow (for without a moral

54 Germain Grisez, *The Way of the Lord Jesus, Volume 2: Living a Christian Life* (1983), 17.
55 John Henry Newman, Letter to Richard Holt Hutton, October 12, 1883, in *The Letters and Diaries of John Henry Newman*, Vol. XXX, 260.

order there can be no social, political, or any other order), the Pope's courageous and just, though I fear...largely ineffectual stand will be accorded the respect and admiration it deserves.[56]

In any case, a key issue here is surely both spiritual and practical, as is pointed out by that great cradle Catholic, Flannery O'Connor:

> The Church's stand on birth control is the most absolutely spiritual of all her stands and with all of us being materialists at heart, there is little wonder that it causes unease. I wish various fathers would quit trying to defend it by saying that the world can support 40 billion. I will rejoice the day when they say: This is right whether we all rot on top of each other or not, dear children, as we certainly may. Either practice restraint or be prepared for crowding...[57]

The Catholic poet and essayist Alice Meynell (1847–1922) stressed the importance of morality in a letter to her daughter Olivia:

> I saw, when I was very young, that a guide in morals was even more necessary than a guide in faith. It was for this I joined the Church. Other Christian societies may legislate, but the Church *administers* legislation. Thus she is practically indispensable. I may say that I hold the administration of morals to be of such vital importance that for its sake I accepted, and now accept, dogma in matters of faith—to the last letter.[58]

There is frequently a great difference between Catholic teaching and that of the tradition of the Enlightenment. This is most obvious and acute on the issue of sexuality. Let us take as an example of this the question of homosexuality. The problem here is expressed very well by Joseph Shaw:

> The Church's position is characterized as holding that homosexuality is a sin, which is nonsense, or that the Church condemns people because of their sexual orientation, which is more nonsense. Acts and vices and agents are condemned; a natural inclination is none of these. The

56 Letter to *The Times*, August 2, 1968, 9.
57 "Letter to Betty Hester," June 27, 1959, in Sally Fitzgerald (ed.), *The Habit of Being: Letters of Flannery O'Connor* (1979), 338.
58 Viola Meynell, *Alice Meynell: A Memoir* (1929), 332–33.

Church condemns "homosexual acts" as they are called (sodomy), as sins; a voluntarily acquired habit of performing such acts, as a vice; and the people who perform them as sinners. But when this is clarified the secular humanist won't be satisfied, for he will say that sexual self-expression is a fundamental right, and that a homosexual inclination is essential to a person's identity.[59]

As a result the secularist will base himself on these two claims and argue that, by his own lights, the Church really does condemn people because of their sexual orientation. Joseph Shaw takes up the case again:

By the secularist's argument the Church arbitrarily picks out one group of people, those with a homosexual inclination, and tells them they may not seek sexual fulfillment: she casts them as second-class citizens, to face either a half-life of impossible self-denial or moral condemnation. And really, the first option is itself a kind of moral condemnation, because the Church is condemning their only route to sexual self-expression. Saying that the Church condemns homosexuality is a convenient short-hand for this argument.[60]

Such problems are magnified by modern conceptions of rationality based on Enlightenment notions centered on the idea that desires give people reasons for action and rational action is any action based on a weighing up of these reasons. Such notions are widely assumed today as first principles. This conception of equality and justice, allowing each person to pursue his own desires without interference, is contrary to the Catholic faith.

In consequence, it is vital that the Church address the issues on which the secularists disagree with her. She must not concede their foundational assumptions. She must get people to see that the hedonism and materialism of modern society are inferior to her own principles. In relation to the state, she must oppose any policy of neutrality between value claims. She must proclaim the true and correct values. The truth, expressed very well by Joseph Shaw, is that "sexuality finds its fulfillment within marriage and its fruits include the relationship of the couple and children, and these

59 casuistrycentral.blogspot.com/2010/02/why-catholic-apologetics-doesnt-work.html.
60 Ibid.

both work best within marriage... [S]ex outside marriage is bad for people."[61] He is, of course, referring to heterosexual marriage.

The following quotation from Edward Feser is a very powerful one:

> Defenders of "same-sex marriage" claim that what really matters in a marriage is just that the partners are lovingly committed to one another. They also claim that marriage is conventional and not grounded in the natural order of things, so that it is up to us to decide what marriage is about in light of changing standards. But given the first premise, there is no way they can consistently rule out the legitimacy of polygamous marriages or incestuous marriages; and given their second premise, there is also no way they can insist in principle on their "loving commitment" criterion for marriage in a way that would rule out "marriages" between people and animals, living people and corpses, or indeed anything whatsoever that someone might want to call "marriage." For someone could always argue that even the "loving commitment" criterion is as arbitrary and open to challenge as the heterosexual criterion is. Yet defenders of "same-sex marriage" also claim that they are opposed to these other purported forms of "marriage." Therefore, their position is incoherent.[62]

Moral Fruits: The enormous benefits which Christian civilization has given to the world.

> Christianity has raised the moral standard, tone, and customs of human society; and it must be recollected that for 1,500 years Christianity and the Catholic Church are in history identical. The care and elevation of the lower classes, the championship of the weak against the powerful, the abolition of slavery, hospitals, the redemption of captives, education of children, agriculture, literature, the cultivation of the virtues of piety, devotion, justice, charity, chastity, family affection, are all historical monuments to the influence and teaching of the Church.[63]

> The history of the centuries of Christendom undoubtedly contains much which betrays belief in a God of love and

61 www.lmschairman.org/2017/09/what-rees-mogg-could-have-said.html.
62 edwardfeser.blogspot.com/2010/09/meta-sophistry.html.
63 John Henry Newman, Letter to John Rickards Mozley, April 1, 1875, in *The Letters and Diaries of John Henry Newman*, Vol. XXVII, 262–63.

which should call the Church today to repent, but it is historically unbalanced not to emphasize as strongly the enormous benefits which Christian civilization has given to the world: in education and care of the destitute and sick; in producing much of the Western world's finest art, architecture, music; in inspiring countless acts of altruism often to the point of heroism in those who have faith in the God of Jesus Christ.[64]

The positive effect of the Faith on civilization is not infrequently an influence in conversions. But it is also often the witness and personal qualities of a friend or neighbor that bring people to the faith. They come to the Church because of actions that move the heart. By no means, then, are most of us led to change our fundamental philosophy of life because of strictly logical reasoning or the strength of historical witness. However, it is still vital for the Church to recognize the importance of an active, visible religious authority with fixed central doctrines present for the potential convert to find. This need is expressed clearly and accurately from a Protestant perspective by the convert poet John Dryden, looking back on his days in the Church of England:

> Our own worship is only true at home,
> And true but for the time; 'tis hard to know
> How long we please it shall continue so;
> This side today, and that tomorrow burns;
> So all are God Almighties in their turns.
> A tempting doctrine, plausible and new;
> What fools our fathers were, if this be true![65]

The point is put more precisely still by G. K. Chesterton: "How can a man know what he wants, how can he even want what he wants, if it will not remain the same while he wants it?"[66]

The decision to enter the Church is usually accompanied by lasting consolation. The case of the American writer Katherine Brégy, to be examined later, is typical:

---

64 Fr. Robin Burgess, "The Case for Atheism," *Heythrop Journal*, January 2001, 67.
65 *The Medal* (1682).
66 "Where Are Women Going?," *Illustrated London News*, January 28, 1922, reprinted in Lawrence J. Clipper (ed), *The Collected Works of G. K. Chesterton, Volume XXXII: The Illustrated London News 1920–1922* (1989), 314.

I should like to record ... that this is the only step of my entire life about which I have never had any subsequent misgiving. I have never, in moments of the most search-ing introspection, questioned its wisdom. I could have said that fair spring day with Sydney Carton (and quite as truthfully): "It is a far, far better thing that I do than I have ever done—It is a far, far better rest that I go to than I have ever known."[67]

Finally, however, and above all, it is God's ineffable grace that is crucial in all cases, and this is extended to all who come to him with a genuine heart and in good faith. Religion, then, from the word *religio*, is, as stated by St Augustine, the link that binds [*religat*] us to the one Almighty God.[68]

With this by way of introduction, it is time to look in some detail at specific cases of notable converts, building into these accounts the reasons given for conversion and also the personal factors involved. Most of the people considered are notable figures in the sense hat they will generally be known to the reader. It must, however, be emphasized that the faith of the simple and anonymous person who makes this final step is not inferior to that of those who are better known, and in fact their devotion to the triune God may be greater. It is more than appropriate, however, to begin with the great John Henry Newman, lately canonized by the Church, and probably the most famous of English converts to the Catholic Church.

67   Essay in Georgina Pell Curtis (ed.), *Beyond the Road to Rome* (1914), 63.
68   *On the True Religion*, 55.

CHAPTER TWO

Newman, Conversion, and the One True Fold

"Ten thousand difficulties do not make one doubt." [1]

ST JOHN HENRY NEWMAN WAS UNDOUBTEDLY the greatest convert of the nineteenth century. He also has much to say to us today. On the matter of conversion to the Catholic faith, it is a very fruitful exercise to examine the last few days of Newman's life as a Protestant and his preparation for reception into the Catholic Church, as recounted in the relevant sections of Volumes X and XI of his *Letters and Diaries* (available now on that excellent site archive.org) and *Apologia Pro Vita Sua* (1864), in which he gave an extensive account of his conversion some twenty years afterward.

At the time of his reception into the Catholic Church, Newman was residing at Littlemore, near Oxford. The Passionist priest Fr (now Blessed) Dominic Barberi (1792–1849), whose mission

1   Newman, *Apologia Pro Vita Sua*, Part VII.

in England was so successful, was soon due to arrive there, and Newman stated that he considered the visit providential. He said to John Dalgairns, who had been received himself in late September and who was on his way to meet Fr Dominic at Oxford, "When you see your friend, will you tell him that I wish him to receive me into the Church of Christ?" The famous meeting between Fr Dominic and Newman is movingly described by Alfred Wilson, also of the Passionist order, in his biography of Fr Dominic:

> Fr. Dominic had traveled all the way from Aston [Hall, Staffordshire] to Oxford on an outside seat of the stage-coach, in pelting rain. According to Fr. Gaudentius, he booked that seat because of his love of poverty and mortification. He left Aston at 10 a.m. and when he reached Oxford, soaked to the skin, at 10 p.m., he was a sorry sight. Very probably he had had no food since morning, and it seems clear that he refused to take any later. He arrived at Littlemore an hour before midnight, and at once began to dry his clothes before a blazing fire in the hearth. The door opened quietly and he stood up, and in a moment, without more ado, Newman was at his feet praying to be admitted into the Catholic Church. Here we have one of the poignant, unforgettable scenes of history which lingers indelibly in the imagination; standing before the fire in the unlit room a humble Italian monk whose squeaky voice transmits only broken English, his misfit clothes still dripping rain, his only arms the arms of the saints; and kneeling at his feet, the fairest flower of English culture, vanquished and victor, the peerless figure whom the English Church had so long venerated; the man whom Dominic had once regarded as the self-assured pope of Anglicanism, and whom he now found to be as "timid as a boy, and one of the most humble and loveable men that he had ever met."[2]

Newman began to make his confession to Fr. Dominic that very evening of the October 8, 1845, finished it the next day, and was received later that same day, October 9. Before all this, on October 3, Newman had resigned his fellowship at Oriel College, Oxford. From then until October 5 he wrote to four persons, indicating what he might do, but only in terms of what was "possible,"

2 *Blessed Dominic Barberi: Supernaturalized Briton* (1967), 308.

"likely," or "probable." He spent October 5, a Sunday, preparing for a general confession. Then, from October 6 to the morning of October 9, Newman wrote no fewer than thirty letters to relatives and close friends, nineteen of which still survive, letters that were, as he put it, "not to go till all was over." In these letters he announced definitively that he was about to be received into the Catholic Church. Two of these letters were to his sister Jemima (Mrs John Mozley [1807–1879]), as he had received a letter from her promptly after sending the first one. The postal service in those days operated somewhat quicker than today!

It is most enlightening (and, of course, moving) to read the texts of the nineteen extant letters. One of the most interesting aspects is how Newman articulates what was about to happen to him. In three of the letters he refers to his prospective "admission into the Catholic Church" and in one to admission into the "bosom of the Catholic Church." One of these letters refers also to his being "received," a term used on its own in three others. More significant, however, is that in five of the other twelve letters (including those to luminaries such as Henry Manning, later Cardinal Manning, Frederick Faber, and Henry Wilberforce) he uses the term "one true fold of Christ" or "one true fold of the Redeemer." In another three (including one to Edward Pusey) the reference is to the "one and only fold of Christ" or the "one and only fold of the Redeemer." On one occasion it is the "one Church and one Communion of Saints"; and three times (notably to Jemima and to Newman's great friend R.W. Church) he uses the term "one fold of Christ" or "one fold of the Redeemer."

It is interesting to note that after Newman's death, R.W. Church claimed that Newman had become a Catholic because only the Catholic Church preserved in full strength the spirit of "devotion and sacrifice of the Church of the Apostles."[3] This evades the true issue by falling back on subjective phenomena (devotion and sacrifice) when Newman was interested above all, as can be seen in the last paragraph, in the evidence of objective truth (the One True Fold).

Now let us move on another 146 years and consider the following. In 1991 Dr William Oddie was received into the Catholic

3   R.W. Church, "Cardinal Newman's Course," in *Occasional Papers, Volume* 2 (1897), 470.

Church. He was an Anglican clergyman and fellow of St Cross College, Oxford. He had, of course, written to the Anglican Bishop of Oxford, Richard Harries, to explain his position. The bishop then issued a press statement, which was widely publicized at the time, in which he stated that Oddie was merely "moving into another room in the same house." What is less well known is Oddie's response to this, which reads as follows:

> When I went to see him, I told him that was simply untrue. The truth was that I had been camping out in a garden shed, some distance from the main house, and one night when the rain was pouring in and the roof leaking, I went to the main house and begged for some shelter. And they opened the door and said "But of course! A room has always been ready and prepared for you. Welcome home!" That was the reality.[4]

There is a world of difference between the approach of John Henry Newman and that of Dr Richard Harries. Does this mean that the Catholic Church's teaching has changed on this most important issue? Well, it is certainly clear what Newman would have thought about Richard Harries' press release in 1991. We know this because of a remarkably similar event. In a letter written by Newman, two months after his conversion, to Dalgairns, Newman describes a meeting with Dr Pusey, who never of course converted, and states that Pusey expected them to act like vinedressers who had merely "transferred to another part of the vineyard."

Equally trenchant would have been Newman's attitude to those who today look forward to a supposed eventual fusion of Rome and Canterbury. He corresponded with such people, notably G. Dawson, an Anglican clergyman, in his own time and left no doubt as to what was the authentic Catholic attitude. In a letter written in 1848 Newman expressed clearly and directly why there could be no fusion:

> The Anglican and the Catholic are two religions. I have professed both, and must know better than those who have professed one only. It is not a case, then, that one believes a little more, and the other a little less; and

4 Joanna Bogle, "Obedience to the Pope Was What He Wanted," *This Rock*, September 2005, 38.

therefore that they could unite. The religions never could unite; they never could be reconciled together.[5]

He expounds this by listing a number of points where the two religions crucially differ, for example in respect to a living authority, one center of jurisdiction, the sacraments, and the question of ordination, concluding:

> It is a dream then to think of uniting the two religions; I speak from experience of both. And, in finding this to be the case, I am recording no disappointment on my part. I joined the Catholic Church to save my soul; I said so at the time. No inferior motive would have drawn me from the Anglican. And I came to it to learn, to receive what I should find, whatever it was. Never for an instant have I had since any misgiving I was right in doing so— never any misgiving that the Catholic religion was not the religion of the Apostles.[6]

It is because Newman held that conversion was a vitally import-ant matter, and, as he put it in 1851 to Mrs Lucy Agnes Phillips, the widow of an evangelical clergyman, "the Catholic Church claims absolute submission to her in matters of faith,"[7] that he insisted that a decision must be made. On the one hand, as he wrote to many correspondents, and to Mrs Phillips herself in the same letter, "unless you believe her doctrines, as the word of God revealed to you through her, you can gain no good by professing to be a Catholic—you are not one really."[8]

Newman emphasized the seriousness and urgency of conversion, and the danger of delaying it beyond a certain point. As he wrote in 1873 to another prospective convert, Mrs Newdigate:

> If your mind has been clear for some time that the Church we call Catholic is the one true fold of Christ, and if you can acknowledge all her teaching, what she teaches and shall teach, it is your simple duty to ask for admittance into her communion, and you cannot delay your actual reconcilia-tion, except the priest to whom you go tells you to delay.[9]

5   Letter to E. J. Phipps, July 3, 1848, *Letters and Diaries*, Vol. XII, 234-35.
6   Ibid.
7   *Letters and Diaries*, Vol. XIV, 292-93.
8   Ibid.
9   *Letters and Diaries*, Vol. XXVI, 341.

Newman kept preaching, especially to converts, that there was only One True Fold, that to belong to it was the key to one's eternal salvation, whereas to postpone endlessly one's conversion might inure one into the treacherous habit of living in sin, the sin of schism. As he wrote to Lord Charles Thynne (1813–1894), another prospective convert, whose conversion is dealt with in a later chapter of this book:

> I should argue, that, if the church be a kingdom, a body politic, visibly, it is impossible that both the Roman and the Anglican communion can be that one body politic—because they are two distinct bodies—Therefore one or other is *not* the Church, or, to use your language, *one or the other is in* schism.
>
> This being the case, if you have a fear of *going into schism* by joining Rome, have a fear too of *living* in schism by not joining Rome. And though of course the *onus probandi* lies with those who would urge you to Rome, the question is whether you have not had the proof made sufficiently clear to you to oblige you to act upon it. The question is, whether, were you dying, you would be satisfied in your not having joined Rome.[10]

So, to return to the question put earlier, has the Church changed its teaching on this issue? Not at all. One only needs to look at the teaching of the Second Vatican Council, especially the Constitution on the Church (*Lumen Gentium*) (1964) and the Decree on Ecumenism (*Unitatis Redintegratio*, 1964), together with a number of important post-conciliar documents. These would include, in particular, the following texts issued by the Congregation for the Doctrine of the Faith: *Mysterium Ecclesiae* (1973); *Notification on the Book of Father Leonardo Boff*, The Church: Charism and Power (1985); and *Dominus Jesus* (2000).

The latest summary and clarification of all this is contained in the CDF's document *Responses to Some Questions Regarding Certain Aspects of the Doctrine of the Church*, issued on June 29, 2007. The crucial passage is the following:

> Christ "established here on earth" only one Church and instituted it as a "visible and spiritual community" that

---

10 *Letters and Diaries*, Vol. XV, 27.

from its beginning and throughout the centuries has always existed and will always exist, and in which alone are found all the elements that Christ himself instituted. "This one Church of Christ, which we confess in the Creed as one, holy, catholic and apostolic.... This Church, constituted and organized in this world as a society, subsists in the Catholic Church, governed by the successor of Peter and the Bishops in communion with him."

In paragraph 8 of the Dogmatic Constitution *Lumen Gentium*, "subsistence" refers to this perduring historical continuity and the permanence of all the elements instituted by Christ in the Catholic Church, in which the Church of Christ is concretely found on this earth. As the Sacred Congregation's 2007 document goes on to say:

It is possible, according to Catholic doctrine, to affirm correctly that the Church of Christ is present and operative in the churches and ecclesial Communities not yet fully in communion with the Catholic Church, on account of the elements of sanctification and truth that are present in them. Nevertheless, the word "subsists" can only be attributed to the Catholic Church alone precisely because it refers to the mark of unity that we profess in the symbols of the faith (I believe ... in the "one" Church); and this "one" Church subsists in the Catholic Church.

In addition, in the *Notification on Leonardo Boff*, the essential points are made very clear indeed. In response to Boff's assertion that the one Church of Christ "is able to subsist in other Christian Churches," the Notification states that "the Council chose the word 'subsistit' specifically to clarify that the true Church has only one 'subsistence,' while outside her visible boundaries there are only '*elementa Ecclesiae*' which—being elements of the same Church—tend and lead to the Catholic Church." This is all part of the connection between Christ and his Church. The real reason the Church is One is that Christ is One. The voice of Christ is not preserved by churches that contradict it.

There is also the *Doctrinal Note on Some Aspects of Evangelization* issued by the Congregation for the Doctrine of the Faith on October 6, 2007, and dealing with the missions. It is completely in line with the documents quoted above.

When, therefore, we look at Newman's reflections on conversion, we can be confident that we are looking at the truth. In addition to the teaching of the Church on this question there is, of course, the force of logic. As that expert on Newman Fr Stanley Jaki writes,

> Newman's words were so many reminders that the Son of God, in whom alone there is salvation, established only One Fold, which therefore had to be the sole True Fold. After all, if God was one, and the Son was Only-begotten and took flesh in only one specific moment in space and time, then the uniqueness of that Fold had to appear a matter of elementary logic.[11]

Finally, there is no better way to express the Catholic faith on this issue than was done by Newman himself in 1851 in a letter to an unnamed woman: "Dear Madam, Of course, my only answer to you can be that the Catholic Church is the true fold of Christ, and that it is your duty to submit to it. You cannot do this without God's grace and therefore you ought to pray Him continually for it. All is well if God is on our side."[12]

Especially recommended on Newman's guidance to prospective converts is Fr Jaki's *Newman to Converts: An Existential Ecclesiology* (2001), published by *Real View Books* and available from the publishers at www.realviewbooks.com.

---

11 *Newman to Converts*, 403.
12 *Letters and Diaries*, Vol. XIV, 423.

CHAPTER THREE
Evelyn Waugh

OUT OF THE
LOOKING-GLASS WORLD

EVELYN WAUGH CHARACTERIZED HIS CONVERSION
and resulting reception into the Catholic Church in a way one might
expect, knowing his character, namely in an existential manner
combined with a touch of Lewis Carroll: "Conversion is like step-
ping across the chimney piece out of a Looking-Glass world, where
everything is an absurd caricature, into the real world God made;
and then begins the delicious process of exploring it limitlessly."[1]

On the question of arguments defending the Catholic faith
one can learn a great deal from considering the process of Evelyn
Waugh's conversion and how that process helped him understand
later threats to the Church. But first of all a brief summary of his

1   Unpublished letter to Edward Sackville-West, July 2, 1948, quoted in
Michael de-la-Noy, *Eddy: The Life of Edward Sackville-West* (1988), 238.

life would be appropriate. Waugh was born on October 28, 1903, at West Hampstead, London. He was brought up an Anglican and educated at Lancing College and then at Hertford College, Oxford. He spent a period as a skeptic before becoming a Catholic. He was known as a socialite and as one of the finest novelists of the twentieth century. His marriage to Evelyn Gardner (1903–1994) was annulled in 1936, and he later married Laura Herbert (1916–1973), from a staunch Catholic family. Waugh served in World War II in the Royal Marines, No. 8 Commando, and the Blues. He subsequently lived the life of a country gentleman on the considerable earnings from his books. Evelyn Waugh died on April 10, 1966, at his home, Combe Florey, in Somerset.

To start, then, with the issue of conversion, one should note that at the age of sixteen Evelyn Waugh informed his school chaplain (he was at an Anglican school) that there was no God. However, at the age of twenty-six Waugh became a Catholic. Many of his writings develop Catholic themes, and in what is still the best biography of Waugh, that by Douglas Patey,[2] the religious, moral, and political themes in Waugh's work appear as a relatively consistent whole. However, the only direct explanations Waugh gave for his conversion are contained in two sources: an interview with the *Daily Express* newspaper[3] and an account for a collection of conversion stories.[4]

In the *Daily Express* article Waugh first of all made it clear that three things had not happened. The Jesuits had not gotten hold of him; he had not been captivated by Catholic ritual; he did not want to have his mind made up for him (as if Waugh ever did!).

So, if these had not led him to the Catholic Church, what did? Waugh made two substantial points here. Firstly, "in the present phase of European history the essential issue is no longer between Catholicism, on the one side, and Protestantism, on the other, but between Christianity and Chaos."[5]

This resulted in his making two discoveries. The first was "that Christianity is essential to civilization and that it is in greater need of combative strength than it has been for centuries."[6] The second

2 Douglas Lane Patey, *The Life of Evelyn Waugh: A Critical Biography* (1998).
3 "Converted to Rome: Why It Has Happened to Me," reprinted in Donat Gallagher (ed.), *The Essays, Articles and Reviews of Evelyn Waugh* (1983), 103–5.
4 "Come Inside," in O'Brien (ed.), *The Road to Damascus*, 10.
5 Gallagher (ed.), 103.
6 Ibid., 104.

discovery was "that Christianity exists in its most complete and vital form in the Roman Catholic Church."[7] Waugh acknowledged the good lives being led by many individual Protestants, but he had come to believe that the religious bodies to which they belonged "are not fitted for the conflict in which Christianity is engaged."[8]

Waugh's second substantial point concerned what he saw as the necessary signs of "completeness and vitality in a religious body."[9] These amounted to establishing (a) "that its teaching shall be coherent and consistent";[10] (b) that there is "competent organization and discipline";[11] and (c) (expressed as most important of all) that "any religious body which is not by nature universal cannot claim to represent complete Christianity."[12] It was these signs that led Waugh to the Catholic Church.

In his contribution to the collection of conversion stories Waugh emphasizes a historical point, and a very important one at that:

> England was Catholic for nine hundred years, then Protestant for three hundred, then agnostic for a century. The Catholic structure still lies lightly buried beneath every phase of English life; history, topography, law, archaeology everywhere reveal Catholic origins. Foreign travel anywhere reveals the local, temporary character of the heresies and schisms and the universal, eternal character of the Church. It was self-evident to me that no heresy or schism could be right and the Church wrong. It was possible that all were wrong, that the whole Christian revelation was an imposture or a misconception. But if the Christian revelation was true, then the Church was the society founded by Christ and all other bodies were only good so far as they had salvaged something from the wrecks of the Great Schism and the Reformation. This proposition seemed so plain to mean that it admitted of no discussion.[13]

Having come to this conclusion, Waugh considered that "it only remained to examine the historical and philosophic grounds

7   Ibid.
8   Ibid.
9   Ibid.
10   Ibid.
11   Ibid.
12   Ibid.
13   O'Brien (ed.), *The Road to Damascus*, 15.

for supposing the Christian revelation to be genuine."[14] This was done to his satisfaction by "a brilliant and holy priest,"[15] Fr. Martin D'Arcy, SJ. There were, of course, other influences on him, notably Christopher Hollis, Douglas Woodruff, and Olivia Plunket Greene. On September 29, 1930, Waugh was duly received into the Catholic Church by Fr. D'Arcy at the Jesuit church on Farm Street in London. This was a conversion of which Arthur Waugh, Evelyn's father, liked to speak as a "perversion" to Rome![16]

Much later in his life, Waugh would discuss his conversion in a *Face to Face* interview with John Freeman on BBC television on June 26, 1960. This is what he said: "Well, I think I'd always, I say always, from the age of sixteen or so, realized that Catholicism was Christianity, that all other forms of Christianity were only good so far as they chipped little bits off the main block. It is a conversion to Christianity rather than a conversion to Catholicism as such."[17]

When Julian Jebb interviewed Waugh,[18] Jebb stated, "it is evident that you reverence the authority of established institutions," and gave as one example the Catholic Church. Waugh said, "No, certainly not. I reverence the Catholic Church because it is true, not because it is established or an institution."

To judge the religious aspects of Waugh's life after his conversion, it is useful to examine his approach to the whole question of accepting the Catholic faith. It so happens that we have an interesting third-party analysis by Fr D'Arcy himself:

> All converts have to listen while the teaching of the Church is explained to them—first to make sure that they do in fact know the essentials of the faith and secondly to save future misunderstandings, for it can easily happen that mere likings or impressions, which fade, may have hidden disagreements with undiscovered doctrines. Another writer came to me at the same time as Evelyn Waugh and tested what was being told him by how far it corresponded with his experience. With such a criterion, it was no wonder that he did not persevere. Evelyn, on the other hand, never

14   Ibid., 14.
15   Ibid.
16   Terence Greenidge, *Evelyn Waugh in Letters*, ed. Charles E. Linck (1994), 11.
17   www.youtube.com/watch?v=UvtjUtoGzKg.
18   "Evelyn Waugh: The Art of Fiction No. 30," *The Paris Review*, Summer-Fall 1963.

spoke of experience or feelings. He had come to learn and understand what he believed to be God's revelation, and this made talking with him an interesting discussion based primarily on reason. I have never myself met a convert who so strongly based his assents on truth.... Nor, though he writes about "little emotion," was his conversion so very matter of fact, because it proved to be an illumination and an inspiration. Hard, clear thinking had with the help of grace given him the answer for which he had been searching, and one can see its effect in his subsequent writings.[19]

Waugh himself is always adamant in playing down the role of emotion in faith. In a letter written on September 17, 1964, to Lady Diana Cooper (1892–1986), he asks her, "Do you believe in the Incarnation and Redemption in the full historical sense in which you believe in the battle of El Alamein? That's important. Faith is not a mood."[20]

In addition, in *Helena* (1950), an account of St Helena's search for the true cross of Christ (interestingly Waugh's favorite of his own books) there is the following passage, expressed in a similar way:

> "Tell me, Lactantius, this God of yours. If I asked you when and where he could be seen, what would you say?" "I should say that as a man he died two hundred and seventy-eight years ago in the town now called Aelia Capitolina in Palestine." "Well, that's a straight answer anyway. How do you know?" "We have the accounts written by witnesses. Besides that there is the living memory of the Church."[21]

After his conversion Waugh devoted himself to defending Christian civilization and contemplating the meaninglessness of human existence without God. Waugh was not in love in any way with modern society, his views of which are represented by Charles Ryder's attitude towards the character Hooper in *Brideshead Revisited* (1945).

One should conclude with some consideration of the sadness of the last few years of Waugh's life, caused not so much by his physical decline as by the loss of venerable practices in the

19 "The Religion of Evelyn Waugh," in David Pryce-Jones (ed.), *Evelyn Waugh and His World* (1973), 59.
20 Mark Amory (ed.), *The Letters of Evelyn Waugh* (1980), 624.
21 *Helena* (1950), 85.

Church which Waugh valued highly. In his comments at the time, he unerringly put his finger on the likely consequences of some proposed changes: a weakening of the sacrificial element of the Mass and the essential nature of the priesthood. He also pointed to the dangers of the version of ecumenism, false to the Council itself, that some sought to promote, involving as it did a dilution of the faith rather than a clarification of what the true faith involved.

In an excellent essay on Waugh, Simon Leys sums up his view of this period: "At the end of his life, with an anguish that came close to despair, Waugh witnessed the dreadful invasion of shallowness and puerility which began to undermine and destroy some of the most precious and venerable traditions of the Church."[22]

Waugh's great friend Christopher Sykes (1907–1986), in his biography of Waugh, was adamant that "[Waugh's] dislike of the reform-movement was not merely an expression of his conservatism, nor of aesthetic preferences. It was based on deeper things."[23] What were those deeper things? Well, they emerge in the course of an article that he wrote in the *Catholic Herald*, in which he does mention "conservatism," but not of the political kind:

> The function of the Church in every age has been conservative—to transmit undiminished and uncontaminated the creed inherited from its predecessors. Not "is this fashionable notion one that we should accept?" but "is this dogma (a subject on which we agree) the Faith as we received it?" has been the question (as far as I know) at all General Councils.... Conservatism is not a new influence in the Church. It is not the heresies of the sixteenth and seventeenth centuries, the agnosticism of the eighteenth century, the atheism of the nineteenth and twentieth centuries, that have been the foes of the Faith turning her from serene supremacy to sharp controversy. Throughout her entire life the Church has been at active war with enemies from without and traitors from within.[24]

Waugh is often criticized as a snob who wants to luxuriate in the life and company of aristocratic Catholics. This is unfair.

22 "Terror of Babel," in *The Hall of Uselessness: Collected Essays* (2011), 200.
23 *Evelyn Waugh: A Biography* (1975), 595.
24 "Changes in the Church: Questions for the 'Progressives,'" *Catholic Herald*, August 7, 1964, 4.

In the *Sword of Honour* trilogy[25] his attitude, as expressed by Mr. Crouchback, the father of the main character, Guy Crouchback, is down-to-earth and eminently practical:

> The Mystical Body doesn't strike attitudes and stand on its dignity. It accepts suffering and injustice. It is ready to forgive at the first hint of compunction. When you spoke of the Lateran Treaty did you consider how many souls may have been reconciled and have died at peace as the result of it? How many children may have been brought up in the faith who might have lived in ignorance? Quantitative judgments don't apply. If only one soul was saved, that is full compensation for any amount of loss of "face."[26]

The function of the Church is not to build up the walls against barbarism, but to bring the whole of humanity in.

Waugh was also very critical of the liturgical changes being suggested at the Second Vatican Council. He died before the *Novus Ordo Missae* came into force, but the transitional changes that he saw during the last three years of his life caused him great distress. Early on he made fun of new practices, such as priests saying Mass facing the congregation, which until the early 1960s had seemed only "fads."[27] But now changes of much broader scope threatened. He mentions them very movingly in the *Catholic Herald* article just referred to:

> Finally, a word about liturgy. "Participation" in the Mass does not mean hearing our own voices. It means God hearing our voices. Only He knows who is "participating" at Mass. I believe, to compare small things with great, that I "participate" in a work of art when I study it and love it silently. No need to shout....
>
> I am now old but I was young when I was received into the Church. I was not at all attracted by the splendor of her great ceremonies—which the Protestants could well counterfeit. Of the extraneous attractions of the Church which most drew me was the spectacle of the priest and his server at low Mass, stumping up to the altar without

25 *Men at Arms* (1952); *Officers and Gentlemen* (1955); *Unconditional Surrender* (1961).
26 *Unconditional Surrender*, 17.
27 See "Ecclesiology," review of Peter Anson, *Fashions in Church Furnishings*, *The Spectator*, April 22, 1960, 581.

a glance to discover how many or how few he had in his congregation; a craftsman and his apprentice; a man with a job which he alone was qualified to do. That is the Mass I have grown to know and love. By all means let the rowdy have their "dialogues," but let us who value silence not be completely forgotten.[28]

Christopher Sykes makes the point that Waugh "believed that in its long history the Church had developed a liturgy which enabled an ordinary, sensual man (as opposed to a saint who is outside generalization) to approach God and be aware of sanctity and the divine. To abolish all this for the sake of up-to-dateness seemed to him not only silly but dangerous.... He could not bear the thought of modernized liturgy. 'Untune that string,' he felt, and loss of faith would follow.... Whether his fears were justified or not only 'the unerring sentence of time' can show."[29]

Well, in the opinion of the present writer, for what it is worth, Waugh was "spot on" in his thoughts on the liturgy. Exactly a year before his death he made this entry in his diary:

Easter 1965: A year in which the process of transforming the liturgy has followed a planned course. Protests avail nothing. A minority of cranks, for and against the innovations, mind enormously. I don't think the main congregation cares a hoot. More than the aesthetic changes which rob the Church of poetry, mystery and dignity, there are suggested changes in Faith and morals which alarm me. A kind of anti-clericalism is abroad which seeks to reduce the priest's unique sacramental position. The Mass is written of as a "social meal" in which the "people of God" perform the consecration. Pray God I will never apostatize but I can only now go to church as an act of duty and obedience—just as a sentry at Buck[ingham Palace] is posted with no possibility of his being employed to defend the sovereign's life. Cardinal Heenan has been double-faced in the matter. I had dinner with him *a deux* in which he expressed complete sympathy with the conservatives and, as I understood him, promised resistance to the innovations which he is now pressing forward. How does he suppose the cause of participation is furthered

28 *Catholic Herald*, August 7, 1964, 4.
29 *Evelyn Waugh: A Biography* (1975), 595.

by the prohibition of kneeling at the Incarnatus in the creed? The Catholic press has made no opposition. I shall not live to see things righted.[30]

Waugh confessed to Nancy Mitford that "the buggering up of the Church is a deep sorrow to me and to all I know."[31] In Easter 1966 he expressed similar sentiments to Diana Mosley:

> Easter used to mean so much to me. Before Pope John and his Council—they destroyed the beauty of the liturgy. I have not yet soaked myself in petrol and gone up in flames, but I now cling to the Faith doggedly without joy. Church-going is a pure duty parade. I shall not live to see it restored. It is worse in many countries.[32]

Evelyn Waugh died on Easter Sunday 1966. He had been earlier on that very day to Mass in the old Latin rite that he loved so much. He was correct in thinking that he would not live to see things righted in respect of the liturgy, but he would no doubt have been gratified at the measures taken by Pope Benedict XVI to bring the old rite of Mass into regular use in the life of the Church. He would also have been impressed by the depth of analysis of this form of liturgy by a number of writers.[33] He would undoubtedly, however, have been distressed by Pope Francis's later decision to restrict the availability of the old rite of Mass. Waugh's wish, as we have seen, was that those with a love for the old liturgy should "not be completely forgotten." By the grace of God his wish has been achieved. As Evelyn Waugh appreciated, and here we can adopt the words of the historian Owen Chadwick, "Liturgies are not made, they grow in the devotion of centuries."[34]

30   Michael Davie (ed.), *The Diaries of Evelyn Waugh* (1976), 793.
31   Amory (ed.), *The Letters of Evelyn Waugh*, 633.
32   Ibid., 639.
33   See, for example, Fr Klaus Gamber, *The Reform of the Roman Liturgy: Its Problems and Background* (1993); Fr Aidan Nichols, *Looking at the Liturgy: A Critical View of Its Contemporary Form* (1996); Martin Mosebach, *The Heresy of Formlessness: The Roman Liturgy and its Enemy* (2003); Dom Alcuin Reid, *The Organic Development of the Liturgy* (2004); Peter Kwasniewski, *Noble Beauty, Transcendent Holiness* (2017) and *Reclaiming Our Roman Catholic Birthright* (2020).
34   *The Reformation* (1972), 119.

CHAPTER FOUR
Holding the Catholic Tradition

EVELYN WAUGH REVISITED

EVELYN WAUGH'S REPUTATION HAS BOTH RISEN
and fallen since his death in 1966. It has risen in the sense that
it has come to be recognized just how fine a writer he was, both
stylistically and from the point of view of plotting, characterization,
and structure. The publicity given to the fine dramatization of
Brideshead Revisited in the 1980s helped in this respect. However,
the counterpart of this is that the message got out that Waugh
was an awkward customer, opposed to all progress, and, worst
of all according to some, devoted to a form of Catholicism now
outmoded. Moreover, or so it was often said, the books were relatively narrow in their theme, marked by a particular form of satire.
As a result of this Waugh tends even now to be characterized as

an old-fashioned conservative (a kiss of death in most academic circles these days), and, even worse, a snob.

However, much true factual information and fair interpretation have resulted from the publication in 1998 of Douglas Lane Patey's *The Life of Evelyn Waugh*. This is undoubtedly the finest biography of Waugh yet to be written. Of course, it must still be conceded that Waugh was in some respects his own worst enemy. In later life he acted up to the part that the media had created for him. One only has to think of the time when, suffering from increasing deafness, he purchased an Edwardian ear-trumpet, seventeen inches long when fully extended, and insisted on using it at public meetings. On one occasion, as Malcolm Muggeridge (1903–1990) rose to speak at a literary luncheon, Waugh managed to deliver a snub on the grand scale by pointedly lowering this "machine," taking it up again only when the speaker sat down.[1] There is, of course, an irony in this, since the position that Muggeridge took on several important issues later in life was relatively close to that of Waugh.

Waugh was a person who delighted to shock and, if pushed in a particular direction, would respond by adopting an even more extreme pose (especially when drunk). But many of these things were just that, a pose. And so emerged the man who did not vote because he did not "aspire to advise my sovereign in her choice of servants";[2] the one who responded to some tedious praise of *Brideshead Revisited* by stating: "I thought it was a good book but if a common boring American woman like you says it's very good, it must be very bad."[3] Some of the famous stories have turned out to be untrue (notably the one in which Pope Pius XI is said to have rebuked Waugh during an audience with the words, "But Mr Waugh, you must remember that I am a Catholic too"), but enough remain to show that they are by no means all apocryphal. One might just add in mitigation that in his diaries and letters there are many examples where he chastises himself for having been uncharitable and prays to be given the virtue of charity. Here is a typically amusing example:

1   Martin Stannard, *Evelyn Waugh: Volume II, No Abiding City, 1939–1966* (Flamingo, 1993), 390–92.
2   "Aspirations of a Mugwump," *The Spectator*, October 2, 1959, reprinted in Donat Gallagher (ed.), *The Essays, Articles and Reviews of Evelyn Waugh* (1983), 537.
3   Christopher Sykes, "Evelyn Waugh—The Man," in Derwent May (ed.), *Good Talk: An Anthology from BBC Radio* (1969), 11.

> Yesterday Laura [his wife] announced to me that a stone
> vase had fallen from a pillar on the head of one of my
> workmen. "O dear is it badly broken?" "It's bleeding
> profusely." "No no I mean the vase." This came out quite
> instinctively. How to reconcile this indifference to human
> beings with the obligations of Charity. That is my problem.
> But I am sure that Dickensian geniality is as far from
> Charity as my indifference.[4]

It is perhaps Waugh's own fault if he has suffered posthumously
from bad publicity, but the time has come to set the balance right
and this has now been done very well by Douglas Patey. It had
already been noted by other biographers that Waugh could be a very
generous individual (and unlike most of today's media stars, he didn't
feel the need to call a press conference to announce an imminent
act of charity). He helped people privately in a significant way when
standing to gain nothing himself. Patey goes further in bringing
these things out in an objective way. He also examines the bemused
attitude of the critics when Waugh himself brought out several of
his more unattractive traits in *The Ordeal of Gilbert Pinfold* (1957).

Waugh has not on the whole been fortunate in his biographers.
The earliest, Christopher Sykes,[5] was too close to him to be objective and lacked the written resources available to later writers.
Martin Stannard[6] gives much detail and is always interesting, but
he lacks that overall sympathy with his subject that is necessary in
order to write biography, something that is particularly notable in
the second volume of his work. Selina Hastings[7] brings out much
valuable detail on a number of issues, most notably surrounding the
nullity proceedings over Waugh's marriage to Evelyn Gardner (on
which certain slurs on Waugh's behavior are shown to be without
foundation). However, there is little of detail and depth in her writings; and the philosophical underpinnings of Waugh's works and
his own views are not explored fully. Philip Eade[8] states that his
biography is not a "critical" one and that it does not seek to assess

4 Artemis Cooper (ed.), *Mr. Wu and Mrs. Stitch: The Correspondence of Evelyn Waugh and Diana Cooper* (1991), 38.
5 *Evelyn Waugh: A Biography* (1975).
6 *Evelyn Waugh: The Early Years 1903-1939* (1986); *Evelyn Waugh, Volume II: No Abiding City 1939-1966* (1992).
7 *Evelyn Waugh: A Biography* (1994).
8 *Evelyn Waugh: A Life Revisited* (2016).

his achievement as a writer, but to paint a fresh portrait of the man. He spends little time on Waugh's writings and much on gossip.

In addition to all this, something of great importance is missing from almost all the other studies of Waugh: the importance of religion in his writing. This aspect is for the first time brought out in great detail and with great skill by Douglas Patey. For example, there is much valuable information about the spirituality of Evelyn Waugh. Though this has never been the subject of any full study, and has been in some circles the object of some cynicism (here again Waugh himself has not always helped the cause), it is of interest in itself. But to those of us (surely the overwhelming majority) who find some of the great mystical saints of the Church somewhat daunting, the faltering stumbling of Waugh's efforts to come to grips with prayer gives consolation of a different kind: the assurance that somebody else has been there and found it just as difficult as we do. Useful remarks along these lines can be found scattered through Waugh's published works, in his novels and non-fiction, in his letters and diaries. The importance of Patey's analysis is that he goes deeper than Waugh's personal spirituality. He brings out in great detail the various religious, moral, and political themes in Waugh's work and shows them to be a consistent whole, something that has not been done before. He even gives copious examples from the early books of this aspect of Waugh's work. For example, if we look at *Labels* (1930), a travel book written before his conversion to Catholicism, we find this passage dealing with contraception, which shows a clear familiarity with, and sympathy for, the Catholic position:

> What a lot of nonsense people will talk about sex repression. In many cases an enforced and unrationalized celibacy does give rise to those morbid conditions which supply material for the jollier passages in the Sunday newspapers. But in healthier psychological organisms, a sublimated sex motive may account for a vast proportion of the beneficial activities of man; copulation is not the only laudable expression of the procreative urge—certainly not copulation in which the procreative motive has been laboriously frustrated. The Christian virtues of charity and chastity have from old time an indissoluble alliance.[9]

9 *Labels* (1930), 50.

Many of Waugh's early novels, such as *Decline and Fall* (1928) and *Vile Bodies* (1930), are generally treated by critics as simply light satirical works, but even here there are important themes of a religious nature dealt with according to a consistent approach. Yes, the themes are introduced with some subtlety, which may have fooled modern critics, but they are there nevertheless. There may be a critical aspect to some of the material at this stage, but it is always linked in with a positive element. In relation to *Decline and Fall*, for instance, Patey shows how the book "mocks modern architecture, modern penology, modern education, modern church-manship—even modern photography—not merely to discredit the new, but to point up the need for a proper ground of value in all these areas, an 'objective ethics' without which man's fallen nature cannot be restrained and his energies fruitfully channeled."[10]

And from where does this proper ground of value come? The hero of *Decline and Fall*, Paul Pennyfeather, like the heroes in all Waugh's early works, finally comes to the knowledge of what is needed to restore order: "The modern world is living on dwindling cultural capital, on inherited institutions deformed by having been cut off from the living Faith that was the source of their authority. Without authoritative institutions, anarchy takes over."[11]

It is relatively easy to identify a "political period" in Waugh's output, specifically between 1930 and 1935, in which he developed a philosophy, a conservative individualism, based essentially on a Burkean pragmatism, and deeply opposed to utopian collectivist schemes.

> In a stream of essays and books, he argued against the Left that liberty and equality are not finally compatible; that the measure of any system of rule is the quality of private life it permits and fosters; and that utopian notions of "progress," either in their nineteenth-century Liberal form or in more modern Marxian guise, rest on a "sentimental belief in the basic sweetness of human nature"...which, reduced to practice, ends in cruelty.[12]

On the matter of politics, the key to understanding Waugh's attitude in the thirties is that he abhorred equally both Fascism

10 Patey, *The Life of Evelyn Waugh*, 59.
11 Ibid., 72.
12 Ibid., 85.

and Communism. His hostility to the latter is often emphasized. He is seen as an old-style right-winger, but both Fascism and Communism were seen by him simply as alternative totalitarianisms, hostile to any form of individualism. And in many ways Communism was seen by him as the greater danger, being a substitute religion and having a creed of its own. Here, as in many other places, Patey makes the point unerringly:

> Fascism had its attractions because Communism, with its longer record of religious persecution and its totalist world-view, appeared the greater evil. Fascism, as Waugh put the case, was a "rough improvisation," its policies merely "opportunist."... But Communism was based on a philosophy: on an explicitly atheistic creed, a utopian "faith like a Christian's" that claimed to encompass all of life, to explain the *telos* of human life and history. In all this Waugh followed the influential analysis of Christopher Dawson, who ... argued ... that "Communism challenges Christianity on its own ground by offering mankind a rival way of salvation," standing over against the Christian Church as a *counter-church* with its own dogmas and its own moral standards, ruled by a centralized hierarchy and inspired by an intense will to world conquest.[13]

Perhaps the clearest statements of Waugh's castigation of the twin evils of Communism and Fascism, as well as his own political beliefs, are to be found in the travel book *Robbery under Law* (1939). Patey shows well how these views are neither eccentric nor original but merely an application of the tenets of the social encyclicals *Rerum Novarum* (1891), on the rights and duties of capital and labor, and *Quadragesimo Anno* (1931), on the reconstruction of the social order. It must be understood that Waugh's proposed individualism, in both politics and literature, is not an economic thesis. It is a theological one. As Patey expresses it, "what finally individuates us, and what must be at the ground of literary characterization, is the unique purpose given each of us by God."[14]

On the aspect of literary characterization here, Waugh himself puts the matter as clearly as possible: "I believe that you can only leave God out by making your characters pure abstractions.

13   Ibid., 145.
14   Ibid., 180.

Countless admirable writers, perhaps some of the best in the world, succeed in this.... They try to represent the whole human mind and soul and yet omit its determining character—that of being God's creature with a defined purpose."[15]

Waugh's politics were clearly influenced by T. S. Eliot (1888–1965) and by the somewhat neglected critic and philosopher T. E. Hulme (1883–1917), who criticized attempts to base notions of ethical value on the purely human and argued that humanism constituted an alternative to religion, which led inevitably to relativism. Hulme's thesis was that it was "'Progress' which is the modern substitute for religion."[16]

Another figure who was very influential in Waugh's view of the world was Christopher Dawson (1889–1970), and allusions to his *Religion and the Modern State* (1935) are particularly noticeable in Waugh's early and later works alike. The following passage from *Religion and the Modern State* is characteristic:

> European culture had already ceased to be Christian in the eighteenth century, but it still retained the inherited moral standards and values of a Christian civilization. And so it attempted to erect these standards into an independent system by providing a rational philosophic justification for them. This was the Liberal idealism that was the faith of the nineteenth century—not a religious faith, but a quasi-religious substitute for one.
>
> But as Liberalism did not create these moral ideals, so, too, it cannot preserve them. It lives on the spiritual capital that it has inherited from Christian civilization, and as this is exhausted something else must come to take its place.[17]

It is the element of individualism, and not any form of elitism, that explains Waugh's frequently expressed hostility to the "common man." The key to understanding Waugh here is to appreciate that, as he put it on one occasion, "The Common Man does not exist. He is an abstraction invented by bores for bores."[18] He saw the use of the term as a device for downplaying the very real individualism of each person in pursuit of a collectivist socialist goal. All of Waugh's

15 "Fan-Fare," *Life*, April 8, 1946, reprinted in Gallagher (ed.), 300.
16 *Speculations: Essays on Humanism and the Philosophy of Art* (1924), 35.
17 Dawson, 54.
18 "Fan-Fare," *Life*, April 8, 1946, reprinted in Gallagher (ed.), 300.

uses of this term, as in the famous "Face to Face" interview with John Freeman (1915–2014), must be seen in this light.

All through the 1930s, notably in *A Handful of Dust* (1934), Waugh continued to develop his critique of humanism, but with an added element taken from Catholic tradition:

> Humanism in its modern, secular form, with its denial of sin and utopian belief in a satisfying human order achievable by purely human means, had been a central target of his satire since *Decline and Fall*. Now Waugh deepens his critique by placing his representative humanists within a sharply defined Catholic view of history, the same history sketched in "Come Inside":[19] "England was Catholic for nine hundred years, then Protestant for three hundred, then agnostic for a century."[20]

A Handful of Dust contains a sustained criticism of modern Anglicanism. The latter "with its picturesque churches, vaguely ethical outlook and fuzziness over doctrine represents in this view the final phase of the Victorians' substitution of sentiment for faith."[21] This latter theme is again one that has been present since *Decline and Fall* and represents a continuing theme of Waugh's criticism of Anglicanism: its "concern with externals rather than a traditional, living, sacramental faith."[22]

Another example of the logical development of themes in Waugh's writing is provided by his biography of the Jesuit martyr Edmund Campion (1540–1581). According to Christopher Hollis, a great friend of Waugh for many years, "it was his study of Campion, his discovery of a man who thought that all must be sacrificed for religion, which was the great turning point in his life."[23] From then on he was to concentrate on a positive Catholic apologetic in his writing. What was shown in the biography of Campion, involving as it did an examination of the Reformation period, was how the world of *A Handful of Dust*, eaten away by humanism and polite skepticism, came into being.[24]

19 An account of his conversion, written in 1949: O'Brien (ed.), *The Road to Damascus*, 10.
20 Patey, *The Life of Evelyn Waugh*, 118.
21 Ibid., 119.
22 Ibid., 65.
23 John St John, *To the War with Waugh* (1975), viii.
24 Patey, *The Life of Evelyn Waugh*, 125.

In relation to the Reformation issues, incidentally, Waugh was clearly influenced by the approach of Hilaire Belloc (1870–1953)[25] to this period, an approach that has now been given added credibility by the researches of so-called revisionist historians such as Christopher Haigh,[26] J. F. Scarisbrick,[27] and, most notably, Eamon Duffy.[28]

It is true, then, that the religious element in Waugh's writing during the thirties, though perhaps understated, is there nonetheless. For example, that masterly novel satirizing the press, *Scoop* (1938), is full of references to false trails, such as the compromise enshrined in High Anglicanism.

The three main later works of Waugh that focus on religious issues are *Brideshead Revisited*, the *Sword of Honour* trilogy, and *Helena*. Patey brings out very well the important religious themes developed there. *Helena*, a fictionalized account of the titular saint's finding of the true Cross, brings out very well the relationship between historical records and Christian faith. It also emphasizes Waugh's belief in the unimportance of this life compared with the next. Finally, and very importantly as we shall see in relation to the other two works, it presents a thesis that was of crucial importance in Waugh's own personal thought: that God put man on this earth to do a special task. This vocation is seen as a call to a "single, peculiar act of service," some unique act: "What we can learn from *Helena* is something about the workings of God; that he wants a different thing from each of us, laborious or easy, conspicuous or quite private, but something which only we can do and for which we were each created."[29]

About *Brideshead Revisited* and the *Sword of Honour* trilogy a great deal might be written. Both works trace the path of the hero's development from "lesser loves to greater, from human loves to God."[30] The theme of personal vocation, as worked out in *Brideshead Revisited*, is seen for example with Sebastian's final act of renunciation in which he helps the unattractive Kurt. The

25 See, e.g., *How the Reformation Happened* (1928).
26 See, e.g., *The English Reformation Revised* (1987).
27 See, e.g., *Reformation and the English People* (1984).
28 See, e.g., *The Stripping of the Altars: Traditional Religion in England, c.1400 to c.1580* (1992); *The Voices of Morebath: Reformation and Rebellion in an English Village* (2001); *Fires of Faith: Catholic England under Mary Tudor* (2009); *Reformation Divided: Catholics, Protestants, and the Conversion of England* (2017).
29 "St. Helena Empress," *The Month*, January 1952, 11.
30 Patey, *The Life of Evelyn Waugh*, 224.

whole chapter in Patey's biography on *Brideshead Revisited* is a tour de force on the profound religious issues explored in that work. The *Sword of Honour* trilogy tells of the development of its hero, Guy Crouchback, from illusions of military honor and grandeur, the identification of modern warfare with a religious crusade, to his "unconditional surrender... to providence and a renewed religious faith."[31] This, again, comes with his acceptance of the notion of vocation referred to above: "Guy Crouchback succumbs in wartime to a series of false notions of heroic purpose before recognizing and embracing that 'small service which only he could perform, for which he had been created. Even he must have his function in the divine plan. He did not expect a heroic destiny.'"[32] As with other aspects of Waugh's fiction, one can trace through the autobiographical elements and draw out the equivalent factors in Waugh's own life. Here we see how his essential melancholy and depression were transcended, albeit transiently and intermittently.

The cure for Guy's "emptiness" and "apathy" is service to Virginia's child and the Jews of Begoy; the thawing of Waugh's own wartime "ice age" came through his invigorating, signal service at the deathbed of Hubert Duggan (1904–1943), the model for Lord Marchmain in *Brideshead Revisited*, followed by the exhilarating months of writing that book, his first explicitly Catholic novel—the book that seemed to confirm his new sense of his writerly vocation—and his work in Yugoslavia. Small services, but real and uniquely his own.[33]

There is a spiritual lesson to be learned here. It is brought out most profoundly in *Sword of Honour*, in connection with the character of Guy Crouchback's father, who is the key to Guy's coming to understand his situation and thereby the key to the trilogy. When Guy hears that Italy has been defeated, he says to his father that the pope should have sat secure and unsullied within the Vatican instead of making the political accommodations that led to the Lateran Treaty of 1929. His father immediately rebukes this "nonsense" with words quoted in an earlier chapter, but equally relevant here:

31 Ibid., 350.
32 Ibid., 296, quoting from *Unconditional Surrender*, 81.
33 Ibid.

That isn't at all what the Church is like. It isn't what she's for. The Mystical Body doesn't strike attitudes and stand on its dignity. It accepts suffering and injustice.... When you spoke of the Lateran Treaty did you consider how many souls may have been reconciled and died at peace as the result of it? How many children may have been brought up in the faith who might have lived in ignorance? Quantitative judgments don't apply. If only one soul was saved, that is full compensation for any amount of loss of "face."[34]

These words are recalled time after time in the later parts of that book. In addition, Guy's act of taking back his wife, whom he no longer loves, in order to adopt the illegitimate son of another man as his own, is the embodiment of his father's words. A friend of Guy reminds him that the world is full of unwanted children; what is one child more or less in all the misery? "It was no good trying to explain, Guy thought. Had someone said, 'All differences are theological differences'? He turned once more to his father's letter: *Quantitative judgments don't apply*."[35] This is the key to an active faith, the way out of sloth and despair, which Waugh himself knew all about. It is charity of this kind that gains actual grace, which is the prompt to further good actions.

A related theme often appears in Waugh's writing: the function of the Church is not to build up the walls against barbarism, but to bring the whole of humanity in. This is interesting, because many have seen Waugh's criticisms of the proposed liturgical reforms in the sixties as representing the Catholic view that everything should be restored to how it was on the death of Pope Pius XII in 1958. A priest friend of the present writer once suggested that there was an article, or even a book, waiting to be written on the subject of "Evelyn Waugh: Victim of Vatican II." That is much too simplistic a description. Far from seeing any ideal model of the Church as existing in the pontificate of Pope Pius XII, Waugh saw several of that pope's reforms as setting the scene for some undesirable later developments.[36] This, together with a whole series of other issues relating to the crisis in the Church over

34 *Unconditional Surrender*, 10.
35 Ibid., 193-94.
36 Patey, *The Life of Evelyn Waugh*, 359-60.

the last sixty years, is certainly a worthy area of research. Once again Patey accurately sifts the truth about Waugh's views of the Conciliar era from the mythology that has grown up:

> Many of Waugh's opponents in the debates sparked by Vatican II thought him motivated merely by traditionalist aesthetic preferences and a snobbish anti-ecumenism. But Waugh always stressed that the "dangers threatening the Church" were to be resisted on graver grounds than the merely sentimental, aesthetic, or traditional: they posed, he believed, a grave threat to piety. Lurking behind this explicit argument was perhaps another fear. "I think the heart of the matter is: do you seek uniformity or diversity in the Church?" Many asked in the wake of the Council whether in sacrificing uniformity, the Church might not also endanger universality. For thirty years, the Church's universality had been the cornerstone of Waugh's thought and a source of profound joy. He had argued that human freedom and diversity were possible only within a framework of accepted moral truth; that relativism frustrated individual and social growth; that an objective ethics could rest only on a religious foundation. Since 1930 he had argued that the most fundamental moral, social and political choice was between "Christianity and Chaos." Was his own Church now taking the first steps towards accommodation with a new brand of modernism, put forward by "traitors from within"?[37]

This conclusion is necessarily sad, but one has the vision of a man doggedly defending the faith, while never allowing himself to be driven from his religious duties, and this itself is uplifting.

37   Patey, 561.

CHAPTER FIVE
Denys Blakelock

ACTOR AND CONVERT

IT IS NOT NECESSARY TO BE A PROFESSIONAL theologian to expound the faith and argue for its truth. Denys Blakelock was an object lesson in this. Despite having no theological qualifications, he was able to put forward immensely powerful arguments for the Catholic faith. More of this shortly, but first of all, a few facts about his life and background.

Denys Martin Blakelock was born on Saturday, June 22, 1901, in Muswell Hill, then a countrified area of London. He was the son of a stern yet sentimental Anglican rector and his cold and reserved wife. He was brought up in a Victorian Protestantism that had its drawbacks:

> Although I very early came to look upon Jesus Christ as someone infinitely loving, endlessly forgiving, and anxious to help and encourage, I am bound to say that, in

my mind, God the Father was a sort of Old Testament Jehovah; loving as long as you were willing and able to do perfectly what he wanted, but who, at the slightest sign of weakness or disobedience, was ready to pounce on you like a Dickensian schoolmaster. [1]

He was treated with great severity by his mother and was beaten and locked in a cupboard for breaking rules. This led him to develop a dual nature. One side was intelligent and kind, the other anxious and depressed, with scruples, claustrophobia, and much uncertainty and doubt. Blakelock reflects on his father's over-scrupulous, worrying mind, especially in relation to sexual matters, and concludes that "the seeds of anxiety planted in my father's mind became seeds of disaster in mine. This ambivalent conception of sex, especially, inevitably handed down to me, was to wind around my life a skein of entanglements so complex that it took the best part of forty years to unravel." [2]

He was serious-minded very early, which was contributed to by the death, when he was twelve and she four, of his sister, and by the bullying to which he was subjected at his private school. He was also a homosexual and fought a lengthy battle to control his desires in that area, as he did to exorcise the other demons in his life. As for religion, in the 1920s and early 1930s he became an ardent "Anglo-Catholic."

Blakelock's career was as an actor, a profession he practiced from 1919 to 1954. He studied at the Royal Academy of Dramatic Art (RADA). He had a successful career, working with many great actors and directors, playing many major roles, appearing on stage, film, and television. However, his career was adversely affected by his claustrophobia and an abnormal terror of forgetting his lines, a particularly serious matter for an actor! As a result he did not reach the real heights, and much of his later life was spent in writing, teaching audition technique and diction at RADA, and broadcasting. He was also a successful poet. He refers to the problem of his physical and nervous inability to live the stage and off-stage life demanded of an actor. In this he was most unlike his close friend Laurence Olivier, who also espoused High Anglican beliefs. Blakelock came to feel disillusioned with the

1   *Finding My Way: A Spiritual Journey* (1958), 7.
2   *Round the Next Corner* (1967), 18.

inability of the Church of England to help him in his situation. He expressed it this way:

> People who "go over" to the Catholic Church from the C. of E. are frequently accused of weak-mindedness; because, it is said, they like to have "their minds made up for them." This is a gross exaggeration of an underlying truth. In a most uncertain world it is surely reasonable to ask that the Church to which you give your allegiance shall be at one within itself, and speak with an undivided voice. Someone once put it rather well when he said that a man might reasonably demand that at least his mother's milk should be pure and untainted. This guarantee could not be logically asked of the Established Church, and to listen for an undivided voice was to listen in vain.[3]

Motivated by such thoughts, Denys Blakelock sought out instruction on the Catholic side of the question. He devotes two chapters of his excellent spiritual autobiography, *Finding My Way* (1958) to this issue, and very powerful writing it is: "My position was that I believed in God, and accepted the historic Christ. I realized that the decision I had now to make must rest on what I believed about the further claims of Christianity, and in particular what Christ meant by his Church."[4]

To Blakelock the keystone of the whole structure of Christian belief was the doctrine of the Resurrection: "If the Resurrection was a historical fact; if it really did take place; then surely everything else falls into position. All the other claims as regards Jesus must be accepted."[5] The next step in the argument is to list the many pieces of evidence of the recorded appearances of Christ at the first Easter. Blakelock sets them out as follows:

> I found the circumstantial evidence in favor of the truth of the recorded happenings of that first Easter overwhelmingly strong. We learn from five different writers the following facts: that Christ lived for forty days on this earth after he rose from the grave; and that during that period he was seen, at least twice, by all the Apostles at once:

3   *Finding My Way*, 35.
4   Ibid., 38–39.
5   Ibid., 39.

That on the second of these occasions the doubting St. Thomas (the only one absent on the first occasion) was invited to touch the wound-marks in Our Lord's hands, and to put his own hand into the spear-wound in Our Lord's side;

That this proof-positive, that it was Christ himself, and not some disembodied spirit, brought forth from St. Thomas his famous confession of belief.

That Christ was seen also: by Mary Magdalen, and at least two other women with her; by two disciples on the Emmaus road, with whom he spent time walking, talking and *partaking of food.* . . .

Again, there was the early morning meeting . . . by the sea of Tiberias. This time he performed one of his miracles [the draft of fishes], and he himself ate with them. . . . And it was then that he had the conversation with St. Peter and asked the thrice repeated question: "Simon, son of Jonas, lovest thou me?" and then that he foretold St. Peter's martyrdom.

Finally, Christ was seen, in one instance, *by more than five hundred people at once.*

If, in spite of all this evidence, I could still cast doubts upon the truth of the Resurrection, I felt I should be raising up a miracle more difficult of acceptance than the Resurrection itself. In this way: only if the Resurrection did take place; only if Our Lord did return to his disciples, after the seemingly tragic failure of that first Good Friday; only then would it have been possible for them to accomplish the amazing things they did accomplish a few weeks later.[6]

Blakelock makes a persuasive case for the Resurrection. Another passage in particular should be quoted at length:

On that Good Friday, the disciples must surely have been hoping against hope for something stupendous to happen at the eleventh hour—something that would end in the complete confusion of Christ's enemies, and the vindication of all his claims. Nothing did happen. He died; it was the end; his enemies had won. And it is extremely doubtful whether to any of Christ's disciples his, to them, rather vague words about the Son of Man rising again on

6   Ibid., 39–41.

the third day meant anything at all. On that first Good Friday afternoon their spirits must have been at a very low ebb indeed. Was I to believe that that small band of uneducated fishermen went out and turned their little world upside down, with the Gospel of the Christ who had failed to implement his claims and fulfill his promises? Was I to believe that these men succeeded in spreading this Gospel throughout the whole world, performing miracles, and *even influencing the Calendar*; so that, up to the present day, most of our public holidays derive their very existence from the birth, death and resurrection of Jesus Christ; the very years being divided into BC and AD—those that were before Christ, and those that are called the first, or the nineteen-thirty-fourth year of the Lord? Was I really to believe that the disciples achieved all this when they themselves were in the depths of disillusion and disappointed hopes? This was altogether too much to demand of credulity. No, the disciples were able to achieve all this just because Christ *did* come back to them on that first Easter Day. Good Friday was *not* the end; his enemies had *not* won. He had triumphed over them; triumphed over the evil in human nature for which they stood; triumphed over Death itself; proving to his followers that there was indeed another life on the other side of the grave, and that all his other claims were more than justified.[7]

All that remained for Denys Blakelock in his quest for truth was to ask what sort of Church Our Lord was referring to when he said to St. Peter: "Upon this rock I will build *my church*." If it was not the "hundred-and-one dissentient voices within the Church of England" but rather, as seemed the case, the one which was to speak with certainty and with an authoritative voice, and to be at unity within itself on all fundamental matters of faith and morals, there was only one Church which could reasonably claim to fit the bill; that Church which called itself the "one true Church" of Christ, and stated that it was *the* Catholic Church. As Blakelock expressed it:

> This Church alone, in the light of history, could logically say that it was the original Church founded by Jesus Christ, from which all the others had broken away; this

7   Ibid., 41-42.

Church alone could say that it had never permitted its teachings to be vitiated and watered down; this Church alone could claim that it had preserved the Apostolic succession and all the sacred functions of the priesthood in an unbroken line; this Church alone had a supreme authority—the Pope, whose final decision on fundamental questions of faith and morals was unquestioned.[8]

Blakelock describes with generosity and humor the course of his instruction at Farm Street with Father Francis Devas, SJ, who was the priest who received Hubert Duggan into the Church—the model for the reception of Lord Marchmain in Evelyn Waugh's *Brideshead Revisited*. Blakelock makes a number of useful points on matters of Catholic doctrine, notably on what he saw as the two crucial issues, the "keys" and the "rock"; also in relation to the second of these, on the doctrine of infallibility; and finally on the disaster of the Reformation in England. On the latter Blakelock poses the question, "What is the result of the great break-away from communion with the Pope by Henry VIII?"[9] His answer is "Chaos and confusion.... An ever-growing snowball of heresy and schism; a snowball from which pieces have broken off; themselves to make other snowballs *ad infinitum*; the whole unhappy process producing the Established Church of England and countless other sects; the whole question of Christianity being desperately confused for the man-in-the-street by this bewildering multitude of bodies, all calling themselves Christian, and some even calling themselves Catholic."[10] Blakelock's account of his conversion is a very moving and compelling account of a life lived and developed, and still retains its freshness today. Suffice it to say that Denys Blakelock was finally received into the Catholic Church in June 1934. He writes movingly of the last stages of that process in words that have a particular resonance today:

> When I looked around and saw the tumult of the world today; when I saw civilization, which had had its very roots in Catholic Christianity, going down and down into the abyss of disbelief and cynicism; as a direct result, it seemed, of breaking away from the one Church, which

8   Ibid., 49.
9   Ibid., 57.
10 Ibid., 57–58.

64

alone could, with any reason, claim to speak authoritatively
and with one voice, the Church which alone could give
civilization any clear positive lead in moral and spiritual matters; when I saw all this, I sometimes glimpsed,
however imperfectly, something of Our Lord's purpose
in safeguarding his Church in this special way, in making
the Pope the linch-pin, as it were, by which the giant
wheel of that great spiritual dynamo could revolve with
perfect safety to the end of time. I saw the reason for it
all—I "saw and believed." Before many weeks had gone
by the parting of the ways became inevitable, and in the
June of that year I was finally received into the Church.
Let me say in conclusion that from that day to this I have
never ceased to be deeply thankful that I took that step:
never had the briefest moment of regret.[11]

In the final pages of *Finding My Way* he writes very well about
his spiritual life and includes several poems exploring such themes.
At this time he became a member of the Third Order of St Francis.
In later life he was also to enjoy a close friendship with the writer
Eleanor Farjeon (1881–1965), who, under his influence, eventually
became a Catholic herself. Blakelock's fine study of this friendship
(*Eleanor: Portrait of a Farjeon* [1966]) has also much of interest in it
about the author himself.

Denys Blakelock died on Monday, December 7, 1970. Sadly, it
seems that some of his demons had come back to haunt him again.
The inquest held at the coroner's court in London determined
that he died from self-administered alcohol and barbiturate poisoning while suffering from depression. The question of suicide
is of course important for Catholics. Some evidence is provided
by Blakelock's friend the novelist Antonia White. She spoke of
his great kindness to her—she had problems of a similar kind
to his. In her diaries she writes of Blakelock's death as follows:

> If he did commit suicide he must have been in such a
> mental state that he couldn't have been responsible....
> Dr. H. had told him to increase his dose of chloral; he
> had taken chloral for years. But he was also taking var-
> ious other things prescribed by other doctors and the
> combination, plus the fact that he was drinking more

11   Ibid., 59–60.

than usual, may have been fatal. I find it hard to believe
that Denys, who had such agonizing scruples about committing "mortal sin," would have deliberately committed
suicide. He suffered terribly from acute claustrophobia.
He alternated between extreme gaiety and self-confidence
("Mr. Playgent") and black melancholy. He was terrified
of his black side, "the tiger."[12]

A fortnight later she was still thinking of Denys Blakelock's
funeral Mass and of him in "that big square coffin and of how
appalling it would be for him, with his acute claustrophobia, if he
were conscious of being in it." She consoled herself by reflecting
that "mercifully that was impossible for, even if he had not left a
proviso in his will for his heart to be pierced, the autopsy could
only have been carried out on a corpse."[13]

All in all, a sad end. So much so that it is better to finish with
his poem, entitled "Conclusion," written in happier times, and
which he saw as a useful summing-up, a way to bring the story
of his spiritual journey to a close.

> Return, return
> To where true love is found
> Bury thy hopes of earthly joy
> Deep, deep beneath the ground;
> Yearn, yearn
> No perfection here to prove,
> Worship no more the image
> Of the face of human love.
> Return, return
> To Him who made the soul
> And keeps it ever without quiet,
> Lest, content, it miss the goal;
> Learn, learn
> The lesson of thy peace,
> Listen to the Voice that stills
> The storm and bids the weeping cease.[14]

---

12 Susan Chitty (ed.), *Antonia White: Diaries 1958–1979* (1992), 220–21.
13 Ibid., 222.
14 *Finding My Way*, 115–16.

CHAPTER SIX
Deathbed Conversions and Near Misses

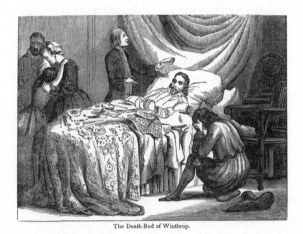

The Death-Bed of Winthrop.

DEATHBED CONVERSIONS TO THE CATHOLIC Church are both dramatic and moving. Having studied the phenomenon of religious conversion for some years now, the present writer finds that when people do convert very close to the end of their lives, they do so pretty well only to the Catholic Church. I may be wrong, but I've not heard of people suddenly being drawn in their last few days or even weeks to the Methodists, the Baptists, or the Congregationalists. The same applies to the Episcopalians in the United States or the Church of England ("Get me an Anglican cleric quick!"). Certainly where literature and published fiction are concerned, the scene is always one of a person being received *in extremis* by a Catholic priest. Here one is referring to a person never before a Catholic and now being received into the Church. There are several novels that focus on such conversions, and it was quite a common theme in England in Victorian times. Alternatively, the convert may, of course, be a "revert," returning to the faith of his or her birth after many years away from it. The classic example of the latter in fiction is probably Lord Marchmain in Evelyn Waugh's *Brideshead Revisited*, someone who was in fact, as we have seen earlier, modeled on a real-life case in which

Waugh, himself a convert, was involved, that of Hubert Duggan.[1]

Lastly in this context, there are what we may call doubtful conversions, where the evidence, such as it is, is inconclusive; and also those who seemed so close to the Church in life and yet never took that final step.

The classic case of a deathbed conversion is that of Oscar Wilde. Much has been written about Wilde's final act—enough to merit dealing with his case in detail, and this is done in a later chapter. Here it is proposed to look at a number of other notable cases, some of which are very moving indeed and contain lessons for us as Catholics. There is also an irony about certain events surrounding the Wilde case itself and that aspect will be noted here. It relates to John Sholto Douglas, 9th Marquess of Queensberry (1844–1900). He was the man who, angered by Oscar Wilde's relationship with his son, Lord Alfred Douglas, was sued for libel by Wilde, whom he had accused of homosexual acts. The libel case was later withdrawn, but it was this that eventually led to Wilde's later criminal trial and imprisonment. The main point here is that Queensbury, a lifelong secularist and atheist, was nursed in his last days by his brother Archie, a Catholic priest, who claimed that Queensberry had been received into the Catholic Church on his deathbed on January 31, 1900. There is no corroborative evidence of this, although his wife, the Marchioness, is known to have converted.

CLARK MAJOR AND MINOR

Two more recent cases of deathbed conversions concern a single family: the Clarks, Kenneth and Alan. About the former, there is no shadow of a doubt. Baron Kenneth MacKenzie Clark (1903–1983), the distinguished art and cultural historian, became famous in his later years for the wonderful television program that he presented in 1969 titled *Civilization*. One can also still find the series' accompanying book,[2] as well as DVDs. In fact, one particular passage in the book gives a clear inkling of the direction in which Lord Clark's mind was moving:

> The great achievements of the Catholic Church lay in har-
> monizing, humanizing, civilizing the deepest impulses of
> ordinary, ignorant people. Take the cult of the Virgin. In

1 See Patey, *The Life of Evelyn Waugh*, 210.
2 *Civilization* (1969), frequently reprinted.

the early twelfth century the Virgin had been the supreme protectress of civilization. She had taught a race of tough and ruthless barbarians the virtues of tenderness and compassion. The great cathedrals of the Middle Ages were her dwelling places upon earth. In the Renaissance, while remaining the Queen of Heaven, she became also the human mother in whom everyone could recognize qualities of warmth and love and approachability. Now imagine the feelings of a simple-hearted man or woman—a Spanish peasant, an Italian artisan—on hearing that the Northern heretics were insulting the Virgin, desecrating her sanctuaries, pulling down or decapitating her images. He must have felt something deeper than shock and indignation: he must have felt that some part of his whole emotional life was threatened. And he would have been right.[3]

With regard to his son, the somewhat notorious Alan Clark (1928–1999), the situation is not so clear. Alan Clark was a barrister and military historian, but is best known as a Conservative politician (on the right of the party) and a great supporter of Margaret Thatcher. Clark was Minister of State at the Ministry of Defense from 1989 to 1992 and became well known for his maverick tendencies. His three volumes of diaries are an often indiscreet record of his political career, plus a number of less public escapades. After his death in September 1999, the story broke that he had been received into the Catholic Church by the high-profile priest attached to Westminster Cathedral, Fr Michael Seed, during a private meeting at Clark's home, Saltwood Castle. Clark's wife, Jane, denied the story, but Fr Seed has never revised his account in any way.[4]

WILLIAM HURRELL MALLOCK

One important character, sadly neglected these days, who gives us a real insight into the Church's concept of revelation is William Hurrell Mallock (1849–1923). Mallock wrote several satirical novels, notably *The New Republic* (1877), in addition to a number of works analyzing politics, economics, and religion from a conservative perspective. He defended the Christian dogmas and opposed the philosophies of radicalism and humanism. The late Msgr Alfred Gilbey, in his beautiful commentary on the 1971 edition of the

3   Ibid., 175–76.
4   For an account of this see Ion Trewin, *Alan Clark: The Biography* (2009).

catechism, *We Believe* (1983), reprinted several times, expounds how truth is by its very nature unchanging and the identity of the Church is unchanging since she continues Christ, who is truth, in corporate form. From this it follows that the Church is her own best evidence, her own authority. Gilbey uses a passage from Mallock's *Doctrine and Doctrinal Disruption* (1900) in order to bring this out. Mallock puts it this way:

> The result which its possession of a complete, organic character has on the Church of Rome as a teaching body is obvious. Being thus endowed...with a single brain, the Church is endowed also with a continuous historic memory; is constantly able to explain and to re-state doctrine, and to attest, as though from personal experience, the facts of its earliest history. Is doubt thrown on the Resurrection and Ascension of Christ? The Church of Rome replies, "I was at the door of the sepulcher myself. My eyes saw the Lord come forth. My eyes saw the cloud receive Him." Is doubt thrown on Christ's miraculous birth? The Church of Rome replies, "I can attest the fact, even if no other witness can; for the angel said Hail! in my ear as well as Mary's."[5]

In this way we are able to see how the Church continues her teaching down the ages yet does so with both greater clarity and greater understanding of that teaching. As Msgr Gilbey puts it, "it is just as a person can understand himself better as he gets older and can expound to others with increasing clarity and precision his deepening, but essentially unchanging, thought."[6]

There is some doubt whether William Hurrell Mallock was ever received into the Church. The entry on Mallock (written by J. N. Peters) in the latest *Dictionary of National Biography* states that "he became increasingly sympathetic to Roman Catholicism in later life, but did not convert" and refers to his death as a sudden one. The entry in the previous edition of the *DNB* (by Alfred Cochrane) says only that "on his death-bed he accepted the ministrations of the Roman Catholic Church." That great convert Ronald Knox, in a letter to Arnold Lunn, then himself on the brink of converting and fearing that he might linger indefinitely on the threshold of the Church, wrote: "There have been people—Mallock is the

5   *Doctrine and Doctrinal Disruption,* 197.
6   *We Believe,* 23.

obvious instance—whose admiration for the Church seemed to kill in them any appreciation of other religious approaches, yet who never, at least till death was upon them, found their way in. I would not have you undergo that agony of soul."[7]

As Lunn himself put it, "Mallock saw the truth, but did not follow it. It was only on his death-bed that a semi-conscious movement was charitably interpreted as a conscious sign of acquiescence by the waiting priest."[8] At the time of Mallock's death the Catholic paper *The Universe* reported that he had been received into the Church. However, in the *New Statesman* the suggestion was made that he was unconscious at the time. So just what happened is unclear.

ROBERT KEABLE

One of the most powerful witnesses to the Catholic faith comes from yet another largely forgotten writer: Robert Keable (1877–1927), who, after graduating with a first in history from Magdalene College, Cambridge, became in 1911 an Anglican minister. He spent some time as a missionary in Zanzibar and Bechuanaland. However, in 1920 he resigned his orders and concentrated on writing. Several of his novels, most notably *Peradventure* (1922), deal with religious issues. Once again, it is Msgr Gilbey, in *We Believe*, who more recently brought Keable's name back into the light. This time he used a passage from *Peradventure* to great effect in showing the nature of faith. The story concerns Paul Kestern, a boy from an evangelical home, who goes up to Magdalene College just before the First World War. There he meets and is influenced by a Catholic priest, Fr Vassall, whose character is clearly drawn from that of the famous priest Robert Hugh Benson, another convert (even down to the stammer that Benson suffered from). Paul begins instruction with the priest and stays for a time at his house in the country. The book is written with great accuracy in its portrayal of Catholicism, and with real sympathy for each character. As Gilbey points out, it is clearly autobiographical and the processes that go through Paul's mind, described in great detail, clearly went through that of Robert Keable himself. There are two passages in the book that are of great power. Here is the first, which takes place on the last evening of Paul's visit. The priest has

7 *Difficulties: Being a Correspondence about the Catholic Religion between Ronald Knox and Arnold Lunn* (1932), 262.
8 *Now I See* (1933), 121.

by now given him a complete exposition of Catholic doctrine. All that is left is for Paul to pray for the gift of faith.

> "My dear," he said, stammering badly, "you g-g-go to-m-m-morrow. And we've kept the tr-truce."
> Paul nodded.
> Silence.
> The priest spoke again. "I don't know," he said. "I can't stick my fingers into your soul. I d-d-don't want to. Only God's been good to you, you know. And—and He's a j-j-jealous God."
> "Oh, I don't know," burst out the boy. "Father, I don't *know*! There's so much for and against. And I've prayed and prayed and prayed, and—and God hides Himself."
> "He's given you all the l-l-light you need. He's shown you! He's sent His Son and appointed His Church and p-p-put it b-b-bang in your p-path. What else do you want? Do you want a special r-r-revelation?"
> "Oh, I don't know," wailed Paul. "I don't KNOW."[9]

On the next morning Paul goes to pray in the chapel as he has been told. The next passage (abridged here for sake of space) vividly describes his situation:

> Paul shut his eyes. He was so tired. He turned deliberately away and thought of Edith. He remembered Hursley Woods, and the brown leaves, and the blue sky. A thrush, too, that looked at them out of beady eyes. And here he was, in a Popish chapel, Father Vassall's chapel.
> He looked up. In the clear morning light, the chapel was all so plain.... A little to the right the white tabernacle veil hung in the folds to which Father Vassall had adjusted it this morning. And behind lay the mystery. If only he KNEW....
> Paul grew afraid. The utter silence of the chapel grew on him, bore down on him, wave on wave. Why wouldn't God speak? Just a word, a flicker of a curtain.... It was all so still. Not even a wind. The silence listened, that was the awful thing; it listened for him to pray. And if he prayed—oh, if he prayed, he would break down like a baby, and surrender, and he would never really have *known*.[10]

9 *Peradventure,* 173–74.
10 Ibid., 175–76.

Msgr Gilbey goes on to explain the awesome significance of this passage, namely that the physical assurance that Paul is looking for would have been no proof of the truth of God's revelation. The act of faith is always a free act depending on a decision of the will to seek and accept God's grace. Keable gets it exactly right and has a real sense of what faith to a Catholic is all about. As Gilbey states:

> That is why there is virtue in the act of Faith. It cannot be simply the result of reason; the mind cannot help go where the reason leads it; whereas with an act of faith the will can be withdrawn and the gift of Faith lost. That is why Catholics believe that the loss of Faith may be blameworthy and is in all circumstances the greatest of all misfortunes.[11]

There is much poignancy in this as regards Robert Keable himself. For the truth is that, despite all, he was never received into the Church. The issue is always a serious and urgent one, ironically expressed elsewhere by the same Fr Vassall, or rather his real persona, Fr Robert Hugh Benson. In his book *The Religion of the Plain Man* (1906) Benson gives an account, also in a fictional form, of a man's journey from Protestantism to the Catholic faith. Eventually the man decides to convert and approaches a priest. The priest sets such cases as Keable's (and possibly Mallock's) in their true context:

> I am very glad, sir, that you have been courageous enough to come. I have known many Protestants who came up to the very door, and then turned back again. They did not ask themselves whether they did or did not believe in the Catholic Church; they only wondered whether they were justified in believing it. They are exactly like the man who said to Jesus Christ that he must first go and bury his father; and for all we know he never saw our Blessed Lord again. No doubt after a few months the impression faded; he congratulated himself on having been so sensible and prudent; and his friends congratulated him too. But what a tragedy!...[12]

One is reminded of the old adage "nothing ventured, nothing gained," or to use the more subtle expression of Newman in his novel *Loss and Gain* (1848): "You must make a venture; faith is a venture before a man is a Catholic; it is a grace after it."[13]

11 *We Believe*, 26.
12 *The Religion of the Plain Man*, 125.
13 *Lost and Gain*, 218.

CHAPTER SEVEN
Royal Defenders of the Faith

HENRY VIII AS *FIDEI DEFENSOR*

In October 1521 King Henry VIII, at his own request, was granted the title *Fidei Defensor* (Defender of the Faith) by Pope Leo X for his treatise *Assertio Septem Sacramentorum (The Defense of the Seven Sacraments)*. He had written this to defend the seven sacraments of the Catholic Church, and the Sacrifice of the Mass, against the assertions of Martin Luther. The book also insisted upon the supremacy of the papacy. Although no mean scholar himself, Henry had benefited from the assistance of a number of leading theologians. Pope Paul II had already conferred the title "His Most Christian Majesty" on King Louis XI of France in 1429, and Pope Innocent VIII had conferred on King Ferdinand of Spain the title "His Most Catholic Majesty" in 1492, and so Henry was feeling rather neglected. He had already suggested such titles as "Defender of the Holy See" or "Apostolic King," and to press home his claim to a papal title he specifically wrote *The Defense of the Seven Sacraments* against Luther. He then sent a presentation copy to Pope Leo X, who after considerable delay issued a Bull,[1]

1 *Ex supernae*, October 11, 1521.

conferring on him the title of his choice, "Defender of the Faith." In the case of France and Spain the papal titles were hereditary. There have been differing opinions expressed on this question in relation to Henry's title. Bishop Milner in his famous work *The End of Religious Controversy* (1818) stated that the title was conferred upon Henry and his successors, but the better view (contained, for example, in the classic account by Fr Thomas Bridgett in his *Defender of the Faith*) is that it was probably intended as a grant to him alone. There is nothing in the Bull to indicate the intention of the pope that this title should descend to Henry's successors. Furthermore, the Bull also states as follows:

> You will rejoice in the Lord, the Giver of all good, to leave this perpetual and immortal monument of your glory to your posterity, and to show them the way, that if they also wish to be invested with such a title, they may study to do similar actions and to follow the illustrious traces of your Majesty.

It would appear from this that the pope intended the title to be hereditable rather than hereditary. The grant was confirmed by Pope Clement VII in 1524, but he did not bestow the title on Henry's successors, and Henry himself was solemnly deprived of the title by Pope Paul III in a Bull issued in 1535 but suspended and only finally put into effect in 1538. Interestingly, Paul III himself bestowed the title "Defender of the Faith" on King James V of Scotland.

Nevertheless, the title was soon converted to a permanent addition to the Royal Style, despite Henry's subsequent rejection of Rome and his excommunication. In 1543 the English Parliament united the title Defender of the Faith with that of Supreme Head of the Church of England and of Ireland, annexing the titles "for ever to the Imperial Crown of his Highness' realm of England." This Act was repealed in Mary Tudor's reign and revived in that of Elizabeth I. In fact, Elizabeth I so prized the title as to set it down before the title "Supreme Governor of the Church." Thus, the title became formally acknowledged as part of the official style of the monarch, which has been borne by every subsequent sovereign. Of course, changes have been made subsequently in the Royal Style, such as the omission of the claim to be King of France, but the title Defender of the Faith has been retained.

In each of these three cases the papal titles indicated the Catholic faith, and the Bourbon heirs to the French throne have largely remained Catholic, as have the kings of Spain. However, in the case of the English sovereigns, "Defender of the Faith" no longer represents the faith of the popes, and has therefore become a misnomer. By a strange coincidence, of all the titles the English sovereigns have acquired over the years, this one, to which they are least entitled, has become the most enduring. Up to the Reformation the popes also addressed the English sovereigns as "Most Religious Majesty" and until the demise of many European monarchies the Emperors of Austria were addressed as "Most Apostolic Majesty" and the Kings of Portugal as "Most Faithful Majesty."

Henry VIII had much promise at the start of his reign. His papal title had been preceded by a gift of the golden rose, a traditional mark of special favor, from Pope Julius II in April 1510. In 1514 Pope Leo X had bestowed the honorific cap and sword, which were presented with much solemnity at St Paul's. Henry received a further golden rose from Pope Clement VII in 1524. Henry died a Catholic but in schism, and by his break with Rome opened the door to the Protestant Reformation under Edward VI and Elizabeth I.

CHARLES II AND JAMES II

No other monarch of England was Catholic until Charles II, and that arose from a deathbed conversion. After the beheading of his father, Charles I, he took over the command of the Royalist troops in the Civil War and led them against Cromwell in the Battle of Worcester in 1651. He was defeated and forced to flee to France, but not before some hair-raising adventures. He narrowly escaped with his life, due mainly to the hospitality of the old Catholic recusant families, who sheltered him while he was on the run. From the reign of Henry VIII Catholics had had to develop skills of concealment in order to survive. Charles II delayed his reconciliation to the Catholic Church until on his deathbed, and in the end it was Fr John Huddleston, OSB, his Catholic Queen's chaplain, who received him at Whitehall Palace. Fr Huddleston was from an old Catholic family that had concealed the king in the past. Before he died, Charles declared that as Fr Huddleston had looked after his body in the past, he now bade him care for his soul. Throughout his reign Charles had done all in his power to defend the Catholic faith and so at least endeavored to live up to the title *Fidei Defensor*.

Charles II was succeeded by his Catholic brother, James II, who did his best to defend the faith, endeavoring to be even-handed and exercising tolerance towards Protestants. However, such was the virulence of anti-Catholic propaganda that William of Orange, the husband of James's daughter, Mary, was invited to make an armed Protestant intervention. The Battle of the Boyne was fought in 1690 and James's army was routed by an army highly trained and twice the size, with a navy larger than the Spanish Armada. James was forced into exile and set up his court at Saint-Germain-en-Laye, just outside Paris, as the guest of King Louis XIV of France. Heretofore he had not been known for his moral integrity, but in exile he embraced his misfortunes as an opportunity to make reparation for his misspent past. His life became punctuated by religious observances and he died in the odor of sanctity. His defense of the faith had lost him his kingdom, but had no doubt gained him the kingdom of heaven.

EDWARD VII AS A LATER DEFENDER OF THE FAITH?

King James II has often been described as the last Catholic monarch to rule England, but recently evidence has come to light to cast doubts on this. This is best studied in the light of the coronation service and the various oaths that the sovereign has to take. Charles II had altered the text of the coronation service in 1661, but the strongly Catholic James II made substantial changes to make it more acceptable to Catholic tradition. However, when the Protestant William III was crowned, many changes were made in favor of Protestantism, including a highly bigoted Coronation Oath. The form of the service has remained essentially the same ever since. Prior to 1910 the new sovereign had to swear to uphold "the Protestant Reformed Religion established by law." King George III defended this oath with the following words:

> Where is the power on earth to absolve me from the observance of every sentence of that oath, particularly the one requiring me to maintain the Protestant Reformed Religion? Was not my family seated on the throne for that express purpose, and shall I be undermined, perhaps overturned? No, No, I had rather beg my bread from door to door throughout Europe than consent to such a measure....

Edward VII's major difficulty was not with the Coronation Oath, but with the more specifically anti-Catholic Protestant Declaration many people confuse it with. In its original form it was simply the test which had been imposed on all Members of Parliament, and upon all officials, in the time of Titus Oates's Plot, requiring denunciation of Transubstantiation together with the "idolatry" of the sacrifice of the Mass and the invocation of the saints, as well as "the worship of the Virgin Mary"! Even after the abolition of the Declaration in the case of subjects of the Sovereign, it still remained to be taken by the Sovereign at the time of Edward VII's coronation. It was reported in *The Tablet* at the time that the king was so ashamed of what he was required to do that he mumbled the Declaration so quietly that only the Lord Chancellor standing before the throne could hear what he was saying. Moreover the king had to pledge that he made this declaration "without any dispensation, or hope of dispensation, from the Pope or any other authority," just in case he was secretly thinking of becoming a Catholic.

One of the reasons for King Edward VII's attitude was that he had strong Catholic sympathies. An indication of these is contained in an interesting article by Sir Shane Leslie entitled "Sidelight on King Edward VII."[2] Leslie notes that his subject was brought up in the narrowest possible Anglicanism, but developed a broadness of mind which made him an Irish sympathizer, a friend of France, and a champion of Catholic equality.

> The King never missed an excuse for attending Mass, but his position allowed him but few occasions. He always attended the Austrian emperor's birthday Mass if he was in the Austrian dominions. He attended the Requiem for the King of Portugal in St. James's Palace.[3] His attitude was to stand within the Sanctuary, which was perfectly consistent with his deep reverence for Catholic belief.[4]

The article also describes activities before the king's succession to the throne which throw light on his (and his wife's) great devotion even then to the Blessed Sacrament:

2 *The Month*, January 1957, 37.
3 This was in 1908 after the assassination of the king, Carlos I. The Mass actually took place in the Portuguese Embassy chapel.
4 "Sidelight on King Edward VII," 37.

The late Fr. Forster was Parish Priest at the Chapel of
the Irish Guards, and used to recount that in old days
he was sometimes summoned to bring the Blessed Sacrament to Marlborough House when any Catholic guest
of the Prince was in need of his services. Fr. Forster on
these occasions found the gates open before him and at
the threshold of Marlborough House was always met
by the Prince and Princess carrying lighted tapers and
conducting him, without saying a word, to and from the
bedroom of their ailing guest.[5]

King Edward VII had no particular friends among the Anglican
bishops, but was a close friend of the famous Catholic preacher Fr
Bernard Vaughan, SJ; also, of Henry, Duke of Norfolk, a notable
Catholic, and of such as the Abbot of Tepl, the Premonstratensian
abbey in the Archdiocese of Prague, and the Marquess de Soverall,
a Portuguese diplomat.

Fr Vaughan was a famous preacher and public speaker, who
resided from 1901 until his death in 1922 at Farm Street in London. In 1898 on the French Riviera Fr Vaughan preached a Lenten
course. His hearers at Cannes included Edward, then Prince of
Wales, who asked for the manuscript of his sermon on St Mary
Magdalen. As there was no manuscript, Vaughan wrote out the
sermon, "The Woman That Was a Sinner," from his notes and
presented it to the Prince, with whom he developed a close friendship. As Prince of Wales, Edward visited Pope Pius IX three times.

The Right Reverend David Hunter-Blair, a Benedictine monk,
gives further such anecdotes.[6] He mentions the King's warm
regard and esteem for Henry Duke of Norfolk. He also states that
Edward's attendance at Mass was more than a mere formality, the
king following "every detail, missal in hand, with attention, vener-
ation, and respect."[7] Further, he points out that Edward VII was
the first English king since the Plantagenets to cross the threshold
of the papal palace in Rome. Edward carried out his intention to
visit Pope Leo XIII on this occasion (in 1903) in spite of the dis-
approval of the prime minister, Arthur Balfour. Hunter-Blair also
recounts the fact that, as Prince of Wales, Edward attended two

5   Ibid.
6   *Memories and Musings* (1929).
7   Ibid.

Nuptial Masses, one "in the Kensington pro-Cathedral, when his Premier, W. E. Gladstone, refused to attend...'lest there should be a popular outcry.'" The other was in 1889 at the London Oratory.

In *The Universe* Catholic newspaper[8] the editor recorded the king's "munificence to the Catholic Church at King's Lynn," not far from Sandringham, and added that practically the last big religious function he attended was the Blessed Sacrament procession at Lourdes. On that occasion he entered the grotto and apparently prayed at La Roque church there. This is further evidence of at least a disposition to become a Catholic.

Sir Shane Leslie confirms that after Edward VII's death there were many rumors of his conversion to the Church, but cites no specific authorities to support this. So, what evidence is there of this claim?

In a letter to *The Universe* newspaper in 1979 the former housekeeper of St Edward's Church, Palace Gate, Westminster, in which Buckingham Palace was then situated, claimed to have seen an entry in the baptismal register recording Edward VII's reception into the Catholic Church. The church is now redundant and the records have been transferred to Westminster Cathedral. However, the same housekeeper described how, when she returned to examine the register some weeks later, the page had been torn out. Was a courtier commissioned to destroy the evidence? There has never been any explanation.

Another intriguing factor is that Paul Cambon, the French Ambassador at the time of the king's death (he was Ambassador from 1898 to 1920 in all), was summoned by Queen Alexandra to pay a final friendly visit to the King as he lay dying and noticed a Catholic priest leaving his bedside. According to Gerard Noel, writing in the *Catholic Herald*,[9] Cambon noted in his memoirs that he knew the priest by sight, but not by name. Certainly, shortly after King Edward VII's death a Catholic Requiem Mass was offered in Westminster Cathedral for the repose of his soul.

With regard to the identity of the priest, there is evidence that it may have been Fr Cyril Forster. His relative Dr Lavinia Braun-Davenport was reported recently by Mary Kenny in her column in the *Catholic Herald*[10] as saying that she was "brought

8   May 13, 1910.
9   June 28, 1985.
10 September 25, 2009.

up with the knowledge that my grandmother's great-uncle, Fr Cyril Forster, had converted the King of England to Catholicism on his deathbed." The king was Edward VII. The suggestion is that Fr Forster was taken by Sir Ernest Cassel, a close friend of the king and a Catholic convert himself (from Judaism), to see the sovereign as he lay dying. It is claimed that Edward there accepted the Roman Catholic faith. Mary Kenny states that it was possible that Cassel brought along Fr Forster. However, her further claim that all the standard biographies of Edward VII agree that Sir Ernest Cassel was the king's last visitor cannot be supported. It also seems to conflict with Cambon's account. Whatever may be the case here, Dr Braun-Davenport's grandmother left a note saying that Edward's conversion was "a 'family secret'—the Old Rake's Repentance!" The matter was treated discreetly, but the lore was passed down through the Forster family just the same. Mary Kenny goes on to ask whether Fr Forster was a reliable witness, if, without betraying the confessional secret, he did not deny the conversion to his own family.

> Apparently he was a man of respected integrity. And he was already well known to the King, and trusted by him. Sir Shane Leslie . . . described Fr. Forster, in 1964, as "a gentleman of the old school, hating cant and advertisement . . . courageous, old-fashioned and transparently honest. . . . The public never heard his name, but as the Royal residences lay in his parish, he had become a friend of King Edward VII, whom, it was supposed, he had at last received into the Catholic fold.[11]

A further contribution comes from Dr Anthony Poole, commenting on an article by the present writer.[12] Dr Poole states that he heard the same story as Dr Braun-Davenport from his father, whose mother, Rachel Augusta *née* Forster, was Fr Cyril Forster's niece. He adds that his cousin once removed, Cecilia Hornby-Waring *née* Forster, wrote to him along the same lines, but that she may have seen an account in an article.[13]

11   Ibid.
12   The article is "Did Edward VII Die a Catholic?" (with Fr Mark Elvins, OFM Cap), *Catholic Herald*, July 16, 2010, 8.
13   supremacyandsurvival.blogspot.com/2014/06/edward-vii-and-catholic-church.html.

Another strand of evidence comes from Niall Diarmid Campbell, the tenth Duke of Argyll. The tenth Duke certainly told acquaintances that Edward VII died a Catholic. The tenth Duke succeeded his uncle, the ninth Duke, in 1914. The ninth Duke was married to Queen Victoria's daughter, Princess Louise, so there was a close court connection.

Fr James Martin Gillis, the famous Paulist preacher, declared in his newspaper column: "Edward VII had the decency to protest against the oath against Transubstantiation. In reward for his courage in that matter, he died a Catholic." He added: "I have direct, authentic reliable inside information on the matter which I could not as a journalist obtain permission to publish. But you may put it down as fact—Edward VII died a Catholic."[14]

Fr Gillis did not reveal the source of the evidence that he claimed to have. This is unfortunate. The conclusion of Shane Leslie in his review of the biography by Philip Magnus of Edward VII is much more nuanced:

> There can be no doubt that Fr. Forster...was one of the king's visitors on his last day but, though much gossip was exchanged, anyone knowing Fr. Forster would know that he would not have done more than assure the king he was dying in good faith. When questioned on the subject he always answered: "I wish I could tell you."[15]

The position, then, is uncertain, although there is more than merely circumstantial evidence supporting the case for conversion. It is, then, interesting to speculate whether Sir David Hunter-Blair is giving us a hint in his comments quoted earlier. In reviewing the two-volume biography of the king by Sir Sidney Lee, he says: "His account of the King's death makes melancholy reading enough; but he, at least, does not know the whole and true history of those last hours."[16]

Finally, Philip Trower (1923–2019), a writer on Catholic issues, describes[17] an account given by one of his great-aunts, who back in the late 1880's married an Austrian professor in Innsbruck. She had two daughters, the eldest of whom married a doctor, Alfons Huber, who eventually became head of the great psychiatric hospital

14 *New York News*, April 13, 1936.
15 *The Tablet*, March 21, 1964, 323.
16 *Memories and Musings*.
17 This account was given verbatim by Philip Trower to the present writer.

in Vienna, Am Steinhof. At some time, probably during the 1920's or 1930's, Mrs Huber was staying with her daughter and son-in-law at Am Steinhof, when two German princesses paid a visit to the hospital and afterwards came to tea. It was during tea that, to everyone's surprise, they said, as if it were something quite well known, that Edward VII had died a Catholic. The identities of the two princesses is not known, and there must have been a considerable number of German princesses at that time, but Mr Trower believes Mrs Huber's account to have been that they were connected with the English royal house. This is not something that his great-aunt would have invented. She was an old-fashioned Anglican and if anything had evidently been rather put out by what she had been told, as witnessed by her tone of voice when asking her great-nephew whether he had heard any such story.

GEORGE V AND THE CATHOLIC FAITH

During the reign of Edward VII, efforts were made in Parliament to change the wording of the Protestant Declaration, but these were frustrated by anti-Catholic pressure. However, after Edward's death on May 6, 1910, a new bill was rushed through Parliament. This modified the wording of the oath to read: "I am a faithful Protestant," and so it was King George V who was to derive the benefit. Like his predecessor, he too had Catholic sympathies and was tolerant of his wife, Queen Mary, attending the Catholic Church of the Assumption, Warwick Street. In a biography of Princess Margaret written by Noel Botham, entitled *Margaret: The Last Real Princess* (1994), we read that Queen Mary herself was received into the Catholic Church with the approval of the king.[18] In this it is claimed that she was guided by a senior Jesuit priest from Farm Street, who would subsequently visit Buckingham Palace each Sunday to say a private Mass for her. It is further claimed that not only had the king been present at his wife's instruction, but that he himself was also received into the Church. Hence, the same priest, with Queen Mary in attendance, gave King George V the last rites of the Catholic Church shortly before he died on January 18, 1936. However, we have to raise some doubts about this testimony. The book is very much a "popular" one and its reliability is uncertain. We know

18   See 364–67.

little regarding the credibility of Mr Botham, but we do know that he worked for several tabloid newspapers and also wrote a book entitled *The Murder of Princess Diana* (2004), which promotes a conspiracy theory. Now, this does not by itself render Botham unreliable on George V, but it does give some cause for concern. After Botham's death the *Daily Telegraph* referred to him as "one of the hard-drinking reporters who made British newspapers the liveliest in the world."[19] Roy Greenslade in *The Guardian* called him "the epitome of a Fleet Street scandal-monger and happy to be regarded as such."[20]

However, there is further evidence from a better source, Canon Reginald Fuller, a priest of the diocese of Westminster and a notable Scripture scholar, at one time assistant at the Church of the Assumption. He stated that he had known a retired Catholic nurse who had been present at Buckingham Palace at the time of King George V's death, and that it was the Queen who had sent for the priest at the Church of the Assumption, knowing the King's attraction to the Catholic Church.

Thus, although largely unknown, two recent British sovereigns may have indeed been hidden defenders of the faith. One cannot be sure, and we would be grateful to those who could add further to this story. On a more serious note, the anomaly of bearing such a Catholic title as "Defender of the Faith" while making an oath to be "a faithful Protestant" indicates vividly the injustice of requiring the monarch to embrace a faith that may be at odds with his or her conscience.

19   "Noel Botham," *Daily Telegraph*, February 4, 2013.
20   "Noel Botham—journalist, author, bon viveur and heroic drinker," *The Guardian*, November 3, 2012.

CHAPTER EIGHT
Eliza Vaughan

HEROIC MOTHER OF
PRIESTS AND NUNS

THERE ARE MANY ACCOUNTS OF THE PROCESS of conversion written by women who have embarked on the experiment of faith and finally made the "journey home" to this one true Church. In the secular society in which we live today it is good to look again at some of these redoubtable women, who in many cases can inspire a reinvigoration of the traditional family, so much under attack in these days. It is difficult to think of a more valuable witness in this respect than that of the nineteenth-century convert Eliza Vaughan, member of a famous Catholic family.

She was born Elizabeth Louisa Rolls on October 8, 1810, but was always known as Eliza. She was brought up in an atmosphere of "earnest evangelical piety" in a family that originally came from

Penrose in Monmouthshire. The family were yeoman farmers in the eighteenth century, but by the time of Eliza's birth they had made a considerable fortune building houses in the London area. However, they lost much money in the depression following the Napoleonic wars and eventually went to live in France at St Omer between 1820 and 1826. While there the family attended an Anabaptist chapel on Sundays, but Eliza did come into close contact with Catholicism as well. On occasion they went to Catholic ceremonies and processions, and we know that she visited a convent on one occasion to see a young woman take the veil. After their return to England in 1827 the family's fortunes revived greatly and much of their fortune was restored.

Eliza was to become the first wife of the Catholic Lieutenant-Colonel John Francis Vaughan of Courtfield, Ross, Herefordshire. The Vaughans were a long-standing recusant family, many of whom suffered for their faith during the centuries following the Reformation. It is not known how John and Eliza met, but we do know that they often attended Mass together before their marriage. The marriage itself took place on July 12, 1830, at St. Mary's Anglican church in Bryanston Square, London. It must be remembered that the civil law in 1830 still required all marriages to take place in the established Church. The couple appear to have been devoted to each other, something that continued throughout their married life together. Eliza soon converted to the Catholic faith, being conditionally baptized on October 31, 1830 at Courtfield by the chaplain, Fr Francis Joseph Daniel.

After her marriage Eliza continued to be impressed by seeing the Catholic faith in action on the Continent. In 1837 she wrote to her husband from Bruges during a stay there:

> Really, the more I see of the churches, of the piety, the ceremonies of this town, the more edified I am.... Last night we went to Benediction at Notre Dame and we both agreed that we had never felt such devotion—the lights, the incense, the dear devout women in their mysterious black cloaks, some with arms extended in silent adoration, all conspired to elevate one's heart above this world.

She also had access to the authentic Catholic tradition in the excellent library at Courtfield, which she herself supplemented. She is reported as having bought every book she heard about on the subject of prayer, her two favorites being *The Spirit of Prayer* by St Alphonsus and *Pensées Pieuses*. She loved also to read the lives of the saints. In relation to prayer she benefited by having as an adviser her own sister-in-law, Sister Frances Angela, a Visitation nun, and another sister-in-law, Sister Mary Chantal of the same Order.

Eliza's character, in addition to one particularly remarkable aspect of her prayer life, is brought out very well by the biographer of one of her children:

> She consecrated herself heart and soul to the service of God. Her religion colored her whole outlook upon the world. It was a favorite saying of hers that she had received all from God, and so must be ready to give everything back to Him. And what more precious had she to give and surrender than her own children? She wanted them all to become priests and nuns. It was not a case of thinking that it would be nice if some younger son made up his mind to study for the priesthood or one of the daughters went to a convent there to pray for the rest; she besought God to send vocations to them all, to Herbert, her eldest born, no less than to the others. For nearly twenty years it was her daily practice to spend an hour from five to six in the afternoon in prayer before the Blessed Sacrament asking this favor that God would call every one of her children to serve Him in the Choir or in the Sanctuary.[1]

Eliza's prayers were certainly answered. She became the mother of thirteen children who lived to maturity (one other child died shortly after birth). All her five daughters entered convents and six of her eight sons became priests. To take them in turn, starting with the sons, Herbert Cardinal Vaughan (1832–1903) was the second Bishop of Salford, then Archbishop of Westminster and founder of St Joseph's College for Foreign Missions at Mill Hill, London. Most Rev Roger William Bede Vaughan (1834–1883) became a Benedictine monk of Downside and later Archbishop of Sydney, New South Wales, Australia. Fr Kenelm Vaughan (1840–1908) was a priest of the Archdiocese of Westminster. Fr Joseph Vaughan (1841–1896) (Dom Jerome in religion) was a Benedictine

1 John G. Snead-Cox, *The Life of Cardinal Vaughan* (1911), Vol. 1, 11.

who established St Benedict's Abbey, Fort Augustus, Scotland. Fr Bernard Vaughan, SJ (1847–1922), was a renowned preacher. Right Rev John S. Vaughan (1853–1925) was Bishop of Sebastopolis and Auxiliary of Salford. Even the other two sons entered ecclesiastical seminaries for a time to try their vocations. Colonel Francis Baynham Vaughan (1844–1919) was Private Chamberlain to Pope Pius X and Reginald Vaughan (1849–1919) was Justice of the Peace for Monmouthshire. It is a remarkable list.

Four of Eliza's five daughters became nuns. Gwladys (1838–1880) joined the Visitation Order in Boulogne; Helen Teresa (1839–1861) entered the Sisters of Charity in London and died shortly afterwards; Clare (1843–1862) became a Poor Clare in Amiens and died after nine months there; and Mary (1845–1884) became prioress of the Augustinian convent in Newton Abbot. The fifth daughter, Margaret, born in 1851, wanted to be a religious sister, but her ill health prevented it. She lived at home, also consecrated to God, and spent her final years in a convent.

As if this were not enough, Eliza was also grandmother of Fr Herbert Vaughan, Catholic priest and Doctor of Divinity; of Fr Francis Vaughan, Catholic priest; and of Rev William Vaughan, lay brother of the Society of Jesus.

An achievement of this kind does not come easily. A profound spirituality is its inevitable foundation. We are fortunate to be able to witness this through the entries that Cardinal Vaughan made in a diary he kept in his twenties:

> After breakfast an hour in the morning was always spent in meditation in the chapel, which was her real home. She generally knelt, slightly leaning her wrists against the prie-dieu. I do not recollect ever seeing her distracted on these occasions, or looking anywhere than towards the Blessed Sacrament or on her book. She often remained with her eyes fixed on the Tabernacle, and while her body was kneeling at the bottom of the chapel, and her face beautiful and tranquil with the effects of Divine Love, her heart and soul were within the Tabernacle with her dearly beloved Savior. Even in those days I was much struck with my sweet mother's ardent love and devotion to the Blessed Sacrament. I used to watch her myself when in the chapel, and love her and gaze upon her. I used often to watch her from the gravel walk in the flower garden,

and marvel to see her so absorbed in prayer. Her love of the Blessed Sacrament was untiring.[2]

Later, Cardinal Vaughan wrote a letter to his biographer in which he reminisced further about his mother and his childhood:

> She made Heaven such a reality to us that we felt that we knew more about it, and liked it in a way far better even than our home, where, until she died, her children were wildly, supremely happy. Religion under her teaching was made so attractive, and all the treasured items she gathered from the lives of the Saints made them so fascinating to us, that we loved them as our most intimate friends, which she assured us they most certainly were.[3]

Eliza was also an example to her children in her works of charity, especially in numerous kindnesses shown to the poor. She was a friend of George Lawrence Bernard Burder, an Anglican curate, who lived nearby. He is considered to have converted under her influence. He later became the second Abbot of Mt St Bernard's Cistercian Monastery near Leicester from 1853 to 1858.

Eliza suffered much from ill health, but her sudden death was still a shock. On January 24, 1853, a few hours after giving birth to her son John, she complained of fatigue and then suffered much pain. After a few hours, conscious and "praying fervently to the last," she died.

One may begin to appreciate the depth of the love in which the memory of their mother was held by all her children by one further fact. When, some years later, their father married Mary, daughter of Joseph Weld of Lulworth, the children never during all the years she devoted to them greeted her with the name of mother. The word had become too sacred from its associations ever again to be used in common speech, and so the second mother was always spoken of and addressed by them all, even by the younger children, simply as Mary.

There are all sorts of ways in which a Catholic apostolate can prosper. Many women have evangelized to great effect in the public forum. Three women are recognized as Doctors of the Church. But we must never forget the Catholic home and hearth, the

2   Ibid., 14.
3   Ibid., 25.

central importance of the family, and the spiritual strength that comes from the domestic life. Eliza Vaughan is a great witness to that vital role. Her contribution is wisely summed up in a recent biography of Cardinal Vaughan:

> Her prayer life was remembered, by those who knew her, as extraordinary. To a few who have read about her, and of her prayer on behalf of her children, she has seemed eccentric. The figure of a young woman praying an hour each day that her children follow a calling to the Church has been misleading. What emerges from her correspondence is the figure of an active mother of a large family, a person with a remarkable prayer life who was at the same time filled with love and affection for her husband and children, her family and friends.[4]

4   Robert O'Neill, MHM, *Cardinal Herbert Vaughan* (1995), 17.

CHAPTER NINE

Resisting the Terror

CONVERT-PRIEST-MARTYRS

Edmund Gennings   *Henry Heath*

ANYONE STUDYING CONVERTS TO THE CATH-
olic faith can only be left in awe by the personal stories, and by
the consistency of the reasons given for moving to Catholicism.
In addition, many of them made great sacrifices, often involving
loss of family contact and verbal attacks. But when one encounters the story of converts who were both priests and martyrs, all
these difficulties pale into insignificance compared with loss of
life in the most horrendous circumstances. These personal stories,
involving such dramatic encounters and a cruel death, move the
soul to a remarkable degree. What adds to this is the realization
that these heroes actually volunteered for a mission involving such
an eventuality as very likely to occur. Such great faith beggars
belief on the human level.

One way of illustrating this is to take just a few of these remarkable stories, perhaps the most remarkable of all in some ways, in
order to show just what spiritual riches lie open to us if we examine this historical phenomenon. To do so we must go back to the
sixteenth and seventeenth centuries in England.

THE CASE OF EDMUND GENNINGS

From the sixteenth century we do have some accounts of reasons given by converts for their journey home to the Catholic Church, but these are not all that common. The reason is probably that the hectic life did not give time and opportunity for considered accounts to be written. Some there were, an obvious example being Fr Edmund Campion (1540–1581), now canonized, but they are relatively few. Here, as in so many contexts, actions spoke louder than words. One of the most dramatic instances of this is the case of the martyr-priest St Edmund Gennings and his younger brother John.

Edmund Gennings, sometimes known by the alias Ironmonger, was born in 1566 in Lichfield, Staffordshire. He was brought up as a Protestant. After his conversion to the Catholic faith in 1583 he was received into Douai College in the same year. His time there was a difficult one. He had always had a sensitive nature and a delicate constitution. Now he made himself ill with study. Seemingly consumptive, he was sent home, but while waiting for a ship at Le Havre, he prayed continuously to be cured. The night before his intended departure he made a sudden recovery, and returned to Douai. His meditations on the responsibilities of priesthood were very intense and induced a shaking of his body like a palsy that remained with him all his life. He spoke constantly of his hope of becoming a martyr. He was ordained priest on March 18, 1590. This was by papal dispensation because he was still under the canonical age.

In April 1590 he was sent to the English mission with two other priests, Alexander Rawlins and Hugh Sewell. Their passage was a difficult one. They were robbed and briefly imprisoned by Huguenots, shot at by pirates, and caught in a storm. Eventually they landed by night under a cliff at Whitby, Yorkshire. Gennings remained six months in the north of England before moving to Lichfield and then on to London. While walking there one day he recognized his one living relation, his brother John, who remained then very anti-Catholic. After working for some time in the London area Edmund was eventually arrested by Richard Topcliffe, a notorious priest-catcher, in November 1591, together with another priest, Polydore Plasden, and several lay Catholics, after he had said Mass in the house of Swithun Wells in Gray's Inn Lane. Edmund was taken to Newgate prison. He was subsequently condemned for his priesthood. He was hanged, drawn, and quartered at Gray's

Inn Fields on December 10, 1591. As he died he was heard to utter, "*Sancte Gregori, ora pro me.*" The *Dictionary of National Biography* gives the following description of his final moments:

> Gennings and Wells were dragged on a sledge to a scaffold set up outside the latter's house. Once again Gennings refused to conform or admit treason. This infuriated Topcliffe, who ordered him to be immediately hung, drawn, and quartered, giving him leave to say no more, and scarce to recite the Pater Noster. With Gennings crying upon St. Gregory his patron to assist him, the hangman astonished said with a loud voice, "God's wounds! His heart is in my hand and yet Gregory is in his mouth."

A very brave death, though one relatively common in those days. What makes the case remarkable is the link with Edmund's brother, John. The latter was born around 1576, also in Lichfield. He was also brought up as a Protestant and in fact had an inclination towards Puritanism. He moved to London where, as we have seen, he accidentally met his brother. This was after eight years' separation. John made no contact with his brother and rejoiced in his death, but shortly afterwards had a conversion experience. This time we can rely on the account given in Joseph Gillow's *Biographical and Bibliographical Dictionary of English Catholics*:

> His conversion bears some resemblance to that of St. Paul. About ten days after the execution [of his brother], he retired to rest after a day's pleasure. He was no sooner alone than his heart grew heavy, and he began to consider how idly he had spent the day. A mysterious feeling came over him as he thought of his brother's death; how he had forsaken all worldly pleasures, and for religion only had suffered such a cruel death. Entering into himself, he compared his own life with that of his brother and, struck with horror and remorse, he burst into tears and implored God to enlighten his understanding that he might see the truth. At that moment he was filled with consolation and joy; strong emotions took possession of his soul, and he vowed on the spot to forsake kindred and country to find out the true knowledge of that faith which his brother had sealed with his blood.[1]

1   Gillow, Vol. II, 120.

John Gennings also trod the route to the English College, Douai. He subsequently entered the English College, Rome, in 1598. He was ordained priest in 1600 and, like so many, his brother included of course, was sent almost at once to the English mission. This was in May 1601 and he worked there for ten years. Finally, in 1611, he was apprehended and imprisoned in Newgate. He did not pay the final penalty, but was released. In 1614 he joined the Franciscan Order and was responsible for restoring the English Franciscan Province (which he served as provincial). He wrote a biography of his brother and finally retired to Douai, where he was buried after his death in 1660 in the church of St Bonaventure. His brother Edmund Gennings was canonized in 1970. Several miracles have been attributed to him.

The story of the Gennings brothers operates on a number of levels, but most obviously it shows clearly how no one is beyond redemption. It also shows how cooperation with God's grace may lead to acts of heroic virtue. The story of Edmund and John Gennings is an inspiration to us all.

Before moving on, however, we must say something about the fate of the other people mentioned in connection with Edmund and John Gennings. Saint Edmund Campion is well known to most and needs no further examination. He is the subject of one of Evelyn Waugh's earliest books and of a very detailed recent biography, *Edmund Campion: A Scholarly Life*, by Gerard Kilroy (2015). Alexander Rawlins had earlier been banished from England as "an obstinate papist." He entered the college in Rheims in 1587. He was ordained a priest at Soissons on March 18, 1590, and sent on the English mission on April 9. Rawlins worked in York and Durham. On Christmas Day 1594 he was arrested at Winston, Durham. In the spring of 1595, he was in York awaiting trial, where he was joined by Henry Walpole, a priest of the Jesuit order. On April 7 they were both hanged, drawn, and quartered at the Knavesmire. Rawlins was put to death first. The hangmen would have cut him down to be disemboweled alive, but they were stayed by a gentleman on horseback who made them wait until Rawlins was dead, and then lower the rope so his body should not fall.[2] Alexander Rawlins was beatified in 1929. Henry Walpole's own

2 Robert S. Miola, *Early Modern Catholicism: An Anthology of Primary Sources* (2007), 151.

story is fascinating. As a young law student he had attended the public debates that Edmund Campion took part in and had been enthralled by Campion's wit and eloquence. Later he attended his trial at Westminster. Walpole stood by the gallows when Campion was put to death and had his elegant clothes spattered with blood from a part of the body tossed by the hangman into the cauldron of boiling pitch. The incident had a profound effect on him and on his future. The next year he went to Rheims and then to Rome and studied for the priesthood. He was ordained on December 17, 1588. After working for several years on the continent he was sent to England with his youngest brother, Thomas. They were soon arrested and taken to York Castle. He also spent time in the tower of London, where he was interrogated and tortured, before being sent back to York. The authorities promised his safety if he would conform, but he refused. His last prayer was the Pater Noster, and he was beginning the Ave Maria when they turned him over the ladder. They let him hang until he was dead. He was canonized in 1970. Polydore Plasden had been educated at Rheims and at the English College at Rome, where he was ordained priest on December 7, 1586. He was sent on the mission in September 1588. On December 10, 1591, he was hanged, drawn, and quartered at Tyburn. By the orders of Sir Walter Raleigh he was allowed to hang till he was dead, and the sentence was carried out upon his corpse. He was canonized in 1970.

A man named Hugh Sewell joined the Augustinian order by 1538. In the aftermath of the Reformation, it would seem that he went over to Protestantism. He appears to have gained high office within the reformed religion. However, there is some evidence of a Hugh Sewell arriving at the English College in Rheims. At the risk of execution if captured, he is said to have been sent back to England and escaped detection. Had the former Augustinian canon, now in his seventies, repented and returned to the old faith? We cannot be sure. Swithun Wells, the only layman among these Catholics, was a country gentleman and one-time schoolmaster whose family sheltered hunted priests. He was not present at the time of the Mass referred to earlier, but his wife, Alice, was. He was arrested and imprisoned on his return. Swithun Wells was hanged outside his own house on the same day as Edmund Gennings. Wells's wife was reprieved, but died in prison in 1602. Swithun

Wells was canonized in 1970. Despite several efforts the present writer cannot locate any more information about Thomas Walpole.

Richard Topcliffe, the notorious priest-hunter, hunted, captured, arrested, and interrogated many prisoners, often using torture. His favorite method was to hang a prisoner by the hands in the gauntlets or manacles. Having seen his prisoners through to trial and condemnation, he would then attend and supervise the executions. Richard Topcliffe died in his bed in November or December 1604 at the age of about seventy-three. The fate of Richard Topcliffe may cause readers to recall the film *A Man for All Seasons*, which recounts the life and death of St Thomas More. The final line of the film notes that the disreputable Richard Rich "died in his bed," in juxtaposition with More's martyrdom and the untimely deaths of other major characters.

TWO FRANCISCAN HEROES

Examining now the seventeenth century, we see that, as in the previous age, great examples of virtue came from the religious orders. Most attention is rightly paid in both periods to the role of the Jesuits, but great examples can also be found in other orders, among them the Franciscan. A vital witness from that venerable Order is provided by the lives of two Franciscan martyrs, Blessed Henry Heath and Blessed John Woodcock.

Henry Heath, whose name in religion was Paul of St Magdalen, was born in about 1599 in Peterborough, Northamptonshire. His parents, who were Protestants, sent him to Corpus Christi College, Cambridge, to study for the ministry. There he studied the writings of the Fathers and later works of controversy, being influenced in particular by the writings of Cardinal Bellarmine. Henry openly exposed the errors of the Reformation and took up a religious way of life. Fearing that the college authorities might take action against him, he fled to London and was reconciled to the Church by Fr George Fisher (better known by an alias, Musket, or sometimes Muscote).

Henry was admitted to the English College, Douai. He became a Franciscan in 1623 and was ordained priest at Douai. For almost nineteen years he resided at the convent of St Bonaventure at Douai, becoming guardian of the convent three times, leading a saintly life, and writing on spirituality. He then went on the English mission, but was apprehended at once and, on confessing himself to be a priest, was committed to Newgate prison. He was found guilty of being a priest and entering the realm. On April 17, 1643 he was hanged, drawn, and quartered at Tyburn. It is moving to note that he reconciled one of the criminals executed with him in the very cart taking him to the scaffold. Such influence also lived on after him, as witnessed by the fact that his father, John Heath, when nearly eighty and a widower, also went over to Douai and was reconciled to the Church in the very convent of St Bonaventure. He became a lay brother in the community, dying there in 1652. There is a beautiful story about him. On the day of his son's martyrdom, he saw a brilliant light ascending to heaven and he knew at that moment that his son had paid the ultimate price. Sometime later, reports reached Douai of Heath's death.

The story of Blessed John Woodcock (who also used the aliases Farington and Thompson, and whose name in religion was Martin of St Felix) is just as remarkable. He was born in 1603 in Leyland, Lancashire, to middle-class parents. His mother was Catholic, but his father conformed to save his estate, which had been in the family for 400 years, and John was brought up in the Church of England. He became a Catholic himself in about 1622, although nothing is known of the reasons for his conversion. It angered his father and John went to live with his maternal grandfather, John Anderton, of Clayton-le-Woods. He then studied at the Jesuit college of St Omer in 1628, and subsequently at the English College, Rome, but did not complete his studies. Instead he joined the Capuchins in Paris in 1630, having sought a strict religious order. His general poor health and inability to learn French led him soon after to transfer to the English Franciscans at Douai. He received the habit in 1631, something which brings together touchingly these two great martyrs, for his habit was bestowed by the very same Henry Heath discussed earlier.

John Woodcock was ordained priest in 1634. He worked in Flanders and then sailed for the English mission in 1643, landing at Newcastle-on-Tyne, but soon working in Lancashire. Things had come full circle as he ended up in his native part of Lancashire. In fact, he was about to celebrate Mass on the night of the feast of the Assumption in Clayton-le-Woods at the house of Thomas Burgess of Lower Woodend Farm, near Chorley, who leased the property from John Anderton, when the house was raided by pursuivants. He hid in the priest's hiding-hole, later said Mass, and later still escaped, but was captured the following morning at nearby Bamber Bridge. After being imprisoned in Lancaster Castle for two years he was condemned on his own confession for being a priest, together with two secular priests, Edward Bamber (alias Reading) and Thomas Whittaker. On August 7, 1646, he was hanged, drawn, and quartered at Lancaster Castle. His agonies were extended, because, as was not unusual, the execution was botched. When he was flung off the ladder the rope broke. Having been hanged a second time, he was cut down and disemboweled alive. His steadfast death makes it only a greater blessing that today we can venerate this great hero of the faith. The Poor Clare nuns at Arundel Sussex possess a relic of his arm bone. Another relic (a piece of cloth) is treasured at Ladywell Shrine, near Preston, Lancashire, along with the altar and vestments that, by tradition, he used at Mr Burgess's house. The Burgess altar[3] was constructed in 1560 by Thomas Burgess, acting bailiff to the Towneley family, near Burnley, so that the family could attend Mass in secret. It was kept, for safety's sake, in the Burgess's hen house, called Dynley farm. The altar was built to resemble an ordinary oak wardrobe, but there was a secret drawer for the vestments and the decorated pediment was made to lift off and be hidden in the lower half of the altar, which was a cupboard. The medallion of Christ in the crib and other decorations were added much later when it was no longer illegal to attend Mass. The altar was moved to different places from time to time. Edmund Campion said Mass on it at Denham Hall in 1564. At Woodend it was also used by another martyr, Edmund Arrowsmith (1585–1628), who worked on the English mission for nearly sixteen years until he was arrested after ministering to Lancashire Catholics at the Arrowsmith house, still standing today, in the village of Gregson Lane. He was hanged, drawn, and quartered at Lancaster. He was canonized in 1970.

These two great martyrs, Henry Heath and John Woodcock, are notable for their spirituality and great bravery under conditions of extreme adversity. They form two out of a steady line of incredible faith. It is noteworthy that both men begged to be sent on the

3   Josie Bolton, "The Burgess Altar," www.documentingdissent.org.uk/the-burgess-altar/.

English mission. They are a great example to us all of how our precious faith has been maintained in this country by the sons of St Francis. Henry Heath and John Woodcock were both beatified by Pope John Paul II on November 22, 1987.

Let us look again at the fate of the other priests, mentioned this time in connection with Henry Heath and John Woodcock. Fr George Musket became Catholic in 1597 at the age of fourteen after being a volunteer attendant on the incarcerated Catholic priests in Wisbech castle. He proceeded to the English College at Douai and was later sent to the English College at Rome. He was ordained priest on March 11, 1606, and left for the English mission in September 1608. He spent many years in confinement, and eventually, in 1628, he was condemned to death. He remained for twenty years under sentence, but operated as before. On the intercession of Queen Henrietta Maria he was reprieved. Later he was president of the English College at Douai. Edward Bamber was a seminarian in St Omer, France, and at the English College of St Gregory in Seville, Spain, where he was ordained priest in 1626. Returning to England he was arrested almost at once, but escaped. For sixteen years he served the Catholic mission, mainly in Lancashire. He was imprisoned again between 1643 and 1646 before being executed at Lancaster Castle. As in the case of Henry Heath, he reconciled a man just before his execution, in this case one condemned for the murder of his brother, giving him absolution on the gallows. Bamber was beatified by Pope John Paul II in 1987. Thomas Whittaker was influenced by the Towneley family mentioned earlier and was sent to Valladolid, where he studied for the priesthood. After ordination in 1638, he returned to England and worked for five years in Lancashire. He was arrested on two occasions, escaping the first time, before being confined in Lancaster Castle, where he was kept for three years before his execution. He also was beatified in 1987.

When one sees what all these men went through, it is a humbling experience. Would we stand fast to the Faith if required to do so, as can come about at any time? Let us end with the prayer of Blessed Henry Heath, which conveys the essence of the actions needed to uphold the Faith in one particular country at least: "Jesus, convert England, Jesus, have mercy on this country; O England, be converted to the Lord thy God!"

CHAPTER TEN
Lost at Sea

THE STORY OF TWO REMARKABLE PRIEST-CONVERTS

Fr Thomas Byles

Fr Basil Maturin

WITNESSES TO THE CATHOLIC FAITH ARE A historical source of immense power. Above all there are the sheer variety and difference in background of these recruits to the faith. They come from all kinds of societies and cultures. Some came to the faith very early, J. R. R. Tolkien at the age of eight and Bishop Challoner at thirteen being good examples. Some were late on the scene. The great Scripture scholar Harold Riley converted in 1995 at the age of ninety-one and was ordained to the priesthood in the same year! George Temple straddled both sides, having been received into the Church in 1919 at the age of eighteen, then, after a great career as a scientist, becoming a priest at the age of eighty-two. Some are scholars; some never really learned their letters at all. Some give us an example of activity, others one of contemplation. Some give us powerful arguments for grasping the faith. Others underline their witness perhaps more surely by their actions.

As a simple illustration of this powerful witness to the faith, it is hard to resist linking together two priests, both of whom converted from Anglicanism: Fr Thomas Byles and Fr Basil Maturin. There is, of course, nothing particularly unusual in the fact that two men in the late nineteenth century should have left the established religion of England and moved to the Catholic Church. What marks them out is the manner of their death, for both of them not only fell foul of the perils of the sea, but did so in perhaps the two most famous sea disasters of the twentieth century, occurring within three years of each other. In the case of one of these priests, it is the very moving witness to the faith by his behavior *in extremis* that offers lessons for us. In the case of the second, there is his labor in the mission fields and his spiritual writing, sealed by his devotion to duty under extreme hazard. Both are worthy of more detailed study.

FATHER THOMAS BYLES

Thomas Roussel Davids Byles was born on February 26, 1870, at Shelton, near Hanley, in Staffordshire. He was the eldest of seven children of Reverend Dr Alfred Byles, the first pastor of Headingley Hill Congregational Church, Leeds. Thomas became an Anglican while a student at Oxford University, where he was a fine scholar, but in 1894 he was received into the Catholic Church. He was ordained priest on June 15, 1902. As a newly ordained priest he listened to a talk given by Herbert Cardinal Vaughan (1832–1903) at the Beda College in Rome on the need for a missionary society for England. It was the Cardinal's vision to begin a society dedicated to the re-conversion of the non-Catholic people of England to the Catholic Faith. Three priests immediately volunteered to be founding members of the society. They were Fr Charles Rose Chase, Fr John Filmer, and Fr Byles, all of whom were converts. The Cardinal later asked his nephew, Fr Herbert Vaughan, and Fr John Arendzen to join this new group. These five priests became the nucleus of the Catholic Missionary Society.

Fr Byles lived with the other priests in a house in Longcott, Gunnersbury, West London, and embarked on his work with the Society by giving talks to non-Catholics in the temporary chapel. These talks were very successful, producing several converts. The work was continued with public missions on the doctrines of the Church.

Later Fr Byles was appointed the parish priest of St Helen's Church, Chipping Ongar, in Essex. It was from there ten years later that he set out on an intended voyage to New York to officiate at the marriage of his brother William, who had emigrated (and was also a convert). What transpired can be explained simply by giving the name of the ship on which he traveled: the *Titanic*. Now, of course, there is a considerable literature concerning the *Titanic* disaster, so that much is known about what happened on board in that fateful time after the ship struck the iceberg. And the actions of Fr Byles are included in the various reports given by survivors of the disaster. We know for instance that he refused to leave the ship, devoting his last moments to the religious consolation of his fellow passengers, notably by hearing many confessions. Take the statement given by Miss Helen Mary Mocklare, a third-class passenger:

> When the crash came we were thrown from our berths....
> Slightly dressed, we prepared to find out what had happened. We saw before us, coming down the passageway, with his hand uplifted, Fr. Byles. We knew him because he had visited us several times on board and celebrated Mass for us that very morning. "Be calm, my good people," he said, and then he went about the steerage giving absolutions and blessings. A few around us became very excited and the priest again raised his hand and instantly they were calm once more. The passengers were immediately impressed by the absolute self-control of the priest. He began the recitation of the Rosary. The prayers of all, regardless of creed, were mingled, and all the responses, "Holy Mary," were loud and strong. One sailor...warned the priest of his danger and begged him to board a boat. Fr. Byles refused.[1]

There is also an account by Miss Agnes McCoy, another third-class passenger:

> I first saw Father Byles in the steerage. There were many Catholics there, and he eased their minds by praying for them, hearing confessions and giving them his blessing. I later saw him on the upper deck reading from his priest's

[1] Msgr D. Shanahan, "Fr. Thomas R. D. Byles, Parish Priest of Ongar and Hero of the *Titanic*," *Essex Recusant* 17, April 1975, 47.

book of hours. Survivors, especially a young English lad, told me later that he pocketed the book, gathered the men about him and, while they knelt, offered up prayer for their salvation.[2]

What is particularly moving here, it is submitted, is the matter-of-fact way in which Fr Byles went about his work, the supernatural element of religion contained within the natural acts.

More detail on Fr Byles may be found in Ann Farmer's article "Priest of Courage: Father Byles of the *Titanic*."[3] In addition, there is a website managed by Fr Scott Archer.[4] At this site can be found, *inter alia*, an article by Mark Fellows, entitled "Fr. Byles and the Ship of Dreams."[5] In addition, Fr John Arendzen wrote the following moving tribute to Fr Byles:

> Father Byles, a first-class scholar with a remarkable academic career, was also hampered with chronic illness, yet to silent humility he worked whenever his frail body would let him. He died on the *Titanic*, gathering the people around him and exhorting and absolving them, till the waves closed over him.[6]

FATHER BASIL MATURIN

Basil William Maturin was born on February 15, 1847, at All Saints Vicarage, Grangegorman, Dublin. He was one of ten children of the Reverend William Maturin, a Church of Ireland clergyman with Tractarian leanings. He was educated at Trinity College, Dublin. On reaching adulthood he became an Anglican rector and a member of the Anglo-Catholic Society of St John the Evangelist. Over many years he worked at times in South Africa and in the United States. He lived in Philadelphia for ten years before his conversion. His stay at St Clement's in that city was a legendary one. It is said that as many as 1,500 people attended church on Sundays to hear his sermons. During his tenure the St Clement's Hospital for the poor was built and the All Saints Sisters of the Poor, who later announced their own submission to the Holy See,

---

2 *New York Telegram*, April 22, 1912.
3 *Catholic Life*, September 2002, 44.
4 www.fatherbyles.com.
5 Published originally in *The Angelus*, May 2004.
6 *Five and Twenty Years, Catholic Missionary Society*, March 13, 2002.

came to work in the parish. His work in Philadelphia combined outreach to the poor with a love of public worship. In his day incense and the highest musical standard were introduced into the parish, as well as a guild for working men and boys.

Fr Maturin's spiritual journey to Rome was a long one. The issue weighed down upon him and he said at one point, "I think I can say without exaggeration that the question was never out of my mind for an hour while I was awake for ten years or more."[7] Some have expressed surprise that he should have remained in a position of uncertainty for so long. But it must be remembered that he was an essentially humble man who respected his superiors and those with whom he worked in the Anglican communion. However, he was eventually received into the Catholic Church at the Jesuit Beaumont College, near Windsor, on March 5, 1897, at the age of fifty. After study at the Canadian College, Rome, he was ordained priest in 1898 and moved to London. There he lived in Archbishop Vaughan's residence and did missionary work in the city. After trying his vocation with the Benedictines at Downside, he returned to London as an itinerant preacher, working some of the time at St James's, Spanish Place. He was then offered simultaneously the parish of the Holy Redeemer in Chelsea and the Catholic chaplaincy at Oxford University. He accepted the latter post, but this was 1914 and the outbreak of World War I left the university with no undergraduates.

A year later, on May 7, 1915, Fr Maturin was the victim of the torpedoing of another famous ship, this time the *Lusitania*. He had gone to New York to give a Lenten series of lectures and was returning home. There are brief accounts of Fr Maturin's activity during the ship's last minutes. He was seen "pale but calm" and giving absolution to several people. Then he was seen handing a child into a lifeboat with the request, "Find its mother." His body was found washed ashore without a lifebelt, and it was generally supposed that he had refused one because there were not enough to go around. His funeral Mass took place at Westminster Cathedral.

Fr Maturin was the author of several devotional and pastoral works, notably *Self-Knowledge and Self-Discipline* (1905) and *Laws of the Spiritual Life* (1907). Some of these works are highly thought of

7   Maisie Ward, *Father Maturin: A Memoir* (1920), anglicanhistory.org/bios/maturin.html.

and have been reprinted in recent years. From the perspective of conversions, however, of more immediate interest is Fr Maturin's description of his own conversion. This is to be found in his book *The Price of Unity* (1912), where he concludes that union with and submission to the Holy See was necessary, rather than merely desirable. The essence of his argument is set out in this passage:

> It is...impossible to hold, or to expect that any man's religion should require him to hold, two doctrines that are directly opposed and mutually exclusive of one another. It is, for instance, impossible to believe that our Lord instituted the Papacy as an integral part of the Divine constitution of the Church, and, at the same time that anything could justify a breach with the Papacy. That a man may believe, as a matter of faith, the divine authority of the Holy See, and at the same time the right of the English Church, which categorically denies it; or, while denying with the English Church the claims of the Holy See, may still assert that the Roman and Anglican bodies are each of them living parts of the same Catholic Church. If the English Church is right in this matter, the Roman Church is wrong, and in teaching such a doctrine as a Truth of Revelation, and insisting upon its acceptance as a condition of Communion, she is in heresy, and has ceased to be any part of the Body of Christ.
>
> For it must be borne in mind that Rome does not allow, in this matter, a distinction between what is of the *esse*, and what is of the *bene esse* of the Church. Some Anglicans maintain that the Papacy is indeed of the *bene esse* of the Church, and that it is their prayer and hope that one day they may be restored to their true allegiance to it. But this is not what Rome teaches, nor what she could accept as a condition of reconciliation. She does not recognize such distinctions in a matter which she believes to be divine, and if an Anglican holds this view, that Union with and submission to the Holy See is desirable, but not necessary, he is really no nearer to clearing Rome from the charge of teaching, as Truth, what is not true, than one who denies the authority of the See of Rome altogether.
>
> It is therefore a direct contradiction—a holding of two things as true, which are mutually exclusive of one another—to assert that the Roman Church teaches as an

article of faith that which is untrue, and insists upon it as one of the conditions of Communion, and at the same time to maintain towards her the attitude that most High Churchmen do maintain.[8]

This is a powerful argument, which forced upon Fr Maturin's High Anglican confreres a logical dilemma of considerable weight. It is not surprising that his contribution as an apologist was a significant one.

A more detailed account of Fr Maturin's life, together with a selection of his letters dealing with spiritual issues and, in some cases, giving guidance to prospective converts, can be found in Maisie Ward's *Father Maturin: A Memoir*, an affectionate account of this great priest. This book has been reprinted in an attractive form and published by BiblioLife. It gives a fascinating insight into his life and thought.

8   *The Price of Unity*, xii–xiii.

CHAPTER ELEVEN

Louis Budenz

COMMUNIST RADICAL
TO CATHOLIC CONVERT

THE QUESTION OF THE RELATIONSHIP BETWEEN faith and freedom, and the related question of politics and religion, has on a number of occasions been a significant factor in conversions to the Catholic faith. Here we will begin with a cradle Catholic: Archbishop Fulton J. Sheen (1895–1979), recently officially recognized by the Church as Venerable. Fulton Sheen should need no introduction, at least to Americans. There is no doubt that he was the leading American Catholic of the twentieth century. He won an Emmy award for "Outstanding Television Personality" and was featured on the front cover of *Time* magazine. His radio and television programs were watched by large sectors of society and his books sold in great numbers.

How does Fulton Sheen fit into this theme? Well, first of all, he was the Church's chief evangelist, a prolific gatherer of converts. Some of these were great celebrities of the day, but many were ordinary souls, drawn in for all sorts of reasons. Of course, much credit is due to Sheen for influencing these conversions, but the great man was always ready to say where the true responsibility lay. He expressed it in the following way:

> The subject of making converts and saving souls is a very difficult one, for it is so easy to believe that we are the agents who cause the results, when actually all we are at best are instruments of God. As it has been said—He can write straight with crooked lines. Pius XII once asked me: "How many converts have you made in your life?" I answered: "Your Holiness, I have never counted them. I am always afraid if I did count them, I might think I made them, instead of the Lord." [1]

Now to the political element. Several of Sheen's converts were former devotees of Communism, some of whom were even convicted of spying against the United States. We are, of course, talking here of the so-called McCarthyite period of American history. Those who have gone along with the "official" history put out by the new establishment and portraying Senator Joseph McCarthy as the incarnation of illiberalism do need to know that the opening up of the Soviet archives after the fall of that regime brought out a very different picture. The majority of the allegations of Communism on the part of high-level officials turned out to be true. [2]

Leaving this particular issue aside, it can truly be said that Fulton Sheen was the right man for this period. He had written extensively on the nature of Communism and the relationship between that "creed" and the Catholic faith. Notable are his books *Communism and the Conscience of the West* (1948) and *The Church, Communism, and Democracy* (1954), but many were the pamphlets he put out on this subject.[3] The most notable of Sheen's converts from the ranks of Communism are Elizabeth Bentley (1908–1963), a spy for the Soviet Union who later became an informer for the United States, and Bella Dodd (1904–1969), a leader in the Communist

1   *Treasure in Clay: The Autobiography of Fulton J. Sheen* (1980), 251–52.
2   See for all of this M. Stanton Evans' detailed study, *Blacklisted by History: The Untold Story of Senator Joe McCarthy* (2007).
3   See *Tactics of Communism* (1936); *Liberty under Communism* (1936); *Communism: The Opium of the People* (1937); *Communism Answers Questions of a Communist* (1937); and *Communism and Religion* (1937).

Party of America (CPUSA) in the 1930s and 1940s who later testified at Senate hearings. Technically Dodd was a "revert" to the Catholic faith, one who had been brought up Catholic and lapsed from the faith but later returned to it. Her story is told in a later chapter of this book. Notable though these two were, perhaps the most notable of Fulton Sheen's converts from Communism was activist and writer Louis Budenz, another revert.

Louis Francis Budenz was born on July 17, 1891, in Indianapolis, Indiana. He was a fourth-generation descendant of German-Irish immigrants. He was brought up in the Catholic faith and was in fact an altar boy. He was educated by the Jesuits at St Xavier University in Cincinnati and St Mary's College in Kansas. He was then admitted to the Indiana State Bar in 1912. He left the Church to marry a divorced woman, but the marriage did not last. Later he married Margaret Rogers, a social worker and atheist, and their children were brought up with no religious beliefs.

He worked for some time as a labor organizer and was arrested many times in that capacity. In 1935 he became a member of the Communist Party and later of its National Committee. For the next ten years he worked for the party's newspaper, the *Daily Worker*, and was later its editor. He was also editor of another Communist daily, the *Midwest Daily Record*, and president of Freedom of the Press Company, a Communist publishing house. During this period he attacked then-Msgr Sheen for his persistent criticisms of Communism, his first shot appearing in the December 1936 issue of the *Daily Worker*. There he challenged Sheen to prove his claims.

The response was very quick, unsurprisingly to anyone who knew Sheen, who worked enormously long hours. Budenz received a manuscript from Sheen entitled *Communism Answers the Questions of a Communist*. Sheen posed the following question: "If Communism is the friend of the downtrodden, why do so many oppressive laws and regulations exist in the Soviet Union?" Sheen then cited page after page of examples of these. The conclusion he drew was blunt and to the point:

> The more I read about Communism, the more I am convinced that its greatest propagandists know practically nothing factual about it. They talk of Russia either in general terms or in stereotyped language of its propaganda.

That is why I believe many Communists are in good faith,
and here I include you, Mr. Budenz.[4]

Budenz's intention was to reply, but he became ill, and by the
time he had returned to work, Sheen had made his next move. He
had written to Budenz informing him that his manuscript had
been published as a pamphlet by Paulist Press. Sheen suggested
they should meet in person. Sheen's behavior at the meeting is
a classic example of how to act in such a situation. He listened
quietly as Budenz set about defending Communism. In his account
of his eventual Catholic conversion Budenz reflected upon Sheen's
tactics: "He was not disposed to contradict me, in our face-to-face
discussion. That would only have aroused my personal pride and
incited me to further argument. What he did, instead, took me
totally by surprise. He simply bent forward and said, 'Let us now
talk of the Blessed Virgin.'"[5] The effect of this on Louis Budenz
can only be described as shattering:

> Immediately, I was conscious of the senselessness and
> sinfulness of my life as I then lived it. The peace that
> flows from Mary, and which had been mine in the early
> days, flashed back to me with an overwhelming vivid-
> ness.... The drabness of life without Divinity, the slaugh-
> ter which science will wreak on mankind without Divine
> Law, pressed in on my consciousness.[6]

When the two men parted, they agreed to meet again, but it was
several years before this took place. Although Budenz continued
to rise in the Communist Party, he was haunted by the meeting
with Fulton Sheen, which he never forgot. Finally, in 1945, he
renounced Communism, took instruction from Sheen (the latter
visiting the Budenz home secretly, at night, for several months) and
returned to the Catholic Church, being received by Sheen himself
on October 10 of that year at St Patrick's Cathedral, New York.

In his autobiography, *Treasure in Clay*, Sheen adds a further
fascinating point:

> I told him I was not interested in discussing Commu-
> nism; I wanted to talk about his soul. Six or seven years

4   *Communism Answers the Questions of a Communist*, 30.
5   *This Is My Story* (1947), 164.
6   Ibid.

passed. Then he wrote and asked to see me again, and returned to the Faith. Only recently did I learn from Mrs. Budenz that he would not allow any radio in the house to be turned on to me while I spoke—so much did he detest me. Later she asked him why he chose to contact me since he bore such animosity. His answer was: "He told me that he was interested in my soul."[7]

In his account of his conversion Budenz was clear that "to be a Catholic is to be of the Communion of Saints, and to be of God's centuries." In his statement to the press he said, "Communism and Catholicism are irreconcilable. Communism, I have found, aims to establish a tyranny over the human spirit; it is in unending conflict with religion and true freedom."

After his conversion, Budenz's marriage was validated. He became an anti-Communist advocate. He testified as an expert witness at various trials of Communists and before many of the Senate and House committees formed to investigate Communists. He confessed that he had spied on behalf of the Soviet Union. Several of his final years were spent teaching at the University of Notre Dame and Fordham University. During this time he wrote books against communism and many articles for Catholic journals. He died on April 27, 1972, in Newport, Rhode Island.

In conclusion, there is a nice twist in the tail of the Budenz tale. His second wife, Margaret (1908-2002), also became a Catholic, at the same time as he did, as did their three daughters, one of whom later became a nun. Margaret had little religious background and was a convinced atheist by her adolescence. Only once in those days did she enter a Catholic church. This was when she was growing up in Pittsburgh. She accompanied a Catholic friend to a novena service at the friend's parish. The preacher on that occasion was a young priest from the diocese of Peoria, an unknown but gifted priest, whose name meant nothing to Margaret. He was Fulton Sheen. As Sheen himself put it in his foreword to Margaret's autobiography: "God's grace! What a mystery!"[8]

---

7 *Treasure in Clay*, 266.
8 *Streets* (1979). On the conversion of Margaret Budenz, see also Kevin Schmeising, "Margaret Budenz: From Communism to Catholicism," *Crisis*, May 2, 2011.

CHAPTER TWELVE
Hugh Ross Williamson

CONVERT FROM THE HISTORY
OF THE ENGLISH REFORMATION

HUGH ROSS WILLIAMSON WAS A VERY FINE HIS-
torian, expert on a wide range of subjects, but has been somewhat
neglected. In the estimation of this writer, his major achievement
was a book only partly concerned with history and written in
response to his daughter's request for a guide to Christianity,
something we shall examine later.

Williamson was born on January 1, 1901. Although the son
of a Congregationalist moderator, he at first followed a secular
career, primarily as a journalist and editor. He then spent some
years (starting in 1942) as a High Anglican clergyman. However,
on October 15, 1955, together with his wife, he became a Catholic.
The specific occasion of this was the so-called South India crisis.
What had happened was that the local mission branches of the

Congregationalists and the Presbyterians had earlier formed a united "church," to be joined later by the Methodists, and finally by the four dioceses of the Church of England in South India. This, of course, was anathema to the Anglo-Catholics. Williamson, espousing this position, expressed things succinctly:

> For myself, preaching on July 6 [1955], I said that "yesterday the Church of England, as we have known it, came to an end." Since that day the body which still calls itself the Church of England is, in fact, only the English branch of the undenominational "Church of South India," and in leaving it I cannot feel that I am deserting the body in which I was ordained priest twelve years ago in the belief that it was "a branch of the Catholic Church." There is no such body left to desert. And with gratitude for the light I see at last that the One Holy Catholic and Apostolic Church into which I, in common with all Christians, was baptized and in which I have, in the Creed, regularly professed my belief is what St. John Fisher called "Christ's Catholic known church," the Church of Rome.[1]

In an earlier passage he had put the position more bluntly:

> What possible theory of Orders, in the Catholic sense, can apply to such a body [the Church of South India], denying the full Christian faith, denying the sacraments, denying the priesthood and denying the Apostolic Ministry? It is a *reductio ad absurdum* without parallel in Christian history that a "Bishop" who is officially not allowed to believe that he is a bishop should ordain a "Presbyter" who is officially not allowed to believe that he is a priest to administer a "sacrament" which he is officially not allowed to believe is a sacrament in the One Holy Catholic Apostolic Church in which he is officially allowed *not* to believe.[2]

What happened on the occasion of the South India crisis has become an ever-recurring phenomenon in Anglicanism. It is expressed perfectly by Williamson's fellow convert Walton Hannah:

> South India provoked a crisis and crises in the Church of England follow a well-defined pattern. A situation arises which is hopelessly compromising to the Anglo-Catholic

1 Anthony Stephenson, *Anglican Orders* (1956), Appendix IV, 76.
2 Ibid., 75–76.

position, but which has the support of the vast bulk of the Church of England. Anglo-Catholics protest against it without avail; some leave the Establishment and become Catholics, but the majority hang on, apparently under the impression that by protesting they clear themselves from complicity. Eventually they get used to it and forget about it, and start talking excitedly about the next crisis, which they say really will split the Church of England.[3]

The main influences on Williamson's conversion were undoubtedly the writings of two other converts, G. K. Chesterton and Robert Hugh Benson. Williamson wrote an introduction to a reissue of Benson's fine work *Come Rack, Come Rope* (1912) and was clearly influenced by the latter's treatment of historical themes. He was also greatly attracted by the notable Chestertonian paradox, developed in another great book, *Orthodoxy*, that only inside the "walls" formed by Catholic doctrine and discipline could one find true freedom. It is, then, no coincidence that Williamson entitled his 1956 autobiography *The Walled Garden*.

Williamson's literary output was both extensive and varied. He wrote histories, novels, plays, religion, theology, and even children's books (*A Children's Book of Saints* [1960]). He was also an active radio broadcaster. In his writings he anticipated some now generally accepted theses, e.g., that Robert Cecil acted as an agent provocateur in the Gunpowder Plot;[4] that Shakespeare was a Catholic or sympathetic to Catholicism;[5] and that the Reformation in England was the "shipwreck of faith."[6] In a chapter devoted to conversion in the context of the English Reformation, one must concentrate on how this latter historical phenomenon informs the process of the former. In this context Protestantism, to Williamson, was a half-way house where one retreated because of a "disinclination to think the matter out to a conclusion." In this context he had respect only for the Catholic and the agnostic, since only they "dare to reach the end of their journeys." One might quibble here with the reference to the agnostic, since, unlike atheism, agnosticism is, in the words of the late Bishop Christopher Butler, "the absence of all positivity."[7]

3 *The Anglican Crisis* (1957).
4 See *The Gunpowder Plot* (1955).
5 See *The Day Shakespeare Died* (1962).
6 See his excellent little study *The Beginning of the English Reformation* (1957).
7 See *An Approach to Christianity* (1981), 21.

In such a large corpus of writing one must be selective. Williamson manages to combine the themes of conversion and history in his *Letter to Julia* (1974), a response to his daughter's request for an apologia for the Catholic faith. There, he deals with all the main issues relating to conversion. In particular he is a powerful witness for the true nature of, and evidence for, the Resurrection. The following extended quotation expresses these things very well:

> The Crucifixion vindicated the verdicts and values of Caiaphas, Pilate, Barabbas and Judas. Dying on the cross, ironically labeled "Jesus of Nazareth, King of the Jews," the wandering Galilean preacher had paid the due penalty for his teaching.... About thirty-six hours later, the body, indubitably lifeless with a lance-thrust through the heart, rose from the dead; and the Resurrection, stupendously reversing the official judgment, proclaimed itself as the final statement of ultimate truth.
>
> Christianity, that is to say, is not about the Crucifixion but about the Resurrection. It should not be necessary to emphasize this, but unfortunately the "religious" climate of today, with a multiplicity of pressures (inside as well as outside the Church) directed to turning God Incarnate into a left-wing humanist martyr, makes it vital.... [T]he perversion of the story is now so usual that it is well to recall the famous mot of Sam Goldwyn who, when it was suggested to him that his film on the life of Christ should include the Resurrection if only to have a "happy ending," retorted: "You forget that to us Jews the Crucifixion is a happy ending."[8]

Williamson stated emphatically to his daughter that "no one, whatever he may call himself, is a Christian who does not believe in the actual physical Resurrection of Jesus of Nazareth."[9] He went on to set out the powerful historical evidence for the Resurrection:

> The Apostles were the men who could bear first-hand witness to this unique phenomenon. After Jesus's death and burial they had met him alive in his body as they could recognize it, bearing still the marks of his suffering. They had spoken to him, walked with him. They had questioned and he had answered. One had doubted and

8 *Letter to Julia*, 81–82.
9 Ibid., 83.

he had given him his body to touch, allowing him to put his finger into the wounds. They had seen the empty tomb, where the grave-clothes lay undisturbed; they had breakfasted with him at a campfire on the shores of the lake where he had first called them to follow him.... Within two months of the Resurrection they had made in Jerusalem more than five thousand converts, for in Jerusalem at least there was no contradiction. The tomb was there for a visit and a verification. The authorities had but to demonstrate that the crucified "King of the Jews" still lay in death where he had been buried, but there was no such answer as "with great power gave the Apostles witness of the Resurrection of the Lord Jesus."[10]

In writing to his daughter, Williamson the historian most powerfully emphasizes also the witness of the English Reformation as an argument in itself for the old faith, the Catholic faith. He pointedly states that the Reformation, often referred to as "the Suppression of the Monasteries," is more properly called "the Great Pillage." A key passage in this book is a quotation from the opening sentences of G. W. O. Woodward's *The Dissolution of the Monasteries* (1966):

In April 1536, at the end of the twenty-seventh year of King Henry VIII, there were scattered throughout England and Wales more than eight hundred religious houses, and in them lived close on 10,000 monks, canons, nuns and friars. Four years later, in April 1540, there were none. Their buildings and properties had been taken over by the Crown and leased or sold to new lay occupiers. Their former inhabitants had been dispersed and were in the process of adjusting themselves to a very different way of life.[11]

Williamson then goes on to explore the unique Anglican heresy, the assertion that the occupant of the throne of England is Head of the Church:

The Oath which every Anglican bishop takes today when he does homage to the Sovereign on entering into his see runs: "I declare that Your Majesty is the only Supreme Governor of this your realm in spiritual and ecclesiastical

10 Ibid., 83–84.
11 Ibid., 120–21.

things, as well as in temporal, and that no foreign prelate or potentate has any jurisdiction within this realm, and I acknowledge I hold the said Bishopric as well the spiritualities as the temporalities thereof, only of Your Majesty." The first part of this is the essential part of the Oath of Supremacy imposed by Henry VIII. Nothing has changed. The issue for which Fisher and More and the first Carthusian saints and martyrs died is, with exactitude, the issue which still separates Catholicism from Anglicanism. But now that the financial and political reasons have vanished, it is easier to discuss the matter in its correct and unemotional terms and ask your Anglican friends why they believe Queen Elizabeth II to be, as far as they are concerned, the successor of St. Peter.[12]

This is deliberately a provocative challenge and it is the measure of the man. There is a pugnacity that is to be respected. He was also someone who had to overcome adversity. Williamson's later years were difficult. The best review of this is by Joseph Pearce in his *Literary Converts* (1999). Williamson was beset by serious illness, and events in the Church caused him particular sadness. He was appalled by the liturgical changes after Vatican II and wrote two pamphlets, *The Modern Mass* (1969) and *The Great Betrayal* (1970), critiquing the *Novus Ordo Missae*. If these may be seen as somewhat extreme at certain points, they can also be seen as a heartfelt plea for what had been. He would of course have been greatly heartened by Pope Benedict XVI's moves to liberate the old rite of Mass; but as in the case of Evelyn Waugh referred to earlier, he would have been greatly upset by Pope Francis's later decision to restrict the availability of that rite. It must also be understood that Williamson was a man who tended to see things in black and white and yearned for clarity of expression. This can be seen most notably in his fascinating examination of a whole series of historical "whodunnits" in his book *Historical Enigmas* (1974)—e.g., Who really murdered the princes in the Tower? Who was the man in the iron mask? Did Buckingham poison James I? Who was Elizabeth I's true father?

Hugh Ross Williamson died on January 13, 1978. He was undoubtedly an integral Catholic. He is not as well known as he should be, perhaps the effect of committing the "English sin" of

12   Ibid., 131–32.

writing on so many subjects. His best work is perhaps on the topic of the historical upheaval in religion in his country. Let us end, appropriately then, with these potent remarks from *The Beginning of the English Reformation*. They are the essence of what he stood for:

> From the vantage point of posterity we see that what is called the Reformation in England was accomplished within the span of a lifetime of seventy-five years.... By 1606, throughout the length and breadth of England, no monastery or nunnery or shrine or chantry existed; to say Mass or to attend Mass, to make a convert to Catholicism or to be a convert were all punishable by death; an Oath asserting that the Head of the Church in England was the successor of Henry VIII instead of the successor of St. Peter was obligatory on all persons of whatever rank under the penalty of exclusion from places of trust and from all the liberal professions; Catholics were required not only to attend Protestant churches but to take Communion there under pain of the confiscation of two-thirds of their property; they were debarred from the legal and medical professions, from the army and the universities, and, if they sent their children abroad to be educated as Catholics, their inheritance was taken away from them and given to their Protestant relations, who were encouraged by liberal bribes to inform against them. In England there was no crucifix to be seen or any statue of Christ's Mother in any public place, and that none should remain as private relics in Catholic homes, Justices of the Peace were given indiscriminate right of search; if any crucifix were there discovered the figure was to be publicly defaced at the Quarter Sessions.[13]

In our own age, where the wearing of a crucifix is often assailed by various authorities and where the secular attack on the Catholic Church is daily increasing, this is surely resonant.

13   *The Beginning of the English Reformation*, 17–18.

CHAPTER THIRTEEN

Ernest Hemingway

CATHOLIC OR NOT?

MY FATHER COULD NEVER UNDERSTAND WHY Ernest Hemingway shot himself. After all, he had everything, hadn't he? Wealth, fame, recognition as a great writer. What else could one want? Well, even as a youngster I suspected that there might perhaps be more to it than that. Suitably prompted, I looked in the local library and there was a copy of *Death in the Afternoon* (1932), Hemingway's magisterial study of Spain and bullfighting. I read the book avidly, as well as poring over the sometimes rather gruesome photos of matadors, both in action and in inaction, the latter usually meaning death or serious injury. How exciting and dramatic it all seemed, and there was the additional frisson that Hemingway himself had put an end to his life by deliberately shooting himself with his favorite shotgun. Not only that, of course. His father Clarence committed suicide and later on his sister Ursula and brother Leicester also took their own lives, as did his grand-daughter, the fashion model and actress Margaux.

For some reason all this did not lead me on to his novels at that stage, but rather to the sometimes pretty poor film adaptations of his work, which tended to put me off his writings. He never figured much after that, and such as Tolstoy and Dostoevsky took center stage for quite some time. When I became a Catholic, it was novelists I saw as obviously Catholic who appealed, and in the context of the United States that meant for me such writers as Flannery O'Connor and Walker Percy. I did note from time to time references to Hemingway's conversion, but these were usually followed by some relatively damning statement to the effect that this was short-lived.

It was only when I came to prepare a book on American converts to the Catholic faith that I decided to look again at "L'Affaire Hemingway," in particular the question whether he was truly a convert to the Catholic Church and, if so, how one should approach this aspect of his life.

On the question whether Hemingway converted there is no doubt. He definitely did. But on the question when this took place there is some disagreement. Once he arrived in Paris in 1921, he soon drifted away from the religious liberalism of his youthful Protestantism (he had been brought up in the Congregational Church). It is definitely the case that his marriage (in 1921) to Hadley Richardson was dissolved by the Catholic Church and that he married Pauline Pfeifer in May 1927 in Paris. He formally converted to the Catholic faith before the marriage to Pauline, but had considered himself Catholic, intellectually and emotionally, from 1918 onward. Some writers consider that he may actually have been received in 1919, but this is not proved.

Hemingway after his conversion is often stated to have been either a "nominal" or "bogus" Catholic. He has also been referred to as a "sentimental humanist," and it has even been said that he had superficial connections with various Christian sects. Neither of these two last things is true. How about the notion that his faith was nominal or bogus? Much has been written about these matters, most of it embodying the skepticism referred to above. Of course, one must not forget that the espousal of the Catholic faith is not necessarily the living of it. Hemingway's vices were

pretty well apparent in a number of areas, notably his relationship with the opposite sex (e.g., divorce from Pauline in 1940 and
marriage in the same year to the journalist and writer Martha
Gellhorn; then divorce from her in 1945 and marriage to Mary
Welsh in 1946). But Christianity is all about sin, repentance, and
redemption, and we poor sinners would be taking risks in pur-
porting to judge someone on incomplete information. There is in
fact much evidence of a more positive side to this complex human
being. Hemingway's close friend, the long-lived A. E. Hotchner
(1917–2020), author of a notable biography, *Papa Hemingway* (1966),
notes that Hemingway went into the cathedral at Burgos to kneel
and pray on his way to Madrid and afterwards said that he wished
he were "a better Catholic." Hotchner also refers to his subscription
to Catholic journals, his contribution to a "badly needed" roof for
a particular Catholic church, and his sympathetic approach to the
film actor Gary Cooper about Cooper's conversion to Catholicism.
He also mentions that when Hemingway placed an advertisement
in the newspaper for a Spanish pickpocket to return his wallet,
he cared most about getting back the "image of St. Christopher
in it." In addition, many sources have pointed out Hemingway's
longstanding devotion to the specifically Catholic pilgrimage of
Santiago de Compostela.

One writer has examined this whole question in greater detail
than has ever been done before. This is H. R. Stoneback, Distinguished Professor of English at the State University of New York
at New Paltz, who bases his conclusions on a detailed examination
of conversations, correspondence, and other unpublished material.
His major conclusions may be found in a series of important texts.[1]

---

1 "From the rue Saint-Jacques to the Pass of Roland to the Unfinished
Church at the Edge of the Cliff," *Hemingway Review*, Fall 1986, 2; "'Lovers'
Sonnets Turn'd to Holy Psalms': The Soul's Song of Providence, the Scandal
of Suffering, and Love in *A Farewell to Arms*," *Hemingway Review*, Fall 1989, 33;
"In the Nominal Country of the Bogus: Hemingway's Catholicism and the
Biographies," in Frank Scafella (ed.), *Hemingway: Essays of Reassessment* (1991),
105; "'Mais, Je Reste Catholique': Communion, Betrayal, and Aridity in 'Wine
of Wyoming,'" in Susan F. Beegel (ed.), *Hemingway's Neglected Short Fiction:
Current Perspectives* (1992), 209; "'The Priest Did Not Answer': Hemingway,
the Church, the Party, and *For Whom the Bell Tolls*," in Rena Sanderson (ed.),
Blowing the Bridge: Essays on Hemingway and For Whom the Bell Tolls (1992), 99;
"Pilgrimage Variations: Hemingway's Sacred Landscapes," *Religion & Literature*,
Summer-Autumn 2003, 49; *Reading Hemingway's* The Sun Also Rises (2007); and

It is impossible here to refer to all the considerable evidence put forward by Stoneback, but in one of his most important articles he presents several pieces of evidence from various sources, elaborated in a detailed appendix, which will give the reader some solid indication of how powerful his case is:

> Some four decades during which Hemingway as a Catholic attended Mass and confession, prayed with great intensity in various phases, named one son after a pope, displayed great pride in [his son] Patrick's confirmation mastery of the catechism, gave money and support to the Church.[2]
>
> Mary [Hemingway, *née* Welsh] had made a real effort to see that the texture of her daily life with Hemingway was Catholic: eating fish on Fridays, observing Lent, singing Christmas carols and fixing the creche under the tree, celebrating Ernest's saint's day, having prayers and Masses said for friends and family, observing Catholic feasts and holy days, driving miles out of the way on journeys to visit and revisit churches and cathedrals, and attending religious processions.[3]
>
> Allen Tate told me in the 1960's that he had gone to Mass with Hemingway in Paris in the 1920's, that Hemingway was "very Catholic," that his attitude toward sport was "rooted in a religious sensibility."[4]
>
> Toby Bruce, Hemingway's longtime friend and associate, thought Hemingway was a "good Catholic."[5]
>
> Hemingway's fishing logbooks have notations of the times he goes ashore and attends Mass. (Do "bogus" and "nominal" Catholics, having a wonderful time boating marlin out in the stream, always come ashore for Mass and to do their "Easter duty"?)[6]

Hemingway's Paris: Our Paris? (2010). See also "Pilgrimage, Poetry, and Song," a fascinating, detailed interview with H. R. Stoneback conducted by Allie Baker at www.thehemingwayproject.com/2018/08/22/pilgrimage-poetry-and-song-an-interview-with-h-r-stoneback/. See also the fine book by Matthew Nickel, *Hemingway's Dark Night* (2013), endorsed by way of a foreword by H. R. Stoneback, who refers to it as "a cutting-edge study."

2 H. R. Stoneback, "In the Nominal Country of the Bogus: Hemingway's Catholicism and the Biographies," in Scafella (ed.), *Hemingway: Essays of Reassessment*, 110.

3 Ibid., 118.

4 Ibid., 120.

5 Ibid.

6 Ibid.

The well-known sportsman George Leonard Herter asserts that Hemingway was "a strong Catholic [whose] religion came mainly from the Apparitions of the Virgin Mary."[7]

In his unpublished memoir, the philosopher Ralph Withington Church recalls his conversations with Hemingway about the "problem of redemption" and Malebranche's "theory of grace."[8]

Hemingway's unpublished letters are filled with references to religion, with clarifications of his Catholicism, especially the letters to various priests, certain letters to Pauline, and the late letters to Adriana Ivancich and Robert Brown. The Adriana Ivancich letters have a consistently Catholic texture, with references to prayer, priests, having Masses said, quotations of St. Teresa of Avila, allusions to Dante, pilgrimages, the Middle Ages, saints and martyrs, the cathedrals of Chartres and San Marco, and the basic stance that people who don't understand their code cannot understand how one can be a serious artist and like to drink and have fun in the sun and go to church. The letters to Robert Brown provide the most precise, succinct summation anywhere of Hemingway's later sense of himself as Catholic. He employs the language of the Church, speaks exactly of states of sin and grace, distinguishes between blasphemy and heresy (and does so using technical language worthy of a student of theology, e.g., bestemnia for blasphemy).[9]

Acting on all this evidence and much other material, Stoneback proposes the following revised outline of the phases of Hemingway's religious sensibility:

1908–1917 Period of more-or-less "cheerful Protestant Christianity."

1917–1925 Period of bitter rejection of Protestantism and discovery of Catholicism, an awakening to an aesthetic sense centered on ritual and ceremony (as in the world of toreo and the Church), and deepening engagement with the sacramental sense of experience and the incarnational patterns of the Catholic Church.

7 Ibid., 121.
8 Ibid.
9 Ibid.

1925–1937   Period of rather intense Catholicity, formalized at the time of the marriage to Pauline but intellectually and emotionally arrived at pre-Pauline.

1937–1947   Period of confusion, aridity, or "dark night of the soul," a cycle of "spiritual dryness" that has for Hemingway aesthetic, moral, and religious consequences; his Catholic marriage ends, betrayal breeds betrayal, his work falters, the self-parodic mythic persona emerges; the role of the Catholic Church in Fascist Spain profoundly troubles him, but he does not reject the Church, knows better than to mix politics and religion.

1947–1960   Period of resurgent belief, coinciding, at first, with Hemingway playing Dante to Adriana Ivancich's Beatrice; partial recovery of creative powers; longing for purgation, for the "grace of a happy death"; Colonel Cantwell, for example, asks himself if he is going "to run as a Christian" (*Across the River and Into the Trees*); best answer given in *The Old Man and the Sea*, where Santiago incarnates Hemingway's lifelong pilgrimage, a quest that issues not in some so-called religion of man or "sentimental humanism" but in a profoundly Catholic sense of expiation and redemption; gives Nobel Prize medal, symbol of life's work, to Virgin Mary.

1960–1961   Period of despair, which Hemingway had earlier noted was the sin against the Holy Ghost, a sin he had not committed—it is not known that electroshock causes despair; it is known that it does not cure it . . . [the last reference is to the illness and severe depression for which he had electro-convulsive therapy, which was unsuccessful].[10]

It might also be added, partly because it involves a moving gesture, that Hemingway named his famous boat after Our Lady of the Pillar, whose shrine he had visited in Spain. As noted by Stoneback, Hemingway went to the shrine to thank Our Lady after winning the Nobel Prize for Literature in 1954, and left his Prize medallion there as a gift to her.

So all is not quite as it seems from reading the standard accounts of Hemingway's life (excluding, of course, Hotchner's). H. R. Stoneback's conclusion is, I submit, a valid one:

10   Ibid., 117-18.

Hemingway was a Catholic, most of his life, and we will have to accept and to understand that. It is not, finally, our business to judge what kind of Catholic he was. What matters most is that it is everywhere in his work, which is fundamentally religious and profoundly Catholic from the earliest good work to the last. Many live in it and never feel it, but it is there, and once we have the biographical record clarified, it is in the fiction that we must undertake the pilgrimage with Hemingway. The route is clearly marked, if we know how to read old maps.[11]

Pilgrimage, seen by him as spiritual travel and something dealt with graphically in his great novella *The Old Man and the Sea* (1952), is, as Stoneback goes on to maintain, at the center of Hemingway's religious vision and his work from his earliest stories to the final, unfinished, and posthumously published novels and memoirs. This must surely act as an incentive to us to read and examine the vision.

Far from being a "nominal" or "bogus" Catholic, Hemingway was a devout practicing Catholic for much of his life. As one of those biographers acknowledged, Hemingway believed that "the only way he could run his life decently was to accept the discipline of the Church,"[12] and he could not imagine taking any other religion seriously. Finally, it is well worth noting that Hemingway's short story "Hills Like White Elephants" (1927) is the most persuasive argument against abortion ever written.

11   Ibid., 122.
12   Carlos Baker, *Ernest Hemingway: A Life Story* (1967), 333.

CHAPTER FOURTEEN

Frank Sherwood Taylor

THE MAN WHO WAS
CONVERTED BY GALILEO

THE GALILEO CASE HAS BECOME AN IMPORTANT part of the mythology of science. The standard account until relatively recently has been that a great revolutionary genius was treated scandalously by the Catholic Church, even to the extent of being tortured for his beliefs. The case has been seen as a triumph of reason and rationality over an obdurate and bigoted institution, still stuck in the supposed ignorance of the Middle Ages.

Well, now that the great work of Pierre Duhem (1861–1916)[1] has been brought into the light, that view of the Middle Ages

---

1 See Stanley L. Jaki, *Uneasy Genius: The Life and Work of Pierre Duhem* (1984); Stanley L. Jaki, *Scientist and Catholic: Pierre Duhem* (1991).

is in any case completely refuted. In addition, modern work by great historians of science has restored some balance to the debate around Galileo. The episode may not have been the high point in the Church's relationship with science, a relationship that has been a very positive one on the whole, but neither is it now seen as an attack on science by the Church.

But there is more. Far from the Galileo case being a reason for turning one's back on the Catholic Church, it has in at least one case played a major part in the conversion to the Catholic faith of an eminent scientist. The person in question is Frank Sherwood Taylor.

THE BACKGROUND[2]

Frank Sherwood Taylor was born at Bickley in the county of Kent in England on November 26, 1897. He was educated at Sherborne School, where he won a classics scholarship to Lincoln College, Oxford. However, World War I intervened and Sherwood Taylor found himself on the Western Front. At Passchendaele he volunteered to take the place of an older man in a front-line action. He was seriously wounded, and lay on the battlefield for several hours before being found. Over the next nine months he underwent fourteen operations. He recovered eventually, though always subsequently walking with a limp. In 1919 he took up his place at Oxford, but was allowed to study chemistry, a subject that had always fascinated him, rather than classics.

Oxford University has always had a fine reputation for chemistry, and Sherwood Taylor benefited from the tuition of Oxford's best in this field. In 1921 he obtained his degree with distinction (degrees for war service candidates, which were shorter in length, were not given classes). From this base Sherwood Taylor embarked on an initial career as a chemistry teacher in a number of schools. During this time his other interest in classics set him on investigating Greek alchemy. He enrolled as a part-time student at University College, London. A preliminary thesis won him the Oxford postgraduate degree of BSc in 1925. The full thesis, "A Conspectus of Greek Alchemy," earned him his London PhD in 1931.

2   For a relatively brief account of Sherwood Taylor's life see *Dictionary of National Biography* (2004). For a more detailed account see A. V. Simcock, "Alchemy and the World of Science: An Intellectual Biography of Frank Sherwood Taylor," *Ambix*, Vol. 34, Part 3, November 1987, 1.

As a school-teacher he produced a number of school and university textbooks on chemistry. In 1933, he was appointed Assistant Lecturer in Inorganic Chemistry at East London College (later Queen Mary College), London University. At this point he did some research work, but his most notable activity was to write the first of several books on general science for the average reader, *The World of Science* (1936).

EARLY VIEWS ON RELIGION

What was Sherwood Taylor's religious background? His father was a solicitor, referred to by his son as a "non-militant Huxleyan agnostic." His mother was a good Anglican. He was baptized and brought up in the manner of most children of his social class at that time. He describes this vividly:

> My religious education was, I fear, almost worthless for one who was destined to emerge into a non-religious society. I attended Matins on Sunday with my parents, I said my prayers and I must have read and been told some bible-stories.... I will not question too much the formal mode of instruction that I received in early childhood: rather would I lay stress on the fact that I did not see the Christian religion manifested. All the family, except, perhaps, my father, regarded themselves as Christians, but our conduct was not regulated with reference to God, but to the social rules which prevailed in the early Edwardian period. The most rigid was that there should be no mixture of classes: whatever might happen in the country, it was imperative in the suburbs that ladies' children shouldn't speak to poor boys....
>
> Prayer was for me like cleaning my teeth, to be done irrationally before bed-time: church was the way women and children spent Sunday morning, while the men—the admirable part of creation—played golf. Nobody prayed in church on weekdays.... In any event it is clear that unless children see their parents and fellows openly acting with reference to God, nothing that they are told about religion will be of any use.[3]

This sort of upbringing was undoubtedly typical for one with his social background at that time in England, with its established

3   Frank Sherwood Taylor, *Man and Matter: Essays Scientific and Christian* (1951), 10-11.

religion. It was no surprise that Sherwood Taylor would react against it when he discovered science: "I had been reading odd bits of popular science since I was eleven but when I reached the age of fifteen I encountered systematized science, which presented a world of logical precision, certainty and order, which gave me the strongest aesthetic pleasure."[4] At this point in his life Sherwood Taylor was prepared to accept the naïve and rather simplistic view supporting mechanism, materialism, and positivism. But even then he had some doubts: "What, then, did I find that could not fit into my mechanical philosophy? First of all my self, which I knew to be alive and thinking. I was not content to be a positivist in this matter.... I could not see how by adding atom to atom we could get life and thought."[5] His doubts regarding the scientific view of mind extended to the scientific view of matter:

> I adopted evolutionary theory as the scheme into which I fitted my ideas of the cosmos, yet found it not wholly satisfactory. There seemed a great dearth of intermediate forms at the significant stages and the whole of nature seemed much too good for its job. Why on earth should a plant produce a wild rose for a business-like brute of a bee who simply wants a pub-sign, the Pollen and Nectar—so to speak? It did not seem to matter whether the beauty was in my eye or in the rose—what place had it in the evolutionary scheme? I could understand seeing beauty in a woman as an inducement to augment the race, but where was the link between women and wild roses? If they and I were designed by the source of Beauty—yes.[6]

GALILEO COMES ON THE SCENE

And then Galileo came to the rescue. In essence what Sherwood Taylor found was that, as he put it, "the case has been disgracefully distorted by the opponents of the Church."[7] Sherwood Taylor recounted the story on a number of occasions, most expansively as follows:

> At this time...I found by the oddest of providences my first approach to the Catholic Church. The Rationalist

4 Ibid., 12.
5 Ibid., 15.
6 Ibid., 16.
7 F. Sherwood Taylor, *The Attitude of the Church to Science* (1951).

Press Association wrote to some other person of my name asking him to lecture: the letter was sent to me in error and I offered my services. What, I wondered, would they like to hear about? What was the greatest crisis for rationalism in the history of science—my specialty? Surely the case of Galileo, of whom I then knew little; I would get up the subject and give them the lecture. I did so, and I went on to write a book about his life. As I studied the documents and detailed histories, I became aware that the usually accepted Galileo-legend was full of deliberate distortions by anti-Catholic and so-called rationalist writers. The Catholic Church did not, it was true, play a very admirable part therein, but it was quite clear that she had been wickedly traduced.[8]

The book that Sherwood Taylor wrote after the original lecture was *Galileo and the Freedom of Thought*, published in 1938. The first impression that one gets from reading it is how little it indicates what later happened to the author. Yes, Galileo was the impetus for his eventual conversion to the Catholic Church, but there was much thinking to be done and issues to be considered before the final step was taken and he was received into the Church. This took place on November 15, 1941.

What was it specifically, then, about the Galileo case that prompted Sherwood Taylor to change his mind and look in a different direction? There are a number of points that he raised and developed.

Firstly, and contrary to what is often claimed, Galileo did not demonstrate that the earth revolved around the sun. Galileo thought he had proofs, of course, the main one relating to his theory of the tides, but his expression of this in the *Dialogue Concerning the Two Chief World Systems* (1632) was shown within a year to be subject to serious mathematical error. Other proposed proofs were his telescopic findings of mountains on the Moon, its rugged surface, the plethora of stars everywhere, the four bodies revolving around Jupiter, and phases in the appearance of Venus. These, though supportive of the Copernican theory, did not provide a physical proof of it. What they did was to demolish geocentrism and the Aristotelian cosmology.

8   Ibid., 19.

In addition, at this time (which was before Newton's discoveries, of course) there were relevant objections put forward to the motion of the earth (even before Galileo it was known that the orbital speed was great), as for example the questions why there were no huge winds blowing all the time across the globe; why falling objects didn't fall backwards; and why everything movable didn't fall off the face of the earth.

Faced with this situation, the Church quite reasonably required Galileo to state his views as a hypothesis only. It was long after Galileo that scientists mustered really convincing proofs. One was Bessel's observation of stellar parallax in 1837, with much improved equipment. Some of Galileo's critics during his lifetime were right in pointing out that the parallax of the nearby stars against the background of the more distant stars was not at all observed (due to the primitive telescopes available at the time).

The other convincing proof was the pendulum experiment, performed by Léon Foucault in 1851. Less significant were two earlier proofs, connected with the deduction in 1675 by Ole Roemer of the speed of light from the observation of the motion of Jupiter's moons and the observation in 1728 by James Bradley of the aberration of light.

The second point that Sherwood Taylor came to appreciate was that although the Roman Curia was entering upon shaky scientific grounds in its approach to the case, everybody at the time knew that no papal infallibility was involved here:

> The Church claims to be infallible only in matters of faith
> and morals intentionally promulgated as articles of faith
> by a Pope or General Council. The decision of 1616 was
> only an opinion of a committee of experts concerning
> what could safely be believed: it was not infallible, and
> has in fact been reversed.[9]

Thirdly, the Galileo case then (as opposed to the Galileo legend) is a much more nuanced matter than many people appreciate. One vital factor here is a severe clash of personalities. Contemporary polemics among learned men at various universities, fueled by knowledge of Galileo's strong temperament (Sherwood Taylor refers to his "sarcastic and witty pen"[10]), were already underway before

9   Ibid., 12.
10 Ibid., 10.

the open conflict with the Holy See. In addition, the Protestant revolt made the case especially sensitive in Galileo's time: "At this period there was very acute controversy as to whether the Church was to be the interpreter of Scripture, as the Catholics urged, or whether the private individual was to be the interpreter, as the Protestants held."[11] It is a great irony that in fact Luther and other Protestant leaders had already, in no uncertain terms, condemned Copernicus (who was feted in the Vatican gardens by a gathering of cardinals and bishops as he lectured there on his theory of heliocentrism). It is probable that at that time the Church was reluctant to contradict the Protestant leaders flatly. Many eminent scientists today are of the opinion that the Church authorities were simply prudent in the Galileo case.

Fourthly, there is the ultimate irony: while Galileo failed in his stated claim of presenting unassailable experimental proofs of the new theory, when it came to the interpretation of the Bible he bested the finest theologians of the Church (see his *Letter to the Grand Duchess Christina* [1615]). Galileo was right when quoting St Augustine on the interpretation of the Bible. Both sides of the debate should have followed St Augustine's wise advice: "We do not read in the Gospel that the Lord said: 'I send you the Holy Spirit to teach you how the sun and the moon go.' He wanted to make Christians, not mathematicians."[12] Galileo himself wrote in the *Letter to the Grand Duchess Christina* that "the Bible was not written to teach us astronomy," and quoted the well-known statement attributed to Cardinal Baronius that "the intention of the Holy Ghost is to teach us how to go to Heaven, not how the heavens go."[13] Sherwood Taylor appreciated also how St Augustine warned against reading hastily our own opinions into the Scriptures and fighting for them as if they were the teaching of the Bible. He summed up this aspect of the case in the following words:

11 Ibid., 11.
12 *Answer to Felix, a Manichean* (AD 404).
13 It is interesting to note that in his *Letter to the Grand Duchess Christina*, Galileo does not refer explicitly to Baronius, but to "a churchman who has been elevated to a very eminent position." The remark, which does not appear in the writings of Baronius (though it is unanimously attributed to him), was probably made by him in conversation with Galileo (we know that the two men, together with Copernicus, visited historical museums on occasions).

It is clear that the Holy Office in 1616 acted foolishly, and that the texts in the Scriptures which seemed to imply that the earth was stationary and that the sun moved were obviously not intended to teach astronomy and were mere figures of speech. We use such figures today, when we speak of "sunrise," knowing well enough that the sun does not rise, but remains stationary relative to the earth's orbit while the earth rotates on its axis.[14]

Little has changed since Sherwood Taylor's day: the insistence of the secularists that Galileo was shamefully ill-treated still persists. This is why Catholics need to arm themselves with the arguments of refutation. In this context, it is worth noting, as Sherwood Taylor himself did, that the sentence of Galileo to house arrest for the rest of his life was also not quite what it seems. He first lived in comfort in the houses of two friends, then retired to his own villa with a handsome pension from the pope, where he continued his studies and was visited by scholars from all over the world. The tale often told that he was tortured is completely untrue, as is the claim that on being forced to recant he said, *sotto voce*, "But it does move" (*Eppur si muove*). This is just scientific hagiography. In addition, and this is a point not made by Sherwood Taylor, it seems pretty clear now that Galileo never dropped balls from the Tower of Pisa or from any other tower.[15] Finally, and what is the ultimate annoyance to the secularists, Galileo of course died as a good Catholic in 1642 and in the company of his daughter, a nun.

ANOTHER ARGUMENT

All the above arguments show that there is indeed a good defense for the Church's decision in the Galileo case. Sherwood Taylor became aware of this and, as we have seen, set out several of the arguments. However, one extra point might be made here. It takes time to make the various necessary arguments and, unhappily, experience shows that in day-to-day life many will not listen. So, as Quentin de la Bedoyere wrote in his always interesting *Second Sight* column in the *Catholic Herald*,[16] it is useful to have to hand

14   *The Attitude of the Church to Science*, 12.
15   See Lane Cooper, *Aristotle, Galileo and the Tower of Pisa* (1935); Stanley L. Jaki, *Galileo Lessons* (2001), 1–8.
16   See Quentin de la Bedoyere, "Enter the Lion's Den," *Catholic Herald*, November 13, 2009, 9.

another kind of argument. This is one that Sherwood Taylor did not make, since he was looking at the issues solely from his own position, but he would have appreciated it. It amounts to that very effective (rhetorical) tactic, *tu quoque* ("You also"). As Bedoyere acknowledges, "it doesn't get you nearer to the truth but it can unsettle opponents, and make palpable hits."[17] So, if the Galileo case is brought up in discussion as an example of the Church's opposition to science, and time is limited, a more direct and effective response is to say, "That's a strange accusation to make given that the history of science is marked by its refusal to accept plain evidence, with far more serious consequences than Galileo."[18]

The point here is that there are many examples of cases where scientists themselves did not follow the evidence. Take for example, as Bedoyere does, the demonstration by William Harvey of the full circulation of blood. He published this in 1628, with experiments and reasoned arguments. But the evidence was rejected by medical scientists for some twenty years. Not exactly a glowing reference for the evidential objectivity of science, one might think.

Bedoyere himself takes as a more powerful illustration the Semmelweis case:

> More dramatic is Ignaz Semmelweis, the doctor who established, with indisputable results, that lack of hygiene led to a high rate of sepsis in midwifery and other medical treatments. This was in the 1840's. Despite the clear evidence his view was rejected time and time again by the scientific community of doctors. It was not until the last decades of the nineteenth century that medical hygiene began to be more widely recognized. Meanwhile, a very large number of deaths, particularly in childbirth, had taken place. It is thought that the mental illness which preceded Semmelweis's death was caused by the continued, tragic rejection of his proofs.[19]

As Bedoyere concludes, "The result of medical science's conservatism was the death of many thousands of innocent people. Galileo only got house arrest."[20]

17 Ibid.
18 Ibid.
19 Ibid.
20 Ibid.

FRANK SHERWOOD TAYLOR'S POSITIVE APOLOGETICS

Now back to Sherwood Taylor. The impact of the Galileo case was not to lead immediately to his conversion to the Catholic faith. What it did was open his mind to the possibilities in respect of this.

> I came to think that if the assertions of [the Catholic Church's] opposition to science were so ill-founded, so also might be all those stories of her wickedness, deceit and superstition which my Protestant and rationalist reading had put into my mind. I did not yet believe—but I now lay open to conviction.[21]

Sherwood Taylor was by no means the only person from the world of science to appreciate the Galileo case in this way. Darwin's "bulldog," T. H. Huxley, looked into the facts while in Italy and concluded that "the Pope and the College of Cardinals had on the whole the best of it."[22] Huxley, however, remained entrenched in his materialist philosophy, but Sherwood Taylor, albeit seven years after giving the original lecture, made the vital move. It is interesting to examine his positive reasons for becoming a Catholic. We shall come to the objective factors in a moment, but first of all it must be said, as so often is the case in the process of conversion, that personal elements played a major role.

> I was fortunate enough to fall in quite separately with two Catholics of personal qualities which throw some light on what Christianity in action could be—and this, in my belief, is an essential in almost every conversion. If a man or woman goes about the world being charitable, humble yet inflexible in the faith, and radiating sanctity to those who have eyes to see it, the people who meet them will find their difficulties disappearing and will tumble one after another into the laver of regeneration. I suspect that one Living Christian is worth a shop full of hortatory treatises or an army of eloquent preachers.[23]

We do not know the names of these witnesses, but we do know that they brought to him also the witness of the Christian mystics

21 *Man and Matter*, 19–20.
22 Letter to Professor St George Mivart, November 12, 1885, in Leonard Huxley, *Life and Letters of Thomas Henry Huxley*, Vol. II (second edition, 1908), 424.
23 *Man and Matter*, 20.

(he had examined supposed thinkers of this kind from the non-Christian traditions, but found them much inferior).

Another vital preliminary came when he wrote a book titled *The Century of Science 1840–1940*:

> Like many scientists I was woefully ignorant of modern social history and I expected to find in that century a smooth, easy triumphal progress. When I was driven to estimate the good and bad effects of science on human life in the years since the industrial revolution, I was brought to quite a different conclusion from that I had expected to find; namely that what had been and still is required by the world is not more knowledge, but better people; and that the scandalous economic cruelty and oppression of the nineteenth century was due to the wickedness of men rather than to ignorance about nature. I saw that as long as men wanted money and power for themselves more than they wanted happiness for others oppression must continue....
>
> I could not see any source of altruistic ethics other than a belief in God, nor could I see any other justification for following truth rather than lies, if the latter were more effective to achieve one's purpose.[24]

Both the witness of Catholics and an appreciation of the significance of good and evil put Sherwood Taylor on the route to Christianity and the Catholic Church. His attitude by now was that "the pagan world was unsatisfactory; was the Christian world credible?"[25] This involved an examination of the relationship between his scientific credo and the Christian faith, basically in respect of two fundamental issues: the existence of what may be referred to as the supernatural, and the historicity of the events recounted in the scriptures.

On the first, Sherwood Taylor was clear that "science could neither affirm nor deny that which does not manifest itself in phenomena that can be treated by the scientific method."[26] And he goes on to emphasize the importance of the measurable, of observable data, to science. This gives us an immediate implicit reference to Fr Stanley Jaki, that doughty champion of the limitation

24 Ibid., 20–21.
25 Ibid., 22.
26 Ibid., 23.

of science to what is empirical and measurable, to what is quantifiable. As Fr Jaki expressed it on so many occasions, "Science, and by that I mean exact science, has quantities for its foundation. Indeed it is nothing else than the quantitative study of the quantitative aspects of things in motion. Nothing more and nothing less than just quantities."[27] So, in the same way it was clear to Sherwood Taylor that although science was not inconsistent with the existence of the supernatural, that matter was actually moved by supernatural agency was not explicable by science. God could not be measured by the methods of science. But if the mind was not reducible simply to matter—and as we have seen, Sherwood Taylor always saw them as distinct in a certain way—then if also the supernatural was analogous to mind, he must regard the supernatural and therefore God as entirely possible. It was from this somewhat agnostic position that he moved forward, though in later life he did write in great detail about both the relationship of science and religion and the question of the proof of the existence of God.[28]

What about the question of historicity? Once Sherwood Taylor became convinced of the limitations of the scientific method, this became gradually easier for him. He understood that the events of the past were no longer observable. There was a radical difference between the kind of evidence on which one asserted that salt crystallizes in cubes and the evidence on which one might assert that Christ did or did not rise from the dead. For the latter, one thing could be said: "The only recorded material was testimony, which could only be assessed as reliable or otherwise by a sort of judgment of value. The Gospels ... read to me like the work of men that were telling the truth: no one could possibly have invented the character of Our Lord."[29]

Previously Sherwood Taylor had always set against the evidence of such testimony the uniformity of natural law. Now, he was able

27 Stated in several conversations with the present writer. For equivalent statements by him to the same effect, of which there are many, see, for example, *Questions on Science and Religion* (2004), 11–24; *Science and Religion: A Primer* (2004), 4–5; *The Drama of Quantities* (2005), *passim*.
28 See *The Fourfold Vision: A Study of the Relations of Science and Religion* (1945); *Two Ways of Life: Christian and Materialist* (1947). In addition, *Man and Matter* contains essays dealing with these themes.
29 *Man and Matter*, 25.

to see the possibility of the modification by God of the course of physical events. This recognition was buttressed by the influence of a particular book, the *Confessions* of St Augustine. This text and its author had a major influence on him, showing on his part an essential humility. "Page by page it went home to me and I said to myself, '*Mutatis mutandis*, this fellow was in the same sort of trouble as mine. He has obviously a far keener intelligence than mine, far greater spiritual powers; why should not his solution be my solution?'"[30]

Sherwood Taylor remained for some time in a state of hesitation, unable to believe any longer in a mechanistic world, but unable to accept more than tentative assertions about the spiritual world. In hindsight he saw that "the gift of faith is a supernatural one and must be divinely infused."[31] His own case at the end involved a veritable Pauline road to Damascus, not usually associated with men of science:

> One day, suddenly and unexpectedly, I heard within me the words, "Why are you wasting your life?" They carried instant conviction and removed all my difficulties. The world was changed: I knew what I was there for, I was endowed with goodwill, and it remained only to throw out the rubbish and rebuild.[32]

He at once sought out the Catholic Church and asked for instruction. It is not surprising, bearing in mind what has been said earlier, that he did not look to the middle-class public-school Anglicanism of his youth. Once more there is an emphasis with Sherwood Taylor on personal testimony. He was well aware of the strength of the formal arguments of Catholic apologetics, and had recourse to them, but again the major force came from elsewhere.

> I will give some personal answers, the first and simplest and truest being that I had not a moment's doubt that it was God's will and intention to call me there. St. Augustine was my master, and again I had no doubt which church, if he were alive today, he would recognize as his own.[33]

30 Ibid., 28.
31 Ibid.
32 Ibid., 29.
33 Ibid.

DEFENDING THE CATHOLIC FAITH

As stated earlier, after his conversion Sherwood Taylor wrote in more detail concerning the relationship between science and religion and the question of possible proofs for the existence of God. He also wrote about the differences between materialism and Christianity. But he came to concentrate on two particular areas. The first, stemming from his original discipline of chemistry, and here his work is still of major significance, is the history of the study of alchemy and early chemistry, out of which came *The Alchemists* (1951), for many years a leading work in its field.

More important in the present context, however, is the work in which he defended the role of the Catholic Church in relation to science. In addition to some general issues, referred to earlier, he set out very clearly an apologia for the Church's almost always very positive relationship with science. As early as 1944 he wrote an article entitled "The Church and Science,"[34] which dealt with several issues, notably the interpretation of Scripture, the case of Galileo, the theory of evolution, and the general relationship between science and the Church. However, his most effective work in this domain appeared in a pamphlet, prepared for the Catholic Truth Society under the title *The Attitude of the Church to Science* (1951). Here we see, in addition to a more detailed treatment of the Galileo case than that in his story of his conversion, an examination of medieval science very much along similar lines to the later research of Fr Stanley Jaki, the successor in some ways to Pierre Duhem. Sherwood Taylor here also takes up certain false tales of the Church's supposed opposition to science. Here can be found an account of particular such stories, including the Flat-Earth story,[35] the stories that the Church forbade dissection and chemistry, and the story that scientific men were burnt for their scientific opinions. In each case he brings out the true position of the Church, which is a world away from the allegations of the secularist camp. Lastly, he shows how certain admittedly unwise

34 *The Month*, April 1944, 1.
35 For a devastating critique of the curiously persistent myth of Catholic belief in a flat earth, see Jeffrey Burton Russell, *Inventing the Flat Earth: Columbus and Modern Historians* (1997). See also the excellent review of that book by David S. Oderberg in *Quadrant*, January/February 1993, 110. See, in addition, Russell's summary of his own book in "Flattening the Earth," *Mercury Magazine*, September–October 2002.

decisions made by the Church in respect of Galileo have never been repeated—how, for instance, the Church has never intruded onto the field of science in respect of the theory of evolution. He would have seen at once the sound sense of a number of writers who have drawn attention to the differences between evolution as a science and evolution as an ideology.[36]

CONCLUSION

We can come to the Catholic Church from many directions. The secular world in which we live is increasingly strident in its opposition to any religious belief and claims that science leads away from belief in God. The example of Frank Sherwood Taylor shows that it does nothing of the sort. It also shows how an openness to the facts and a reasoned approach to this question can lead one, under God's grace, into communion with the one true Church.

36   See, for example, the following texts by Fr Stanley L. Jaki: *Evolution for Believers* (2003); *Questions on Science and Religion* (2004); *Darwin's Designs* (2006); "Evolution as Science and Ideology," in *Lectures in the Vatican Gardens* (2009), 169.

CHAPTER FIFTEEN
Joseph Sobran and God's Showering of Blessings

IT IS NOW GENERALLY ACCEPTED THAT WILLIAM Shakespeare was a Catholic or at least sympathetic to Catholicism. I don't know if this was a relevant factor in the process of conversion of Joseph Sobran, but I do know that Shakespeare was a very significant person in his life. Sobran, who died on September 30, 2010, wrote commentaries on a number of the plays (*Hamlet*; *Julius Caesar*; *A Midsummer Night's Dream*; *Henry IV, Part I*; and *Twelfth Night*). However, he is chiefly remembered in this context for his book *Alias Shakespeare: Solving the Greatest Literary Mystery of All Time* (1997), where he argued that Edward de Vere (1550–1604), the 17th Earl of Oxford, was the true author of the plays usually attributed to William Shakespeare of Stratford-on-Avon. I don't want to get involved with that thesis here. It is obviously very controversial. Sobran himself is usually thought of as something of a controversial character anyway, but this is probably because he wrote with a bluntness and a political incorrectness that is frankly refreshing in our era. He also wrote with a style and humor that are appealing. Furthermore, there is a power and a persuasiveness in his writings on Jesus Christ and the Catholic faith that are very compelling and should be examined closely.

Michael Joseph Sobran (he used the name Joseph and was often called simply "Joe") was born on February 23, 1946, in Ypsilanti, Washtenaw County, Michigan. He was raised by lapsed Catholic parents who divorced when he was seven or eight. His parents gave him no instruction, never had him given the sacraments, and never sent him to Catholic school. He started to read about the faith and, when fourteen years old, decided he wanted to be a Catholic. His public high school teacher attempted to talk him out of it, but he persisted and made his first Communion as a teenager in 1961. Sobran graduated from East Michigan University in English. After graduation he lectured on a fellowship at the university in Shakespeare and English. He then worked at the *National Review* from 1972 to 1993. He practiced the faith irregularly during the late 1970s and the 1980s, but then returned to the Church during the papacy of John Paul II. He was removed from the *National Review* in controversial circumstances in 1993. He was a commentator on the CBS Radio *Spectrum* program for twenty-one years and a syndicated columnist with a number of newspapers and journals, including the *Los Angeles Times*, *The Wanderer*, *Catholic Family News*, *Human Life Review*, and *Chronicles*. In addition, he published his own newsletter, *Sobran's*, still available online, from 1994 to 2007. For most of his career he was identified as a paleo-conservative.

Sobran did not write about his conversion when it happened, but he produced many apologetic works in his later years. The size of his corpus inevitably requires here a strict process of selection, but what follows will give more than a flavor of his writings on several important issues and an appreciation of their power. As indicated at the end of this chapter, we are fortunate indeed that much of his best writing has been republished, most notably in the book *Subtracting Christianity* (2015).

He is keen to emphasize the importance of the historical evidence for Christ. On several occasions he takes up his sword against those who argue that Our Lord was a great moral teacher who never claimed divinity but preached a simple message of love, which was corrupted by his followers and ended up with layers of doctrine and repressive morality. Sobran replies with a simple question:

Why would anyone want a man crucified for preaching an innocuous message of benevolence? Jesus was accused of blasphemy for equating himself with the Father: "I and the Father are one." "No man comes to the Father but by me." And if his claim were untrue, the charge of blasphemy would be fully justified.[1]

In any case, he adds, "the trouble is that nearly everything we know about Jesus stems from the four Gospels, all of which were written by believers in the Resurrection, the central dogma."[2] Nevertheless, the hunt goes on for a supposedly "real" Jesus behind the Gospels. But still the problem remains: "The only documents we have attest a life of miraculous deeds, supernatural orientation, and eschatological purpose; the belief that a stripped-down 'natural' life of Jesus can be reconstructed is totally at odds with the records."[3]

Next, when one looks at the Gospels, says Sobran, each one (and it is the same with the Epistles) portrays the same recognizable and unique man. This phenomenon of many writers conveying the same impression of the same human being is unique in world literature. Christ is incomparable and never reminds us of anyone else. How on earth could four unpracticed amateur writers create the most vividly virtuous personality in all literature?

In addition, there is another unparalleled fact. We know, it is in fact notorious, how difficult it is to write about a good human being and make that person both good and memorable. So often evil characters are more interesting than good ones. But the Gospel writers succeeded in this awesomely difficult task, even to the extent of making the best of all characters, one who positively exudes holiness—indeed he is sinless—so fascinating. They succeeded where famously John Milton, in *Paradise Lost* and *Paradise Regained*, made Satan a more vivid character than either God or Christ. As Sobran points out, "World literature boasts many convincing villains but few convincing saints. And no literary saint has ever spoken words with the lasting impact of Jesus' teachings."[4] And to think that the ones writing were no professionals or literary geniuses!

1   "The Man They Still Hate," *Sobran's*, December 1999.
2   "The Optional Jesus," *Sobran's*, July 1998, reprinted in Fran Griffin and Tom Bethell (ed.), *Joseph Sobran: Subtracting Christianity* (2015), 259.
3   Ibid.
4   "The Man They Still Hate," *Sobran's*, December 1999.

In a very real sense, Sobran affirms—as did the poet Tennyson, who referred to them as "his greatest miracle"—it is the sheer power of Christ's words that are enough to prove his claim to be God:

> Physical miracles might be feigned, but not these verbal miracles. Yet he apparently never wrote them down; he spoke them, often off the cuff, trusting them to "carry" by their inherent power. Most writers are flattered if their words are remembered at all. But the spiritually demanding words of Jesus—which condemn even looking at a woman with lust—are still carried in the hearts of millions after 2,000 years, even though we know them only in translations from translations (Jesus spoke Aramaic, but the Gospels are written in Greek). Even conveyed to us so indirectly, those words have "carried" like no others in all history, because so many people have found them true and compelling.[5]

Sobran also points out that it is impossible for anyone to invent a single saying worthy of Christ. And there are so many of them. Such phrases as "Heaven and earth shall pass away, but my words shall not pass away" or "Whoever among you is without sin, let him cast the first stone" become part of us. They are eternally new, even when we have heard them all our lives, and they always reward meditation. Sobran poses a challenge to us:

> Some day when you have nothing better to do, try improving on the Lord's Prayer. "Forgive us our trespasses, as we forgive those who trespass against us." Don't all religions agree on that? No. In most religions—see the *Iliad,* the *Koran,* and the *Psalms,* for example—it is normal to pray for revenge. Forgiving and praying for one's enemies are among the hardest duties of a Christian. Being "nice" is far from the same thing as being a Christian; after all, Jesus was not tortured to death for urging good manners on his disciples.[6]

What about other religious leaders? Some say that Christ was no different from them in reality—just a teacher. Sobran is scathing about this claim:

> Do other religions have prayers like the Our Father? Did the ancient Greeks ask Zeus to "forgive us as we forgive

5   Ibid.
6   "The Incomparable One," *The Reactionary Utopian,* June 4, 2009, reprinted in *Subtracting Christianity* (2015), 15.

others?" Did the Aztecs pray like that? How many other religions command their votaries to rejoice, be of good cheer, have no fear? ("Trust in Poseidon?") And many other religious figures, we are told, have performed miracles every bit as impressive as those attributed to Jesus. Really? Did they cure blind men and cripples while assuring them that their sins were forgiven? And did they, even after they had died (and risen again, it goes without saying), make converts who would die for what they had taught? Did any of them ever give a speech like the Sermon on the Mount? If so, where can I find a copy?[7]

So there we are. The Gospels, so often derided by liberal critics, do satisfy a series of important tests. Sobran sums it up in this way:

If you want to contend that the Gospels are packs of lies and that Jesus never said all those things or performed all those wonders, you should at least admit that Christianity is the most brilliant hoax of all time. Everything fits so well. How could a few unlearned and provincial Jews invent such a supremely memorable character, endow him with the ability to speak immortal words on all occasions, then make virtually all the details of his story cohere so well, tallying even with Old Testament prophecy?[8]

Finally, on the question of the divinity of Christ, Joe Sobran asks what greater proof there could be than that he is still resisted, even hated, after two thousand years. As he expresses it, "Nobody hates Julius Caesar any more; it's pretty hard even to hate Attila the Hun, who left a lot of hard feeling in his day. But the world still hates Christ and his Church."[9] Of course, this fact is only to be expected, since Our Lord himself affirmed it. In respect of looking for the true Church, there is a link here with the writings of Archbishop Fulton Sheen, who always said that if he were a non-Catholic and looking for the true Church in the world, he would look for the Church which the world hates.[10] Getting back

7 "Happy Easter!," *Sobran's*, April 2007, reprinted in Griffin and Bethell (ed.), *Subtracting Christianity*, 15.
8 "Jesus' Simple Message," *Chronicles*, January 2008, 13.
9 "The Words and Deeds of Christ," *Sobran's*, November 2000, reprinted in Griffin and Bethell (ed.), *Subtracting Christianity*, 4.
10 See, e.g., Preface to Fr Leslie Rumble and Fr Charles M. Carty, *Radio Replies, Volume 1* (1938), ix.

to Christ himself, Joe Sobran well understood that "Christ always has been, still is, and always will be too much for the human race at large to accept or assimilate. Exactly as he said he would be. The world keeps proving the truth of his words."[11]

On the question of which body was the one Church chosen by Christ, for Joe Sobran the "clinching argument" was simply that the authority of the Bible itself rested on the Church:

> It was the Church herself that had established the Scriptural canon, long before Luther. Unless she was divinely guided, how could Protestants be sure that she had chosen the right books out of the welter of gospels, epistles, and other early Christian literature? And if she was divinely guided, by what authority did the Protestant reformers reject several books of the Old Testament that had been accepted by all Christians until the sixteenth century? The daily life of Christians was sacramental rather than Scriptural.[12]

In addition to this, as he pointed out, it was several centuries after Christ before the canon was defined, and the Bible as we know it now hardly existed until the invention of the printing press and the spread of literacy.

Joe Sobran also wrote significantly about the Real Presence of Our Lord in the Eucharist. He could not see how anyone could deny that Christ meant the words "This is my body.... This is my blood" literally, or that his disciples took them literally:

> The Last Supper was the most solemn moment of his life, the very moment at which we would expect of him a stupendous revelation, not a mere metaphor or figure of speech. And it came. Here was the body that would be sacrificed, the blood that would be shed in redemption, under the appearances of bread and wine (foreshadowed in his miracles with bread and wine). For him to have demanded a mere symbolic memorial of himself would have been wholly inadequate to the occasion.[13]

11 "The Words and Deeds of Christ," *Sobran's*, November 2000, reprinted in Griffin and Bethell (ed.), *Subtracting Christianity*, 5.
12 "My Faith: A Brief Defense," *Sobran's*, June 2002, reprinted in Griffin and Bethell (ed.), *Subtracting Christianity*, 35.
13 Ibid., 38.

Sobran would have appreciated the great work of Friar Basile de Soissons, the chaplain to Queen Henrietta Maria, widow of the English king Charles I. Basile gave many sermons on the Eucharist in the Queen Mother's London chapel and gained many converts. These sermons were collected and printed in 1676 under the title *Invincible Defense of the Orthodox Truth of the Real Presence of Jesus Christ in the Eucharist, Proven by Nearly Three Hundred Arguments, of which the Major are Taken from Scripture.*

The main emphasis placed by Basile in *Defense Invincible* was on clarity. He pointed out that Jesus used the clearest words possible when he said, "This is My Body," and "the bread that I will give is my flesh for the life of the world." At this time his audience, mainly Protestants, believed that Scripture was clear to the average reader in all things necessary for salvation. Therefore, Basile asks how they can teach that the word of God is clear and then expect a simple man who reads "This is My Body" to understand that Christ means "This signifies My Body."[14] In addition, Jesus took a solemn oath when he was about to reveal something important that no one has ever heard of before, as when he swears to Nicodemus that one must be born again. In John 6 he swore four double oaths of "Amen, Amen" before promising that his flesh would be present in the Sacrament. Basile went on to examine several aspects of the exact grammar of the key biblical text "This is My Body" to demonstrate that it cannot be read as a figure of speech. All of this was the fulfillment and explanation of the "hard saying" in chapter 6 of John's Gospel, which led many disciples to leave him. The fact that Christ let them leave was further endorsement of his teaching, since if he had been misunderstood, he could simply have put the matter straight. Joe Sobran would have understood the significance of the above teaching:

> The key to Catholicism is the Eucharist, the Body of Christ, which requires the priesthood, the hierarchy, the Magisterium, apostolic succession, and all the rest. Eliminate the Eucharist, and every form of heresy and license follows naturally; this is the history of Protestantism in a nutshell. "Reforming" Christ's Church nearly always turns out to mean relaxing her morals.[15]

14 *Defense Invincible*, 29.
15 "Eccentric Catholicism," Universal Press Syndicate, May 28, 1998, reprinted in Griffin and Bethell (ed.), *Subtracting Christianity*, 258.

Sobran would no doubt have had a similar reaction of approval to a more informal endorsement of the Real Presence. This was by his compatriot, the great writer Flannery O'Connor. As a young woman O'Connor was at a dinner party hosted by the noted novelist, Mary McCarthy. O'Connor, very much the outsider, listened quietly to the conversation in which McCarthy, a former Catholic with a convent education, mentioned her loss of faith at age fifteen. What happened next is told by O'Connor in a manner Sobran would have appreciated:

> Well, toward the morning the conversation turned on the Eucharist, which I, being the Catholic, was obviously supposed to defend. Mrs. Broadwater [Mary McCarthy] said when she was a child and received the Host, she thought of it as the Holy Ghost, He being the most "portable" person of the Trinity; now she thought of it as a symbol and implied that it was a pretty good one. I then said, in a very shaky voice, "Well, if it's a symbol, to hell with it."[16]

There are many memorable passages in Joe Sobran's extensive writings. They have a remarkable power and persuasiveness. If you delve into his work you will find finely tuned arguments for the Catholic Church, rebuttals of attacks on that body, and moving passages containing refreshing and personalized advice. I would like to finish with a lengthy quotation from one of these.

> The loveliest argument I know against unbelief was made by a woman whose name I have forgotten,[17] quoted by the theologian John Baillie in *Our Knowledge of God*; it boils down to this: "If there is no God, whom do we thank?"
>
> The force of this hit me on a mild November evening when I was oppressed by woes; I prayed for a little relief and tried counting my blessings instead of my grievances. I've long known that a great secret of happiness is gratitude, but that didn't prepare me for what happened next.
>
> It wasn't a mystical experience, just a simple mental one (speaking of simple messages). I began by comparing my lot with that of countless others, many of whom are starving or dying of horrible diseases. Then, I reflected that the modern world teaches us to be ingrates. What else

16 Sally Fitzgerald (ed.), *The Habit of Being: Letters of Flannery O'Connor* (1978), 125.
17 The woman referred to was in fact the writer Katherine Mansfield.

is political life for? Democracy is obsessed with supposed rights, injuries, and entitlements.

Within a few minutes, as I munched a cheeseburger, my mind told me how unlikely my own existence was: My parents' meeting (remarkably improbable, too, just in mathematical terms), the love they gave me, my living in the Christian Era, my later Baptism (I became a Catholic at age fifteen), the priests who taught me, my dear stepfather and his holy parents, my friends, my children, and on and on—in spite of all my own sins. I could hardly think of anything in my life that couldn't be seen as a gift from God. Now I was over sixty-one, still showered with blessings every day, despite all my attempts to make myself unhappy by brooding on my petty dissatisfactions.

As one of the characters in *Lear* tells his father, "Thy life's a miracle." Of whom is that not true?

The more we reflect on the sheer oddity of our very existence and, in addition, of our eligibility for salvation, the deeper our gratitude must be. Amazing grace indeed! To call it astounding is to express the matter feebly. Why me? How on earth could I ever have deserved this, the promise of eternal joy?

And given all this, in comparison with which winning the greatest lottery in the world is just a minor fluke, how can I dare to sin again, or to be anything less than a saint for the rest of my life?

Yet I know that my own horrible spiritual habits will keep drawing me downward every hour. Like most men, or maybe more than most, I am my own worst enemy, constantly tempted to repay my Savior with my self-centered ingratitude. When I think of my sins, the debt of thanksgiving itself seems far too heavy to pay. No wonder He commands us to rejoice. It's by no means the easiest of our duties.[18]

Many of Joseph Sobran's writings (notably those in his newsletter, *Sobran's*) can be found on the Internet by googling his name. In addition, published in 2012 was a book, *Joseph Sobran, The National Review Years: Articles From 1974 to 1991*, edited by Fran Griffin. Moreover, there was published in 2015 a further set of his writings, *Joseph Sobran: Subtracting Christianity: Essays on American Culture and Society*, edited by Fran Griffin and Tom Bethell.

18   "Jesus' Simple Message," *Chronicles*, January 2008, 13.

CHAPTER SIXTEEN
Siegfried Sassoon

CONVERT WAR POET

SIEGFRIED SASSOON WAS ONE OF THE VERY finest of what may be called the First World War poets. His career in that capacity (and also his distinguished prose writing) have been pretty exhaustively examined by various writers. Less well known, and also of great interest, is that Sassoon was a convert to the Catholic Faith. He did not take that step into the Church, however, until much later in his life, in fact on August 14, 1957. It is well worth looking in more detail at this process and at the grounds for his conversion, as far as we know them.

Siegfried Loraine Sassoon was born in Weirleigh, Benchley, in the county of Kent, England, on September 8, 1886. He was the son of Alfred Ezra Sassoon, a financier and sculptor, but was brought up entirely by his mother. He was descended on his father's side from a Jewish family, but he was brought up Anglican. He went up to Clare College, Cambridge, but left without taking a degree. It is something of an irony that although he became a pacifist and publicly protested against the war, he was awarded a Military Cross for his actions during this time. He gave much assistance to the other major war poet, Wilfred Owen. In his study of Sassoon, Paul Moeyes brings out the frankness of Sassoon about those earlier years and the question of religion:

> I was a complete ignoramus about religion. It amazes me to look back on it. I never said a prayer, never consulted any religious book, or *thought* about doctrine. Just went blindly on, clinging to the *idea* of God, unable to believe that salvation applied to *me*, though firmly convinced of the existence of a spiritual world and heaven above. Again and again in these past years, I have asked myself how I endured it, so unendurable it seems in retrospect. *Was* it some kind of dark night of probation?[1]

As to the personal influences on Sassoon's conversion, the most straightforward and direct was perhaps Cardinal Newman: "Reading Newman, I wonder what effect it would have made if someone had given it to me ten years ago. Everything I needed is there, waiting for me! All clear as daylight. And as simple as falling off a log—just unconditional surrender!"[2] Other significant influences were Msgr Ronald Knox (another great convert of course), Hilaire Belloc, Mother Margaret Mary McFarlin, the Mother Superior at the Assumption Convent in Kensington Square, the nuns of Stanbrook Abbey, and finally the Asquith family. Sassoon's Catholic faith undoubtedly gave him great comfort and joy in his last years. He died on September 1, 1967, at Heytesbury House, near Warminster, Wiltshire, and is buried in St Andrews churchyard, Mells, Somerset, not far from the grave of Ronald Knox.

There are a number of questions one might ask about Sassoon's conversion. In answering them we are now assisted greatly by modern research. Around the turn of the last century there appeared no fewer than three biographies. First came Jean Moorcroft Wilson's two volumes: *Siegfried Sassoon: The Making of a War Poet, 1886-1918* (1998) and *Siegfried Sassoon: The Journey from the Trenches, 1918-1967* (2003). The two single-volume works are John Stuart Roberts, *Siegfried Sassoon, 1886-1967* (1999), and Max Egremont,

---

1 Paul Moeyes, *Siegfried Sassoon: Scorched Glory* (1997), 245-46.
2 John Stuart Roberts, *Siegfried Sassoon* (2000), 316.

Siegfried Sassoon (2005). These works make full use of the many resources available concerning Sassoon. All of them discuss his conversion.

The first question is simple: why did he do it? The experience and conversation of the persons listed above were obviously very important. In addition Dennis Silk, a first-class cricketer and public school headmaster, and close friend through a mutual love of cricket, believed that a decisive factor in Sassoon's turning to Rome was his despair over world events, Korea and Suez in particular. Sassoon became very disillusioned and no doubt saw Rome as the body which, through thick and thin, in season and out of season, continued to witness to the Christian message. This was clearly and unsurprisingly a factor impressing itself on Sassoon, though it was in no way the only one.

If Rome was long-standing, what was Sassoon's own process of development? As Max Egremont points out, "there can be no doubt that although Sassoon's conversion was some long time coming, it was not, like that of J. H. Newman, the result of long intellectual reasoning. Nor did the light come in a sudden burst, as experienced by St. Paul."[3] The same author points out that "what happened had come slowly, encouraged by a slow falling away of much that had seemed worthwhile in his life, a process that began as far back as what he saw as the betrayal of his sacrificial idealism during the First World War."[4]

In this context John Stuart Roberts brings out the mystery of the process of conversion and mentions also that for Newman as well, some aspects of whose conversion he had examined earlier in the book, it was not simply an intellectual journey.

> As to what happens at conversion nobody can explain—
> except that there is a before and after; the crossing of a
> border: a moving between states—darkness to light; chaos
> to order and everything made new. Sassoon in the spring
> of 1957 was aware of an "instant release." His puzzlement
> was why he had taken so long to understand that it was
> not an intellectual argument but just . . . unconditional
> surrender.[5]

3   Egremont, 488.
4   Ibid.
5   Roberts, 315–16.

In looking for specific factors, Jean Moorcroft Wilson, perhaps harking back to Sassoon's several homosexual relationships (though later came marriage and family), sees as of great significance the issue of guilt:

> One of the powerful attractions of the Catholic Church for Sassoon appears to have been the notion of confession and absolution. "Could I but be absolved of what my years have wrought," he had written in an unpublished poem of 1947; and two years later had argued, in a letter to [H. M.] Tomlinson, that the whole point of life was "to try to rise above one's waistline." There is no doubting the sense of guilt he carried with him up to his entry into the Church.[6]

A similar question is "Why Catholicism?" Why did Sassoon choose to become a Catholic? Why did he not simply go back to the Anglican faith in which he had been brought up? Jean Moorcroft Wilson probes this too:

> In responding to Tomlinson, who sympathized with his spiritual needs but found his choice of Church puzzling, he told him that the Catholic Church gave him a "suste-nance" the Church of England could not; it seemed "so real" and its followers so different from the "inhibiting reticence" which characterized the average Anglican.[7]

But what was it that conveyed to Sassoon the "sustenance" and "reality" that he saw in the Catholic Church, as opposed to the perceived "inhibiting reticence" of Anglicanism? It is clear from all the sources that this hinged upon the issue of authority. In his search for religion, the aspect he was most attracted by was, as he put it, "the complete authority of the Church." There is something of an irony here, because, as Max Egremont points out, "this was odd ... after his rebellious record in the First World War."[8]

Jean Moorcroft Wilson, in dealing with the authority issue, refers again to the witness of Denis Silk: "He also maintained that Sassoon 'wanted to be told what to do' in his old age, and that the Catholic Church, with its claim to be the 'One True Church'

6 Wilson, 393.
7 Ibid., 395.
8 Egremont, 490.

and belief in the infallibility of its leader, the Pope, provided that authority."[9] Further evidence comes from Maurice Wiggins, who met Sassoon towards the end of the latter's life, and suggested that his "instinct for order" was very important to him.[10]

Sassoon himself, in an effort to explain his decision to convert, had written that Catholicism "makes Anglicanism seem unreal and ineffective. The faith I am now blessed with came to me through Catholic influence."[11]

Max Egremont summarizes well the main ideas going through Sassoon's mind:

> Authority was what he wanted, not the soft, apologetic Church of England. The Abbot of Downside surely would "put the fear of God into me." And Sassoon longed to be "put in my place." "Be ye as little children": he yearned for those reassuring words and "never to be lonely and forsaken again."...
>
> Roman Catholicism brought authority—an end to questioning, the return of a certainty.... It brought an understanding, and forgiveness, of everything about him that was wrong. In the Church, he belonged, at last, to a definable and (to him) an admirable world, an elect drawn together by religious mystery, by the idea of the unknowable which he believed was at the core of the most important part of his life: his poetry. The search for utopia—recreated in his prose books—ended with monks, nuns and priests, the holy Catholics of his last years. Sassoon's Catholicism also had beauty and history, even glamour, exemplified by what he saw and loved at Mells [home of the Asquith family], the Roman Catholicism of *Brideshead Revisited*. When his new faith began to manifest itself in inexplicable visions and mysticism as well, his joy in it became an ecstasy greater than anything that he had ever known.[12]

The reference here to the Asquith family is important. There is a very moving passage written by Hilaire Belloc to one of the family, Katherine Asquith, which has often been referred to by

9 Wilson, 395.
10 Ibid.
11 Ibid.
12 Egremont, 486–89.

other converts. Sassoon came across it in Robert Speaight's biography of Belloc and adopted it for himself:

> The Faith, the Catholic Church, is discovered, is recognized, triumphantly enters reality like a landfall at sea which at first was thought a cloud. The nearer it is seen, the more it is real, the less imaginary: the more direct and external its voice, the more indubitable its representative character, its "persona," its voice. The metaphor is not that men fall in love with it: the metaphor is that they discover home. "This was what I sought. This was my need." It is the very mould of the mind, the matrix to which corresponds in every outline the outcast and unprotected contour of the soul. It is Verlaine's "Oh! Rome—oh! Mère." And that not only to those who had it in childhood and have returned, but much more—and what a proof!—to those who come upon it from the hills of life and say to themselves, "Here is the town."[13]

Sassoon wrote to Dame Felicitas Corrigan, a Benedictine nun and author, of that moment: "Belloc's magnificent words settled it once and for all. 'That's done it,' I said. My whole being was liberated."[14] It is, of course, the reference to "coming home" that is the crucial one. How often does one find such language in accounts of conversions to the Catholic Church? Time after time. It is no surprise, then, to find a reference to it in respect of Siegfried Sassoon.

Sassoon referred to the process of conversion in one of his own poems, *Lenten Illuminations*, and it is accordingly highly appropriate to give this convert poet the last word on his conversion.

> This then, brought our new making. Much emotional stress—
> Call it conversion; but the word can't cover such good.
> It was like being in love with ambient blessedness—
> In love with life transformed—life breathed afresh,
> though yet half understood.
> There had been many byways for the frustrate brain,
> All leading to illusions lost and shrines forsaken...
> Our road before us now—one guidance for our gain—
> One morning light—whatever the world's weather—
> wherein wide-eyed to waken.

---

13   Speaight, *The Life of Hilaire Belloc* (1957), 377.
14   Dame Felicitas Corrigan, *Siegfried Sassoon, Poet's Pilgrimage* (1973), 181–82.

CHAPTER SEVENTEEN

Deathbed Conversions and the Case of Wallace Stevens

AS STATED IN A PREVIOUS CHAPTER, YOU DON'T tend to hear about deathbed conversions to anything outside of the Catholic Church. Certainly the classic examples are of those who grasp the last chance open to them to join that august body. For some it is a matter of moving from some other religious organization to full communion with the Church. With others there may have been no previous religious affiliation. In yet other cases it is more an example of someone returning to the faith of his childhood, along the lines of the fictional case of Lord Marchmain narrated by Evelyn Waugh in *Brideshead Revisited*, based, as stated earlier, on a true story, that of Hubert Duggan, brought back to the faith predominantly by the efforts of Waugh himself.[1] The novel presented this event quite faithfully.

In the present writer's book *Roads to Rome: A Guide to Notable Converts from Britain and Ireland from the Reformation to the Present Day*

1 See Patey, *The Life of Evelyn Waugh*, 210.

(2010), there are references in the main entries to seven death-bed conversions about which we can be pretty certain, the most notable historically being King Charles II and, in more modern times, Oscar Wilde, of whom more will be said in a later chapter. The others are art and cultural historian Sir Kenneth Clark; poet Robert Hawker (1803-1875); diplomat Richard Lyons (1817-1887); musician, composer, and antiquary Robert Pearsall (1795-1856); and diplomat Conrad Russell (1878-1947). Then there are four others who may well have converted on their deathbed, but about whom there are some doubts. These are Anglican churchman Godfrey Goodman (1583-1655); writer William Hurrell Mallock, dealt with in an earlier chapter; classical scholar Gilbert Murray (1866-1957); and John Sholto Douglas, the ninth Marquess of Queensbury. If this last case is genuine, then there is much irony there, since this is the man who was Oscar Wilde's accuser.

In my later book *The Mississippi Flows Into the Tiber: A Guide to Notable American Converts to the Catholic Church* (2014), there are fourteen such cases. The book deals with converts from North America, and the deathbed converts come, as in the previous book, from very different backgrounds. Here they are in alphabetical order: author and judge Alfred Arrington (1810-1867); political and social commentator James Burnham (1905-1987), a revert; soldier and showman William Frederick Cody ("Buffalo Bill") (1846-1917); politician and soldier John Floyd (1783-1837; some have doubts about this one); political columnist Sam Francis (1947-2005); college football player George Gipp (1895-1920); the great golfer Bobby Jones (1902-1971); actress, dancer, and singer Dixie Lee (1911-1952); political leader Sir Alan Napier MacNab (1798-1862; the one Canadian here); philosopher and political activist Frank Straus Meyer (1909-1972); actress and dancer Ann Miller (1923-2004); mobster Dutch Schultz (1901-1935; referred to in detail in a later chapter of this book); poet Wallace Stevens (1879-1955); and film star John Wayne (1907-1979).

Some converts tell us very little about their journey to the Catholic faith. For them it remains a private thing; they never seek to give public expression to their reasons for converting. This is the case with the overwhelming majority of the above names. And, of course, there is the obvious extra factor in such cases that those who convert on their deathbed would have little, if any, time to set out their reasons in some publicly verifiable way! However, in the case of Wallace Stevens, widely considered the greatest American poet of the twentieth century, things are somewhat different. One can only come to the conclusion that in a very real sense, no matter when he was received formally into the Church, this was not essentially a deathbed conversion of the traditional kind. We shall see that his poetry is one long attempt to escape from modernist subjectivism and solipsism. This was a long, drawn-out conversion, a work in progress as it were, until finally realized at a time very close to his death. This chapter will attempt to map out this process and evaluate it.

Wallace James Stevens was born on October 2, 1879, in Reading, Pennsylvania. His father was a lawyer who himself wrote occasional poems. Stevens was born to Pennsylvanian Dutch Puritan parents. His family had been farmers for several generations. He was brought up as a Presbyterian, but attended a school which had a Lutheran church attached to it. So he was from provincial, small-town America, not the usual background then for one attending Harvard University, to which he proceeded after his schooling. While there he was a close friend of George Santayana (1863–1952), the philosopher, poet, essayist, and novelist, who influenced him considerably. He was subsequently at New York Law School, graduating in 1903. When at university he moved away from Christianity, and his reading focused on Coleridge, Nietzsche, and Bergson. Stevens worked as a lawyer in New York until 1916, but spent most of the rest of his life in Hartford, Connecticut, where he worked in a legal capacity for the Hartford Accident and Indemnity Company. He died on August 2, 1955, in Hartford.

In order to assess Stevens' work at all one must look first at Santayana. He was born in Spain and raised a Catholic, spending his early childhood in Avila, but from the age of nine he lived and was educated in Boston (later at Harvard). Influenced by nineteenth-century rationalism, he decided that he did not and could not believe that Christianity was true. However, he had been brought up with a philosophical interest in Catholic theology and this never left him. It should be noted in passing that he taught and had influence over another poet, one who converted later to Christianity of the Anglican kind, namely T. S. Eliot. Santayana's religious beliefs became Unitarian, followed by a kind of agnosticism, although, as we shall see, late in his life he once again espoused something very close to the Catholic belief he had rejected earlier.

Santayana's effect on Stevens is significant indeed. It is well described by Lucy Beckett, who gives a very interesting account of Santayana's influence on both Stevens and Eliot:

> This was the man who gave to the young Wallace Stevens... not only the certainty that to believe Christianity is true was no longer possible, and the certainty that the vocation of the poet was the highest possible calling in a world that had lost religious conviction, but also a sense of the substance and value of the Catholic faith as "a real religion" that remained in the back of Stevens' mind for the rest of his life.[2]

Under the encouragement of Santayana, Stevens did well at Harvard, succeeding in becoming something of a literary figure there. The legal work to which he proceeded took up the whole of the rest of his life and he became a wealthy man. Thus, he became a man of business, but also a very focused and dedicated poet. Early on there is already a positive attitude in him towards religion. Take for example the following extract from his journal: "The feeling of piety is very dear to me. I would sacrifice a great deal to be a Saint Augustine but modernity is so Chicagoan, so plain, so unmeditative.... I'm completely satisfied that behind every physical fact there is a divine force. Don't, therefore, look at facts, but *through* them."[3]

Maria J. Cirurgião points out the continuing influence of St Augustine in Stevens' life and work:

> It was no passing fancy, but the beginning of a lifelong companionship of the mind and heart. Not only are Augustinian writings and teachings echoed throughout Stevens' *Collected Poems*, but the acute reader cannot miss the importance of the great Church Father as the moral compass by which the poet measured the integrity of his verse.[4]

2   *In the Light of Christ: Writings in the Western Tradition* (2006), 435.
3   Holly Stevens (ed.), *Letters of Wallace Stevens* (1966), 482.
4   "Last Farewell and First Fruits: The Story of a Modern Poet," *Lay Witness*, June 2000; www.catholiceducation.org/en/culture/art/last-farewell-and-first-fruits-the-story-of-a-modern-poet.html.

On the influence of religion on Stevens, many writers have pointed also to the fact that in the years he spent alone in New York he often could be found in St Patrick's Cathedral. He sometimes attended Mass there, but spent much time "in the dark transept where I go now and then [probably more often in fact] in my more lonely moods."[5]

Furthermore, his journal at that time identified a division in himself between the divine presence that he sensed walking in the countryside and the God he encountered in the Cathedral.

> The priest in me worshipped one God at one shrine; the poet another God at another shrine. The priest worshipped Mercy and Love; the poet, Beauty and Might.... As I went tramping through the fields and woods I beheld every leaf and blade of grass revealing or rather betokening the Invisible.[6]

In her fine study, Lucy Beckett makes the very valuable point that Stevens had no one to connect the two presences for him, as, say, Gerard Manley Hopkins (1844–1889) had connected them.[7] Stevens himself refers to what might be termed his bipolar view in a letter written in 1907 in which he encouraged his future wife, Elsie Moll (1886–1963), to join a church (one assumes a Protestant one):

> One can get a thousand benefits from churches that one cannot get outside of them.... Don't *care* about the Truth. There are other things in Life besides the Truth upon which everybody of any experience agrees, while no two people agree about the Truth.... I am not in the least religious. The sun clears my spirit, if I may say that, and an occasional sight of the sea, and thinking of blue valleys, and the odor of the earth, and many things. Such things make a god of a man; but a chapel makes a man of him. Churches are human—I say my prayers every night—not that I need them now, or that they are anything more than a habit, half-conscious. But in Spain, in Salamanca, there is a pillar in a church (Santayana told me) worn by the kisses of generations of the devout. One of their kisses is worth all my prayers.[8]

5 *Letters of Wallace Stevens*, 32.
6 Ibid., 58.
7 *In the Light of Christ*, 437.
8 *Letters of Wallace Stevens*, 96.

This led Stevens, encouraged by the writings of Santayana, to the idea that in an age of loss of religious faith poetry may be able to meet the need for spirituality. This was something of a poisoned chalice, since, as Lucy Beckett points out, "Santayana opened to the young Stevens a glimpse of the European Catholic past but also closed for him, for almost all Stevens' life, the possibility that Christianity might be true."[9] In line with this, Stevens has become well known for his statement that "After one has abandoned a belief in God, poetry is that essence which takes its place in life's redemption."[10]

Stevens' work covers a wide range of issues, but always in the background, and often in the foreground, is this philosophical position. For example, in his earliest great poem, "Sunday Morning," written at the outbreak of World War I, he writes of the meditation of a woman (but really of anyone) on religion and the meaning of life. Stevens gives expression to the simple natural beauties of the earth, but relates *that* as all the beauty there is. There is, he says, "no imperishable bliss," for "death is the mother of beauty." As so often in his work there is a sense of ambiguity. There is a more positive reference to the Incarnation in the poem, but it ends with a stanza that begins by bringing in the Christian story and specifically the Resurrection in a negative way:

> She hears upon that water without sound,
> A voice that cries, "The tomb in Palestine
> Is not the porch of spirits lingering.
> It is the grave of Jesus where he lay."

Stevens was already forty-four when his first book of poetry, *Harmonium* (1923), appeared. The shorter poems in the book included several later accepted as great ones, but the book was little noticed at the time. Perhaps in consequence Stevens wrote hardly any new poems in the next ten years. However, he then began to write a relatively large amount and produced three books. He won the Pulitzer Prize for Poetry in 1955 and the National Book Award in 1951 and 1955. His poetry during this period continued to characterize the philosophies outlined earlier. It is almost as if he is working in a laboratory, trying to reconcile the opposing

9   *In the Light of Christ*, 439.
10   *Opus Posthumous* (1957).

philosophical ideas. Lucy Beckett captures this sense when she refers to his thinking and writing: "his experimental way toward something that would, perhaps, confirm that his responsiveness to beauty, his love for the earth and his sense that poetry was for him a serious lifelong vocation all had somewhere, somehow, a sufficient meaning."[11] Stevens himself expressed a key part of this philosophy in a letter he wrote at this time:

> I ought to say that it is a habit of mind with me to be thinking of some substitute for religion. I don't necessarily mean some substitute for the church, because no one believes in the church as an institution more than I do. My trouble, and the trouble of a great many people, is the loss of belief in the sort of God in Whom we were all brought up to believe. Humanism would be the natural substitute, but the more I see of humanism the less I like it.[12]

Maria Cirurgião deals further with this:

> Poetically speaking, he kept a vacillating foothold on each side of the abyss between Christianity and the paganization of the Christian conscience—modernism. Stevens' poetic voice is a voice of ambivalence. In the ambivalence, though, he made room for grace, and his poetry can truly be said to be a poetry of conversion.[13]

What emerges from an analysis of his major poems on this theme is that Stevens is haunted by the old truths of Christianity, but seems unable to grasp them. However, the figure of Christ never really left him and at times he seems very close, as Lucy Beckett puts it, to "the God of truth, goodness and beauty, ... to God revealed in Christ."[14] The themes of these later poems are many, among them an ongoing tension between subjectivism and true realism. Stevens emphasizes the power of imagination. Sometimes this seems no more than a subjective feeling, the poet's resource (available to anyone else as well) against "the pressure of reality." Stevens himself expresses this belief in *The Owl's Clover* (1936):

11 *In the Light of Christ*, 459.
12 *Letters of Wallace Stevens*, 348.
13 "Last Farewell and First Fruits."
14 *In the Light of Christ*, 463.

> The idea of God is a thing of the imagination. We no
> longer think that God was, but was imagined. The idea of
> pure poetry, essential imagination, as the highest objective
> of the poet, appears to be, at least potentially, as great as
> the idea of God, and, for that matter, greater, if the idea
> of God is only one of the things of imagination.

Thus, as a matter of philosophy, this makes God a thing of the imagination, rather than imagination being a thing created by God.

However, on occasions it looks like Stevens is resisting a desire to acknowledge that there is no more to be said on this question. This is in the sense that imagination can be seen as the invisible or even the soul. Stevens seems on many occasions to be less than fully accepting of his philosophy. Many of his later poems are rich in matters relating to the fundamental question of whether God exists in reality. Stevens is never sure that one can leave God behind and reduce him to a figment of the imagination. Lucy Beckett speaks of "the never quite abandoned possibility that the imagination, the soul, the invisible, has also to do with the truth."[15] At times he definitely acknowledges this, but often there is a turning away from this and its implications. Interestingly, however, in "The Sail of Ulysses," a poem of 1954—just too late to be included in *Collected Poems*, published the same year, but published in his *Opus Posthumous*[16]—he acknowledges clearly and directly the grace of God:

> Yet always there is another life,
> A life beyond this present knowing,
> A life lighter than this present splendor,
> Brighter, perfected and distant away,
> Not to be reached but to be known,
> Not an attainment of the will
> But something illogically received,
> A divination, a letting down
> From loftiness, misgivings dazzlingly
> Resolved in dazzling discovery.

How did it all end up for Wallace Stevens? Well, in 1952 he wrote as follows to an Irish friend, Thomas MacGreevy, a devout Catholic: "At my age it would be nice to be able to read more and think more and be myself more and to make up my mind

15   Ibid., 465.
16   2nd edition, 1989.

about God, say, before it is too late, or at least before he makes up his mind about me."[17] Also, an indication of the direction in which his mind was going can be gleaned from his statement to Anthony Sigmans, one of his closest business associates, that he belonged to no church, but if he ever joined a church it would be the Catholic Church. Incidentally, and on a lighter note, according to Sigmans, Stevens (always a joker) once arranged a hotel reservation for them both in Boston by writing to the Statler Hotel and saying, "I would like a room overlooking the Common. I will have with me Sigmans, who could be assigned a room overlooking most anything." Sigmans took no offense!

Moving on from that, there is good evidence that during his final days, when he was in St Francis Hospital, Hartford (in passing, it seems not insignificant that he chose a Catholic hospital), suffering from stomach cancer, he was baptized and received into the Catholic Church by Fr Arthur Hanley, chaplain of the hospital. His alleged deathbed conversion was disputed, particularly by his daughter Holly, and there is no record of his baptism, but there was testimony in favor by Dr Edward Sennett, the head radiologist, and by the sisters at the hospital.

The statement given by Fr Hanley is well worth looking at in detail, in particular for the insight it gives to the process of conversion. It is evident also that by this time Stevens was well on in the process of conversion, having a much more definite notion of the reality of God, perhaps induced to some extent by his repeatedly expressed belief that to reject God leads to isolation and darkness. By this time also Stevens was concerned, not with general notions of the validity of God, Christ, and the Church, but with very specific questions about certain dogmas.

> He really wanted to talk. There was something bothering him all the time. He believed strongly in God. When he went to New York, he told me, he used to spend at least a couple of hours at St Patrick's Cathedral, meditating. He said he got so much peace and enjoyment that he always, when he went to New York, went to St Patrick's Cathedral. I think he had such a marvelous idea of what God was. The absolute idea of God. "Everything," he said, "has been created. There is only one uncreated." And that was God.

17   *Letters of Wallace Stevens*, 763.

He was unusual in this respect. He said, "I think I ought to be in the fold, but there's one thing that bothers me. That is that I don't see how a just God could construct a place like hell, because I do think that a merciful God, knowing the weakness of mankind, would not fashion a place like that to punish anyone—not even a dog." So we went through all that business about whereas God is merciful, He is also just. And in His justice, He must recognize that some people, no matter what grace is given them, will repudiate Him. I said, "As far as we know, we don't know that there's anyone specifically in hell except the devil and his cohorts."

I think he was a bit upset by the mysteriousness of the world. That was one thing that bothered him, the evil in the world. And he was always coming back to the goodness of God: how could a good God allow all this evil in the world? So we went into free will and all that business. But he was more of a poet than a Scholastic philosopher.

He gave me the impression he knew quite a bit about the Church. The impression he gave me was there were just a few little things that kept him from being a Catholic, and that was this hell business. I told him hell was mentioned fifty-seven times in the Bible and that our Lord said there was a hell, so we believe what our Lord said. "Well," he said, "that sounds logical."

So we talked along that line quite a bit, and he was thinking and thinking and thinking. One day he had a bit of a spell. He called for me, and he said, "I'd better get in the fold now." And then I baptized him, and the next day I brought him Communion.

In 1977 Fr Hanley wrote to Professor Janet McCann about Stevens' conversion. The account is very engaging and compelling.

Dear Janet: The first time he came to the hospital, he expressed a certain emptiness in his life. His stay then was two weeks. Two weeks later, he was in, and he asked the sister to send for me. We sat and talked a long time. During his visit this time, I saw him 9 or 10 times. He was fascinated by the life of Pope Pius X. He spoke about a poem for this pope whose family name was Sarto (meaning tailor) at least three times, he talked about getting into the fold—meaning the Catholic Church. The doctrine of hell was an objection which we later got thru that [sic] alright.

He often remarked about the peace and tranquility that he experienced in going into a Catholic church and spending some time. He spoke about St Patrick's Cathedral in N. Y. I can't give you the date of his baptism. I think it might be recorded at the hospital. He said he had never been baptized. He was baptized absolutely. Wallace and his wife had not been on speaking terms for several years. So we thought it better not to tell her. She might cause a scene in the hospital. Archbishop at the time told me not to make his (Wallace's) conversion public, but the sister and the nurses on the floor were all aware of it and were praying for him. At the time I did get a copy of his poems and also a record that he did of some of his poems. We talked about some of the poems. I quoted some of the lines of one of them and he was pleased. He said if he got well, we would talk a lot more and if not—he would see me in heaven. That's about all I can give you now. [Signed] God's Blessing, Father Hanley.[18]

Later still, Milton Bates, author of *Wallace Stevens: A Mythology of Self* (1985), investigated Fr Hanley's evidence, through interviews and written correspondence with the priest. He was impressed by Fr Hanley's frankness and credibility and concluded that the account was "more or less a fact." Further to this, Sigmans and his wife Mary were, he learned, the godparents.

There is a sense in which Stevens' life came full circle and corresponded in an important way with that of his old mentor George Santayana. Santayana had moved to Rome in 1941, where he lived in a convent. In 1946 he published *The Idea of Christ in the Gospels*. For the most part this book is a bold and unreserved presentation of sound Christian belief. Here are examples:

> The gifts of grace, like those of nature, require active acceptance and exercise.... [19]

> Christ, being God, reflects God's whole glory. For us, also, there is no difference between God entering into us and our attaining our special perfections and reflecting our appointed part of the good.... [20]

18   Janet McCann, "A Letter from Father Hanley on Stevens' Conversion to Catholicism," *Wallace Stevens Journal*, Vol. 18, Spring 1994, 3–5. The letter was dated July 24, 1977.
19   *The Idea of Christ in the Gospels*, 95.
20   Ibid., 251.

In his very last piece of writing, "On the False Steps in Philosophy," left in a sealed envelope to be opened after his death, Santayana nails his colors to the mast: "If once the Father has existed and created a world ... the idea of that creation will have been raised for ever from the realm of essence to the realm of truth.... Our participation in truth is final and intimate, and raises us, as far as it goes, above our mortal condition."[21]

We do not know whether Stevens read *The Idea of Christ in the Gospels*. However, it is pretty likely that he did and was influenced by it, and some support for this may be found in the fact that he referred often to Santayana in his later writings. This is the case most notably in the most celebrated poem of his final years, "To an Old Philosopher in Rome," written in 1951, and addressed clearly to his old mentor.

In light of the life and work of Wallace Stevens, two particular things occur to the present writer, either of which might have provided the impetus to Stevens to convert fully at an earlier point if only he had been aware of them. The first relates to a writer particularly notable for his imagination, J. R. R. Tolkien. If for Stevens until his last days Christianity was not the truth but perhaps myth, albeit valuable in relation to our spiritual feelings, this was exactly the claim that Tolkien addressed in the celebrated discussion with C. S. Lewis and Hugo Dyson as they took a stroll around Addison's Walk in Oxford on the evening of September 19, 1931. In his biography of Lewis, George Sayer sums it up in this way:

> Jack [i.e., C. S. Lewis] said he loved reading and thinking
> about myths, but that he could not regard them as being
> at all true. Tolkien's view was radically different. He said
> that myths originate in God, that they preserve something
> of God's truth, although often in a distorted form....
> Tolkien went on to explain that the Christian story was
> a myth invented by a God who was real, a God whose
> dying could transform those who believed in him. If Jack
> wanted to find the relevance of His story to his own life,
> he must plunge in. He must appreciate the myth in the
> same spirit of imaginative understanding that he would
> bring to, say, a Wagnerian opera.[22]

21 Santayana, The *Birth of Reason and Other Essays* (1995), 167.
22 *Jack: C. S. Lewis and His Times* (1988), 134-35.

The reference to Wagner is appropriate, since here was another person intent on a projected replacement of religion, in this case with art generally.

The second particular thing is the constant and powerful rebuttal of subjectivism, a philosophy close to Stevens' heart, in the writings of one Joseph Cardinal Ratzinger, subsequently Pope Benedict XVI. A good example comes from a discussion of subjectivism in relation to conscience in ethical issues that is also applicable to subjectivism in relation to doctrinal truth:

> For modernity, the realm of religion and morality has been confined to the subjective sphere, since there is no trace of objective religion and morality in an evolutionistic conception; religion and morality are reduced to a complete subjectivism. Beyond the subject, no roads or further horizons open up. The ultimate confidence of the subject, who cannot transcend himself and remains closed within himself, is thus expressed in a certain conception of conscience, according to which man is the measure of himself. As much as he might make use of aids and criteria outside himself, in reality his subjective conscience is what has the last and decisive word. The subject thus becomes really autonomous, but in a dark and terrible way, because he lacks the light that could really give his subjectivity value. This conception of the self-enclosed subject who is the ultimate criterion of judgment is overcome only in the classical concept of conscience, which expresses, on the contrary, the human being's openness to divine light, to the voice of the other, to the language of being, to the eternal *logos*, perceptible in the subject's very interior. It seems to me, then, that it is necessary to return to this vision of the human being as openness to the infinite, in whom the infinite light shines through and speaks. [23]

Despite not having this kind of openness, Stevens finally came through. We may wonder whether it was philosophy that directly showed him the way. Lucy Beckett points to other longstanding and more down-to-earth motives: "his lifelong love of France and of the Spanishness of Florida and Cuba and the Catholic friends of his old age." [24] In this context it is interesting to note that

23 "The Renewal of Moral Theology: Perspectives of Vatican II and *Veritatis Splendor*," *Communio*, Summer 2005.
24 *In the Light of Christ*, 468.

Stevens never crossed the Atlantic: "his keen sense of Europe, particularly France, was nourished only by books, paintings and postcards from friends."[25]

To conclude with something both practical and spiritual, and of still greater importance for Stevens, we may perhaps go back to the fact that this meditative poet chose to visit St Patrick's Cathedral in New York for meditative purposes. As we have seen, Wallace Stevens wrote in his journal in 1902, "I go [there] now and then in my more lonely moods."[26] Maria Cirurgião concludes:

> [He] never outgrew his need for St. Patrick's. The quiet hours in the pews left a stamp on his poetry that is hard to miss, in verses such as: "Now both heaven and hell / Are one, and here, O terra infidel."... Likely, these verses give us all the insight we shall ever have into why it was St. Patrick's Cathedral that beckoned irresistibly to Wallace Stevens; why he made St. Augustine the companion of his meditative hours; and why he chose St. Francis Hospital when terminally ill.[27]

And why, it might be added, he ended up, albeit very late in his life, coming home at last to Holy Mother Church.

ADDENDUM: THE STEVENS VS. HEMINGWAY FIST FIGHT

Since we have now considered the conversion of both Ernest Hemingway and Wallace Stevens, it might be appropriate to link the two together by recalling how they once came together in a somewhat disreputable incident, a fist fight, if only to show again that there is hope for all of us.

The evidence can be pieced together from an account by Hemingway in a letter to Sara Murphy (immortalized by F. Scott Fitzgerald as Nicole Diver in *Tender is the Night*) and from other sources. The incident took place in February 1936. Stevens was in Key West, Florida, visiting a business friend. It seems that he and Hemingway had not been getting along. Here is Hemingway's account of the encounter between "the 50-something hard-drinking poet and the 30-something hard-drinking novelist."

25 Ibid., 458.
26 *Letters of Wallace Stevens*, 32.
27 "Last Farewell and First Fruits."

Nice Mr. Stevens. This year he came again pleasant like
the cholera and first I knew of it my nice sister Ura was
coming into the house crying because she had been at
a cocktail party at which Mr. Stevens had made her cry
by telling her forcefully what a sap I was, no man, etc.
So I said, this was a week ago, "All right, that's the third
time we've had enough of Mr. Stevens." So headed out
into the rainy past twilight and met Mr. Stevens who
was just issuing from the door having just said, I learned
later, "By God I wish I had that Hemingway here now
I'd knock him out with a single punch."

So who should show up but poor old Papa and Mr.
Stevens swung that same fabled punch but fortunately
missed and I knocked all of him down several times and
gave him a good beating. Only trouble was that first three
times put him down I still had my glasses on. Then took
them off at the insistence of the judge who wanted to
see a good clean fight without glasses in it and after I
took them off Mr. Stevens hit me flush on the jaw with
his Sunday punch bam like that. And this is very funny.
Broke his hand in two places. Didn't harm my jaw at all
and so put him down again and then fixed him good so
he was in his room for five days with a nurse and Dr.
working on him. But you mustn't tell this to anybody.

Anyway last night Mr. Stevens comes over to make
up and we are made up. But on mature reflection I don't
know anybody needed to be hit worse than Mr. S. Was
very pleased last night to see how large Mr. Stevens was
and am sure that if I had had a good look at him before
it all started would not have felt up to hitting him. But
can assure you that there is no one like Mr. Stevens to go
down in a spectacular fashion especially into a large puddle
of water in the street in front of your old Waddel Street
home where all took place.... I think he is really one of
those mirror fighters who swells his muscles and practices
lethal punches in the bathroom while he hates his betters.[28]

The story is confirmed by Stevens' biographer Joan Richardson,[29]
who writes that Stevens returned home to his wife and daughter

28 Carlos Baker (ed.), Ernest Hemingway: *Selected Letters 1917–1961* (1981).
The reference to "Ura" is to Hemingway's sister Ursula, who also committed
suicide and is referred to in the earlier chapter on Hemingway.
29 *Wallace Stevens: The Later Years, 1923–1955* (1986).

in Hartford in March with a still-puffy eye and broken hand, and that Stevens himself told versions of the story throughout his life (his first had been a postcard to his wife blaming his bad handwriting on a fall down a flight of stairs, the same cover story Hemingway reports he and Stevens agreed on after making up). This account is basically confirmed in a later, and excellent, biography of Stevens, Paul Mariani's *The Whole Harmonium: The Life of Wallace Stevens* (2016).

There ended what has been referred to as "this most unlikely of modernist battles," one fought in the streets rather than in the seminar room. You just couldn't make it up!

CHAPTER EIGHTEEN

Walker Percy

A GREAT AMERICAN
LITERARY CONVERT

IT IS POSSIBLE TO CLASSIFY AMERICAN CON-
verts to the Catholic faith in several ways, such is their variety. One
way is by profession, vocation, or career. Among these there are
a fair number of literary figures, novelists, poets, and dramatists.
The most notable are perhaps, in alphabetical order, F. Marion
Crawford, Caroline Gordon, Ernest Hemingway, Robert Lowell,
Walker Percy, Allen Tate, and Tennessee Williams. No doubt many
readers will respond at this point, pretty accurately, that Williams
is hardly worthy of the name "convert." It has even been claimed
that he converted "only for one day" at a time when he was having
severe personal problems. Others will point out that Stevens only
made it to Catholicism on his deathbed, though there is much
in his earlier thought and writings that is in harmony with the
faith. As for Lowell, well, he went backwards and forwards so
often between the Catholic Church and Episcopalianism that he
must have found it difficult to decide at any one time to which

he belonged! With regard to Hemingway, many people continue to think that he was merely a nominal Catholic, but I showed in an earlier chapter that the research of H.R. Stoneback brings out a person much more integrally Catholic than is often supposed. Crawford and Gordon were relatively pious, and Tate never formally renounced his faith, though his personal life during his last years did not always adhere to Catholic teaching.

However, from a whole series of perspectives, I would maintain that the most notable and interesting of these literary converts is that great Southern writer Walker Percy. Much has been written about both his novels and his non-fiction, but not a great deal about his conversion. It is true that it is dealt with in the two biographies—by Jay Tolson, published in 1992, and Patrick Samway, published in 1999—but not in any great depth. So an attempt will be made here to fill this gap.

Walker Percy was born on May 28, 1916, in Birmingham, Alabama, into a distinguished and prosperous Southern Protestant family. Tragedy was a frequent companion of this family. Percy's grandfather (in 1917) and father (in 1929) both committed suicide, thus providing another link with the Hemingways. In 1931 his mother died in a car crash when she drove off a bridge. This was probably an accident, but Percy always wondered whether this too may have been suicide. He and his two brothers were then adopted by his bachelor uncle, William Alexander Percy ("Uncle Will"), a lawyer and poet, and moved to live with him in Greenville, Mississippi. Percy was brought up agnostic, though nominally liberal Presbyterian. He was educated at the University of North Carolina at Chapel Hill. He then trained as a medical doctor at the University of Columbia, but contracted tuberculosis when serving as an intern in a pathology lab. He spent the recovery time reading literature and philosophy. He was influenced particularly by the writings of Fyodor Dostoevsky and Søren Kierkegaard, but also by St Augustine and St Thomas Aquinas, and decided that Christianity offered the most realistic assessment of human nature. In 1945 he said to a friend, "If you take the claims of Christianity seriously, then it seems to me that Catholicism is where you have to end up,"[1] but he was not ready then to take that step. Other

---

1   C. Stuart Chapman, *Shelby Foote: A Writer's Life* (2003), 102.

influences on his conversion were his friend Caroline Gordon and the broadcasts of Msgr Fulton Sheen. Percy was finally received into the Catholic Church on December 13, 1947, together with his wife, Mary Bernice Townsend (known as "Bunt"; 1921–2012). After an outstanding literary career, producing such works as *The Moviegoer* (1961; winner of the National Book Award for Fiction in 1962), *The Last Gentleman* (1966), *Love in the Ruins* (1971), *The Second Coming* (1980), *Lost in the Cosmos* (1983), and *The Thanatos Syndrome* (1987), Walker Percy died on May 10, 1990, in Covington, Louisiana. He is buried in the grounds of St Joseph Benedictine Abbey in Benedict, Louisiana.

All of Percy's major works were written after he became a Catholic. However, one can see from that later perspective strands of thought in both his fiction and non-fiction that would have moved him towards the espousal of a Catholic position. In the former his chief concern is with "the dislocation of man in the modern age," with the sense of ennui and meaninglessness that has shadowed so many lives. In the latter he questions the ability of science to explain the basic mysteries of human existence: "The burden of my non-fiction is a demonstration that man is different from other creatures. That he has this extraordinary capacity to know things, a certain freedom, and he can find himself in a predicament. You can't explain these things by deterministic biology."[2] On one occasion he summed this up by saying that science "explained everything under the sun, except one small detail: what it means to be a man living in the world who must die."[3] At the same time he opens up the possibility of conversion:

> I think my writings reflect a certain basic orientation toward, although they're not really controlled by, Catholic dogma. As I say, it's a view of man, that man is neither an organism controlled by his environment, nor a creature controlled by the forces of history, as the Marxists would say, nor is he a detached, wholly objective, angelic being who views the world in a God-like way and makes pronouncements only to himself or to an elite group of people. No, he's somewhere between the angels and

2 Jan Nordby Gretlund, "Laying the Ghost of Marcus Aurelius?," in Lewis A. Lawson and Victor A. Kramer (eds.), *Conversations with Walker Percy* (1985), 205.
3 *Signposts in a Strange Land* (1991), 188.

the beasts. He's a strange creature whom both Thomas Aquinas and Marcel called *homo viator*, man the wayfarer, man the wanderer.[4]

Walker Percy's most detailed presentation of his view of man can be found in *The Message in the Bottle* (1975). It should be noted that Percy's view of the history of science is in line with this type of thinking (and, incidentally, completely in line with the writings of Fr Stanley Jaki, referred to in an earlier chapter in connection with Frank Sherwood Taylor): "The great paradox of the Western world is that even though it was in the Judeo-Christian West that modern science arose and flourished, it is Judeo-Christianity which the present-day scientific set of mind finds the most offensive among the world's religions."[5]

How did these views lead Percy to move directly to religious conversion? He wrote relatively little about his conversion. There is evidence, however, from a close friend, Robert Coles, that Percy experienced a very serious religious crisis during 1946 and 1947, which led him eventually to the Church. Coles is clear that there was no dramatic moment of conversion. Rather, he maintains, this was a case where "a deeply introspective and somewhat withdrawn man gradually began to make commitments, and affiliation to a particular faith was one of them."[6]

One researcher, Robert H. Brinkmeyer Jr, brings out further factors in Percy's conversion. First, there was a great attraction to "the great historical authority of the Catholic Church, the original bride of Christ, the Church of Peter and John and the Apostle Paul."[7] Secondly, Brinkmeyer emphasizes Percy's attraction to the writings of the philosopher Søren Kierkegaard. Percy himself said, "If I had to single out one piece of writing which was more responsible than anything else for my becoming a Catholic, it would be that essay of Kierkegaard's ['Of the Difference between a Genius and an Apostle']."[8] Brinkmeyer goes on to explain the great attraction:

4   John C. Carr, "An Interview with Walker Percy," *Georgia Review*, Fall 1971, 317; reprinted in Lewis A. Lawson and Victor A. Kramer (ed.), *Conversations with Walker Percy* (1985).
5   *Signposts in a Strange Land*, 312.
6   Robert Coles, *Walker Percy: An American Search* (1979), 68.
7   *Three Catholic Writers of the Modern South* (1985), 124.
8   Ibid.

Percy was fascinated by the dichotomy Kierkegaard drew between what he called the genius and the apostle. A genius, says Kierkegaard, is a man who discovers truth; he uses the example of a scientist who works in the realm of the immanent; he can discover truth anywhere, anytime, anyplace. The apostle, however, bears news, his realm is the transcendent, and he speaks with divine authority. Those who hear the apostles are faced with a choice, as Kierkegaard describes, using the example of an apostle's message: "These words were spoken by Him to whom, according to His own statement, is given all power in heaven and on earth. You who hear me must consider within yourselves whether you will bow before this authority or not, accept and believe the words or not." Walker Percy heard the message of the modern apostles, whom he saw as present-day Catholic priests, and he believed.[9]

The point about the importance of history and the longevity of the Church is brought out graphically by Percy himself in an article entitled "A 'Cranky Novelist' Reflects on the Church":

We Catholics have a way of taking things for granted, the very sort of things which other people find extraordinary. I'll give you one example. The other day I happened to read a short review of a book in a magazine. The book was a new edition of the Rule of St. Benedict, published to celebrate the sesquimillennium of the saint's birth. Do you know what a sesquimillennium is? I had to look it up. It is 1,500 years. Now, that is remarkable. What struck me as even more remarkable is that no one seemed to find this remarkable. Yet every day we hear about this or that anniversary celebration: five hundred years since Luther's birth, two hundred years since Goethe's birth, seventy-five years since the Wright brothers' flight, a stamp commemorating James Audubon or Joe Louis. This is all very well. But here is a man who was born 1,500 years ago, who lived in a critical, disorderly time with certain resemblances to our own, who devised a rule for living in a community, a practical, moderate, yet holy rule which apparently is quite as useful now as it was 1,500 years ago. 1,500 years. I call that remarkable. Yet very few

9 Ibid.

people seem to find it remarkable—very few Catholics. Maybe the Benedictines do, but they don't say much about it, and the Jesuits practically nothing.[10]

So we see that Percy's conversion was intellectually based. However, it must be emphasized that there was much passion and emotion in the process. Walker Percy describes an incident at Mass that he once experienced:

> The Mass was going on, the homily standard—that is "true" but customary. A not-so-good choir of young rock musicians got going on "Joy to the World," the vocals not so good but enthusiastic. Then it hit me: What if it should be the case that the entire cosmos had a Creator, and what if he decided for reasons of his own to show up as a tiny baby, conceived and born under suspicious circumstances? Well,...you can lay it on Alzheimer's or hang-over or whatever, but—it hit me. I had to pretend I had an allergy attack so that I could take out my handkerchief.[11]

In line with this theme, Jay Tolson shows in his biography how Percy arrived at the Christian position "precisely out of this powerful sense of his own unworthiness."[12] Tolson continues:

> Indeed, it seemed to him the principal brilliance of the Christian "anthropology" (a word that he liked to use in its radical, non-academic sense) was that it put human corruption and inadequacy at the center of its picture of man, and furthermore, that it taught that recognition of this inadequacy was the first step in hearing the Christian message.[13]

Walker Percy himself comments on the importance of the personal element in conversion in his fine foreword to a book on convert stories:

> One can write about conversion two ways. One way is to put the best possible face on it, recount a respectable intellectual odyssey. Such as: Well, my tradition was scientific. I thought science explained the cosmos—until one day I read what Kierkegaard said about Hegelianism, the

10   *The Quarterly*, Summer 1983, 1.
11   Fr. Gerald O'Collins, *Incarnation* (2002), 125–26.
12   Jay Tolson, *Pilgrim in the Ruins: A Life of Walker Percy* (1992), 199.
13   Ibid., 199–200.

science of his day: that Hegel explained everything in the universe except what it is to be an individual, to be born, to live, and to die. And for me this "explanation" would be true enough, I suppose. But then there is this. When I was in college, I lived in the attic of a fraternity house with four other guys. God, religion, was the furthest thing from our minds and talk—from mine, at least. Except for one of us, a fellow who got up every morning at the crack of dawn and went to Mass. He said nothing about it and seemed otherwise normal. Does anyone suppose that one had nothing to do with the other? That is, thinking about Kierkegaard's dilemma and remembering my roommate's strange behavior—this among a thousand other things one notices or remembers, which, if they don't "cause" it, at least enter into it, at least make room for this most mysterious turning in one's life.[14]

Finally, it is instructive to look at Percy's attitude towards things happening in the Church after he became a Catholic. This is best expressed in a fascinating piece where the great man, somewhat frustrated by constant visits for the purpose of interviews by graduate students, decided to write his own "interview" in which he himself both asks the questions and supplies the answers:

Q: How is such a belief [in the dogmas that the Catholic Church proposes for belief] possible in [the present] age? A: What else is there?

Q: What do you mean, what else is there? There is humanism, atheism, agnosticism, Marxism, behaviorism, materialism, Buddhism, Muhammadism, Sufism, astrology, occultism, theosophy. A: That's what I mean.

Q: I don't understand. Would you exclude, for example, scientific humanism as a rational and honorable alternative? A: Yes.

Q: Why? A: It's not good enough.

Q: Why not? A: This life is much too much trouble, far too strange, to arrive at the end of it and then to be asked what you make of it and have to answer "Scientific

14   Dan O'Neill (ed.), *The New Catholics: Contemporary Converts Tell Their Story* (1989), xiii.

humanism." That won't do. A poor show. Life is a mystery, love is a delight. Therefore I take it as axiomatic that one should settle for nothing less than the infinite mystery and the infinite delight, i.e., God. In fact I demand it. I refuse to settle for anything less....

Q: But isn't the Catholic Church in a mess these days, badly split, its liturgy barbarized, vocations declining? A: Sure. That's a sign of its divine origins, that it survives these periodic disasters.[15]

Percy goes on in similar manner, rather like a baseball batter striking a series of pitches clear out of the stadium, and culminating in this final flourish:

Q: But shouldn't faith bear some relation to the truth, facts? A: Yes. That's what attracted me, Christianity's rather insolent claim to be true, with the implication that other religions are more or less false.

Q: You believe that? A: Of course.[16]

Strong stuff! And there is more of it throughout Percy's corpus. His forthright tone and depth of knowledge, not only on theological and philosophical questions but also on how to pass on the faith, make him a powerful witness in the mission of evangelization. If you doubt me, have a look at the following: "A View of Abortion with Something to Offend Everybody," *The New York Times*, June 8, 1981, A-15; "If I Had Five Minutes with the Pope," *America*, September 12, 1987, 127; "Why Are You a Catholic?" in Clifton Fadiman (ed.), *Living Philosophies* (1990); and the collection of essays in *Signposts in a Strange Land* (1991), which contains most of his major non-fiction writings. Walker Percy was far more than just a novelist, as his non-fiction writings show clearly. He was a formidable advocate of Catholic truth and is missed now more than ever.

15 "Questions They Never Asked Me So He Asked Them Himself," *Esquire*, December 1977; reprinted in Victor A. Kramer and Lewis A. Lawson (ed.), *Conversations with Walker Percy* (1985), 175–77.
16 Ibid.

CHAPTER NINETEEN
Father Oliver Vassall-Phillips

A GREAT BUT NEGLECTED CATHOLIC APOLOGIST

AT THIS TIME, WHEN THE CATHOLIC CHURCH is beset with problems of all kinds, threats from outside in the form of the "new atheists" and the like and threats from inside, as illustrated by the happenings at the Synod on the Family called by Pope Francis, the need for sound religious apologetics and a solid defense of the Catholic Church is great. Of course, in a sense all converts make a contribution to these. Those who argue for the faith generally do not in fact get as far as those who witness to the faith by living it from day to day, often through adversity. We have looked already at several converts who provided reasoned arguments for the faith. The best example is probably Saint John Henry Newman, but there are many others, and many more to follow. One who is well worthy of being added to the list is a priest who has been virtually ignored since his death, but who contributed to apologetics in a most vibrant way, and whose writings are as fresh today as they ever were.

Oliver Rodie Vassall-Phillips (he was originally Oliver Vassall, but assumed his maternal grandfather's name in 1901) was born in 1857. He was brought up in an old-fashioned Protestant home and educated at Eton and Balliol College, Oxford. He became a Catholic when an undergraduate at Oxford, being received there on March 18, 1878, at St Aloysius church. The main influence on his conversion was Newman, whose *Essay on the Development of Christian Doctrine* (1845) and *Apologia pro Vita Sua* (1864) he "devoured" as a boy of sixteen ("To Cardinal Newman I always feel that, under God, I owe my very soul"). Another influence in his conversion was the Benedictine monk Dom David Oswald Hunter-Blair, another convert.

Vassall-Phillips joined the Redemptorist Order in 1880 and was ordained priest in 1884. He was successively rector of Mount Alphonsus, Limerick; Bishop Eton, Wavertree, Liverpool; Bishop's Stortford, Essex; and of Kingswood, Bristol. He became well-known during his lifetime as a preacher and controversialist. He died on May 8, 1932 (at sea while returning from a lecture tour of South Africa).

Fr Vassall-Phillips was a prolific writer and one of considerable power of expression. It is impossible to do justice to his work within these confines, so emphasis will be placed on his works on apologetics. An account of his own conversion, and the essential reasons behind it, can be found in an essay printed in a book edited by J. G. Raupert, entitled *Roads to Rome* (1901), containing many fascinating convert stories. The essay was written in 1878, the year of Fr Vassall-Phillips' conversion. During the course of it the author puts to the reader a number of challenging questions, leading, he argues, to a particular conclusion:

> Why should I not accept the testimony of the Catholic and Roman Church? The fathers at the Council of Chalcedon cried out, *"Petrus per Leonem locutus est"* (Peter has spoken through Pope Leo). Why am I to be forbidden to believe them? Why am I to be forbidden to believe St. Ambrose when he says, *"Ubi Petrus, ibi Ecclesia"* (Where Peter is, there is the Church)? Why am I to be forbidden

to submit myself to the Shepherd to whom our Blessed Lord when about to leave this world committed all His sheep and all His lambs; for whom He prayed specially that his faith should not fail, and to whom alone He gave a new name, and the keys of the kingdom of heaven?[1]

Fr Vassall-Phillips' earliest full-length book is *The Mustard Tree, or The Truth of the Christian Religion: An Argument on Behalf of the Godhead of Christ*, originally published in 1912, a second edition appearing in 1923. This is a remarkable book, both for its content and for another thing, to which I shall return. As to the former, the author, after giving an exposition of the nature of divine and human faith, examines in great detail a series of factors leading to proof of the divinity of Christ, namely the Catholic Church as such, the Papacy, the Sacraments (especially the belief of Catholics in the Real Presence), devotion to the Blessed Virgin Mary, and the religious life. He then shows the essential unreasonableness of certain alleged barriers to conversion and concludes with the image of the Church as "the mustard seed, sown first in the soil of Palestine, when still it was the smallest of all seeds, but stretching its boughs at this hour over all the world, over hill and dale, over woodland, vale and pasture."[2]

The other remarkable thing here is what might be called the character references for this book. Believe it or not, the introduction was written by G. K. Chesterton, the preface by Msgr Robert Hugh Benson, two great converts themselves of course. But, in addition, there is an epilogue by that great Catholic Hilaire Belloc. My poor recommendation must be seen in this light!

Fr Vassall-Phillips' next book was *Catholic Christianity: or The Reasonableness of Our Religion* (1920). The book is divided into three sections: "Is the Christian Religion True?"; "Is Catholicism True?"; and "What Does Catholic Christianity Give?" The first two contain detailed apologetic arguments. The third consists of a powerful statement of the doctrines held by the Catholic Church. A good example of the cogency of the author's writing can be found in the very first section, where he expresses himself in a way that makes one wish he were here today to put the key points to such as Richard Dawkins:

1   Raupert (ed.), *Roads to Rome*, 272.
2   *The Mustard Tree*, 475.

The principle of causality may be expressed by the formula: "Every being that now exists, but does not exist *necessarily*, is the effect of a cause." To deny the truth of this proposition would be not only to deny the truth of religion, but also to make all science impossible....

No one can admit the existence of an infinite series of secondary causes without involving himself in a manifest absurdity and contradiction, since a secondary cause is of its very nature finite; in other words, it had a beginning. So we are driven by our reason (if we would save it) to a primary or First Cause, which exists *necessarily*, and is therefore Uncaused, but is the ultimate cause of all. In other words, from the finite, visible creation, which is undeniably an *effect*, we rise to the conception of the Creator, who is the First Cause. We call Him God. He is Essential Being. As such in the Bible He is represented by the two solemn words: *I Am*.[3]

Each chapter of the book is free-standing and deals with all the major apologetic issues, for example the evidence for theism, the nature of faith, the evidence for miracles (most notably of course the Resurrection of Christ), the arguments from experience and prophecy, and an analysis of the marks of the Church. The last section is primarily an examination of the sacraments. Altogether, the book is a fine exposition of our Catholic faith. Before leaving it one should note the frank statement in the preface about the author's own conversion, which illustrates the Christo-centric character of his writing:

When I became a Catholic I did not attempt to judge the evidence for Christianity at all. I became a Catholic, knowing at the time practically nothing about that evidence, simply because I knew *in my conscience* that it would be a sin for me to turn my back on Christ, and because I was absolutely convinced in my mind that loyalty to Christ involved for me submission to the Catholic Church.

I found myself unable to go on saying: Thou art the Christ, unless I was prepared unreservedly to believe Christ when in His turn He said to His disciple: Thou art the Rock. I saw as clearly as I saw the sun in the heavens that Christ was committed to the plain consequence of His

3 *Catholic Christianity*, 17-20.

words, their fulfillment in history which He foresaw, and
the indefectibility of the Church which He founded on
a foundation of His Own choosing. If Catholicism failed,
Christianity had failed also. That much at any rate was then,
and always has been since, perfectly clear to my intellect.[4]

Fr Vassall-Phillips followed up this book with a detailed account
of Our Lady's role in salvation, *The Mother of Christ: or The Blessed
Virgin Mary in Catholic Tradition, Theology, and Devotion* (1922). Then
came a very different work, *Tom Smith's Conversion* (1925). This was
originally a series of articles written for *The Universe* newspaper. It
takes the form of a fictitious account of a series of instructions given
by a priest to a young non-Catholic man engaged to be married
to a Catholic girl. The book is a concise yet profound guide to the
Catholic religion. A flavor can be given by the following passage,
in which the priest brings up a very important apologetic issue,
namely one of the marks of the true Church, its apostolic nature:

> If you think of any of the Protestant Churches, you can
> tell exactly who founded them. The Lutherans, for example,
> were founded by Martin Luther, the Calvinists by John
> Calvin, the Presbyterians by John Knox, the Wesleyans
> by John Wesley, the Salvation Army by General Booth,
> and so on....
>
> As for the Reformed Church of England as a whole,
> we know too well the names of the men responsible for
> her separation from the Holy See—they are among the
> most horrible in all history. Lord Macaulay, no lover of
> Catholicism, has summed them up—Henry, the murderer
> of his wives; the Protector Somerset, the murderer of
> his brother; Elizabeth, the murderer of her guest, and
> the like. With regard to the separated Churches of the
> East, we know the exact dates when they separated from
> Catholic Unity, and the names of the men who effected
> the separation—the Nestorians were made a separate body
> by Nestorius, the Eutychians by Eutyches, the Greeks first
> by Photius, and then—after they had been reconciled
> to Catholic Christendom—again by Michael Cerularius.
>
> It has often been asked: "Where was Protestantism
> before Martin Luther?" The answer is "Nowhere. It did
> not exist." And if it should be asked: "Where was the

4 Ibid., x.

Church of England before Henry the Eighth, or the Greek Church before Photius?" the only answer that can be given is: "In union with the Catholic and Roman Church." The Catholic Church alone goes back straight, without break, to the Holy Apostles Peter and Paul: but it was not founded by St. Peter and St. Paul. It was founded by Jesus Christ, the Apostles' Lord.[5]

Fr Vassall-Phillips returns to this theme in his autobiography, *After Fifty Years* (1928), where he states that "from the earliest days of Protestantism, 'Where was your Church before Luther?' was a deadly question." He goes on to anticipate and refute a possible Protestant response: "Equally deadly is the question: 'If your theory be true as to the old Church having become corrupt in her teaching—the theory on which, admittedly, alone can your history and actions be defended or justified—what has become of the promises of Christ?'"[6]

Central to all of Fr Vassall-Phillips' writing is his view of the relationship of Christ and the Church, and this can be seen in several places in this book. Here is a particularly forceful statement of it:

> Christ is the one great Fact in the world's history without measure or parallel with which it may be compared. No other life that has ever been lived in the story of humanity may be placed in the same category as His; and closely dependent upon Christ, from the hour that He sent His Holy Spirit to dwell with us, on the first Whit Sunday, is the other great outstanding Fact—the Fact of the Catholic Church, visible to all who will open their eyes to see, unique, standing alone as Christ stands alone, refusing to be ignored, whether throughout the history of Christendom since Christendom was, or throughout the world today, peremptory in its claims—in this again like to Christ and representing His attitude—teaching "with authority and not as the scribes."[7]

Such statements as these are just as powerful today as they were then. *After Fifty Years* is a delightful account of the author's religious development leading to his conversion, followed by a

5   *Tom Smith's Conversion*, 57-58.
6   *After Fifty Years*, 139.
7   Ibid., 96.

consideration of his spiritual contentment once inside the Church. Incidentally, it also contains two photographs of the author, one of which shows him as a student, a diminutive figure sporting a mustache, pictured with other Catholics at Oxford in 1878, the year of his conversion. One of the others in the picture is the poet Gerard Manley Hopkins, another convert, and by this time a Jesuit priest. The other photograph shows Fr Vassall-Phillips in 1928, by now rather more rotund, though making a dignified figure in his cassock and biretta.

Fr Vassall-Phillips' last book, published in the year of his death, is *Apostolic Christianity: or the Witness of the Apostles to Christ* (1932). This work, as may be supposed, is a study of what might be referred to as the apostolicity and continuity of the Church, but set out in an innovative way. One substantial argument put forward here is that few people consider with sufficient seriousness all that is involved in the way of intellectual difficulty by the rejection of Christianity. The author proceeds to give three examples of this. The first stems from the fact that before her Son was born the Mother of Christ, an unsophisticated Jewish maiden and the espoused wife of a carpenter, declared publicly that, in consequence of her Motherhood, all generations should call her blessed. Pretty astonishing, but see what follows:

> This is a declaration which has been fulfilled ever since she spoke the strange words; it is being fulfilled before our eyes today. When, then, she made this prediction, who will deny that either she was mad or inspired by God? The undeniable fact, for such it is, that her words have been verified—that they have come to pass—goes to prove that they came to her from heaven. There seems to be no alternative in reason.... How then, we may ask, do unbelievers in Christ attempt to account for his Mother's words? Such an attempt is never made. The facts are simply left alone; if they remain unchallenged, it can only be because the conclusion is seen to be unchallengeable. To anyone who does not believe in Christ, the prophecy of his Mother defies reasonable explanation.[8]

Secondly, Christ permitted a woman who had led a sinful life, on her repentance, to pour a vase of very precious ointment over

8   *Apostolic Christianity: or The Witness of the Apostles to Christ* (1932).

his feet and wipe them with her flowing hair. As the author states, this is another astonishing fact—it is described as an act of homage and gratitude and love for his person. Moreover, not only did he permit this, but he actually declared that wherever what he alluded to as his "Gospel" should be preached throughout the world, there that which the Magdalen had done should be made known for her praise as a memorial of her.

> What could have seemed at the time to be more extrav-
> agantly unlikely of accomplishment, if Christ were as
> other men? Yet that it has been accomplished is beyond
> a doubt. Throughout the world the Gospel of Christ has
> as a fact been preached, and throughout the world, as a
> direct result of this preaching, the name of the Magdalen
> is known, loved and venerated.... If Christ be what the
> Catholic Church believes him to be, it is easily understood
> and follows inevitably from his Godhead, but if he were
> not, how explain the fulfillment of those words of his?[9]

Thirdly, on the night before he suffered, Christ observed the ceremony of the Jewish Passover together with his apostles. He then declared that his body should be broken for them as bread is wont to be broken, that his blood should be shed for them and for many for the forgiveness of sins—and he then commanded them to "do this" (using sacrificial words) in commemoration of him. In consequence of this action of his and of this command, to this day thousands of Catholic priests offer each morning a Sacrifice for the living and the dead which they believe to have been instituted by him, to continue until he should come again in majesty to judge the world. Fr Vassall-Phillips goes on to set out the significance of this last example in the context of his own personal circumstances:

> Not very long ago I was endeavoring to say Mass in
> the face of some difficulty, and I asked myself *why* I was
> taking so much trouble to do this thing to which I had,
> alas, not been brought up by the traditions of my family.
> Without hesitation I answered my question: Because of
> what Christ had done nearly two thousand years ago. I
> desire each day to be mindful of his passion and death
> in the manner which he commanded. Then it came over

9 Ibid.

me with overwhelming force—something which I need hardly say I knew already—how unthinkable it was that this holy rite should have lasted through all the ages, that such vast importance should have been attached to it in all parts of the world, unless Christ were in truth what he claimed to be. It is offered "in memory"—as a memorial of him. But of whom? Is there another "memorial" of any other who has passed away with which we may compare or liken it? If not, once again the conclusion seems inevitable; he is not as other men.[10]

It will be seen, then, that we have a doughty fighter here for the Catholic faith, and it is submitted that we need at this juncture in the life of the Church many more of his kind. This is shown to be undoubtedly so by Fr Vassall-Phillips himself. In chapter one of *Catholic Christianity* here is what he says: "That we exist—that the world exists—that God exists—that Jesus Christ is in some sense different from other men—here we find firm certainties possessed by almost every English boy and girl."[11] Well, that was perhaps true then, in 1920, but it sure isn't true today. Now, of course, what is true is that different issues do come to the fore at different stages in the history of apologetics. But, nevertheless, the same basic principles apply today as they did then. The truth does not change. Great is the need for witnesses to the Faith and the arguments for an integral Catholic Christianity. Those arguments are available in a profound form in the writings of Fr Oliver Vassall-Phillips. His books are hard to find in bookshops and more is the pity. But they are available online secondhand or as reprints, and some of them can be read on-screen from such sites as the remarkable archive. org. I can only advise all readers to make a beeline for them, and I assure them that they will have no regrets at having done so.

10   Ibid.
11   *Catholic Christianity*, 6.

CHAPTER TWENTY

The Conversion of Dietrich von Hildebrand

FIGHTER AGAINST THE NAZIS

IF ONE LOOKS FOR EXAMPLES OF HEROIC CHRIS-
tian Resistance to the Nazis, the choice of a subject among notable
converts to the Catholic faith is an easy one. In 2014 the first English
translation of a book entitled *My Battle against Hitler* was published.
The book was originally a memoir written in German and left
unpublished; John Henry Crosby has rendered a great service with
his translation. The original author? None other than the great German philosopher, theologian, and convert Dietrich von Hildebrand.

The book is an edifying account of a crucial part of the author's
life. It deals, *inter alia*, with his struggles against the Hitler regime,
his flight from Germany to escape capture by the authorities there,
his role as the editor of an anti-Nazi newspaper, and his being

sentenced to death *in absentia*. He ended up in the United States, where he embarked on a most successful writing career, dealing with philosophical and theological issues of great moment. He also took part in much controversy, most notably expressing his concerns about the Church during and after the Second Vatican Council.

It is tempting to concentrate here on these fascinating issues, but my task is to examine Dietrich von Hildebrand's conversion and the light that it sheds upon the Catholic faith and the apologetics of conversion. The man himself did not write a detailed account of his conversion, though he does mention it from time to time and gives clues to the influences behind it. By far the most detailed analysis is given by his second wife, Alice von Hildebrand, whom he married after the death of his first wife. This is contained in *The Soul of a Lion* (2000), her account of his life up until 1940. This is done most specifically in chapter two, "University Years and Conversion 1906–1914." She also appeared on the EWTN program *The Journey Home*, where she gave an account of her husband's conversion. This is available for viewing on the internet.

Dietrich Richard Alfred von Hildebrand was born on October 11, 1889 (coincidentally the same day as another notable convert, Christopher Dawson) in Florence to a German family. His father was a sculptor. Dietrich spent a very happy childhood in a beautiful house on the outskirts of Florence, where he had the privilege of meeting many outstanding artists and thinkers. In his early years he was educated exclusively by private tutors. He was given no religious education, but in an article now available on the internet he writes in a very positive way about his family and his own early religious development:

> Though my parents had no Christian faith, and religion played no role at this period in the lives of my five sisters, all older than myself, the great gift of faith in the divinity of Christ and the love of Christ was granted to me at the age of five. My parents, full of respect for every interest arising spontaneously in the souls of their children, never tried to shake my convictions. [1]

As early as the age of fifteen, it became evident to him that philosophy was his vocation, and this conviction never altered. In

1   www.catholicauthors.com/vonhildebrand.html.

relation to the growth of this vocation, two philosophers were vital: Adolf Reinach and Max Scheler, both phenomenologists. Another philosopher, Edmund Husserl, who established the school of phenomenology, was a lesser but still important influence. Regarding conversion, one persistent and very important belief that remained with him throughout his life was a detestation of moral relativism.

Max Scheler was also important to Dietrich's religious and spiritual development. It must be remembered that despite being born and raised in a Catholic country, Dietrich had never met a Catholic and knew nothing of Catholic doctrines until his meeting with Scheler. Yes, he had often visited churches and was educated in their artistic beauty, but his parents appreciated nothing of their sacred character. Dietrich soon came to relish conversations with Scheler, who was not only a great intellect but a most attractive personality with a warm and personal touch. It was Scheler, ironically a fallen-away Catholic, who asserted that the Catholic Church was the one true Church of Christ, and when Dietrich expressed himself baffled by this, Scheler brushed aside the prejudices against the Church that his interlocutor had picked up from his tutors and his milieu. Alice von Hildebrand brings out very well her husband's willingness to learn and his receptivity towards better-instructed minds, and emphasizes the importance Scheler ascribed to holiness:

> Scheler told him that the Church produced saints. "What is a saint?" the young man inquired. Once again, Scheler deployed the full scope of his genius. He applied all his gifts to sketching the essence of sanctity, and he illustrated his teaching by mentioning Francis of Assisi, describing his life in the most vivid terms. Scheler's arguments about holiness were so powerful that they convinced his young friend that the life of a Saint Francis of Assisi could not be explained by purely natural ethical categories; his holiness had to come from another source. Unwittingly, Scheler had opened for his young friend the path to conversion. Slowly but surely, the face of the Holy Catholic Church began to shine more and more clearly. It was a slow process. It took several more years for Dietrich von Hildebrand to enter the Church, but, thanks to Max Scheler, he was on his way.[2]

2   *The Soul of a Lion,* 74.

These things had taken place while Dietrich was a student at the University of Munich between 1906 and 1909. In the latter year, Scheler spent the summer vacation in Austria and Dietrich visited him there, soaking up the Catholic spirit of the country. Later that same year, however, Dietrich went on to the University of Gottingen, where he completed his doctorate in philosophy under Edmund Husserl and Adolf Reinach.

By this time the influence of Max Scheler had reached the point where Dietrich began to give his whole time to the question of religion and whether to become Catholic. It is something of an irony that one final prompting to him came from his sister Lisl (1879-1957), the last of his five sisters he would have expected this from as she was the least religiously inclined, when she herself decided to become Catholic. Dietrich, together with his first wife, was present in the Roman catacombs when Lisl made her first Communion. Alice von Hildebrand recounts an important incident that took place after this ceremony:

> On the way back ... Lisl shared a carriage with her brother and, with great seriousness, urged him not to delay his own conversion. "Grace knocks at the door of one's soul," she said solemnly, "and if one does not answer the knock, it may never be repeated. Promise me that when you go back to Munich, you will take instruction."[3]

Dietrich was deeply affected by this and soon afterwards both he and his wife went to a Franciscan friar, Fr Heribert Holzapfel,[4] at the Franciscan church in Munich and embarked on this process.

A key factor in his acceptance of the Catholic faith was the question of the importance of authority in relation to such belief:

> Up to that time, his opinions, his wishes, his outlook had been the decisive factor in the decisions he made. He had been his own ultimate authority. Through God's grace, he discovered that every true authority comes from Him, the Master and Creator of all things, and that Christ, the Son of God and the Redeemer of the world, had delegated this authority to His Holy Bride, the Roman Catholic Church. Just as Christ had taught authoritatively "and not like the scribes and pharisees" (Mk 1:22), now the Church, and

3 Ibid., 128.
4 Author of *History of the Franciscan Order* (1909).

she alone, who had been given the keys of the kingdom, was to teach erring man the path leading to salvation. Her teaching was infallible in matters of dogmas and morals, and all that he was called upon to do was to be receptive to her teaching and gratefully accept it.[5]

It is in fact a tribute to Dietrich's essential humility that he, a man of great intellectual self-assurance, should act in such a way. This arose from the fact that although he would defend a proposition with great vigor and believed that man's mind could reach absolute truth, he had also learned, in his wife's words, "that man's mind is fallible and that the best and the greatest have fallen into errors and ambiguities."

Dietrich, who knew so little about Catholicism at this stage, had no difficulty accepting all the Catholic dogmas except one. The one in question is especially topical given the history of the Church since that time. It related to the question of contraception. Dietrich was astonished to hear from Fr Holzapfel that artificial birth control was condemned by the Church and that he could not be received unless he accepted this. There was no question of picking and choosing. The Church's teaching must be accepted in its totality. Dietrich's reaction was immediate and unequivocal. He submitted. "The Church had spoken; that was enough. Who was he to dare contest her holy teaching. He truly lived the words *'Credo ut intelligam'* (I believe in order to understand), the famous phrase of Saint Augustine, repeated and developed by Saint Anselm of Canterbury."[6] Shortly afterwards he came to see the rightness and profundity of Catholic teaching on this question and was amazed that he had not grasped this before. From then on he championed the Catholic position, beginning with a trenchant article criticizing the 1930 Lambeth Conference's reversal of the position held hitherto by the Church of England. And when the encyclical *Humanae Vitae* was issued in 1968 he immediately sprang to the defense of the pope. The whole incident with Fr Holzapfel drove home to him the importance of humility in the intellectual life.

Dietrich von Hildebrand was received into the Catholic Church (along with his wife Gretchen) on Holy Saturday, April 11, 1914, in

5 *The Soul of a Lion*, 133.
6 Ibid., 132.

the Franciscan church of Munich. There is no doubt that he was filled with joy to have come home to Holy Mother Church. Added to his great love for beauty and natural truth was, in the words of his second wife, "a beauty that was infinitely more ravishing—the face of Christ and His Church and the supernatural message they convey, the path of humility and love leading to holiness."[7] It must be added that his influence also led many of his family members into the Church, and all five of his sisters became Catholic.

Dietrich's joy over his conversion never waned and he went on to become one of the great philosophers of the twentieth century. He taught for many years at the University of Munich, but was forced to flee from the Nazis and arrived in 1940 in the United States, where he continued his career with great success. He wrote several important studies on particular philosophical and theological issues. In addition, he was undoubtedly one of the very first writers to express concern over the way certain things in the Church were going after the Second Vatican Council. These views of his should not be taken as extremist. In fact, right up until the end of his life (he died on January 26, 1977), he was held in great honor by major figures in the Church. Pope Pius XII referred to him as "the twentieth-century doctor of the Church." Pope John Paul II said to Alice von Hildebrand, "Your husband is one of the great ethicists of the twentieth century." Finally, Joseph Cardinal Ratzinger, later to become Pope Benedict XVI, writing the foreword to *The Soul of a Lion*, summed it all up with a general conclusion, which is particularly relevant in view of all that Dietrich had to face: "When the intellectual history of the Catholic Church in the twentieth century is written, the name of Dietrich von Hildebrand will be most prominent among the figures of our time."[8] With statements of such significance for all to see, there can be no hesitation in recommending the two major works on the Council and post-Conciliar developments, namely *The Trojan Horse in the City of God* (1967) and *The Devastated Vineyard* (1974). In respect of both doctrinal and liturgical issues, Catholics today would be well advised to consult these major texts, in which Dietrich von Hildebrand's honesty and love for the Church positively shine out.

7 Ibid., 12.
8 Ibid.

CHAPTER TWENTY-ONE

How to Steal Heaven

THE STORY OF DUTCH SCHULTZ

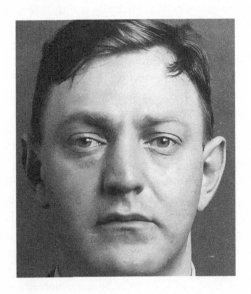

IT IS CERTAINLY THE CASE THAT CONVERTS come in all shapes and sizes. It is a tribute to the many sources of grace that they should come from all sorts of backgrounds. There are historians, politicians, writers, figures from the media, and sports celebrities, to mention only a few. And yes, there are also those previously to be characterized as reprobates. Two of the latter were the spies Elizabeth Terrill Bentley (1908–1963) and Bella Dodd, the latter of whom is the subject of a later chapter. But perhaps the most surprising is the notorious gangster born Arthur Simon Flegenheimer, better known as Dutch Schultz. The life of Schultz and the circumstances of his conversion to the Catholic faith raise important questions relating to the nature of faith and redemption.

Dutch Schultz was born on August 6, 1901, in The Bronx, New York City, to German-Jewish immigrants Herman and Emma Flegenheimer. When he was fourteen his father abandoned the family. Schultz left school to find work and at first did legitimate jobs, but he moved into crime and was sent to prison for burglary. He got involved with mobsters, and during the Prohibition period he brought liquor and beer from Canada into New York City and became a wealthy man. He worked in a speakeasy and gained a reputation for violence. He became a partner in the firm and opened more operations with the profits. He was involved in conflict with rival gangs, and other mobsters were murdered by him or on his orders, enabling him to gain overall control. After the end of Prohibition he found new sources of income from the numbers racket, and from extorting restaurant owners and workers.

He was said by some to have converted to Catholicism at this time in order to better relations with Charlie "Lucky" Luciano, a rival mobster, but this is almost certainly untrue. Schultz asked the Mafia Commission for permission to kill his enemy, U. S. Attorney Thomas Dewey, who had been appointed to break up the rackets. The Commission refused and decided to kill Schultz instead. He and his main associates were shot by hit-men at the Palace Chophouse, Newark, New Jersey, on October 23, 1935. Schultz was taken to a hospital, where he was registered as a Jew. Before surgery he was baptized and given the last rites at his request by a priest (Fr Cornelius McInerney). He died the next day. He was buried in Gate of Heaven Catholic Cemetery in Westchester County, New York. Then all hell was let loose.

There was outrage in many quarters that such a notorious person had been permitted burial in sacred ground. What right, people said, did that man have to be laid to rest with the rites of the Catholic Church? A Jesuit priest, Fr John A. Toomey, stepped into the fray in an article in the Catholic weekly *America,* noting at the outset that there were thousands of people saying that "if a guy like that can go to heaven there won't be anybody in hell." Fr Toomey addressed this as follows:

> To these thousands, glaring contradictions appeared to be involved. Here was the Catholic Church, which always had impressed on her children a horror of even the slightest sin; which had ceaselessly warned them concerning the danger of presuming on the chances of a death-bed conversion; which had ever inculcated high ideals in asceticism, in selflessness, in heroic virtue; here

was the Catholic Church beckoning into her fold a man who through his entire life had represented everything which the Church abhorred and condemned.

Dutch Schultz with the angels! Dutch Schultz whose beer-trucks once rumbled over the Bronx, whose gorillas blustered through the sidewalks! Dutch Schultz associating with the holy saints in Heaven! He to get the same reward as valiant souls who have clung to the Faith through a ceaseless hurricane of trial and temptation. It seemed more than unjust. It seemed ridiculous, preposterous, almost laughable. [1]

However, Fr Toomey was clear that the Catholic Church was not at fault and that a number of things had not been taken into account by her critics. He dealt with them under a number of headings, summarized as follows:

1. There is just One in the entire universe who is capable of accurately judging the complex skein of a man's life. The influence of bad example, of environment in general; of heredity; the lack of religious training; the exact strength of temptations. That One is God Almighty. No one else can even begin to do the job.

2. The time of mercy for sinners does not expire until the moment of death; there is no crime and no series of crimes which God will not forgive, this side of eternity, to the truly contrite of heart.

3. The dynamic power of Divine Grace to move the most obdurate heart to repentance was also omitted from the consideration. Indeed, in Fr Toomey's view, "the intimate and essential connection of grace with final salvation is widely overlooked."

4. Another important bit of evidence that was neglected is that nothing happens in this world without the permission of God. The reason Schultz was not killed instantly was because it was God's will that he be not killed instantly, and so he was conscious the morning after, and able to receive the grace of conversion, a grace that comes from God.

The point here is that if Schultz's conversion was sincere, it means that, in the words of Fr Toomey, "God gave him a last chance to save his soul, and that Dutch took advantage of the offer. It does not mean that God, or His Church, condoned the

---

1 "The Death and Burial of Dutch Schultz," *America*, November 16, 1935, 128.

evil life of Schultz but that ... God judged he should be given another opportunity to save his soul...."[2] Fr Toomey spelled out the implications of this for his fellow Catholics:

> After all, Heaven belongs to God. If He wants Dutch Schultz to be there, it is difficult to see what we can do about it. Perhaps, instead of worrying about Schultz, a somewhat more profitable occupation for us would be to do a little more worrying about our own salvation—to make sure we get there ourselves. We may not be given the opportunity for a death-bed repentance. Relatively few are given that chance.[3]

But there is a final, and perhaps more conclusive, point to be made about that fateful evening in 1935. It is dealt with, albeit briefly, by Fr Toomey himself, when he observes that "whether we meet Schultz in Heaven or not, there is one individual we are certain to encounter there; a gentleman who was in more or less the same line as Schultz—the Thief who, as he was dying on Calvary, asked the Man on the next Cross for forgiveness and who heard that Man say: 'This day thou shalt be with Me in Paradise.'"[4]

This crucial point was treated in more detail at that time by Msgr John L. Belford (1861-1951), the celebrated pastor of the Catholic Church of the Nativity in Brooklyn. This was in a defense of Fr McInerney's ministrations to Schultz in an article for *The Monitor*, a church publication. Msgr Belford brings out the point very powerfully:

> Was Dutch Schultz worse than the penitent thief? He was a criminal. He seemed unworthy of the least consideration. Perhaps he was. But who will close the gates of mercy? The fact that he received the sacraments is no guarantee that he received God's forgiveness. If he was not really penitent, the priest's absolution had no effect. Yet that priest did right when he baptized or absolved him. The dying man said he was sorry he had offended God; he declared he would do all in his power to avoid sin in the future and to repair the harm he had done. If he meant this, God ratified the action of the minister.[5]

2 Ibid.
3 Ibid.
4 Ibid.
5 See FestungArnulfinger.blogspot.com/2007/06.

Msgr Belford also made a most important point when he emphasized that the sinner contracts two debts: the debt of guilt and the debt of pain. "God can forgive the former and insist on payment of the latter. He could forgive Schultz and yet keep him in purgatory until the end of time to atone, so far as man can atone, for his wickedness."

So, as often in these situations, the Church is seen to be proclaiming the true teaching of its founder. To that dying criminal on Calvary the Son of God himself promised paradise. It has been said in respect of the good thief that he was a robber to the last; he even stole heaven. Christ's Church continues to do what Christ did.

There is a lesson for us all in this story and it is expressed perfectly by Victor R. Claveau in his article "Stealing Heaven":

> The good thief, traditionally called Dismas, received Christ's precious promise because he cooperated with the great grace that God gave him. In a moment, a truly great sinner became a saint. In the face of this fact, how can any sinner despair? To every one of us, God gives His bountiful grace. We must follow the good thief's model of repentance and his cooperation with grace. And then, in cooperation with that grace, we must strive to live a life of faith, to follow Christ.[6]

CHAPTER TWENTY-TWO
Adolphe Retté

FRENCH CONVERT AND
CATHOLIC APOLOGIST

IT IS A FACT OF SOME NOTORIETY THAT A REL-
atively large number of literary figures considered to be part of
the Decadent movement ended up converting (or reverting) to the
Catholic Church. In Britain obvious examples of this phenomenon
are Oscar Wilde, Aubrey Beardsley (1872–1898), and Ernest Dowson
(1867–1900). The same is true about France, where such as Joris-Karl
Huysman (1848–1907), Léon Bloy (1846–1917), and Paul Verlaine
(1844–1896) come to mind. In this context the name Adolphe Retté
is rarely mentioned now. He is, however, a figure of considerable
importance whose neglect should be a matter of concern.

Adolphe Retté was born on July 25, 1863, in Montmartre in
Paris. His father was Auguste-Frédéric Retté, who came from a
Lutheran family and soon after his son's birth went to Russia to
tutor in French the children of the grand duke Constantine. He

returned only briefly before dying in 1880. Adolphe's mother, Elise, who was from a Catholic family, was a talented musician. Her father was Claude-Joseph-Adolphe Borgnet, a history professor at the University of Liège (and for a time rector of the university), who had become very anti-clerical and objected to all religious instruction. Retté was baptized into the Catholic religion by his maternal grandmother, a practicing and pious Catholic. His parents later separated, and he was brought up by his grandparents. On his father's insistence he attended a Protestant college from 1874 to 1880. While there he retained a vague theism but disliked the dryness of the Lutheran religion. After his father's death his mother withdrew him from the school and took him to Paris. He enlisted in the army and served from 1881 to 1886. He adapted to discipline, but lost all spiritual outlook and by all accounts surrendered to "the evils of sensuous living." In 1887 he settled in Paris and devoted himself to literature, joining the movement which was christened first Decadent and later Symbolist. When in the army he met Louise Rachel ("Lia"), who followed him to Paris. They lived together before going through a civil marriage in 1893, but she died in 1901.

Retté had a first great success with *Thulé des Brumes* ("Mists of Thule") in 1891. He then went through an anarchist and revolutionary phase from 1893 to 1896 and formed a hatred for Christianity. From 1896 to 1901 he was a pantheist and wrote from the perspective of a return to nature, advocating art in the service of revolution, and believing in the triumph of science. His work, which combined eroticism with blasphemy, was by now anti-clerical, though containing much religious imagery. However, his life began to change, slowly at first. He began to lose his faith in science and in progress, and religious questions tormented his mind. In this context, a fascinating incident—taking place at Fontainebleau, a place particularly linked with Retté, as we shall see—is described by Dom Antoine Marie, OSB, of the Abbey of Saint-Joseph de Clairval, Flavigny:

> One evening in Fontainebleau, he boasted in front of about thirty workers the limitless progress of science, which explains everything. "War on the priests, war on the capitalists...!" he exclaimed. As everyone was leaving, four listeners took him aside, and one of them, a gardener,

asked him, "We know that there is no God. But since the world wasn't created by anyone, we would really like to know how 'everything' began? Science must know about it . . ." Retté would have been able to drown his listener in an impenetrable torrent of words. But the good faith of these poor people touched him. "I would have wanted to die if I had deceived them," he wrote. "So?" the gardener asked again. "So," I said, urged on by truth, "science cannot explain how the world began." Yet the question echoed in Adolphe's head: "Who made the world?" The following night, he couldn't sleep, and the next morning, he asked himself, "And yet, if God existed...?" A century after Retté's avowal of his powerlessness, science has made much progress in knowledge of the universe, but the more it advances, the more arduous the difficulties it meets, and it still cannot answer the simple gardener's question.[1]

It was to be only a matter of time before an incident of greater significance proved to be the decisive step towards Retté's final conversion. This took place in 1905, again at Fontainebleau. It is described in detail by William Kenneth Cornell of Yale University in his book entitled *Adolphe Retté (1863–1930)*, published in 1942. This book, volume twenty in a series entitled *Yale Romantic Studies*, is an excellent piece of work, going into great detail about all aspects of Retté's life and work, and is undoubtedly the definitive biography of the subject. As Cornell shows, Retté was greatly influenced by reading Dante, whose work made him recognize the hollowness of his own aims and the necessity of belief in a Creator:

Retté, in a somber and repentant mood after a week of folly, was walking toward the Grotte des Montussiennes. In his hand he held one of his favorite books, *The Divine Comedy*, a work he had read many times and which had always seemed to him a fantastically beautiful story told by a poet of genius.

Reading as he walked, he had arrived at the second canto of the *Purgatory*, at the beautiful description of the swift ship piloted by the angel and bearing happy souls to the island where they may atone for their sins. Then a wonderful thing happened. Retté was suddenly overcome

1   Spiritual Newsletter, November 21, 2000, www.clairval.com/lettres/en/2000 /11/21/2221100.htm.

by what he describes as an inner radiance. He let the book fall, and resting his hand for support against a near-by tree, remained trembling in the silence of the forest while the monstrous picture of his vices presented itself to his mind. At the thought of being able to redeem himself, he wept. From the moment of these tears began the year-long struggle which ended in complete acceptance of the religious beliefs he had so long held up to ridicule.[2]

This was the decisive moment, although the culmination of the struggle was not immediate.

During the months that followed, this imparted radiance was to be a lambent flame that sometimes flickered and grew dim. There were days of demoniac assault, and hours when the struggling soul cried out for deliverance through death. But by the very intensity of the struggle the poet's inner life was completely changed. A man was in the agonizing process of rebirth, and by 1906 Retté had turned away from expression of personal mood and sentiment, from concern for material well-being among men, even from love of literary art. Until his death the new Retté was to keep his attention fixed on the problems of redemption and salvation through Christ and through the Church.[3]

In his own account of his conversion, *Du Diable à Dieu: Histoire d'une Conversion* ("From the Devil to God"), written in 1907, Retté analyzes his mental struggle with great frankness and sincerity. He gives a real emphasis to the groundwork on which his future existence was to be built, namely his complete obedience to the Church and his continual struggle not to weaken in his faith. He was to suffer many attacks of doubt, against which he fought with great integrity. Cornell tells of another moving scene that took place in the same location as earlier:

Walking through the quiet Fontainebleau Forest...he examined past creeds in his life, discarded them all, and found as his only refuge the idea of God. Particularly did his mind dwell on the firmness of the Catholic Church, fixed and unyielding against repeated assaults of unbelief.

2   Cornell, 164–65.
3   Ibid., 165.

For the first time since his fifteenth year he knelt in prayer, asking for guidance.

At this moment came one of those strange coincidences which strengthened so much his belief in the divine tutelage of which he was the recipient. A few minutes after his voiced request for aid, Retté saw an old priest approaching the tree where he was standing. As the aged man (the priest was Abbé Parys, who was for some time chaplain of the Carmelite convent at Beaune) passed near, his breviary in his hand, he uttered distinctly the lines from the Angelus: "*Et Verbum caro factum est: et habitavit in nobis.*" To the listener these words were as a revelation of divine grace. He hastened after the priest, asked him to pray for him and received his benediction.[4]

Retté was finally received into the Catholic Church on October 13, 1906, his mother following him into the Church shortly afterwards. The most immediate personal influence on Retté's conversion, though, was the poet and novelist François Coppée (1842–1909), himself a revert to the Catholic faith. When Retté was at such a low point during his struggle against temptations that he was on the verge of suicide, Coppée behaved towards him with great charity, and inspired him to regain his moral strength.

After his conversion Retté rejected much of his earlier published work, regarding it as "fit for the dung-heap." He formed a great devotion to St Teresa of Avila and to St John of the Cross. Furthermore, in 1908, as the expression of gratitude for his conversion, he made a pilgrimage on foot to Lourdes. His visit there is of great importance for his later writings in support of the Catholic faith and is worthy of more detailed consideration. Cornell's account summarizes well the process of Retté's thought here:

> Since he regarded himself as the object of a miracle, he wished to carry his homage to the grotto of abundant miracles, to Lourdes.... Retté thought that a beneficent influence was exerted at Lourdes in a great many ways. When he saw how he and his companions, unused to the care of the sick, were able to accomplish efficiently their dismal and painstaking task; when he saw sufferers, forgetful of their own anguish, in prayer for the one

4   Ibid., 172–73.

who was being lowered into the waters, he felt that the cures operated were not the only supernatural manifestations in the place. But he also saw some miraculous healings and received accounts of miracles from Doctor Boissarie. In addition he carefully studied testimonials from physicians.

After collecting sufficient documentation, Retté was led to refute the objections he heard from unbelievers. For those who attributed recovery from bodily affliction to the chill of immersion, he cited cures operated by a few drops of water and even by the passage of the Holy Sacrament. He discounted auto-suggestion, both because it had never been successfully employed in the medical world, save in certain cases of nervous disorder, and because many of the recipients of instant healing were not at all hopeful at the moment of their cure. Finally he cited the healing of children utterly incapable of understanding what was happening.

Retté was most wroth at an explanation given in Zola's *Lourdes*. In that novel Zola had spoken of a sanitive fluid which was disengaged from crowds in an ecstatic state of prayer. Refuting this idea, Retté cited healings, such as those of Léonie Levêque and Mlle Rouchel, which occurred in absolute solitude.[5]

However, there was a further important question, clearly relevant in any Catholic apologetic: Accepting the miracles of Lourdes as a divine gift from the Blessed Virgin, why are only a few cured and why do the prayers of the faithful often go unanswered?

> This was the first time he tried to give a disquisition on a theological matter and he borrowed his method from the early Church fathers. His reasoning, destined to prove that in the working of divine will there is neither disorder nor injustice, runs somewhat as follows: (1) Man, corrupt through original sin, constantly violates God's will; (2) the human race must pay for all its evil doing, and the payment is often exacted through suffering; (3) the miracles are merely a sign that some of the evil has been redeemed through good deeds, but good persons may be obliged to continue to suffer for wrongs committed by their forebears or relatives. Retté asserts that God's justice is further proved by the fact that the

5   Ibid., 181, 186–87.

poor and lowly are generally the recipients of miraculous cure. He is certain that the small number of miracles in the twentieth century is directly proportionate to its lack of faith.[6]

This last issue is, of course, just as relevant to us as it was in Retté's day. The forces of secularism, present at that time, are on the march still, and the Church is under real attack from such as the "new atheists" and their fellow travelers. Retté's writings are as timely now as then. After his conversion he pursued the life of a militant churchman, writing eighteen volumes of meditations, biographies, and memoirs, and two of critical essays. He attacked the materialism and atheism of his age and was very influential in effecting conversions. The tragedy is that very little of his work has been translated into English and Cornell's biography, although profound, is really the only substantial source of information in the English language on this great Catholic writer. A great apostolate is open for a scholar who would translate the major works, and especially the great story of Retté's conversion.

Finally, it should be noted that Retté's own Catholic apostolate was not only one of words. Exempt from military service because of age, he served in a hospital unit on the Western Front during World War I. He also tried unsuccessfully on several occasions to see if he had a monastic vocation.

Adolphe Retté died in poverty at Beaune on December 8, 1930, after much illness. He is buried in the cemetery there. The quotation on his tombstone is from Psalm 30: "*In te Domini, speravi. Non confundar in aeternum*" ("In thee, O Lord, have I trusted. Let me never be confounded"). Even in his own country of France he is not exactly well known. He deserves much wider recognition there and throughout the world.

6   Ibid., 187.

CHAPTER TWENTY-THREE

Elizabeth Sarah Kite

CATHOLICIZING
AMERICAN HISTORY

COULD THERE EVER BE SUCH A THING AS A
pagan path to Christ? Could a pagan influence lead one directly
to Christ and then on to his Catholic Church? Clutching at straws,
one might think about the writer and publisher Milton Waldman (1895–1976). In his latter role he was an advisor to several
well-known authors, notably J. R. R. Tolkien. Why Waldman in
this context? Well, there is a curious reference in the account of
his life given in that authoritative resource the *American National
Biography*: "A picture of Waldman would be incomplete without
any mention of his devout Catholicism, to which he formally
converted in the mid-1940s, partly as a result of his research into
the lives of the Medicis and Joan of Arc." The reference to Joan of

Arc is perfectly understandable, but the notion of someone being converted to the Catholic faith through research into the Medicis does seem somewhat odd. In the biographical material relating to the Medicis there are perhaps some pagan-like elements, even though they may not be of the traditional kind; why they would lead directly to a conversion to Catholicism is a little puzzling. So Milton Waldman must be left behind, I'm afraid, since nothing further seems to emerge to solve that particular puzzle.

In his place one should focus on another American. This is the redoubtable Elizabeth Sarah Kite, who can be described as a historian and social scientist. How, then, to develop the link with paganism in her case? It is not all that easy, I'm afraid, and perhaps a stretch, but it is worth trying, and even if one fails, her life is of interest as a conversion story.

In his book *Catholic Converts: British and American Intellectuals Turn to Rome* (1997), Patrick Allitt, who is the main modern source of information on Elizabeth Kite, draws attention to a common theme in the work of several notable historians. He makes reference to Carlton Hayes, Ross Hoffman, Gaillard Hunt, and, of course, Elizabeth Kite herself. The common theme is referred to in the following terms and stems from the way that all four of these historians denied that the intellectual origins of the U.S. Constitution could be traced to the English philosopher John Locke: "All of these were also converts and all argued that the U.S. Constitution embodied the wisdom of the 'great tradition' of natural law political philosophy which traced its roots back through the pagan-Christian synthesis in Aquinas to the principles of Augustine's *City of God*."[1] So perhaps, in the light of Elizabeth Kite's own historical work, one may be justified in looking at her in terms of pagan influences duly Catholicized. We shall see. Certainly her progress towards and into the Catholic Church and her subsequent historical writing are worthy of close examination.

Elizabeth Sarah Kite was born in Philadelphia in 1864. She came from a venerable Protestant family and was brought up in a strict Quaker household. She was close to tragedy from a relatively early age, as her mother, brother, and sister all died when she was in her early twenties. Furthermore, other relatives died, later leaving her responsible for five nephews and nieces. Her own personal

1   *Catholic Converts*, 137.

life did not always run smoothly. She found out that the man she loved was already married. After discovering this she took a vow of chastity. She then studied for six years in England, France, Germany, and Switzerland. While living in London she became aware of a growing "spiritual hunger" and had a series of religious experiences. Her conversion process is of particular interest. The first part of the story, essentially a clearing away of false religions, is recounted in Patrick Allitt's book:

> Feeling intellectually and spiritually dissatisfied after flirt-
> ing with socialism, Hinduism, and theosophy around the
> turn of the century, she attended a sermon in Westmin-
> ster Abbey, only to find the preacher dispensing the cold
> comfort of the historical-critical method: "I was a starving
> soul begging imploringly for the bread of life, but all
> the minister had to offer were stones, stones, stones, or
> rather baked clay tablets from old Babylon, with which
> he frittered away the whole Gospel narrative as an absurd
> myth.... It seemed to me that Almighty God had per-
> mitted me to hear the very worst this evidently popular
> speaker could do in the way of giving a so-called higher
> criticism interpretation of the Christian religion, so that
> never again would I turn to the Church of England when
> in search of spiritual food." [2]

However, her experiences in Catholic France and in Algiers during a trip with friends were positive influences on her. Back in England, in London, she began to pay visits to a Catholic Church and it was there that she had what might almost be termed a "blinding flash" conversion. Allitt takes up the story again:

> She found herself there on Holy Thursday, 1904, joining
> a procession to kiss the feet of the crucified Jesus. As
> she did so she experienced an intense psychological or
> spiritual sensation: "As I rose the corpus as it were came
> alive and as I gazed, a glance from under the partly closed
> lids struck to the inmost centre of my being, cleaving me
> in twain. For I, from above the feet, distinctly saw myself,
> even to the dress I wore that day, with head bowed and
> downcast eyes, join the retreating line of worshippers. At
> the time I did not understand, but I now see that what

2   Ibid., 134–35.

had happened was the miracle of *Belief*—a pure gift from the divine heart of Jesus."[3]

Within a few weeks she had taken instruction and was then received into the Catholic Church. She was fortunate in that she received no criticism from her relatives and her Quaker friends continued to behave in a kindly fashion towards her. She was a devout Catholic for the rest of her life.

After her conversion she became a Franciscan tertiary. Several notable British converts were also Franciscan tertiaries. There seems to be a link here with the arts, for several were writers by profession. One of them was an actor, William Farren (1825-1908), but it is the written word which joins together Cecily Hallack (1898-1938), Bartle Teeling (1851-1906), and Peter Anson (1889-1975), the last of whom was also noted for his paintings. Anson also wrote specifically on Franciscan themes, notably in *The Pilgrim's Guide to Franciscan Italy* (1927). In addition, he and Hallack co-wrote the delightful *These Made Peace: Studies in the Lives of the Beatified and Canonized Members of the Third Order of St. Francis of Assisi*, last revised in 1963. However, when it comes to American converts, the link seems much less strong. Elizabeth Kite is the one major example.

After becoming a Catholic Elizabeth Kite returned to the United States and worked as a teacher in private schools. In relation to her post-conversion scholarly activities, there is, in the light of the Catholic faith, a positive and a negative. Her dual career involved working in a field which was fully in line with the Catholic faith. However, it also involved work in an area of research in conflict with that faith. Let us start with the positive aspect. This is Kite's major contribution to scholarship and it involves her work in the field of history. She had studied at London University with Emil Reich, a Hungarian Jewish professor and his influence on her was crucial. He caused her to see Catholicism as a great *historical* religion. In this context she began to research the history of France's role in the American Revolutionary War and in *The Catholic Part in the Making of America* (1936) argued that without the aid of France and its pious king, Louis XVI, the United States would never have become independent. Patrick Allitt draws attention to another crucial incident that backed up Kite's thesis of the vital importance of history in the development of religion:

3   Ibid., 135.

[Emil Reich's] lecture on the confrontation of Emperor Henry IV and Pope Gregory VII in the snowy Alps had an effect on Kite almost as profound as had her religious conversion.... Reich's description of a moment when the pope enjoyed a great victory over the temporal power showed Kite Catholicism in a new light, as a great *historical* religion, the "miracle of the ages," which combined "perfect democracy with perfect authority." History became for her a quasi-religious vocation.[4]

Elizabeth Kite's particular vocation, then, was to persuade honest patriots to admit that the United States as a nation, even if there was much anti-Catholic prejudice, owed its genesis to the selfless work of Catholics. She was, of course, not the only historian to work along these lines. In order to appreciate this one only has to think of such fine scholars as the aforementioned Carlton Hayes, Ross Hoffman, and Gaillard Hunt. All these were also converts and all argued that the U. S. Constitution embodied the wisdom of the "great tradition." Kite's work on Franco-American relations contributed a new dimension to this extensive effort to identify a crucial Catholic element of American history. She aimed to show that American independence had been made possible through the aid of a Catholic power and that this aid had been based not just on political considerations, but on religious feeling. In the process of reaching these conclusions, her meticulous research involved much time in the major libraries of London, Paris, and Washington, helping to reform utterly the holdings of the last in French diplomatic history. In this process she reduced the importance of the role in the Revolution of the freethinking Marquis de Lafayette (1757–1834), and helped to advertise the role played by previously unrecognized and sound Catholics, for example Louis Duportail (1743–1801) and Pierre-Augustin Caron de Beaumarchais (1732–1799). Her major works were *Beaumarchais and the War of American Independence* (1918), *Brigadier-General Louis Lebegue Duportail* (1933), and *The Catholic Part in the Making of America* (1936).

In recognition of this work she received the Cross of Chevalier de la Légion d'Honneur, and was the first laywoman to receive the degree of doctor of literature at Villanova University. She

4   Ibid., 135–36.

was also archivist for the American Catholic Historical Society of Philadelphia.

Now, let us move to what Catholics loyal to their faith would take to be the negative aspect of Elizabeth Kite's post-conversion experience. The fact is that before her conversion she was an enthusiast for eugenics, believing that heredity outweighed environment in the transmission of desirable traits, and undertook research under the guidance of Henry H. Goddard, a leading psychologist and eugenicist, into issues relating to those then referred to as the feeble-minded. Of course, eugenics, now rightly deplored as a tool of social policy, was seen at that time by many liberals as something progressive and a way of improving the population. However, Catholics were opposed to eugenic reforms, such as the proposal to limit marriage to those granted a eugenic health certificate by the state and laws permitting sterilization of the mentally defective. It may be noted that Elizabeth Kite also translated the work of Alfred Binet on the IQ test, seen by Catholics as a further example of a eugenic approach.

It can be said that Kite was never as extreme as some in her approach to eugenics. There is no evidence of how, if at all, she reconciled these beliefs with her Catholic faith. She did, however, concentrate in her later years on her historical research. All that can be said by way of comment is that she was not the first, and will not be the last, to bring into her new faith beliefs and sentiments developed before her conversion that did not conform to the outlook of her new faith.

Elizabeth Kite died on January 6, 1954, in Wilmington, Delaware. She is buried at the Friends Burial Ground, Philadelphia. Her conversion is of importance on two levels. The first is her work on the role of the Church in history. The second relates to her work on a domestic level, since in the years following her conversion she persuaded no fewer than fifteen members of her extended family to convert also.

The Elizabeth S. Kite Collection is at Rutgers University, New Jersey, and contains in typescript *A Conversion Story from Quakerism to the Catholic Church* and her unpublished autobiography *The Beggar Maid and the King*. Her progress towards and into the Catholic Church, and her subsequent historical writing, are worthy of close examination.

CHAPTER TWENTY-FOUR

Historians Converting for the Truth

THE CASE OF WARREN CARROLL

CATHOLIC CONVERTS AMONG HISTORIANS SEEM
plentiful. If one starts by focusing on America and confines one's
researches to notable persons whose principal activity was the study
of history, the following names emerge: Marshall Baldwin, Thomas
Brady, Warren Carroll, Elizabeth Fox-Genovese, Eugene Geno-
vese, John Hassard, Carlton Hayes, Ross Hoffman, Gaillard Hunt,
Frederick Kinsman, Elizabeth Kite, Daniel Sargent, and Thomas
Woods—thirteen in total then. If one turns to notable converts from
Britain and Ireland, many more names emerge. A representative list
embraces the following: Colin Amery, A. C. F. Beales, Edmund Bishop,
Fr Thomas Bridgett, Jonathan Clark, Eveline Cruickshanks, Chris-
topher Dawson, Fr Francis Edwards, Sheridan Gilley, Agnes Head-
lam-Morley, Anne Hope, Christopher Lee, James Lees-Milne, Shane
Leslie, William Maskell, John Morrill, Edward Norman, William

Pantin, Edgar Prestage, Dom Daniel Rees, E. E. Reynolds, Anthony Rhodes, Jonathan Riley-Smith, Jean Stone, Jocelyn Toynbee, David Watkin, and Hugh Ross Williamson. Twenty-seven in total this time.

That is quite a difference between the American and the British totals. I do not intend to speculate on the reasons. As always these converts on both sides of the Atlantic come along several different routes. In addition, some tell us nothing about their reasons and motivations.

These converts discuss many things that led them to the Church. Not surprisingly several of them cite their historical researches and findings as contributing, often in a major way, to their conversion. Some themes occur in several cases: for example, what might be called the C. S. Lewis/G. K. Chesterton argument for the divinity of Christ, that he must be either God or a bad man. This is a major part of Ross Hoffman's conversion in particular[1] and, as will be seen, that of Warren Carroll.

Yet here it is important to explore another facet of the conversion of historians looking for the truth, something that is very specific and bears upon the craft of writing history and the nature of historical evidence itself: this is the banning of the supernatural from historical writing. In order to do this it is useful to concentrate on just one of the historians referred to above, Warren Carroll, and in particular to his argument for a certain thesis. But first a short account of his life may be appropriate.

Warren Hasty Carroll was born on March 24, 1932, in Maine. He was not baptized as a child. His father was an agnostic. His mother did believe in God, but refused to join a church, since, as she put it, they were "always fighting and criticizing one another." As a child Carroll himself believed in God, but knew nothing about Christ. He loved the C. S. Lewis interplanetary books, but did not appreciate the Christian undertones. He became what he described as a "pagan deist with a strong desire for the truth."

Carroll received an MA and PhD in History from Columbia University. Between 1955 and 1961, he served two years with the U. S. Army Signal Corps and worked for the Central Intelligence Agency, serving in the anti-communism division as a propaganda analyst. He worked as an assistant command historian for the Second Air Force, Strategic Air Command.

1   See "The Verdict of History," in O'Brien (ed.), *The Road to Damascus*, 76.

Between 1962 and 1964 he attended law school. From 1967 to 1972 he served on the staff of California State Senator, later U. S. Congressman, John G. Schmitz.

His conversion to the Catholic faith was very much influenced by the pious example of his cradle Catholic wife Anne, *née* Westhoff, the author of *Christ the King, Lord of History* (1986) and *Christ in the Americas* (1997). Warren Carroll was received into the Church on December 7, 1968.

After his conversion Carroll worked for the Catholic journal *Triumph*, becoming its education director, dealing with issues of Catholic education, and in charge of its catechetical section, the Christian Commonwealth Institute. He coordinated weekend lecture series throughout the United States and oversaw *Triumph*'s summer program in El Escorial, Spain.

His main literary achievement consisted in many books on history, including a five-volume history of Christendom, written from a Catholic perspective, with the papacy as its unifying thread. The main titles are as follows: *1917, Red Banners, White Mantle* (1981); *Our Lady of Guadalupe and the Conquest of Darkness* (1983); *The Founding of Christendom* (1985); *The Guillotine and the Cross* (1986); *The Building of Christendom* (1987); *70 Years of the Communist Revolution* (1989); *Isabel of Spain: The Catholic Queen* (1991); *The Glory of Christendom* (1993); *The Rise and Fall of the Communist Revolution* (1995); *The Last Crusade* (1996) (a history of the Spanish Civil War); *The Cleaving of Christendom* (2000); *The Revolution against Christendom* (2006; with Anne Carroll); and one published after his death, *The Crisis of Christendom* (2013; with Anne Carroll).

Being concerned after the Second Vatican Council at the effect of the cultural revolution on Catholic education, he founded Christendom College, Front Royal, Virginia, in 1977, to provide a truly Catholic liberal-arts education faithful to the Church's magisterium. He was the first president of the college until 1985, as well as the chairman of the history department until he retired in 2002. He returned to give many public lectures at the college. Among several honors was that he became the first recipient of the Pius XI award for history given by the Society of Catholic Social Scientists. Carroll's teaching became famous for several memorable phrases: "History can be summed up in five words: Truth exists. The Incarnation happened"; "You can never bribe a pope"; "One man can make a difference."

From 1997 onwards he suffered several strokes, and died on July 17, 2011, in Manassas, Virginia. He is buried in the grounds of Christendom College.

Now to the specific argument referred to earlier. It is not something directly related to his conversion as such, but it is indirectly related. Let us allow Carroll to express it himself, which he did very precisely in 1996 in an important article:

> Scholarly history, as written today and for the past forty years, has banned everything supernatural as though it were an intellectual plague. The very possibility of action by God in history has become academically taboo. This prohibition applies not only to miracles and apparitions, but even to the power of prayer. So universal is this ban, so chilling its effect even on the minds of historians who personally believe in the supernatural, that its imposition has gone virtually unchallenged the past forty years. Indeed, in all honesty I must say that since I began writing scholarly Catholic history thirteen years ago I have found no other contemporary historian who writes in defiance of this ban.[2]

Carroll is rightly appalled by this "ban." As he explains, the great Catholic historians of the past would have no truck with such an approach. He cites Eusebius of Caesarea (265–339), St Augustine (354–430), Caesar Baronius (1538–1607), the first modern Catholic historian, and Jacques-Bénigne Bossuet (1627–1704). From the middle of the twentieth century he cites the works of Hilaire Belloc, G. K. Chesterton, and William Thomas Walsh. These historians gave their account of history on every occasion both powerfully and from the Catholic viewpoint, "which puts God and His Son and the Church He founded at the center of history."[3]

As an illustration of this last point, let us take just one example. It comes from Hilaire Belloc's book *The Battle Ground* (1936) and could not be put better, though the expression is thoroughly tongue-in-cheek:

2   "Banning the Supernatural: Why Historians Must Not Rule out the Action of God in History," *Catholic Social Science Review* (1996), 73. Available online at pdfs.semanticscholar.org/b411/187684d4b40f1399e8ba388979c-8c2fe2ed9.pdf.
3   Ibid.

This book needs a brief apology. The writer has not only
taken it for granted that there is a God, but also design
in the Universe and in the story of Mankind. He has
affirmed a special design in the story of Syria and particularly of Israel, reaching a climax at the Crucifixion. He
even seems to imply the Divinity of his Savior.

All this must sound so unusual today that it may be
thought an affectation, deliberately assumed to startle and
offend. Such a feeling will be enhanced by the discovery
that he takes the gospel of St. John to have been written
by St. John and even allows some historical value to the
Old Testament.

The sole excuse he offers for his extravagance is that
the present Generation is tolerant of novel ideas, and that
he therefore may hope for indulgence.[4]

Carroll was adamant that the older approach should be allowed
to continue. He emphasized the fact that the Christian and Catholic faith is preeminently a historical faith, one which believes
that God, the Creator and Sustainer of the universe, entered
history, incarnate as the man Jesus Christ, at a particular time
and place. This is something absolutely unique, unclaimed by any
other religion.

In support of his case Carroll refers to some powerful words
of G. K. Chesterton, that doughty champion of the Christian and
Catholic faith, in his great work *The Everlasting Man* (1925):

Right in the middle of all these things stands up an enormous exception ... nothing less than the loud assertion
that this mysterious maker of the world has visited his
world in person. It declares that really and even recently,
or right in the middle of historic times, there did walk
into the world this original invisible being, about whom
the thinkers make theories and the mythologists hand
down myths; the Man Who Made the World. That such
a higher personality exists behind all things had indeed
always been implied by all the best thinkers, as well as
by all the most beautiful legends. But nothing of this
sort had been implied in any of them. It is simply false
to say that the other sages and heroes had claimed to be
that mysterious master and maker of whom the world

4   Preface to *The Battle Ground.*

had dreamed and disputed. Not one of them had ever claimed to be anything of the sort. Not one of their sects or schools had ever claimed that they had claimed to be anything of the sort. The most that any religious prophet had said was that he was the true servant of such a being. The most that any visionary had ever said was that men might catch glimpses of the glory of that spiritual being; or much more often of lesser spiritual beings. The most that any primitive myth had ever suggested was that the Creator was present at the Creation. But that the Creator was present at scenes a little subsequent to the supper parties of Horace, and talked with tax collectors and government officials in the detailed daily life of the Roman Empire, and that this fact continued to be firmly asserted by the whole of that great civilization for more than a thousand years—that is something utterly unlike anything else.... It makes nothing but dust and nonsense of comparative religion.[5]

If Chesterton is right on this, as he is on so many things, then, as Carroll puts it, "we should never allow ourselves to be persuaded or pressured to consent to any field of study—especially history—being declared off limits to it."[6] On this issue Carroll then aligns himself with another great figure, Dom Prosper Guéranger, OSB (1805-1875), Servant of God, who served for nearly forty years as Abbot of the monastery of Solesmes:

> History ought to be Christian, if it is to be true: for Christianity is the truth complete; and every historical system which disregards the supernatural order in its explanation and evaluation of the facts is a false system which explains nothing, and which leaves the annals of humanity in chaos and permanent contradiction with all the ideas that reason forms on the destinies of our race here below.[7]

So, what went wrong and when? Carroll puts some of the blame at the feet of "the last great avowedly Catholic historian," Christopher Dawson. He maintains that Dawson was "much more cautious, seeking academic acceptance as he was for his presentation

5 *The Everlasting Man*, 265-66.
6 "Banning the Supernatural," 74.
7 *Le Sens Chretien de l'Histoire* (1858), 6-7.

of Christian culture; and since Dawson, even Catholic historians have generally accepted, without even a protest, the academic ban on the supernatural, which consequently now reigns supreme."[8]

Perhaps Carroll slightly overstates the point regarding Christopher Dawson, but certainly one can agree with his overall conclusion:

> The arbitrary *a priori* assumption that apparitions and miracles and the Incarnation itself could not have happened, that historical events never transcend the natural order, is not a critical standard. It is a flagrant bias that ought to be firmly rejected. Jettisoning this prejudice is a reasonable and fair position to demand even from non-Christian historians. For the Christian historian it is nothing less than a duty.[9]

Warren Carroll goes on to quote once again what he refers to as "the hard-hitting but just words of Dom Guéranger":

> The Christian has not only a duty to believe, but also a duty to confess what he believes. This double obligation, founded in the doctrine of the Apostle [Paul] (Rom 10:10), is the more binding in ages of naturalism, and the Christian historian ought to understand that it is not enough for him to declare his belief, in passages here and there in his book, if its Christian character then immediately disappears.[10]

Carroll goes on in this same article to explain how this process of downplaying God, Christ, and the Church in historical works operates. Space precludes examination of this here, but Carroll's account is worth reading. It may be that overall he slightly overstates his critique of modern Catholic historians. Among those sometimes referred to today as Catholic revisionist historians, for example, one can see more than just an element of what Carroll is advocating as the authentic Catholic approach. Whatever one's views on this, there is no doubt that Warren Carroll himself saw clearly the importance of "history as if truth mattered" and wrote vigorously to uphold it. The Catholic faith is always at the center of his work. "It is the pivot around which true history revolves,"

8 "Banning the Supernatural," 74.
9 Ibid., 79.
10 *Le Sens Chretien de l'Histoire*, 27–28.

THE HOUSE WITH A HUNDRED GATES

he explained, "and the one standard by which the importance of every historical event and figure should be judged."[11]

Finally, to return to the topic of conversion, it has been indicated earlier that Warren Carroll is yet another who was heavily influenced in his conversion by C. S. Lewis. As Lorene Hanley Duquin states, "When Dr. Carroll's search for truth led him to examine Christianity, he turned back to C. S. Lewis. After reading *Mere Christianity*, *Miracles*, and *The Problem of Pain*, he became convinced of the divinity of Jesus Christ: 'Lewis does not let you evade the fundamental question: Who was this Man? He shows you why you must answer that He is God Himself.'"[12]

This new understanding of faith altered the course of Carroll's life. As he himself explained, "I had never been a Christian until I was finally convinced that Jesus Christ is God. Now I knew I must put Jesus at the center of my life, because His Godhead is truth."[13]

11 "Banning the Supernatural," 79.
12 Lorene Hanley Duquin, *A Century of Catholic Converts* (2003), 171.
13 Ibid., 172.

CHAPTER TWENTY-FIVE
Maurice Baring

THE NEGLECTED THIRD OF THREE

THAT GREAT CATHOLIC WARRIOR HILAIRE BEL-
loc had many friends, and two of the closest were converts. We
hear much about the friendship and association between Belloc
and G. K. Chesterton, the so-called "Chesterbelloc," but little is
said, at least nowadays, of someone who might be referred to as
the third member of a triumvirate. This is Maurice Baring (or
the Honorable Maurice Baring, to give him his full title). The
three were great friends and we can still, as it were, view them
together in the celebrated painting by James Gunn (1893–1964).

Whereas there has been renewed interest in both Chesterton
and Belloc in recent times, Maurice Baring has been forgotten,
which is a great shame. Yes, it must be admitted that in comparison with the other two, he is a minor character (virtually anyone
would be in the company of those two intellectual giants!), but
there is much about him that is well worth remembering and
some compelling statements by him on reasons for conversion

to the Faith. He himself was a notable convert in his time and the following account considers him primarily from that aspect.

First of all, then, a summary of his life would be useful. Maurice Baring was born on April 27, 1874, in Mayfair, London. He was a member of a famous banking family and was the eighth child and fifth son of Edward Charles Baring, first Baron Revelstoke. His background was Protestant, though lacking serious denominational ties. He was a freethinker in his teens, but his thoughts began to move towards the Catholic Church. He was educated at Eton and Trinity College, Cambridge, but left the university without taking a degree. Baring was a great linguist and entered the diplomatic service. He was attaché in Paris, Copenhagen, and Rome, and after that worked in the Foreign Office in London before resigning the service in 1904. He then became a correspondent for the *Morning Post* in Manchuria, and later in St Petersburg and Constantinople. He also represented *The Times* in the Balkans. Baring deferred his conversion to the Catholic Church until 1909, partly due to family objections. He was finally received on February 1 of that year at the Brompton Oratory in London by Fr Henry Sebastian Bowden (1836–1919; a convert himself, who achieved some small notoriety as the priest who nearly converted Oscar Wilde in the 1870's, and was the superior of the Oratory for two periods of time). Baring referred to his conversion as "the only action in my life which I am quite certain I have never regretted."[1] His sister, Elizabeth, Countess of Kenmare (1867-1944), was received earlier and his niece, Daphne Pollen (1904-1986), an artist, converted in 1926. Baring was in the Royal Flying Corps, the embryonic RAF, during World War I. His main literary achievements were a series of novels, verse plays, memoirs, and studies on Russia. The last are well worth reading today as fine character studies and depictions of a society. In his final fifteen years Baring suffered from Parkinson's Disease. He died on December 14, 1945, at Beaufort Castle, Beauly, Inverness-shire, in Scotland.

Why did Maurice Baring convert? He never wrote a full account of why he came to espouse Christianity and the Catholic Church. As to the former, Baring is yet another of the significant number of people who have come to believe in the divinity of Christ on the basis of a version of the "bad, mad, or God" argument. This

---

1   *The Puppet Show of Memory* (1922), 395-96.

argument's most famous advocate in modern times is C. S. Lewis, but it should be noted that a powerful form of the argument can be found in the writings of G. K. Chesterton, notably in *The Everlasting Man* (1925). Here is what Baring himself puts forward in a letter to Desmond McCarthy written in 1916:

> It doesn't solve the mystery, if Christ was only a man, of how and why such an astounding thing could happen.... Given the fact that the existence of this person changed the whole face of the world, all this is very difficult to explain. If, that is to say, the man was only a man. Some explanation is necessary. You have either to say "Yes, but he was a very good man" or that he was mad, went mad. Neither explanation [is] adequate. Because no other very good man has [had] quite the same effect. Nobody, for instance, has believed that Socrates or even Buddha or Mahomet was God and madmen have not inspired people to die for them rather than deny them. On the other hand you have the Church which claims to have been founded by that Person and claims the gospels as the title deeds of her estate and an uninterrupted tradition from the days of Christ and his contemporaries. To be in fact the representative of the Divine on earth. If you admit that this claim is substantial, the whole matter is simple....
>
> But this, you will point out, entails believing that Christ was God. And you will say this is difficult. I admit the difficulty. But I maintain it is not more difficult than it is difficult for you... or anyone else to believe that He was not God. Because once your faith in Him as a man and ordinary like Shakespeare or Mahomet is sure and certain, once you really believe that He was not God, a host of difficulties arise. You are forced to find some explanation in order to account for the rise and growth and existence of the Church.[2]

As to the choice of the Catholic Church, Baring tackles this issue on a number of different occasions. What he has to say is very persuasive, and he is at pains to thank Hilaire Belloc—in a letter written in 1934. There he wrote, "But for you I should never have come into the Church: you were the lighthouse that showed

2 Jocelyn Hillgarth and Julian Jeffs (ed.), *Maurice Baring Letters* (2007), 107–8.

me the way, the beacon, and once I was there you remained a tower of strength in times or moments of difficulty."[3] It should be added, in relation to influences on conversion, that Baring also mentions *En Route* (1895), the autobiographical novel of the French novelist Joris-Karl Huysmans as an influence.

Baring's argument for the Catholic Church has a similar structure to his argument for the divinity of Christ. It is one of those either/or arguments similar to the "bad, mad, or God" argument. Here is an example taken from his novel *Passing By* (1921):

> Riley said there were only two points of view in the world: the Catholic point of view or the non-Catholic point of view. All so-called religions which I could mention, including my layman's common-sense view, were either lopped-off branches of Catholicism or shadows of it, or a blind aspiration towards it, or a misguided parallel of it, as of a train that had gone off the rails, or a travesty of it, sometimes serious, and sometimes grotesque: a distortion. The other point of view was the materialist point of view, which he could perfectly well understand anyone holding. It depends, he said, whether you think human life is casual or divine.

A similar strain of thought on the part of Baring is brought out by Gordon Albion in an article on Baring's novel *C* (1924):

> C. who had never in his life discussed religion is suddenly asked by a new poet acquaintance: "Are you a Catholic?" "No," said C., "I'm nothing"—"Of course not, if you're not a Catholic," said Bede, "There is either that or nothing. There is no third course." "And one can't very well become a Catholic," said C. "Why not?" asked Bede. C. stammered and did not answer.... It was not, however, necessary, for Bede poured out a stream of argument and exposition to the effect that Catholicism was the great reality; the only thing that mattered; the only thing that counted; the only creed a thinking man could adopt; the only solace that satisfied the needs of the human heart; the only curb to the human passions; the only system that fulfilled the demands of human nature and into which factors such as love and death fitted naturally; the unique and sole representative of the Divine upon earth. The English had

3   Ibid., 148.

gone wrong because they had fallen into a rut from the straight road of the true inheritance: Catholic England, Chaucer's England, to which the whole of Shakespeare was the dirge.[4]

The same sort of approach is evident once more in a letter of 1913 to H. G. Wells, quoted in an article by Julian Jeffs:

The difference which separates [Protestants and Catholics] is not in any special dogma but in the authority in which all dogmas root, Protestants basing their authority on the Bible which Catholics do also.... But the Roman Catholic Church's first doctrine is her own perpetual infallibility. She is inspired, she says, by the same Spirit that inspired the Bible—this voice is equally the voice of God.... Catholicism is the only real living religion at this moment that is influencing humanity. That it is a gigantic fact, that no discoveries of science which shake Bible-founded Protestantism or any Bible-founded Sect to its foundations have the slightest effect on it.[5]

Finally on this theme Baring wrote to Dame Ethel Smyth in 1919 that he became a Catholic because "at one moment I came to the conclusion that human life is either casual or divine. If divine it meant a revealed representative. Where was this? The Catholic Church. And then everything follows down to the holy water. But if it is not divine, then the only alternative would be for me complete agnosticism."[6] For Baring, then, there is no middle way.

Maurice Baring also had a real historical sense. He wrote a biographical novel, *The End Is My Beginning* (1931), about Mary Stuart. In one of his letters to Dame Ethel Smyth, this one in 1914, he brings out powerfully the historical connections within the Mass:

I went to Mass this morning, and it was nice to think I was listening to the same words, said in the same way with the same gestures, that Henry V and his "contempt- ible little army" heard before and after Agincourt; and I stood between a man in khaki and a French Tommy, and history flashed past like a jeweled dream.[7]

4 "Catholicism in Maurice Baring's 'C'," *The Month*, May 1948, 303.
5 "The Conversion of Maurice Baring," *Chesterton Review*, February 1988, 83.
6 Hillgarth and Jeffs (ed.), *Maurice Baring Letters*, 131.
7 Ibid., 86.

The matter of history and historical criticism gives Baring the opportunity to make perhaps his most profound point on reasoned grounds for conversion. There is a delightful paradox in the argument that he adopts. He actually manages to use the case given by the French philosopher and critic Ernest Renan (1823–1892) for leaving the Church as a case for joining her! Here is the way that Baring expresses his argument, which is a considerable one, contained in his book *Have You Anything to Declare?* (1936) and worth setting out in some considerable detail:

> To the young of my generation there was a certain excitement in reading Renan. We chuckled at his irony, thinking he had helped to emancipate us once and for all from many tedious superstitions, sham conventions, and false traditions. But his influence did not end there. It would have surprised Renan to hear that his histories of the origin and vicissitudes of the early Church, and his touching account of the laceration he suffered when he abandoned the thought of the priesthood and left the Church, should have been instrumental in bringing more than one agnostic into the Catholic Church. Such, however, is the truth. The reasons are briefly these. First of all, his histories of the early Church reveal to the agnostic who has had for sole religious education at school a certain amount of translating and construing of the New Testament, and some "talks" prior to confirmation, the astonishing fact that there was an early Church, of which the Apostles were the pillars; secondly, Renan informs them that his reasons for leaving the Church are not the so-called abuses of the Catholic Church, that is, the so-called "errors of Rome." For him, the Reformed Churches have not a leg to stand on. "*Malheur au vague! mieux vaut le faux,*" he says. "I regretted at moments," he writes, "not being a Protestant, so that I could continue to be a philosopher without ceasing to be a Christian. Then I realized that it was only the Catholics who were logical." Nor was it because he found it impossible to swallow Catholic dogmas.
>
> His reasons, he tells us, were based entirely on philology and criticism; and had nothing to do with metaphysics, politics or morality. Such categories of ideas as the last-named seemed to him intangible and easily molded to any

shape. But the problem of deciding whether there were discrepancies between the fourth Gospel and the synoptic Gospels was entirely palpable. To him the evidence of such discrepancies was so conclusive that he was ready to stake his life on it, and consequently his immortal soul, without a moment's hesitation....

What drove him out of the Church was neither dogmatic difficulties nor the misdeeds of the Papacy, but his belief in the infallibility of the German higher criticism of the biblical texts.... It was German textual criticism that cut the Gordian knot for him. He swallowed German criticism whole. He admired it, he says, all the more because he did not perceive its limits.... Renan probably never read the German higher criticism of Shakespeare, with a Shakespeare beside it in the original; but others did, and that shattered their faith once and for all in the German higher criticism. Once one has read portions of that—however little one knows and whatever its merits may be—one can no longer believe German higher criticism to be infallible.... For instance, if we read a scholarly and detailed argument written by a German, setting out to prove a possible thesis, say that *Richard III* was entirely the work of Marlowe, we may be duly impressed by the author's scholarship, ingenuity and labor, we may think he has made out a good case; there is much to be said on his side; but if at the same time we are personally convinced, after re-reading the play, that some passages have an authentic Shakespearian ring, and could not have been written by Marlowe, we do not on account of the thoroughness of German scholarship, learning and industry, renounce our opinion which we consider was based on common sense; we adhere to it. And after a course of the higher criticism of Shakespeare, we become aware that it is possible, as Father Knox has so brilliantly shown, to prove that *In Memoriam* was written by Queen Victoria; and when we see the German higher criticism at work upon the Gospels, and they tell us that certain of Our Lord's answers to Pontius Pilate are authentic, but that others are not, we merely reply, "Sez you!"...

[Renan] is partly responsible for the conversion of more than one agnostic, not only to belief from unbelief, but to belief in the Catholic Church; because his arguments lead to one conclusion, and to one conclusion only: namely, that if Christianity is true and has not been proved false by the German higher criticism of biblical texts, then the Catholic Church is its only possible and logical manifestation on earth.[8]

However, while appreciating the strength of the Catholic case, Baring never forgot the various factors, many stemming from ignorance or prejudice, that kept many from embracing it themselves. He expressed this thought to Hilaire Belloc in a letter written in 1916:

Take my advice. Never never talk theology or discuss the Church with those outside it. It is not a subject that can be discussed from the outside. People simply don't understand what one is talking about and they merely (a) get angry, (b) come to the conclusion one doesn't believe in the thing oneself and that one is simply doing it to annoy.[9]

During his own lifetime Baring was a very popular writer who wrote many volumes on a series of topics, summarized by one critic as "novels, plays, anthologies, poetry, memoirs, and reportage." Much of his work is now out of print. His writings on Russia, a country he loved and where he spent much time, are very fine and were a great influence in the increasing popularity of Tolstoy, Dostoevsky, and Chekhov. His two major novels, C (1924) and Cat's Cradle (1925), are well worth reading. Although somewhat superficial in their characterization, they handle Catholic themes with great skill. There is a study of his work by Dame Ethel Smyth, Maurice Baring (1938); a biography by Emma Letley, Maurice Baring: A Citizen of Europe (1991); and a memoir by his friend Laura Lovat (who nursed him during his last illness), Maurice Baring: A Postscript (1947). Baring himself wrote an autobiography, The Puppet Show of Memory (1922). Paul Horgan put together a selection from Baring's writings, Maurice Baring Restored (1970). There is, in addition, a fascinating recent volume comprising a selection of Baring's letters, quoted from earlier, Jocelyn Hillgarth and Julian Jeffs (eds.), Maurice Baring Letters (2007). Several of his letters relating to Catholic themes are included. It also contains his own concise apologia for the Faith, with which it is well to conclude:

8 *Have You Anything to Declare*, 127–34.
9 Hillgarth and Jeffs (ed.), *Maurice Baring Letters*, 115.

Anglicanism seemed to me a lopped branch and ten years in Russia convinced me that the Orthodox Church (more attractive to me outwardly than R. C.dom) was not a lopped but a bent schismatic branch and suffered from that, i.e., instead of one Pope you had a million (State creeping in) and *tout ce qui s'ensuit*. So directly I came to the conclusion *inside* that life was for me divine and that I had inside me an immortal thing in touch with an Eternal Spirit, there was no other course open to me than to become a Catholic.[10]

10   Hillgarth and Jeffs (ed.), *Maurice Baring Letters*, 131–32.

CHAPTER TWENTY-SIX

Robert Speaight

A CONVERT FROM THE STAGE

ROBERT WILLIAM SPEAIGHT, KNOWN TO HIS friends as "Bobby," was born on January 14, 1904, at Corner Cottage, St Margaret's Bay, Kent, England. Both of his parents were fervent Protestants and both of his godfathers were Anglican clergymen. Robert Speaight was brought up in the Tractarian tradition. He was a senior scholar of Haileybury School and a history scholar of Lincoln College, Oxford, graduating in 1926. Already as an undergraduate he was a noted actor at Oxford. Speaight describes himself as being at this time "markedly pagan," but shortly afterwards had an impulse to become a Catholic. He resisted it, "because I feared it was a 'hangover' from Oxford where my closest friends were Catholic and where conversions to Catholicism have always been rather *chic*."[1] After a visit to Bavaria

1   Robert Speaight, *The Property Basket: Recollections of a Divided Life* (1970), 116.

and to the Oberammergau passion play, "I suddenly felt with quite overwhelming force that I wanted to become a Catholic."[2]

Not long afterwards he did indeed become a Catholic, being received on October 31, 1930, by the eminent Jesuit Fr Martin D'Arcy, at Farm Street, London. Of course, Speaight did have contacts with G. K. Chesterton, Christopher Hollis, Compton Mackenzie, and Hilaire Belloc, three of whom were converts. However, the man he most admired was Maurice Baring, another convert, whose story was told in the last chapter.

It may be useful to give an outline of Robert Speaight's adult life. He was a very fine actor indeed. Relatively early on he played leading Shakespearean roles, but the public came to know him best as the creator of Thomas à Becket in the first production of T. S. Eliot's *Murder in the Cathedral*. He was also the principal character in Dorothy L. Sayers' wonderful sequence of radio plays on the life of Christ, *A Man Born to Be King*. His performance as Thomas More in *A Man for All Seasons* is also frequently noted. After publishing four novels, he devoted himself to a second career writing biography and literary criticism and giving lectures. He was remarkably prolific in these fields. His works include a detailed and impressive biography of Belloc in *The Life of Hilaire Belloc* (1957), followed up in the following year by a selection of Belloc's letters. He wrote also on three other Catholic figures, St Thomas of Canterbury (1938), Eric Gill (1966) and Msgr Ronald Knox (1965), the latter book being written with Fr Thomas Corbishley (1903–1976). Speaight wrote several books specifically on theater, including one from a Catholic perspective, *The Christian Theatre* (1960); there is also an earlier work on acting (1939). Then there were several studies of Shakespearian drama (1955, 1973, and 1977) and one on the work of George Eliot (1954). There are also books by him about two great French writers, George Bernanos (1973) and Francois Mauriac (1976), plus a guide book to Burgundy (1975). A very active and creative life indeed! He was in addition visiting professor at several American universities, including the University of Notre Dame. In 1958 he was appointed CBE for his services to literature and the stage. Robert Speaight died on November 2, 1976, at Campion House, near Benenden, Kent.

What were the reasons behind Speaight's conversion? One of the best indications of this is contained in an essay contributed by

2   Ibid., 115.

Speaight to a collection of conversion stories contained in a book edited by Maurice Leahy and published three years after Speaight was received. The essence of Speaight's account is contained in the following passage:

> [The Catholic Church's] body was one; her voice was clear; her dogmas were immutable; her testimony was consistent; her teaching was harmonious.... The choice of the modern world, as it seemed to me, lay between Catholic transcendentalism and a purely Pragmatic materialism of which Communism was the most serious and intelligent example. To these the ecstasies of art, the quest of science, and the fastidious delights of humanism were no proper alternatives; and the Papal claims seemed strictly necessary to ensure the maintenance of true theological belief and the preservation of moral order.[3]

I venture to say that Speaight was living in a time when the Church's voice truly was expressed clearly and authoritatively. We are not so lucky today, when great confusion has arisen among Catholics. I refer to the unanswered *dubia* issued by four cardinals relating to communion for the divorced and re-married, a matter not simply of discipline but involving issues of dogma. A situation where the same thing can be at the same time recommended in Germany and seen as a grave sin in Poland is not one to inspire confidence in a budding convert regarding clarity of voice and immutability of dogma. There is also the diminution in beauty in much of what passes for Catholic liturgy today. In his autobiography, Speaight himself refers to the "ruins of the liturgy"[4] after the Second Vatican Council. However, in respect of all these things, we must not forget that such periods do occur in the history of the Church. As Speaight himself put it in that autobiography:

> It was plainer than the midday sun that Newman was right in seeing mankind involved in some "aboriginal calamity"; and that Baudelaire was right in refusing to recognize progress as anything else but a "diminution of the results of original sin"; and that T. E. Hulme was right in dismissing the aesthetic attractions of Catholicism, such as they were, and in declaring that he could

3 *Conversions to the Catholic Church: A Symposium* (1933).
4 *The Property Basket*, 122.

swallow the décor for the sake of the dogma, not the other way about.[5]

Speaight's apologetic is centrally within the Catholic tradition, as can be seen by his approach to the major doctrines of the faith:

[I] could not see why a dogma which was thought credible yesterday should suddenly be dismissed as incredible today. Either the Resurrection was a fact of history, or it was not. If it happened, it interested me very much; if it did not happen, I was not in the least comforted to regard it as a significant myth.[6]

And this leads naturally into the question of the link between the Incarnation and the Church:

If Christ's promise meant anything should there not be an authority to decide [questions] for me? Either the Church was divided and effective authority was in abeyance; or, as Catholics believed, the Church of Rome was the repository of revealed truth and its divinely inspired interpreter. The claim was a gigantic one, and only the Church of Rome was bold enough to make it. The question therefore was this: Did the Church of Rome, by the coherence of its doctrine, the witness of its saints, the continuity of its tradition and its international character, substantiate this claim?...

That in basic matters of doctrine the Church must be regarded as infallible seems to me now, and even seemed to me then, incontestable.... I was not shocked that a body which prided itself on "proceeding confidently in the doctrine of God" should do so with a certain manifestation of self-confidence....

Once the Incarnation was admitted, I could see no reason to stop short of the Papal claims if these were sensibly interpreted. The Incarnation was the crux—was it conceivable, and was it necessary?[7]

Having established his thesis, Speaight goes on to pull everything together and takes up again the relationship between religion and dogma:

5   Ibid., 128.
6   Ibid., 119-20.
7   Ibid., 120.

The idea that you could have a religion without dogma was as silly as the idea that you could have a car without a carburetor. You could not run your life any more than you could run your car without knowing how the gears worked, and how or when to put on the brakes. Anything that worked was dogmatic. And so the Incarnation, improbable as it might appear and strictly unimaginable as it undoubtedly was, came as the realistic answer to man's infirmity; and in so far as man responded he was cured. This, at least, I did not have to take on trust; it was manifest in history, and in the lives of many I had known.[8]

It is true that in Speaight's autobiography there are occasional signs of what may be characterized as temporary enthusiasms about certain novelties. For example, Speaight went so far as to write a biography of Teilhard de Chardin and took a relatively positive approach to his subject, although he did express several reservations. In addition Speaight made a pretty halfhearted response to the encyclical on birth control, *Humanae Vitae*, as did a number of public figures at the time. If he had seen the way that history has made Pope Paul's teaching seem prophetic in the materialistic and secularist maelstrom that we have had to suffer since—and remember, Speaight was writing back in 1970—I venture to suggest that Robert Speaight today would have aligned himself squarely behind Church teaching.

All in all, Speaight was still a valuable Catholic author and personality. His essay, referred to earlier, on his reasons for his conversion, is excellent, as is the Belloc biography. His other books are well researched and put together. Also, his autobiography is a fascinating account of an age now gone by, and we would do well to value it in several respects. As the entry for Robert Speaight in the *Oxford Dictionary of Biography* (DNB) says, he was "a Catholic intellectual in the great European tradition."

8   Ibid., 128.

CHAPTER TWENTY-SEVEN
Passionate Reason and the Conversion of Algernon Cecil

IT IS SOMETIMES SAID THAT IN THE SEARCH for true love, reason and feelings are opposed. Well, on the subject of conversions to the Catholic Church, it is interesting to reflect on the relationship between reason, albeit directed towards something that may instill an element of passion, and romantic feeling.

There are certainly some converts about whom one can say that a feeling of romance was a contributing factor in the step they took. For example, novelist and poet Gilbert Frankau (1884–1952) became a Catholic in the very last years of his life. The Church of Rome is said to have appealed to the romantic in him.[1] In addition, for the landscape painter Atkinson Grimshaw (1836–1893) it is said that majestic Roman ceremonial (something certainly less readily available today) suited his romanticism. Hopefully, however, both men had solid, reasoned arguments for their entry into the Catholic Church. A mere romantic feeling is not going

1 Hugh Cecil, *The Flower of Battle: British Fiction Writers of the First World War* (1995), 213.

to be enough when difficult times arise in an individual's life and his or her faith comes under threat. As for reason, well, many are the reasons put forward for becoming a Catholic, and different things appeal to different persons. The Catholic faith has a wealth of riches and therefore motivating factors can come in many different forms.

In addition, although the Catholic faith consists of a definitive set of doctrines, and truth does not change, different aspects appeal at different times. If the Church is to go forward, we must identify these. They may come from many directions, but basically they stem from philosophy (reasoned argument) or history. If the convert is to persevere in the faith, then what better foundation can there be but the necessary linking in that person's mind of reason and history with the Mass and Our Lord's Passion? A very good illustration comes from the experience of Algernon Cecil (pronounced "Sissil"), a talented but sadly long-forgotten barrister and writer.

Algernon Cecil was born on January 31, 1879. He was the son of Lord Eustace Cecil, a Conservative politician and a member of Parliament between 1868 and 1885. Algernon's uncle was Robert Gascoyne-Cecil, 3rd Marquess of Salisbury (1830–1903), Prime Minister of the United Kingdom on three occasions. The Cecil family was heavily involved earlier in that act of looting and piracy known as the English Reformation. So there is a touch of irony in this later Cecil being received into the Catholic Church. Furthermore, Algernon Cecil was a cousin of Lords Hugh and Robert Cecil, sons of the 3rd Marquess. Now, these two men were opponents of disestablishment of the Welsh Church from the Anglicans. It was they who drew from Lloyd George the famous taunt in which he reflected on the deeds of their sixteenth-century ancestors:

> Look at the whole story of the pillage of the Reformation. They robbed the Catholic Church, they robbed the monasteries, they robbed the poor, and they robbed the dead. Then they come here when we are trying to seek at any rate to recover part of this pillaged property for the poor, and they venture, with hands dripping with the fat of sacrilege, to accuse us of robbery of God.[2]

2 *Hansard 5C*, 38.1326.

Algernon Cecil converted in 1915, having been instructed by the famous Jesuit Fr Herbert Thurston, by whom he was received into the Church. His sister Blanche (1872–1945) was also received, in 1921.

Algernon Cecil wrote on history, biography, politics, and international relations. His earliest published work was a contribution to the anthology *Five Stuart Princesses: Margaret of Scotland, Elizabeth of Bohemia, Mary of Orange, Henrietta of Orleans, Sophia of Hanover* (1902). This was followed by the study *Six Oxford Thinkers: Edward Gibbon, John Henry Newman, R. W. Church, James Anthony Froude, Walter Pater, Lord Morley of Blackburn* (1909) and then by *Essays in Imitation*, a series of reviews of contemporary culture written in the style of Thomas Carlyle, Jonathan Swift, and Charles Lamb (1910). His insight was such that his utterances were sometimes prophetic. As early as 1925 he had warned in his collected Catholic essays that liberalism and socialism threatened society itself: "Let parents part from one another when they please, and children be advised to think about religion as they like, and the inheritance of property be identified with theft and a whole civilization will be presently put out, and that civilization one that has served us well."[3]

Notable among his output were three biographies: *A Life of Robert Cecil, First Earl of Salisbury* (1915); *A Portrait of Thomas More: Scholar, Statesman, Saint* (1937); and *Metternich, 1773–1859: A Study of His Period and Personality* (1947). He also wrote two books focusing on foreign policy, *British Foreign Secretaries, 1807–1916: Studies in Personality and Policy* (1927) and *Facing the Facts in Foreign Policy: A Retrospect and a Prospect* (1941). Cecil's final work was *Queen Victoria and Her Prime Ministers* (1953).

Algernon Cecil died on April 13, 1953. There is no detailed record of his reasons for becoming a Catholic, although we do know that he converted from the Anglicanism he had adhered to as a student at Oxford University. However, and this is surely relevant to the theme of passionate reason leading to true love, Cecil recounts in his autobiography, *A House in Bryanston Square* (1950), a particular event in which he was involved. He tells of assisting at an Easter Mass at St Peter's in Rome in about 1930. What happened was something that, as he put it, "invited an interpretation of human history far more searching and satisfying than all the rest":

3   *A Dreamer in Christendom: Or What You Will* (1925), 297.

If God continued, according to Pascal's formula, to con-
ceal Himself from prying eyes, St. Peter's bade fair to
betray the secret of His policy. The pressure of historic
circumstances was in fact such that the significance of the
Thing done at Calvary could with difficulty, as it seemed
to me, be concealed from any eye trained to assess political events and consequences. Christ had been lifted up
in Jerusalem; but, if the matter had stopped there, one
might well wonder whether He could in any convincing
sense be said to have drawn all men unto Him.[4]

So, what made the difference? Algernon Cecil brings out the
historical evidence in this way:

It was Christian Rome which had fully understood that
the Eucharist was no mere feast of remembrance but a
continuation of Calvary with both a major and minor
Elevation of the Host implicit in its significance. Here lay
drama more moving than any that the mind of man had
yet come on—drama so touching that, as is well known,
St. Louis was moved to salute it as an act done for love
of him once long ago by One he had never seen.... Here
as elsewhere it would have been well for the world if the
spirit of finesse had been more active. The Mass can be
said, as it has been said, an infinite number of times, but
the event of Calvary quite obviously cannot be repeated.[5]

Cecil is clearly trying to emphasize the incomparable historical
impact of Christ on Calvary. It is all the more remarkable in that
no greater impact has been made on countless people through an
event witnessed by so few, namely Mary Magdalene, then some
other women, next Peter and then the eleven. In order to illustrate
this, and to give it a more philosophical basis, Cecil brings in an
often-cited anecdote. This relates to a remark which Talleyrand,
the laicized Bishop of Autun, politician and diplomat, is supposed
to have addressed to one who thought up a new religion called
"Theophilanthropia." It is said that the poor man found that his
purely intellectual religion failed to make converts, and he complained to Talleyrand, who then gave him the best conceivable
advice. This is set out most concretely in four places by the priest-
physicist Fr Stanley Jaki, who quotes Talleyrand as saying, "If you

4   *A House in Bryanston Square*, 339.
5   Ibid.

want to make converts perform miracles. Cure the sick, revive the dead, allow yourself to be crucified and rise on the third day."[6] Algernon Cecil astutely uses this story to make his point:

> Talleyrand's Voltairean advice to the enterprising rev-olutionary who proposed to invent a new religion and inquired how best to begin is here in point. The Bishop, formerly of Autun, blandly recommended that Sieyès (if Sieyès it was[7]) should get himself crucified and rise again

6 Jaki, *God and the Sun at Fatima* (1999), 65; "The Catholic Intellectual," in *The Gist of Catholicism and Other Essays* (2001), 28–29; *Science and Religion: A Primer*, 21–22; *The Litany of the Sacred Heart* (2006), 132.

7 The Theophilanthropists were a deistic sect formed in France during the later part of the French Revolution. The sect was set up by Thomas Paine with other disciples of Rousseau and Robespierre. John-Baptiste Chemin wrote the *Manuel des Théoanthropophiles*. The Convention gave them the use of the church of St Catherine in Paris. The sect developed slowly until Louis Marie de La Révellière-Lépeaux, an influential member of the Directory and bitterly hostile to Christianity, acted on its behalf. After the Revolution of 18 Fructidor it was given some of the great churches of Paris, including Notre Dame de Paris. In spite of opposition from Catholics and other groups, it became very influential with the masses. The Catholic reaction came from Pope Pius VII, who on May 17, 1800, placed an interdict on the churches that had been desecrated by the deistic rites. In addition, Cardinal Consalvi, during the negotiations regarding the Concordat of 1801, demanded that a quick end should be put to the profanation of the Catholic churches. The sect was brought to an end by the Directory when the First Consul set his face against it. Later attempts to revive it were unsuccessful.

Algernon Cecil refers to the Abbé Emmanuel Joseph Sieyès. He was a Cath-olic priest, but was one of the chief political theorists of the French Revolution, and also played a prominent role in the French Consulate and First French Empire. His 1789 pamphlet *What Is the Third Estate?* became the manifesto of the Revolution. He was indeed a supporter of the Theophilanthropists. However, he is not usually named as the recipient of the advice given by Talleyrand. That is usually identified as Louis Marie de La Révellière-Lépeaux, although some sources have Talleyrand speaking to a group belonging to the sect. Whether, in fact, the advice was given, and if so to whom, is not certain. This story is usually told without any citation. I first came across it when reading the works by Fr Stanley Jaki referred to in the previous note. Fr Jaki, with whom I worked for several years, was a stickler for correct referencing, but even he gave none here. In fact, a search of the Internet on the subject of Talleyrand and the Theophilanthropists reveals an article by the English lawyer and phi-losopher Sir James Fitzjames Stephen, "The Unknowable and the Unknown," published in 1884 in the periodical *Nineteenth Century*. There Stephen states that the anecdote attributed to Talleyrand is to be found in François Guizot's book *Méditations sur L'Essence de la Religion Chrétien*, giving 1864 as the date of publication, but a search of that book revealed no such account there. However, there is an account of the Talleyrand incident in the second edition of the

the third day, and thus incidentally said the last word upon all subsequent projects of new religions.[8]

The last phrase is the crucial one and it reveals that aspect of the theme of love that emphasizes its overwhelming importance, whether stemming from romantic feelings or passionate reason. Cecil concludes movingly:

> There will be no successor to Christianity, if only because Love can no further go.... The Great Lover has come, has been raised to the Cross and will be sacramentally in agony until the end of the world. No man can steal the genius of that drama from Him, nor substitute another in its place.[9]

Fr Jaki comments that Talleyrand's remark should be "engraved over the entrance of all departments of 'Christian' theology where each new set of faculty starts all over the business of reinventing the Church according to ever-new molds of intellectual fancies."[10] He is thinking of the doctrinal uncertainty in the Church over the last fifty years or so, and his warning includes both those Christians who want to be catholic though not Catholic, those who "advocate the liberty of choosing from the catholic banquet table according to one's own preferences, and if necessary or desirable, not to feed on items that smack of Catholicism."[11] As the litany of the Sacred Heart puts it, "*Cor Jesu, vita et resurrectio nostra*" (Heart of Christ, our life and resurrection). Algernon Cecil's own conclusion reinforces the need to hold on to the traditional faith.

---

book, which was published in 1866, where it is related as follows: "*Je n'ai qu'une observation à vous faire lui dit M. Talleyrand qu'il entretenait de son plan: Jésus-Christ, pour fonder sa religion, a été crucifié et est ressuscité. Vous devriez tâcher d'en faire autant.*" Guizot gives no further authority for the statement in his book, but does identify Louis Marie de La Révellière-Lépeaux as Talleyrand's interlocutor. Stephen's version in English is quite close to that of Guizot: "Gentlemen [presumably this refers to a group of Theophilanthropists], when Jesus Christ established a new religion he found it necessary to be crucified, dead, and buried, and to rise again the third day from the dead; go and do likewise, and your religion will be worth discussing." Of course, whether the words were said or not makes no difference to the point being made, which is a powerful one.

(Many thanks to my good friend Antonio Colombo for help in finding all the references in this footnote.)

8   *A House in Bryanston*, 339.
9   Ibid.
10   *The Gist of Catholicism and Other Essays*, 29.
11   Ibid.

CHAPTER TWENTY-EIGHT
Katherine Brégy

CONVERSION AND CATHOLICIZING LITERARY CULTURE

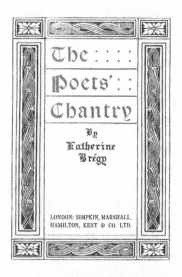

AN INTERNET SEARCH FOR REFERENCES TO Katherine Brégy brings up very little of significance, comprising for the most part brief references to a few of her books. At one time she was very well known in the United States. Undoubtedly her work has fallen into neglect. However, one can still find positive evaluations of her and, of course, a writer's public reputation can depend merely on the vagaries of fashion. The major emphasis should be upon the reasons for Katherine's conversion to the Catholic faith and her contributions to Catholic culture, which were substantial.

First, a biographical outline. Katherine Marie Cornelia Brégy was born in 1882 in Philadelphia. She had French and Irish Catholic ancestors, but her parents were Protestant and she was brought up used to a "dignified, moderately 'high' Episcopal ritual."[1] She

1   Essay in Curtis (ed.), *Beyond the Road to Rome*, 59.

was educated at the University of Pennsylvania. Katherine Brégy remained unmarried for the whole of her life and died in 1967.

Briefly, then, on the literary aspects of her work. She wrote much poetry and prose (the majority of the latter being literary criticism) for both British and American journals. She was elected president of the Catholic Poetry Society of America in 1939. In respect of poetry, leaving aside her own work, much of which is contained in *Bridges with Other Verse in Varying Moods* (1930) and in *Ladders and Bridges: A Book of Verse* (1936), she assisted in a very significant way the revival of the poetry of Gerard Manley Hopkins and wrote appreciations of the poetry of Joyce Kilmer, Francis Thompson, and Robert Southwell. A notable achievement was that in the mid-1920s she won a *Commonweal* competition prize of a thousand dollars for a five-thousand-word essay on Dante. She also wrote *Queen of Paradox: A Stuart Tragedy* (1950), a novel about Mary Queen of Scots. Her main prose works are *Poets and Pilgrims: From Geoffrey Chaucer to Paul Claudel* (1925), *From Dante to Jeanne d'Arc: Adventures in Medieval Life and Letters* (1933),[2] and *The Story of Saint Francis de Sales: Patron of Catholic Writers* (1958).

Now to the question of Katherine's conversion. Thankfully, she wrote about this in some detail in an essay contributed to Georgina Pell Curtis's *Beyond the Road to Rome* (1914). This volume consists primarily of accounts by converts of their experience within the Church, though several contributors, including Katherine, discuss what brought them into the Church in the first place. Katherine's account of her conversion is a fascinating piece of work and should be read in full. It is available at no cost on archive.org. What follows here deals with the essentials of the case she sets out. To begin with, it is clear that Katherine was attracted early by Catholicism; she refused to be confirmed in the Protestant Episcopal Church. It seems that it was not so much intellectual considerations that turned her mind to the Catholic Church, but, as happens in so many cases, brief contacts with other aspects of this venerable and ever-powerful force. She expresses what is in essence the mystery of grace:

> Theoretically, at least, the Church idea was not new to
> me. Then somehow—I cannot say whether it was through

2   The competition winning essay is reprinted there as "Dante's Dream of Life."

constantly passing a hospital of the Sisters of Charity, or
through dipping into the Memoirs of Mme. Navarro [the
actress Mary Anderson, a devout Catholic, who was also
billed as Mary Navarro during her silent film career and
whose memoirs, *A Few Memories*, were published in 1896],
or through accidentally hearing a description of the office
of *Tenebrae*—I woke up to the fact that this Church idea
was still a vital force in the world. I was just a school-girl
at the time: I had never been through a convent or spoken
to a priest in my life. But the immensity of the thought
did certainly arrest me. That simple linking of past and
present was so vivid, so majestic, so incredibly thrilling![3]

What did she do next? The answer will be a familiar one to
many converts. It involves an element of secrecy and romance,
culminating in assurance and a credible voice of authority.

I did not talk much about the subject (never being able
to talk of deep things without a certainty of sympathy in
the listeners), but I began to read. First it was every scrap
of Catholic news in the daily papers, the magazines, the
encyclopedias—prolific sources, if dubious! Then, like a
thief in the night, I stole off to a little Catholic bookshop,
where I happened very fortunately upon the *Baltimore
Catechism* and Father di Bruno's *Catholic Belief*. I was more
interested in these than (even!) in the Shakespearian dra-
mas in which I had immersed myself for months before.
Considering my age, I think I was abnormally interested!
I suspect I gave my first romantic love to that venerable,
tangible, mystical thing known as Catholicism. I had been
accustomed to a very "respectable" religion: here I found
sanctity and the seven deadly sins. I had been used to the
compromises of Anglicanism: here I found one "speaking
with authority, and not as the scribes."[4]

With regard to Fr di Bruno's marvelous little book, nothing could
be more concisely compelling than his citation of St. Augustine's
powerful argument for the central truth of the Christian religion:

St. Augustine argues thus: Either the Resurrection happened or it did not. If it did, then we have all the proof
we need. If it did not, then the Apostles preached a lie

3 Curtis (ed.), *Beyond the Road to Rome*, 59.
4 Ibid., 59-60.

and the world accepted. But that would itself be a miracle, that twelve such men should impose the doctrinally difficult and the morally hard principles of Christianity on all sorts of men, in the teeth of their passion and pride, in virtue of a supposed event which men knew could not possibly happen.[5]

Katherine Brégy obviously found this period of her life to be fascinating, "a great joy, this secret of mine."[6] As Patrick Allitt puts it, "she channeled her emotional energy into the Church itself and wrote about her approach to conversion in the language of romantic love."[7]

However, the next stage in the process was not so pleasant. It is part of the process that will also be familiar to many converts. As she put it, "the pearl had its price.... I drew the traditional storm upon my head. It was quite electrical for a while."[8] The storm came from the family pastor, who called and talked vaguely about the Forged Decretals! (The Forged Decretals, sometimes referred to as the False Decretals, refer to a number of documents alleged to be written by early popes, but forged in the ninth century by an author using the pseudonym of Isidore Mercator. Anti-Catholic apologists often claim that Catholic doctrines on the primacy and infallibility of the pope are founded upon them.) In addition, other well-meaning folk brought her books in which "all the vile accusations of nineteen hundred years were gathered together against the 'Scarlet Woman.'"[9] Fortunately Katherine's own reading served her well:

> I had read my New Testament rather attentively, and the charges sounded familiar. The Christ of Galilee and Jerusalem had been called seducer and liar and worldling and blasphemer, I seemed to remember; St. Peter was charged with tyranny and St. Paul had to defend himself against preaching that the end justified the means.[10]

Katherine found comfort in these cases, but she goes on to acknowledge that the real historic scandals of the Church, of which

5 *Catholic Belief* (1957), 3.
6 Curtis (ed.), *Beyond the Road to Rome*, 60.
7 *Catholic Converts: British and American Intellectuals Turn to Rome*, 141.
8 Curtis (ed.), *Beyond the Road to Rome*, 60.
9 Ibid., 60–61.
10 Ibid., 61.

she was aware, hurt her bitterly. She responded with prayer, but once again her reading was a source of assistance:

> I had to remember the apostles once again—and the pitiful earthen vessel which bore the Treasure age after age. It was a lesson I needed to learn: that everything had happened before and might happen again; and still Mother Church would travel on, clothed with the sanctity of God and the frailty of man—infallible yet nowise impeccable—"doing the King's work all the dim day long" [a quotation from Robert Browning's poem "How It Strikes a Contemporary"]. To apprehend this early in the religious life saved me, I think, from that sorry disease of "taking scandal" which so often afflicts the newly received.[11]

It was during what she calls "those troubled days"[12] that she first began to read Cardinal Newman, "perhaps the strongest literary influence of my life."[13] It was Newman who moved her on from a position that was essentially emotional, though giving a good grasp of the faith, to one that made her an able expounder of the rational arguments supporting the Catholic position:

> His keenness of thought, his lucidity of form, his snow-white elevation of soul enchanted me. I literally sat at the great Oratorian's feet for a year and a half, and while reading the *Apologia* I was as conscious of his personality as of any actual living friend. He made faith an intellectual rather than an emotional thing to me. He taught me conclusively that Catholicism was the true Church of the Past; and I stood quite ready to burn my bridges on the strength of "development" and Patristic testimonies....[14]

Katherine's parents objected to her becoming a Catholic, but consented later. As a result she was received into the Church on May 27, 1904 by the widely influential Paulist priest Fr John Burke (1875–1936), editor of the *Catholic World* from 1903 to 1922. She expressed in no uncertain terms her gratitude for having taken this step:

11 Ibid.
12 Ibid.
13 Ibid.
14 Ibid., 61–62.

I should like to record ... that this is the only step of my entire life about which I have never had any subsequent misgiving. I have never, in moments of the most searching introspection, questioned its wisdom. I could have said that fair spring day with Sydney Carton (and quite as truthfully): "It is a far, far better thing that I do than I have ever done—It is a far, far better rest that I go to than I have ever known." [15]

Finally, some thoughts on Katherine Brégy's contribution to Catholic culture. Here there is a clear link with the writings of another American woman, the historian Elizabeth Sarah Kite, whose efforts to uncover a crucial Catholic element of American history have been dealt with earlier in this book. Patrick Allitt explains the relevance of this for the current context:

> What Kite had attempted for American history, Brégy attempted for English and American literature, arguing that its explicitly Protestant character was really no more than a thin covering over sturdy Catholic timbers and that all the really inspiring elements of post-Reformation literature could be traced to the old faith.... Brégy maintained that *Pilgrim's Progress*, though undeniably the work of a Protestant, owed what strengths it had to Bunyan's familiarity with the great Catholic tradition.... "In the light of present-day vagaries the Catholic reader is often surprised to note the orthodoxy of these seventeenth-century dissenters—their hold upon Christ, upon the Holy Trinity, and many cardinal points of faith." Even so, she emphasized, the Reformation had impoverished the tradition of Christian allegory, so that "one turns back with a sigh to the wholesome, unstudied sanity of pre-Reformation standards." [16]

Katherine Brégy stated that her life was dedicated to "an appreciation of Catholic poetry as the beauty of holiness." [17] In addition, this appreciation of the Catholic element in literature is combined with an appreciation of Catholicity through history. Katherine brings this out in the course of a visit to Europe, something which also reinforced her commitment to Catholicism:

15   Ibid., 63.
16   *Catholic Converts: British and American Intellectuals Turn to Rome*, 142.
17   "Of Poets and Poetry," *Catholic World*, February 1939, 525.

Some five years after becoming a Catholic, I paid my first visit to the Old World I had long so passionately loved. This again was very much like going home, and my citizenship in the Church Catholic proved in a new sense a citizenship of the World. More poignantly than ever was I aware of my kinship with the past. I felt it, kneeling at the tomb of Peter or gathering poppies along the Appian Way. I felt it in the high seriousness of Oberammergau, in the beautiful, tragic triviality of Versailles, in the chateau-fort of my school-time hero, Godfrey de Bouillon. In the mysterious gloom of Notre Dame de Paris it enveloped me—nor was it far away in the noble, outraged shrines of old Westminster.... [18]

Katherine's visit undoubtedly had a great influence on her, bringing a new quality to her religion and her "whole mental and spiritual viewpoint." [19] There was an aspect not only of Catholicity, but also of aesthetics and a common inheritance:

For one thing, the ancestral note had been accentuated— I was less a convert than ever before. I had absorbed something of that curious toleration of the Romance nations, and something of their hunger after beauty. Beyond all this, a sense of the largeness and fullness of life possessed me. One phase of this was an exhilarating, almost intoxicating delight in the enormous heritage of culture which is, as it were, the birthright of every child of historic Christendom. To find Catholicity, then, means more even than to find religion: we may save the soul (if we can) and the mind, too, by her immemorial wisdom! It is a heartening thing to feel that we reap not only where the martyrs have sown in blood but where the doctors have sown in brain—where Dante and Chaucer and the Troubadours have sung—where the Tuscans and Umbrians, the Spanish and Flemish have wrought their rainbow canvases—even where, century after century, the French have talked so exquisitely. [20]

A further inspiration to her was that "the great universities of Europe were as authentically our own as the great cathedrals" [21]

18 Curtis (ed.), *Beyond the Road to Rome*, 71–72.
19 Ibid., 72.
20 Ibid., 72–73.
21 Ibid., 73.

247

THE HOUSE WITH A HUNDRED GATES

and that "under normal conditions Catholicity stands committed not to ignorance, not even to mediocrity, but to culture of the entire spirit."[22]

Summing up, then, she refers to the distinction sometimes made to the effect that the Dominican ideal placed Truth as the highest Love, while the Franciscan placed Love as the highest Truth. To Katherine, "Beauty becomes ... the synthesis of this Truth and this Love; and the beauty of holiness becomes the last word in religion. It is the leaven which permeates the whole mass of Christian life—the key to that wisdom which 'stretches from end to end mightily and orders all things sweetly' [Wisdom 8:1]."[23] It is important here to state, as Katherine does, that "Beauty is not merely a sensuous thing; although certainly the sensuous side—the delight of color and music and form and movement—is not to be despised. Nor is it wholly an intellectual thing, nor absolutely a moral thing. It is an all-embracing sense of the harmony of life, reaching up to God as the primal Artist, the first and final source of 'whatsoever things are lovely' [Philippians 4:8]. I do not hesitate to affirm that my own religion has become increasingly a worship of Beauty—and that Beauty seems to me the most satisfying synonym for God Himself."[24]

When one reads the writings of Katherine Brégy, one is saddened by the neglect of her work today. Her account of her conversion to the one true faith, her Catholicizing of literature, and her efforts to reconcile the claims of emotion and intellect are all worthy of a contemporary audience.

22 Ibid.
23 Ibid., 74.
24 Ibid.

CHAPTER TWENTY-NINE

How Two Jane Austen Admirers Came to the Catholic Church

Sheila Kaye-Smith	*G. B. Stern*

GOOD, QUIET AUNT JANE

It is not an easy task to write on Jane Austen from a Catholic perspective. One might well do so from the perspective of Christianity generally. A very good summary of this aspect of Austen is given by Dr Peter Mullen in an article commemorating the bicentenary of her death at the age of forty-one.[1] The title given to the article is perceptive: "Jane Austen was Low Church but she had high religious ideals."

Jane was the daughter of a clergyman, George Austen, "a devout and faithful country parson who lived among his people and cared for them."[2] Her brother was also a clergyman. Mullen recounts how Jane and her sisters sewed and provided clothes for the local poor. A related point should be emphasized: "It's worth noting that she was granted burial in the north aisle in Winchester Cathedral not on account of her undoubted literary

1   *Catholic Herald*, July 18, 2017.
2   Ibid.

249

stature—for she published her novels anonymously—but because of her charitable work in the local churches."[3] As Peter Mullen goes on to say, there is nothing in Jane Austen of George Eliot's "sensual enthusiasm for the Methodist revival" or Dickens' "sentimentalization of Christianity": "She was not the sort of Protestant who protests against anything. She was Low Church: the common sense and very English version of Christianity summed up by the words 'Do as you would be done by.'"[4] Throughout her novels "she shows a benign affection for the Church of England, which in her day was the dominant presence in the countryside,"[5] and Mullen gives several examples of a Christian moral response in her characters "as the best means of attaining to the life worth living."[6] However, and this is a significant truth, "she had little understanding of how hard it was to be a Catholic in England in her day, and she died twelve years before the Catholic Emancipation Act of 1829."[7]

So, how does this fit in with the question of conversion to the Catholic faith and Church? Well, if Jane Austen did not come to Catholicism, one can at the very least take a look at two Catholic converts who co-authored two fine analyses of the writings of Jane Austen, the friends Sheila Kaye-Smith and Gladys Bertha Stern (the latter known as "Bronwyn" and who wrote under the name G. B. Stern). The first of their books is *Talking of Jane Austen*, published in 1943 (some versions are published under the title *Speaking of Jane Austen*). This work was followed by *More Talk of Jane Austen* in 1950. Curiously, this book also appears on occasions under another title, this time *More about Jane Austen*.

These two women explore the novels of Jane Austen in some detail. Space precludes doing the same in their cases, and of course their merits as novelists, which both were, are nowhere near as great as those of "good, quiet Aunt Jane," as Austen was called by her first biographers. However, Kaye-Smith and Stern, especially the former, are of great value to those looking for reasons for an individual's conversion to the Catholic Church, and it is this aspect that we are to examine.

3   Ibid.
4   Ibid.
5   Ibid.
6   Ibid.
7   Ibid.

G.B. STERN

Gladys Bronwyn Stern, born Gladys Bertha Stern and known as G. B. Stern, was born in London on June 17, 1890. She wrote nearly fifty novels, plus short stories and plays, two biographies, film scripts, and much journalism. Having to leave her on the sidelines is disappointing as she wrote an excellent book, *All In Good Time* (1954), telling the story of her conversion culminating in her reception into the Church in 1947. However, her account is so personal as not to be generally applicable to converts. She also had a tendency to wander off-topic when her curiosity took over! Having said that, one cannot leave her without sharing the following anecdote contained in a later book in which she gives an account of her early years within the fold of the Catholic Church. She had been introduced to a woman of "the Modern School of Thought" who proceeded to deride prayer and religion generally:

> I should like ... to have achieved a twist in space, and included our young realist among a crowd heckling Frank Sheed at the Catholic Evidence Guild one wet and windy Sunday evening on a street-corner in Liverpool; "If I couldn't make a better world than God, I'd be ashamed!" shouted a burly opponent. And Mr. Sheed turned to him and said, oh so winningly, on such a coaxing note: "Make us a rabbit now, just to establish confidence!" And the heckler oozed away.[8]

Delightful!

SHEILA KAYE-SMITH

So, onto Sheila Kaye-Smith, who was born on February 4, 1887, at St Leonards-on-Sea, Sussex, England. Her father was a doctor. She was privately educated and brought up as an Evangelical. Later on she became a High Church Anglican, referring to herself as Anglo-Catholic, about which she wrote *Anglo-Catholicism* (1925). She is best known for her novels about Sussex, gaining the moniker "the storyteller of the Sussex Weald." Her writings reflect an interest in questions of religious faith and include, besides novels (perhaps the most notable being *Joanna Godden* [1921] and *The End of the House of Alard* [1923]), ballads, plays, stories,

8   *The Way It Worked Out* (1956), 30–31.

and criticism. She married Sir Penrose Fry (1892–1970), a High Anglican clergyman, in 1924. Kaye-Smith was received (together with her husband) into the Catholic Church in October 1929 by the great Jesuit Fr Cyril Martindale (1879–1963), also a convert, at Farm Street, London.

After her conversion she wrote a number of novels on Catholic themes, notably *Superstition Corner* (1934) and *Gallybird* (1934). Kaye-Smith was influenced by the example of St Thérèse, but became a Tertiary of the Order of St Dominic. Her house, Little Doucegrove, was later owned by Rumer Godden (1907–1998), another convert novelist. Sheila Kaye-Smith died at her home on January 14, 1956. She was buried beside her husband in the grounds of St Thérèse of Lisieux church, Little Doucegrove, which she and her husband had built for the Catholics in that area. She was buried in her Dominican tertiary's habit, her rosary in her hands.

Sheila Kaye-Smith cited three main reasons for her conversion. The first emphasizes her move away from High Anglicanism based on her acknowledgement that the Anglican Church had broken away from the Catholic Church and could not be seen as a branch of that body. In her spiritual autobiography, *Three Ways Home: An Experiment in Autobiography* (1937), she is very frank about her belief even during her Anglo-Catholic period, noting that "four hundred years ago the Catholic religion was forcibly suppressed in this country."[9] Here is how she sets out in a very direct fashion the problem that arose for her. This is contained in an essay, available in several different collections of conversion stories:

> Once one conceives the Church as a living personality, it is impossible to see it divided and yet remaining alive. The hand cannot say to the foot: "I have no need of thee." My branch theory would not work once I saw the Church no longer as a mere organization but as the living Body of Christ.[10]

The second factor was something that altered her attitude to the Catholic Church rather than prompting her conversion. It

9 *Three Ways Home*, 183.
10 Maurice Leahy (ed.), *Conversions to the Catholic Church* (1933). Reprinted as "Unadulterated Catholicism," in Severin and Stephen Lamping, OFM (ed.), *Through Hundred Gates* (1939), 67; and as "Only One Thing to Do" in John A. O'Brien (ed.), *The Road to Damascus* (1949), 228.

was the effect of a visit with her husband to Sicily in September 1928 and the impact of the fundamental difference in practical application between Catholicism and Anglicanism:

> We arrived in Palermo and visited the cathedral.... It was full of the population of the city hearing Mass..., being baptized, getting married, saying its prayers, talking, resting or walking about. It was, in fact, a spiritual version of the streets of Palermo.
>
> We found it impossible to keep comparisons with Anglican cathedrals out of our minds. These certainly are not a spiritual version of the cities in which they stand, but something select and apart, museums rather than market-places they stand; frequented chiefly by tourists, except for rare intervals when religion comes in and the tourists go out.[11]

Sheila Kaye-Smith began to see the superiority of the Catholic Church as essentially spiritual, and the appeal it made "was to that wider Catholicity which concerns not only dogma but sex, class and temperament, a democracy of the spirit."[12] In addition, she learned at Palermo that she definitely belonged to the Church of England at this point, and that the Anglo-Catholic mindset was a curious rationalizing process by which certain people ranged themselves in opposition to the body with which they were factually in communion.

It was undoubtedly the spiritual appeal of the Catholic Church that Sheila Kaye-Smith had come to find overwhelming. At this stage it came through the life of St Thérèse of Lisieux, whose canonization had just taken place, only thirty years after her death. Kaye-Smith describes it in her autobiography:

> It is difficult to describe the impression this young saint made upon me. It was not only the beauty of her life, the charm, wit, and sweetness of her recorded words or the lovely simplicities of her Little Way. It was rather the realization of that sanctity, that heroic virtue, that sublime love, being offered to the modern world. Here was a saint who, if she had been alive today, would scarcely have been old—a saint of our times, showing the world that the

11 *Three Ways Home*, 207.
12 Ibid., 213.

> *Acta Sanctorum* is no closed book, no worn papyrus of the
> Early Church or illuminated tome of the Middle Ages,
> but an up-to-date serial illustrated with photographs.[13]

In an article published in 1930 with a very appropriate title for
one converting from Anglo-Catholicism, "Dropping the Hyphen:
A Story of a Conversion," she repeated the first part of this passage, referring now to "this saint of our time whose features and
expression have been given us, not only by the painter and ecclesiastical image-maker, but by the photographer," and concluded
by further emphasizing the point at hand:

> In Lisieux are still living men and women who knew her
> and spoke to her, including her own sisters; her can-
> onization miracles were not found in documents or in
> tradition, but on the lips of living witnesses. And when
> I looked at her I saw not merely myself, but the living,
> unfailing fountain of sanctity which is the Church that
> made her what she was.[14]

Sheila Kaye-Smith contrasted that with the position in the
Church of England, where "one is given the impression that sanctity
as well as miracles came to an end with the early Church. The
Anglican Calendar is astonishingly poor and bare; it was drastically
cleared after the Reformation, and no name has since been added
to it (with the doubtful and disputed exception of King Charles I),
till the Revised Prayer Book cautiously inserted a few commem-
orations, the latest of which is some five hundred years old."[15]
She discusses the process of saint-making, bringing out very
powerfully the logic of the Catholic Church:

> I shall naturally be told that Sanctity is not an affair
> of the Calendar, and if the Church of England has no
> official saints later than the twelfth century, it does not
> follow that she fails to encourage or to recognize holi-
> ness, but merely that she does not record and publish it.
> To which one simply retorts: Why not? Presumably a
> Church's greatest glory is her holiness, and her holiness
> is the holiness of her members. It seems strange that

13 Ibid., 217–18.
14 "Dropping the Hyphen," *Dublin Review*, 1930; reprinted as *Dropping the Hyphen: A Story of a Conversion* (Catholic Truth Society, 1938 and 1941).
15 *Three Ways Home*, 218.

she should ignore and suppress her achievements in the only field where success is really worthwhile. One cannot imagine a country that should ignore its great men, its heroes, its poets, its philosophers and scientists. If one were inconceivably to hear of such a country, one would conclude either that it had no great men, or, worse still, that it was indifferent to their merits.[16]

Finally, she brings all the previous themes together:

I was disturbed by the holiness of Rome—or rather, I should say, by the fact that I was cut off from it. This surely was the heart and blackness of schism. I was cut off from the Altar of the Saints—of St. Thérèse of Lisieux, of St. Teresa of Avila, of St. John of the Cross, of St. John Vianney, and all the rest of that great cloud of witnesses—just as I was cut off from the altar of the people—the people of Palermo, Preston, Peking, every part of the world where the Catholic Church draws together all classes, colors and races. I was cut off, not by any personal conviction but because I belonged to a Church which had deliberately cut itself off four hundred years ago.[17]

Sheila Kaye-Smith combines both doctrinal reflection and the practical pursuit of the spiritual life. Her writings were neglected for some time following her death, but there has been a resurgence of interest in her. This is characterized by the formation in 1987 of the Sheila Kaye-Smith Society, and the publication of a biography in 2017, *The Shining Cord of Sheila Kaye-Smith*, by Shaun Cooper. In addition, there is much interesting information about her on the Internet. Finally, her husband Penrose Fry also wrote an account of his own conversion, containing much food for thought, in his book *The Church Surprising* (1932) and in his own essay for the Leahy Symposium referred to earlier.

16   Ibid., 218–19.
17   Ibid., 219.

CHAPTER THIRTY
The Story of Bella Dodd

FROM CATHOLICISM TO COMMUNISM AND BACK AGAIN

SEVERAL OF THE PERSONS WHOSE CONVERSION is related in this book were originally Communists or Communist sympathizers. One such is Bella Dodd, who took the step into the Catholic Church after being caught up in the awful legacy of the Soviet Union.

Bella Dodd was born Maria Assunta Isabella Visono in October 1904 in Picerno, Basilicata, southeast of Naples, Italy. From her maiden name and her place of origin one can perhaps conclude already that we are not talking here about a convert, but about a "revert." By this is meant someone who was a cradle Catholic and lost the faith, but eventually came back to it. But more about that later.

Bella was the youngest in a family of ten children. The rest of the family had moved to the United States when her mother had to return to Italy to deal with problems relating to her farm there. Bella was born during that trip and spent her first five years there with foster parents before going to the United States. She was indeed brought up in the Catholic faith, but then rejected it. Hardship came to her very early, since at the age of twelve she was involved in a trolley car accident, necessitating the amputation of her left foot.

Bella was educated at Hunter College, New York, and had clear impressions of this period in her life:

> Since we had no common basis of belief, we drifted into laissez-faire thinking, with agnosticism for our religion and pragmatism for our philosophy.... We had no real goals because we had no sound view of man's nature and destiny. We had feelings and emotions, but no standards by which to chart the future.[1]

She then did graduate work in political science at Columbia University and in 1930 received the Doctor of Jurisprudence degree from New York University. In the same year she married John Dodd, but this ended in divorce in 1943. In 1931 she was admitted to the New York State bar. She taught political science at Hunter College from 1935 to 1944.

On the political front, Bella was active in several labor organizations and a leader in the Communist Party of America (CPUSA) in the 1930s and 1940s. However, she became disillusioned by her experience with Communism (especially the purges of members and personal attacks she faced) and broke with the party, resulting in her formal expulsion. She eventually converted to the Catholic Church. She was influenced in her reading by St Augustine and by St Thomas Aquinas, but most notably by the witness of Fulton Sheen, who welcomed her into the Church at St Patrick's Cathedral, New York, on April 7, 1952.

What brought this woman of strong beliefs back to Holy Mother Church? She explained in most detail primarily in two places, her book *School of Darkness: The Record of a Life and of a Conflict between Two Faiths* (1954) and her article "I Found Sanctuary," in one of Fr John A. O'Brien's five collections of conversion stories, *The Road to Damascus, Vol. IV: Roads to Rome* (1955).

1 *School of Darkness: The Record of a Life and of a Conflict between Two Faiths* (1954), 28ff.

The first book gives a powerful account of the evolution of Bella Dodd's thought. A key factor for Bella was what she referred to as "this cataloguing of people" as either "right" or "left." She believed this to have led to "more confusion in American life than perhaps any other false concept," something which today one can apply with a good degree of truth to the Church. To stick to the purely political issue, however, Bella believed that this dichotomy sounded so simple and so right, but contained a dangerous trap:

> By using this schematic device one puts the communists on the left and then one regards them as advanced liberals—after which it is easy to regard them as the enzyme necessary for progress.
>
> Communists usurp the position of the left, but when one examines them in the light of what they really stand for, one sees them as the rankest kind of reactionaries and communism as the most reactionary backward leap in the long history of social movements. It is one which seeks to obliterate in one revolutionary wave two thousand years of man's progress.[2]

Working on from this, Bella began to see that there were many things that she had not really understood:

> I had regarded the Communist Party as a poor man's party, and thought the presence of certain men of wealth within it accidental. I now saw this was no accident. I regarded the Party as a monolithic organization with the leadership in the National Committee and the National Board. Now I saw this was only a facade placed there by the movement to create the illusion of the poor man's party; it was in reality a device to control the "common man" they so raucously championed.[3]

What Bella Dodd realized was that "with the best motives and a desire to serve the working people of my country" she, and many like her, had been led to "a betrayal of these very people." Unwittingly she had been on the side of those who sought the destruction of her own country:

2   Ibid., 40.
3   Ibid., 228.

What now became clear to me was the collusion of these two forces: the Communists with their timetable for world control, and certain mercenary forces in the free world bent on making profit from blood. But I was alone with these thoughts and had no opportunity to talk over my conclusions with friends.[4]

Fortunately for Bella, she went to Washington early in the fall of 1950 and ran into an old friend, the congressional representative of the old East Bronx area of her childhood, Christopher McGrath. The latter was clearly concerned, believing that, given her developing views, she was potentially in danger and offered FBI protection, which she refused. He said he would pray for her safety. From the viewpoint of divine providence, what happened next is of great interest and much credit is due to Christopher McGrath. She tells how he looked at her for a moment as if he wanted to say something else. Then he put what turned out to be the crucial question: "'Bella, would you like to see a priest?' Startled by the question, I was amazed at the intensity with which I answered, 'Yes, I would.' 'Perhaps we can reach Msgr Sheen at Catholic University,' he said."[5] An appointment was made for her late that same evening at the Msgr's home. One can imagine her feelings on the journey there. She expresses herself as having been assailed by a thousand fears. Many of them related to the natural fear that Sheen might insist on her seeing the FBI, with the possibility of having to testify against her erstwhile colleagues in the Communist Party. Would he see her at all? This was a traumatic time in the political life of the United States.

For us, however, of more relevance are her thoughts on the religious issue. She gives expression to some of these:

> All the canards against the Catholic Church which I had heard and tolerated, which even by my silence I had approved, were threatening the tiny flame of longing for faith within me. I thought of many things on that ride, of the word "fascist," used over and over by the communist press in describing the role of the Church in the Spanish Civil War. I also thought of the word "Inquisition" so skillfully used on all occasions. Other

4   Ibid., 229–30.
5   Ibid., 231.

terms came to me—reactionary, totalitarian, dogmatic, old-fashioned. For years they had been used to engender fear and hatred in people like me.[6]

Putting the political thoughts together with the religious ones, she began to see the dramatic nature of the position she could soon be in:

> And then before my mind's eye flashed the cover of a communist pamphlet on which was a communist extending a hand to a Catholic worker. The pamphlet was a reprint of a speech by the French Communist leader [Maurice] Thorez and it flattered the workers by not attacking their religion. It skillfully undermined the hierarchy in the pattern of the usual communist attempt to drive a wedge between the Catholic and his priest. By what right, I thought, was I seeking the help of someone I had helped revile, even if only by my silence? How dared I come to a representative of that hierarchy?[7]

Bella Dodd describes the interview with Fulton Sheen, how she began to thank him for letting her come, and then broke down in tears and wept at the unjust allegations the Communist Party had been making against her. Sheen said, "Don't worry. This thing will pass," and led her gently to a little chapel.

> We both knelt before a statue of Our Lady. I don't remember praying, but I do remember that the battle within me ceased, my tears were dried, and I was conscious of stillness and peace. When we left the chapel Msgr Sheen gave me a rosary. "I will be going to New York next winter," he said. "Come to me and I'll give you instructions in the Faith."[8]

In his autobiography, *Treasure in Clay* (1982), Fulton Sheen gives a similar account of their meeting. What is undeniable is that it gave Bella Dodd a real appreciation of how well the priest understood the human condition. As she writes:

> He knew that a nominal Christian with a memory of the Cross can easily be twisted to the purposes of evil by men

6   Ibid., 231–32.
7   Ibid., 232.
8   Ibid., 233.

who masquerade as saviors. I thought how communist leaders achieve their greatest strength and cleverest snare when they use the will to goodness of their members. They stir the emotions with phrases which are only a blurred picture of eternal truths. In my rejection of the wisdom and truth which the Church has preserved, and which she has used to establish the harmony and order set forth by Christ, I had set myself adrift on an uncharted sea with no compass. I and others like me grasped with relief the fake certitude offered by the materialists and accepted this program which had been made even more attractive because they appealed for "sacrifice for our brothers." Meaningless and empty I learned are such phrases as "the brotherhood of man" unless they have the solid foundation of belief in God's Fatherhood.[9]

Bella speaks about her instructions in the faith and of how she, generally skeptical and argumentative, now found that she asked few questions.

Week after week I listened to the patient telling of the story of God's love for man, and of man's longing for God. I listened to the keen logic and reasoning that have lighted the darkness and overcome the confused doubts of others of my group who had lost the art of reasoned thinking and in its place had put assertive casuistry. I saw how history and fact and logic were inherent in the foundations of the Christian faith. I listened to the Bishop explaining the words of Jesus Christ, the founding of His Church, the Mystical Body.[10]

As in the case of many others coming from a similar position, Bella Dodd began to appreciate true "communism," if it can be put that way. As she expressed it, she "felt close now to all who received communion in all the churches of the world. And I felt the true equality which exists between people of different races and nations when they kneel together at the altar rail—equal before God. And I came to love this Church which made us one."[11] In the article cited earlier, Bella Dodd refers again to the impact made upon her by the faithful kneeling in reverence and

9 Ibid.
10 Ibid., 243-44.
11 Ibid., 244.

in thanksgiving: "Here were the masses I had sought, the people I wanted to love. Here was the brotherhood of men, cemented by their love of God."[12]

In that same article she again reflects on the peculiarity of a philosophy like Communism, which "believes in nothing except that which one can see or feel."[13] In addition, she wonders how "a Messianic ideal dedicated solely to the purely animal well-being of man should have captivated so many young people."[14] In reality, the effects of original sin, of course, help account for this. And in this context, one is reminded of the tragic effect on our own society of the sexual revolution fostered by such as Wilhelm Reich and Michel Foucault. Bella Dodd suggests an analogy from her own time:

> We were the sex-saturated generation who did not have the power to love and who understood love only in its twisted manifestations. I lived through twenty staccato years in this kind of atmosphere. My personal life was meaningless and chaotic, and my spiritual life was void. So blind was I that the murder of 5,000,000 farmers (called kulaks) in Soviet Russia in the name of a class-less society and a planned economy aroused only a small twinge of conscience. And the word "liquidation" meant not the murder of those who did not agree with the leaders of world Communism but the purification of the party.[15]

She tells how little by little her conscience started to affect her and how she now appreciated the contradictions between what the Communists preached and what they did.

> I no longer saw Communism as an unadulterated doctrine of social betterment. I began to see it as a dominant, aggressive force which contained many evil features of the existing materialist society and added new ones. Individual life and liberty were expendable in the interest of the class.[16]

12 "I Found Sanctuary," in John O'Brien, *The Road to Damascus, Volume IV: Roads to Rome* (1955), 70.
13 Ibid., 79–80.
14 Ibid., 75.
15 Ibid., 76.
16 Ibid.

After becoming a Catholic, Bella Dodd was a vocal anti-communist. In 1953 she testified before the U.S. Senate about widespread Party infiltration of labor unions and other institutions. She asserted that the Communist Party's structure "was in reality a device to control the 'common man.'" She lectured at St John's University, Brooklyn (now in Queens), and practiced law. Between 1952 and 1957 she was subpoenaed and testified several times before the Internal Security Subcommittee of the U.S. Senate, which investigated communist activities of teachers. In 1955 she formed the law firm Dodd, Cardiello, and Blair, which represented the interests of the disadvantaged. She twice (1965 and 1966) failed in attempts to be elected to the New York State Supreme Court as a conservative. In 1968, again as a conservative, she made an unsuccessful bid for a New York State congressional seat. Bella Dodd died on April 29, 1969, in New York City.

Since Bella Dodd's death little has been written about her. However, in the light of the difficulties that have undoubtedly arisen in the Church in recent years, it is perhaps not altogether surprising that one particular story has surfaced from time to time. It was presented most notably in an article under the title "Present at the Demolition," an interview with Dr Alice von Hildebrand, in the Summer 2001 issue of *Latin Mass Magazine*. Here is what Dr Hildebrand said:

> I can only tell you what I know. It is a matter of public record, for instance, that Bella Dodd, the ex-Communist who reconverted to the Church, openly spoke of the Communist Party's deliberate infiltration of agents into the seminaries. She told my husband and me that when she was an active party member, she had dealt with no fewer than four cardinals within the Vatican "who were working for us."[17]

In the early 2000s Dr Hildebrand confirmed that Bella Dodd had said: "I, myself, put some 1,200 men in Catholic seminaries." Dr Hildebrand said that Dodd had originally desisted from talking about the seminary infiltration at the request of Fulton Sheen. She also provided an affidavit from Paul Leininger and his wife Johnine, both devout Catholics, who witnessed Dodd

17 www.latinmassmagazine.com/articles/articles_2001_SU_Hildebran.html.

making the public statements. The Leiningers confirmed that there were others who could also verify that Dodd made the statements about seminary infiltration. The present writer is no conspiracy theorist, but such machinations by an avowed enemy of the Church such as the Communist Party would not exactly be surprising. Whether Bella Dodd is a credible witness is another question, although she seems straightforward in her statements and the Hildebrands have a deservedly high reputation as witnesses to the Catholic faith. In any case, and leaving this last matter aside, Bella Dodd describes with accuracy many matters of significance, both doctrinal and spiritual, in relation to the ever-important task of Catholic apologetics.

CHAPTER THIRTY-ONE
Newman and the Need for the Supernatural

THE CASE OF
LORD CHARLES THYNNE

ON THE QUESTION OF CONVERSION TO THE Catholic Church, it is important to stress something that John Henry Newman, a person with almost unmatchable knowledge and experience of the subject, himself stressed to his convert friends. This relates to the crucial distinction between natural and supernatural talents. In a letter to J. Spenser Northcote in 1862 he wrote: "Samuel was disappointed when he saw Eliab, that the Lord's anointed was not before him. 'I ever tell friends that they must look among Catholics, not for natural excellence, but supernatural. *But many Catholics do not like to allow this.*'"[1] The italicized words were emphasized by the late Fr Dermot Fenlon, Cong Orat, in his superb article "De-Christianising

1 *Letters and Diaries*, Vol. XX, 209-10; letter dated June 18, 1862.

England: Newman, Mill and the Stationary State."[2] Fr Fenlon went on to claim that "in those few italicized words, we can see summarized the history of the collapse of the Catholic Church in the twentieth century West. Religion as utility; education as the road to the top, in Manning's marvelous phrase, 'the key to Grosvenor Square'; Newman as the exemplar of a worldly eminence."[3]

Newman himself had seen this misinterpretation of the Catholic mission; he stated in one of his sermons at the newly established Catholic University in Dublin that "they think we mean to spend our devotion upon a human cause, and that we will toil for an object of human ambition."[4]

However, long before this time Newman had seen what Fr Fenlon refers to as "the doctrine of Oriel College, of [Richard] Whately, Thomas Arnold and Rugby School—a broad, comprehensive, nationally based, useful religion, with few doctrines."[5] He adds that Newman "knew it as a personal temptation while at Oriel College 'to prefer intellectual to moral excellence.'"[6] Newman himself, in his *Apologia pro Vita Sua*, describes how the death of Newman's sister Mary in 1826 "taught him the truths which he was to communicate to a generation intent on substituting political welfare for eternal welfare."[7]

Fr Fenlon brings out very powerfully the way in which in our own day Newman has been misinterpreted and proposed wrongly as "the patron and exemplar of a worldly eminence."[8] As Fr Fenlon puts it, "the twentieth century seized on him as the promoter of an educated laity."[9]

> This was Newman circulated to advantage. But Newman as the promoter of a supernatural excellence, rather than a purely natural one, of that—scarcely a word. Newman's vision tended to elude us. Perhaps I should say we eluded him. That has been the great betrayal of the twentieth century.[10]

2 See Dermot Fenlon, "De-Christianising England: Newman, Mill and the Stationary State," in Luke Gormally (ed.), *Culture of Life—Culture of Death* (2002), 27.
3 Ibid., 44.
4 Ibid.
5 Ibid., 38.
6 Ibid.
7 Ibid.
8 Ibid., 44.
9 Ibid.
10 Ibid.

Fr Fenlon then points out how the climax came in 1968 with "the deployment of Newman as the supposed promoter of the rights of conscience in the reproductive act against *Humanae Vitae*."[11] Fr Fenlon is rightly appalled at how supposedly educated Catholics made use of a false understanding of Newman's views of conscience to appeal against the pope and support dissent. The dissidents went so far as to quote Newman's famous words in his letter to the Duke of Norfolk: "If I am obliged to bring religion into after-dinner toasts (which indeed does not seem quite the thing) I shall drink—to the Pope, if you please—still—to conscience first, and to the Pope afterwards."[12] As Fr Fenlon points out, however, the correct construction of those words is that "Newman's appeal to conscience, 'the aboriginal Vicar of Christ,' was to conscience as confirmed in matters of doubt by the certitude of faith and morals enunciated by Christ's living vicar the Pope."[13]

It is instructive to consider Newman's approach to his close associates in the Oxford Movement. He believed that, in the words of Fr Stanley Jaki in his excellent book *Newman to Converts* (2001), "they had been so much imbued with Catholic principles and perspectives that they could not easily claim invincible ignorance as to the identity of the true Church, the Church of Rome, to which he kept fondly referring as the only ark of salvation."[14] Not a word from Newman about anything except the crucial issue. Here is how Fr Jaki explained it:

> He felt not only that they had a grave obligation to move toward the Church of Rome, but that he had a grave responsibility to nudge them forward in that move so that they might save their souls. This and nothing else was in Newman's eyes the sole rationale for conversion. He did not call others into the Church as if it were a fuller depository of truth and a more satisfying source of spiritual experience. For him, belonging to the Church was a matter of life and death, eternal in both cases.[15]

What a world away from this is the statement by Bishop Robert Barron in his televised interview with the Jewish commentator Ben

11 Ibid.
12 Ibid., 45.
13 Ibid.
14 *Newman to Converts*, 8.
15 Ibid.

Shapiro. There Bishop Barron said that Christ is merely "the privileged route" to salvation, made no mention of baptism or faith, and had the gall to cite Newman as being in favor of this approach. [16]

Let us, then, examine a specific case of a potential convert dealt with by John Henry Newman, that of Lord Charles Thynne. The latter was born on February 9, 1813. He was the seventh and youngest son of the second Marquess of Bath. He was also the son-in-law of Richard Bagot, Anglican Bishop of Oxford, who denounced the effort of Newman to give in *Tract 90* a Catholic interpretation of the Thirty-nine Articles of the Church of England. Thynne was also the brother of Charlotte Montague-Douglas-Scott, Duchess of Buccleuch.

Charles Thynne was an Anglican rector and canon of Canterbury. He had much correspondence with Newman about the differences between Anglicanism and Catholicism. Early on in their correspondence Thynne asked Newman why he maintained that his communion was the true Church. Newman replied as follows:

> The Church is a *kingdom*—so Our Lord says. Now does this mean a kingdom only as when we talk of the "animal kingdom," or the "vegetable kingdom"? Impossible. Is it an *invisible* kingdom? No Anglican will say so. Well then if it be a visible kingdom, where is such a kingdom, visible and yet spiritual, all over the earth except the Catholic Church?... I want to know *what* religion is embodied in a kingdom except the Catholic? The Queen's Supremacy simply deprives the Establishment of the characteristic of a *kingdom*.... The Greek Church, the Russian Church, neither are kingdoms, it will be found—whereas the Catholic Church is only known as a kingdom.... [17]

Newman remarks that one may say "that Methodism, or the Freekirk, is something of a kingdom in like manner." [18] Yet when either of these bodies is spread over the earth, "like the Mustard plant," or endures for a few hundred years, then they may put in their claims—"but as yet I do not think anyone would allow them." [19]

We do not have the text of Thynne's letters to Newman, only the replies. From these it seems clear that Thynne raises the usual

16 www.wordonfire.org/resources/video/bishop-barrons-interview-with
-ben-shapiro/5978/.
17 *Letters and Diaries*, Vol. XV, 19-20.
18 Ibid., 20.
19 Ibid.

points, of which there are three main ones, contained in different letters. As always, Newman takes these head-on and stresses the need to correct them. The first one is that Anglicans "are apt to say that Greece, Rome, and England make up *one kingdom.*" Newman replies to this with precision and with illustrative examples:

> I ask, "visible or invisible"? I suppose invisible, and then they are simply Lutherans or Evangelicals—for it is impossible to say that Greece, Rome, and England make up one *visible* kingdom. A *Race* is not synonymous with *kingdom* or *state.* The United States and we are both Anglo-Saxons—the *race* is the same, yet no one would call it one *kingdom* with the Americans; and in like manner, even admitting that Greek and Roman and Anglican Christians are all descendants in a spiritual line from the first Christians, this would not make Greeks, Romans, and Anglicans members of one *kingdom* (i.e. visible).[20]

The second point, raised by Thynne in a later letter, relates to this notion of the Church being a "kingdom," claiming that the Roman and the Anglican communion together constitute that one kingdom. Newman is very direct in his rejection of this and again proceeds to give clear examples supporting his answer:

> Indeed it seems so strange to call Rome and England *one kingdom....* It is like saying that Buckingham Palace and the National Gallery are one house. I attach no sense to the words. I understand those who say that there is *no* kingdom—or that the Church is *not visible*—but how can it be visibly one, when there is a visible duality, not individuality.[21]

The third point, which is dealt with in a further letter, relates to the crucial question of unity. Newman is adamant in stressing the key distinction in this context between "kinds" and "degrees":

> Unity does not admit of degrees but of kinds—sanctity admits of degrees. You cannot talk of "more one," you can talk of "more holy." The degree of holiness, to which the Church should attain, is *not* specified—we cannot say that any thing has failed—On the contrary our Lord distinctly foretold "Offences"—and said His Church was to be a net. But if He has said His Church should be one, it either

20 Ibid.
21 Ibid., 27.

is one or it is not. His word is either fulfilled altogether, or has failed altogether. You have a right to say that in this *sense* it is one, and that it is not—and here I have set down *in what sense* it ought to be taken—viz. in the sense of a kingdom.[22]

In relation to the points made earlier about Newman's general approach, it is interesting to note that on two occasions during the correspondence between the two men Newman does not hesitate before putting the central question in simple and forceful terms: "The question is, whether, were you dying, you would be satisfied in your not having joined Rome."[23] And again: "The simple question is, am I in the Church? This is the question for me—others have not had this question brought home to them, I have. I am not as others."[24]

Lord Charles Thynne eventually became a Catholic in 1852, being received with his wife, Lady Harriet Frances (1816-1881). His daughter, Gertrude Thynne (1840-1913), Countess of Kenmare, was received in 1853. His sister Charlotte was received into the Church by Cardinal Manning in 1860.

After the death of his wife, Thynne was ordained a Catholic priest in 1886 (in Rome by Cardinal Manning) and served at Ditton Park, near Slough, residence of his sister, until his death there on August 11, 1894.

In conclusion, it is valuable to look in some detail at the letter written by Thynne to his former Anglican parishioners shortly after his conversion to Rome. There one finds the effect of the two questions that Newman put to him:

> I left you because I could not honestly hold the position in which I had been placed. By this, I mean that I did not consider it to be the act of an honest mind to believe one thing and to teach another. I will give you some instances of this. I believed, that in order to obtain the remission of our sins by absolution, it was necessary to confess them to someone possessed of authority to receive confessions, and to give absolution. I believe this to be necessary for all who have fallen into sin after baptism. But . . . it appeared to me,

22 Ibid., 58–59.
23 Ibid., 27.
24 Ibid., 63.

both from the practice of the Church of England, as well as the testimony of the Bishops, that it did not sanction confessions, except in extreme cases, and as a kind of religious luxury for the dying. I mentioned this to the Bishop of Salisbury, and asked his opinion upon the subject. He very candidly told me that, as a minister of the Established Church of England, I could not enforce the necessity of penance, which is a sacrament in the Catholic Church of Christ, and of which confession forms one important part.

Conceive, then, my distress of mind. The very peace which I felt to be so necessary, I could neither obtain for myself, nor lawfully apply to others equally in need; nay, more, I could not even encourage them to seek it, so long as they continued to be members of the Church of England. That blessed fountain for the remission of sins has been closed against the people of England for three hundred years. Ever since the Reformation, successive generations have passed away unabsolved and it seems to be the intention of the Church of England (so long as it shall remain) that future generations shall pass away in the same uncomforted, unhopeful state.[25]

Lord Charles Thynne's reasons for his conversion are in line with Newman's approach. Fr Jaki expresses it well:

[Newman] kept in focus that one's eternal existence was at stake in the decision about whether or not to convert. He singled this out as his *sole* reason for converting. As a Catholic he never ceased to underline this point by calling prospective converts' attention to the Roman Church as the "One True Fold," that is, the only legitimate framework of salvation.[26]

This is the authentic approach. The Church has not changed its teaching, but sadly pastoral practice has on occasions taken a downturn. It is grossly misleading to refer to Christ as merely "the privileged route" to salvation and not even to mention that a potential convert is bound by the Law of God to believe in the Lord Jesus, be baptized, and join the Catholic Church.

25 *A Letter to His Late Parishioners* (1853).
26 *Newman to Converts*, 9.

CHAPTER THIRTY-TWO
Justine Ward

MUSICAL EDUCATOR AND CONVERT

THERE CAN BE NO DOUBT THAT SINCE THE
Second Vatican Council many Catholics have had to suffer from
a massive decline in the quality of liturgical music. It may be
that things are starting to improve, partly as the result of the
restoration of tradition, in particular in those Benedictine monasteries, for example at Le Barroux and Fontgombault in France,
that have reverted to the old missal and liturgical books. What
the present writer would maintain, however, is that if the work
of the musical educator Justine Bayard Ward had been kept in
mind during this period, things would have developed in a much
more, dare I say it, Catholic way.

Justine Ward (*née* Cutting) was born on August 7, 1879, in Mor-
ristown, New Jersey. She was the second of four children of an
Episcopalian family. Her father, William Bayard Cutting, was an
enormously wealthy businessman and philanthropist (when he died
his estate was valued at $10,906,480, colossal wealth for that time).
She was mainly privately educated and skilled at music. In 1901 at
the Brompton Oratory, London, she married George Cabot Ward,
a lawyer and a Catholic, but the marriage was annulled in 1911.

Justine Ward had been received into the Catholic Church on January 27, 1904, in New York. She developed a system for teaching music to children, which became known as the Ward Method. She strongly believed in the liturgical superiority of chant over other music in view of the latter's dance and secular connotations. In 1916 she founded in New York, at Manhattanville Academy, run by the Sacred Heart nuns, the Pius X Institute of Liturgical Music, using her great wealth to assist in her mission. She was also influenced, as many others were, by the Benedictines of Solesmes. Her aim was to further the liturgical and musical reforms of Pope Pius X by teaching children sight-singing skills. Her method was very successful and spread throughout the United States, Europe, and other parts of the world (at its basic level it did not require music specialists as instructors), and trained many thousands of school children. She expressed the great value of this as follows: "The little Catholic school child is learning to pray, not only in words, but also in song; not only in the Church's language, Latin, but in her musical language, Chant; and when these children grow up, our choirs will be the whole Catholic world." [1]

Justine Ward also trained many adults to teach the method, and the School of Music building of the Catholic University of America was donated by and named for her. She died in Washington, DC, on November 27, 1975.

Before looking at the principles behind Ward's musical work, which are of great value, it is helpful to set this in context by examining her relationship to the Catholic Church. She never put in written form the grounds for her conversion, but did write an essay in 1913 setting out her impressions after living the Catholic life for several years. This was published in Georgina Pell Curtis's *Beyond the Road to Rome* (1914). In this essay there are some brief indications of the reasoning behind her move from Episcopalianism:

> Before becoming a Catholic, the exterior unity of the Church is what strikes the convert. After a few years of experience as a Catholic the exterior unity becomes valuable—not only in itself—but as a figure of the interior unity which the Catholic Church alone supplies. The whole interior life is ordered and at peace; not with the peace of

1   "The Reform in Church Music," *Atlantic Monthly*, April 1906, 462.

inactivity and passive acceptance, as is so often supposed
by those who judge by the shell, but the peace of ordered
activity of mind and heart that springs from a common
source and motive power; that allows no deep disquiet
to take root in the soul; permitting storms to ruffle the
surface but never to penetrate to the interior of the soul. [2]

When I entered the Church it was not through any feeling
of attraction, but through a forcible overcoming of a deep-
seated aversion. Indeed it was only the conviction that I
could no longer be a sincere person and remain outside
the Catholic Church which forced me to enter. There
has been no Catholic practice that I have not approached
with dislike, and later learned to love, as the prejudices
which arose from a supernatural knowledge melted away
before a deeper understanding. [3]

Justine Ward was also able at this time, having entered the Church,
to explain the rationale behind what was for her a new attitude:

The puzzles that agitated the heart before as to the reasons for things, the apparent inequalities and injustices
of life, the meaning of sorrow and of physical pain—all
these things, with many more, suddenly fall into place.
    One becomes conscious of a new motive power: love.
Before, the love of Christ was, and in a sense could only be,
the cold impersonal admiration, or enthusiasm, that one
feels for a historical character, a person known through
a book. After coming into close personal contact with
Christ, day by day through the Sacraments, He is known
and loved as an intimate friend. [4]

Ward wrote more volubly of her musical work, giving a detailed
account of this under the title "The Reform in Church Music."
Her stated intention was "to bring out as clearly as possible the
fundamental principle of the art of musical prayer, in order that
principle, and not caprice, may be brought to bear to the solution
of the problem." [5]

Let us examine this further. She begins by setting out a test of
Church music, an explicit standard of artistic value. She complains

2 *Beyond the Road to Rome*, 406.
3 Ibid., 410.
4 Ibid., 407.
5 "The Reform in Church Music," 455.

that "we have been too long content to make beauty in the music *as music* the Alpha and Omega of such test."[6] Such a standard is wholly inadequate here:

> Church music is an art made up of two elements, music and prayer, and it cannot be judged by the value of one of its elements tested as a separate entity. We need a test that applies to the art as a whole, and we find it in the simple formula "*Lex orandi lex cantandi.*" Here the crux of the whole matter; the law of prayer must be the law of song, both that our prayer (I use the word *prayer,* not in the sense of a mere petition, but in its wider meaning, a lifting of mind and heart to God) may be good art and that our art may be good prayer. Prayer and music must so combine as to make *one art;* the music must pray, the prayer must sing. Otherwise the prayer is forgotten in the detached beauty of the music, or the music is forgotten in the detached beauty of the prayer. Unless the prayer and song thus rise to heaven as a single "spiritual groaning," unless they become one, merged in a true marriage of the spirit, their association is an offense both artistic and devotional.[7]

This, then, is the true test of a musical composition for the Church: Does it conform to the law of prayer? If so, it is good art. Does it seek independent paths of edification? If so, it is bad art.

Moving on from this, Ward makes the point that in the Catholic Church the music is not merely an accessory, but an integral part of the ritual. She states that words and music form together "a complete artistic whole."[8] Ward goes on to show, and here is the lesson for certain moderns who cannot resist tinkering with things, that the ritual of the Catholic Church is fixed. Why so? Because "the idea is fixed of which ritual is the outward manifestation. And so long as we remain human beings, the spiritual must take an outward form—of word, of gesture, of action—that it may be part of our nature."[9] As she points out, "even God became man that He might be fully apprehensible to His creatures; He translated Himself into terms of the

6 Ibid.
7 Ibid.
8 Ibid., 456.
9 Ibid., 457.

tangible; which is, indeed, the sacramental principle. And so we must have ritual."[10] But this ritual must really express what is behind it; it must bear a very logical relation to faith, even as the gesture does to the thought. Herein lies the true importance of Church music. For, in Ward's words, "it is not enough that it should not hide the faith; it must reveal it, even interpret it, and, through the outward manifestation of faith, raise the heart to an understanding of its inner meaning; it must, by means of the natural, help the weak human heart to rise to the heights of the supernatural."[11]

Here Ward refers to the *motu proprio* on Church music, *Tra le sollecitudini*, issued by Pope Pius X in 1903. What she has said explains why the pope attached such importance to this reform in music and in particular why the liturgy should feature a certain type of music in preference to others. What is the music whose use the pope wishes especially to encourage? It is the Gregorian Chant. The pope was not against other forms of music. He simply reaffirmed the primacy of Gregorian chant, which had largely fallen out of favor. In relation to polyphony, he asserted the superiority of the Renaissance form, especially that of Giovanni Pierluigi da Palestrina (1525-1594), over other, later styles of music. He recognized that some modern compositions are "of such excellence, sobriety and gravity, that they are in no way unworthy of the liturgical functions," but warned that they needed to be "free from reminiscences of motifs adopted in the theaters, and be not fashioned even in their external forms after the manner of profane pieces."

Why, according to Ward, is Gregorian chant superior to any later form of liturgical music? First of all she refutes the argument that the Gregorian is an antiquated art form, a musical archaism. As she says, an art form does not become antiquated through mere lapse of time, since "Greek architecture and Greek sculpture, which date still farther back, remain the standard in plastic art."[12] The Catholic liturgy is, as we have seen, fixed in its general character and scope; the form that best expresses it, then, need not be the latest fluctuation of popular taste; it need

10   Ibid., 456.
11   Ibid.
12   Ibid., 457.

not even be the form which is most interesting, judged from a purely musical standpoint. But the highest art will be the form that best fits the liturgical form. Granting, even, that music, as an art, has advanced and developed since the days of St Gregory, the question remains, which, for us, is the important one: has it advanced and developed along the lines of prayer, or the reverse, in religious or in secular channels? For if it has not advanced along the lines of prayer, then the earlier form will be the best art for our specific purpose.

Ward makes the point that in the development of every art we have a form, at first crude, then gradually perfecting itself until it reaches the classical period when idea and form become synonymous. Any further development of form is at the expense of the idea and is the beginning of decadence. Gregorian Chant represents the culmination of the melodic idea, the highest conceivable development of unisonous music, and further development had to take the form of polyphony. "The important question, then, is not whether we ought to go back to antiquity, but whether, by so going, we shall or shall not find the classical period in the art of musical prayer: the moment when the idea—prayer—and the form—music—became identical."[13] Ward is adamant that the Gregorian form, and that form only, succeeds in translating the liturgy into music, in fitting that particular idea with form, thus proving its value as an art.

> The liturgy of the Catholic Church serves a twofold purpose: to pray and to teach. The latter, her teaching function, is defeated by the use of any but unisonous music, because polyphony makes the words, in a greater or less degree, incomprehensible. In Chant the words are not repeated, twisted, turned upside-down, inside-out, and hind-part-before; they are uttered slowly, distinctly, pensively, each syllable lingered over as though with tenderness. It is a "musing," a quiet spiritual breathing. We can hear the Word of God and absorb it. Thus the teaching function of the Church demands the use of Chant.[14]

In addition to these structural issues, the aesthetic demands of the Church are no less clearly exhibited by chant.

13 Ibid.
14 Ibid., 457–58.

This prayer has, first of all, dignity; it is addressed to Almighty God. For this reason our modern rhythm, the outgrowth of the dance movement, is out of place, the form being too trivial to express the idea. I am speaking on purely artistic grounds. Again, prayer must have spontaneity; any insincerity kills prayer as prayer. For as we have seen a form attracting attention to itself detracts from the idea, and the idea in this case is God. Thus a prayer in rhyme would so obtrude its form as materially to detract from the idea. In precisely like manner is a prayer in music inferior to a prayer in Chant. Music, with its fixed measure, its regular strong and weak beats, is a formal garden, cut and trimmed into conventional avenues, adorned with hothouse plants. Chant is nature, the beauty of the fields and the forests. The formal garden has indeed its own place, its proper functions; but prayer trimmed into a formal garden is an anomaly. The spirit bloweth where it listeth. Music moves with the regular rhythm of poetry; Chant with the free rhythm of prose, the cadence of a fine oratorical period. [15]

Modern music has two scales, or modes (the major and the minor). Chant has eight. It is evident that eight modes give greater variety of expression than two. The ancient modes, with their eight scales, as opposed to the less flexible two of modern music, combine, in Ward's words, "a solemnity, a grandeur, with the most tender and fervent devotion," resulting in "true prayer: reverence in love—the prayer that, like David's, rises as incense before the altar." [16]

Many knowledgeable observers have written that the post-Vatican II reforms to the liturgy have not led to positive results; see, for example, the works of Aidan Nichols, *Looking at the Liturgy: A Critical View of Its Contemporary Form* (1996); Klaus Gamber, *The Reform of the Roman Liturgy: Its Problems and Background* (1993) and *The Modern Rite: Collected Essays on the Reform of the Liturgy* (2002); Martin Mosebach, *The Heresy of Formlessness: The Roman Liturgy and Its Enemy* (2003); and most notably Cardinal Ratzinger, later to become Pope Benedict XVI, *The Feast of Faith* (1986), and more recently, the works of Lauren Pristas, Alcuin Reid, Claude Barthe, Michael Fiedrowicz, and Peter Kwasniewski, among many others.

15   Ibid., 458.
16   Ibid., 459.

Certainly attendance at Mass has massively decreased during this period of time. In addition, and leaving aside the musical issues, another important point is that made by Francis Brancaleone in his article "Justine Ward and the Fostering of an American Solesmes Chant Tradition":

> I cannot but remark on the strong religious emphasis permeating the concept. The Method was not just about teaching music, it was also preparing little souls for more meaningful participation in Catholic liturgy. Over time, with the changes brought about by the Second Vatican Council, particularly those dealing with the advocacy of the vernacular and the movement away from Latin and Gregorian chant, the Method's influence necessarily began to wane.... [17]

This is very sad, especially when one thinks of the very large lapsation rate of young Catholics these days, many of whom have departed long before leaving school.

On the directly musical issues Brancaleone states that after the liturgical changes of the 1960s, Justine Ward's "indomitable spirit, conviction, and some of her disappointment" come through in a trenchantly expressed letter to Dom Gajard, the renowned choirmaster at Solesmes, with whom she is pictured at the start of this chapter:

> They [some of the theologians interpreting the Second Vatican Council's documents] wanted to lower the prayer of the Church to mud level in order to attract the most ignorant people. My opinion is completely different: I know that souls can be raised to the level of the Liturgy, by elevating the souls. Children have no preconceived ideas; if they are taught to pray in beauty, they are delighted. [18]

How bitterly disappointed Justine Ward must have been as in the years from the end of the Second Vatican Council to her death in 1975 she looked on at the erosion of her valiant efforts. It must have been especially galling for her in the light of the fact that the Vatican II document on the liturgy, *Sacrosanctum Concilium*, states

17 *Sacred Music*, Fall 2009, 23.
18 Ibid., 25.

that "the Church recognizes Gregorian chant as being specially suited to the Roman liturgy. Therefore, other things being equal, it should be given pride of place in liturgical services."[19]

Brancaleone, writing in 2009, sums up the situation well:

> When the Church adopted the easy popularity of guitars, amplification and charismatic group participation which could be accomplished by a relatively untrained congregation and moved away from the solitary introspection of personal prayer and training in Gregorian singing, the Ward Method came to be viewed as out of touch and therefore not a profitable promotional tool. However, the book on the Ward Method is not yet closed because of its intrinsic musical value (which may have to be redefined), staying power, and as its centenary approaches, who knows, Pope Benedict XVI's recent relaxation of restrictions on celebration of the Latin Mass may yet provide a catalyst for renewed life.[20]

Undoubtedly the promptings of Pope Benedict did result in a renewal of the liturgical traditions of the old-rite Mass, which is available on many more occasions now, and, mainly in consequence of this, Gregorian Chant has made something of a comeback. However, since the beginning of the pontificate of Pope Francis it seems that there is no longer papal encouragement for these developments. That, however, is another story, one which will undoubtedly have to be grasped at some stage. When that happens Justine Ward may hopefully yet gain the victory she so greatly deserves.

19 Chapter VI, n. 116.
20 *Sacred Music*, Fall 2009, 26.

CHAPTER THIRTY-THREE
Elizabeth Anstice Baker

AN ANGLO-AUSTRALIAN CONVERT

ELIZABETH ANSTICE BAKER (KNOWN TO HER friends as "Bessie") was a fascinating character. With her wide-ranging interests, she is best described as an intellectual and social activist. But before looking at that a short account of her life would be useful. She was born on September 24, 1849, at the family mansion, Morialta, at Magill, today a suburb of Adelaide, South Australia. She was the sixth of eight surviving children. Her father, John Baker, an English-born politician of broad-church persuasion, had emigrated and became the second Premier of South Australia.[1] Her mother, Isabella, née Allan, was a low-church Evangelical from Scotland. Her older brother was Sir Richard Chaffey Baker, the first President of the Federal Senate of Australia.

---

1   His position as premier was short-lived, as he only held office for twelve days.

Elizabeth was educated at home and in 1860–1863 in Paris. She then returned to Adelaide and joined in Church of England services with her family, playing the organ and teaching Sunday school classes. She became independent and wealthy after her father's death in 1872 and returned to Europe with her mother and sisters in 1876. She is described as being "small in stature, with fine features and expressive, dark eyes," and "elegantly simple in hairstyle and dress."

Living in London she came under high-church influences, but was later impressed by an article by a Unitarian minister, Robert Suffield (once a Catholic priest), to the effect that his creed and Catholicism are the only logical options. She also had discussions with Pusey and Newman before her own conversion. Another influence was Robert Hugh Benson, also a convert of course. This period of her life was one of very intense study and reflection and was characterized by a realistic approach to things. For example, she was "not so illogical as to suppose that any number of abuses should make the slightest difference in my estimate of Catholicism, or to expect perfection in all the members of a Church of which Judas had been a Christ-appointed priest, and in which he had held the position of Bishop and Apostle." [2]

On November 25, 1876, the feast of St Catherine of Alexandria, Elizabeth Baker heard a Dominican friar preach at the church of St Augustine in Paris.

> The preacher began by asserting the concord of Faith and Science, and maintained that real contradiction between them was utterly impossible, for the Creator of the Universe and the Author of Revelation are one and the same, and all Truth is revelation of the God of Truth. The laws of Nature are God's laws and the voice of the Church is God's voice, and He cannot contradict Himself. [3]

The friar then presented a fuller account of the faith and its effect on the life of St Catherine. Elizabeth Baker now came to appreciate, as she had never done before, "that Catholicism is no theory of creation, no mere logical deduction, no problem to be solved by the intellect alone, but devotion to a Person, union

2 *A Modern Pilgrim's Progress* (1906), 227.
3 Ibid., 235.

with a living God."[4] She made inquiries and found the preacher to be Rev Père Etienne Le Vigoureux, a friar of the Dominican Convent in the Faubourg St Honoré. The next day she called upon him and arranged to receive instruction. In December 1877, she was finally received into the Catholic Church at the Carmelite Church in the avenue de Messines by Père Etienne, who was to remain her spiritual guide.

Elizabeth Baker returned to Adelaide in 1879, but visited Europe again in 1881, by which time her mother had also become a Catholic. After her conversion Elizabeth Baker worked actively for the alleviation of poverty, both material and spiritual, and for Church and charitable ventures. She provided or found accommodation, counseling, and financial support for many women in need. She also initiated the migration to Adelaide in 1883 of English Dominican sisters, led by Mother Rose Columba (Sophia) Adams. In addition, with financial support from her mother, she established in 1883 Adelaide's first Catholic hospital, in Strangways Terrace, and managed it and its successful school of nursing from 1884.

Elizabeth Baker moved to England in 1901, where she became an active supporter of women's suffrage. She was a voluntary helper of the Catholic Missionary Society. However, she was dubbed a "Refuge for Sinners" for opening her big house in Brompton, London, to a variety of misfits! Nothing daunted, she helped to found the English Catholic Women's League in 1907, through which she worked to spread the message of the Church in England and Wales. After contracting influenza, she died of pneumonia on October 16, 1914, at her home in Kensington, London. She was buried in the churchyard of St Thomas, Fulham, London.

Elizabeth Baker's contribution to the promotion of the Catholic faith can be seen on two levels, one philosophical and literary, the other practical and organizing. Dealing with the former, it is clear that she maintained broad intellectual interests throughout her life, read widely, and wrote journal articles on a range of topics, most notably the relationship between religion and science. Most important in this context is her book referred to above, *A Modern Pilgrim's Progress*. This contains a description of her slow

4   Ibid., 237.

journey from agnosticism to Catholicism. She referred to it as a "psychological history" of her beliefs. The book was widely reviewed and ran to several editions. Fr Robert Hugh Benson wrote a preface to one of the editions, as did the Oratorian Fr Henry Sebastian Bowden, another convert. The book brought, in the words of Benson's biographer Fr C. C. Martindale, SJ, "incalculable help to souls touched slightly, it may be, by the *maladie du siècle*, but anyhow utterly impervious to the customary pious or apologetic literature."[5] The whole of *A Modern Pilgrim's Progress* is well worth examining in detail. Two major points dealt with in the book may be cited as evidence of its overall importance. The first brings out the simply staggering nature of the Incarnation and the significance of this. In order to convey this, an introduction is required.

The present writer, lucky to spend much of his childhood on a farm, later came across that wonderful book written by Richard Jeffreys, *Bevis: The Story of a Boy* (1882), which recounts the adventures of a young boy also on a farm. The Anglican theologian J. S. Whale refers to this very book as follows:

> You may remember the reference to the Crucifixion in ... *Bevis*.... "The Crucifixion hurt his feelings very much; the cruel nails; the unfeeling spear; he looked at the picture a long time and then turned the page saying, If God had been there, he would not have let them do it."
>
> If God had been there! That artless comment discloses the whole glory and mystery of the Incarnation. Shakespeare himself could not have made dramatic irony more complete. For the whole of the Christian religion rests on the fact that God *was* there. It is a matter of historic experience that out of this lowest depth to which the race of men could go down, God made his highest revelation. God's mind and act are shown forth out of the very stuff of events which supremely illustrate man's mind and act. This is the Lord's doing and it is marvelous in our eyes.[6]

What is crucial here is for Christians to appreciate the importance of getting this matter right. That doughty woman Dorothy L.

5   Fr C. C. Martindale, SJ, *The Life of Monsignor Robert Hugh Benson*, Vol. II (1916), 211.
6   *Christian Doctrine* (1941), 98.

Sayers was worried as early as the late 1930s that those responsible for promoting the Christian message, notably on the BBC, were holding back. This is all linked with the central apologetic argument of such as C. S. Lewis, which the present writer has emphasized on more than one occasion.[7] It is the classic argument regarding Christ and is often referred to as the "bad, mad, or God argument" or, as expressed often in Latin, *"aut Deus aut malus homo."* It is expressed most simply by St Thomas More: "Surely if Christ were not God, he would be no good man either, since he plainly said he was God."[8] Here, then, is Sayers emphasizing the central Christian doctrine in a letter to one of the religious officials at the BBC:

> What does the Church think of Christ? The Church's answer is categorical and uncompromising, and it is this: That Jesus Bar-Joseph, the carpenter of Nazareth, was in fact and in truth, and in the most exact and literal sense of the words, the God "by whom all things were made." His body and brain were those of a common man; His personality was the personality of God, so far as that personality could be expressed in human terms. He was not a kind of demon or fairy pretending to be human; He was in every respect a genuine living man. He was not merely a man so good as to be "like God"—He *was* God.[9]

Sayers deplored the fact that even then just about the only religion that people seemed to hear about from what she referred to as "the Churches"—she was an Anglican of course—was "a little mild theism (as preached, no doubt, by an itinerant preacher in Galilee)."[10] Where was the faith of "Jesus Christ and him crucified," which needed to be addressed to "everybody totally unaware that Christianity is about the death of God and the redemption of the world by the suffering of the innocent"? She was utterly frustrated by the fact that "they've got the most terrific story in the world and they don't tell it." As she said in a later letter, "Tell

7 See "C. S. Lewis, Conversion, and the 'Mad, Bad, or God Argument,'" *Saint Austin Review*, May/June 2013, 27; and "C. S. Lewis and the 'Mad, Bad, or God Argument': An Addendum," *Saint Austin Review*, November/December 2013, 30.
8 *Dialogue of Comfort against Tribulation* (1553), Book 3, Ch. XIV, 179.
9 *The Greatest Drama Ever Staged* (1938), 7–8.
10 Letter to Dr. J. W. Welch, Director of Religious Broadcasting at the BBC, February 11, 1943.

them who God is, and what He does and did. Tell them God was crucified, and that they have got to be crucified too. Because that's what they want to know—they want to know that their suffering makes sense."[11]

Elizabeth Baker does not hold back either; and remarkably she expresses the point here by quoting directly from, of all people, her Unitarian friend Robert Suffield:

> To say there was on earth eighteen hundred years ago a little baby in a manger cradle, growing up in the workshop, preaching and dying on the cross, who really was almighty God, maker of the world? If true, it is the only truth worth knowing at all. Every other fact in history is not worth teaching and knowing. If it is true, then the course of life to be prescribed is to act on that truth. There is nothing else worth living for—God-man—God, dying on the cross for man. It is simply infinite in its signification.[12]

In the words of Fr Aidan Nichols, OP, the Incarnation is "the key belief of the Church, on which everything else turns";[13] what he refers to as "the Great Assertion,"[14] something that is, even if expressed in slightly unusual language, "the ultimate in 'gobsmackers!'"[15] Such it may be, but no less powerful for that. As Christopher Hollis said, "It is hardly possible to see a madman in the preacher of the Sermon on the Mount and the figure who has stood as the comfort for tribulations of the world for two thousand years."[16]

From her standpoint, Elizabeth Baker is able to push further and see this principle operating within the Catholic Church itself, again, ironically, citing Robert Suffield as follows:

> The Church of Rome recognizes the Incarnation as the foundation of the supernatural, and carries it into the whole life of man.... Take one doctrine—the central doctrine of the Church of Rome—Transubstantiation. It has afforded abundant food for laughter and

11 Letter to Dr. Welch, November 11, 1943.
12 *A Modern Pilgrim's Progress*, 57.
13 *Come to the Father: An Invitation to Share the Catholic Faith* (2000), 48.
14 Ibid.
15 Ibid., 49.
16 *Noble Castle* (1943), 186.

counter-arguments of Protestants, but I cannot see the difference between the doctrine that a little baby lying in its cradle is Almighty God, and saying that a wafer exalted amid a thousand lights and worshipped by thousands is Almighty God. The one thing is quite as rational or irrational, as possible or impossible, as the other. When I can believe the one, I will accept the other.... Looking on the Incarnation as the fount of all these doctrines of the Church of Rome and of the doctrine especially of hell—for hell corresponds to the Incarnation—the two dogmas will stand or fall together; to save men from infinite punishment, you have this infinite remedy of God-made man. If hell is put aside, why then did God come upon earth to die upon the cross?[17]

The second major issue point in *A Modern Pilgrim's Progress* is the fundamental difference between Protestantism and Catholicism:

One teaches that God came on earth, taught the truth, went away leaving a creed, a system, or a book in His place; in the other He is the Way, the living abiding bridge between earth and heaven—not a bridge once built and then destroyed, not a Christ who saved the world and then left it, but a Christ who abides substantially in that Church which is the pillar and ground of the Truth and who speaks through his Vicar, whose infallibility is the very mortar by which the stones of that pillar are held in their respective places.[18]

She continues: "other religions professed to tell us of a God who is in heaven, Catholicism of One who is here, close to the human will and close to the human heart; other religions professed to tell us about God, Catholicism to teach man how to obtain union with Him here as well as hereafter."[19] As a consequence, not only did Catholicism teach man to worship God, but "by the Eucharist it professed to unite the creature with the Creator, and thus answer to all the needs of humanity."[20]

It would be unfair to leave the subject of Elizabeth Baker without emphasizing the other aspect of her work, the organizing and

17 *A Modern Pilgrim's Progress*, 58–59.
18 Ibid., 232.
19 Ibid., 234.
20 Ibid.

practical part. We have seen already her pastoral and charitable work, but there is more. A simple example will suffice. In 1911 the Motor Mission, with its remarkable automobile chapel, took to the roads in England for the first time to spread the Catholic Faith, to refute the cries of "No Popery" with the response, in Fr Bernard Vaughan's phrase: "Know Popery!" The preacher was Fr Robert Hugh Benson. Elizabeth Baker played a notable part in preparing for the various missions. In his biography of Benson, Fr Martindale refers to Miss Baker's organizational ability, even though suffering from severe deafness:

> "Did I understand you to say," murmured Miss Baker, "that you wanted the galleries cleared?" ... A moment later, a stir was noticeable in the hall. Distant tiers of seats were being evacuated.... The front rows on the floor were filling up.... In less than seven minutes this deaf old lady had effected the results despaired of by princes and by prophets.[21]

However, there is a need for balance, and that was always present in the case of this great worker for the faith. As Fr Martindale recognized, it would be quite wrong to leave the impression of "an ardent, exterior, and perhaps impertinent activity": "Her tenderness and infinite tolerance, in which a Christian love and a deep knowledge of the world and of human hearts helped each other, were more secret, perhaps, but not less real or loved."[22] Elizabeth Anstice Baker was a true Catholic heroine who advanced the understanding of Christian witness in both theory and practice.

21 *The Life of Monsignor Robert Hugh Benson* (1916), 211–12.
22 Ibid., 212.

CHAPTER THIRTY-FOUR

James Higgins, Conversion, and the Assumption of Our Lady

Assumption of Mary *(Titian)*

AS CATHOLICS WILL KNOW, THERE IS AN ancient and important tradition behind the Church's belief in the Assumption of the Blessed Virgin. It is traceable back to the fifth century in Jerusalem and the sixth century in the east. By the seventh century it made its appearance in Rome and by the thirteenth century it was the general belief of Catholics in both east and west. However, the belief in Our Lady's bodily assumption into heaven, called in the eastern Church the "falling asleep" of Our Lady, the Dormition, was not finally made a formal dogma

289

of the Catholic faith until Pope Pius XII defined it on November 1, 1950. It appears also that all Catholic books of dogma assert that neither Sacred Scripture nor the Church Fathers mention it. However, although they all agree that the doctrine is not stated explicitly in Sacred Scripture, the claim is that it is stated implicitly. Most theologians refer to Luke 1:28, which speaks of Mary's "fullness of grace." They also refer to Genesis 3:15. Fr Kenneth Baker puts it in this way: "Since by the seed of the woman they understand Christ, and by the woman, Mary, it is argued that as Mary had an intimate share in Christ's battle against Satan and in his victory over Satan and sin, she must also have participated in his victory over death."[1]

These Scriptural texts are not exactly decisive proof, but a few years ago I came upon what I would submit is a very strong argument that the view stating that this dogma is not to be found in Sacred Scripture is false and that there is powerful evidence of scriptural witness for it. This all came about as a result of discovering an excellent Catholic scholar-convert. The story is worth telling in conjunction with that of his conversion.

In 2009 I came across a published article of great quality. It had the somewhat daunting title "St Thomas's Pedagogy—Ignored, Rediscovered, and Applied."[2] It was written by someone completely unknown to me. Little did I know then that he had written three articles for a periodical for which I had also written, the *Downside Review*, published by the Benedictine monks at their abbey in Somerset, England. The man in question was James Higgins, a convert to the faith. The value of his writings should be advertised; they are all of outstanding merit and the present writer has benefited hugely by being exposed to them. First some facts about his life and conversion to the Catholic faith as recounted to the present writer.

FROM OXFORD TO ROME

James Higgins was born on April 15, 1931, in Oxford. He was the eighth of nine children, seven of them boys, born to an Anglican family. His father died in 1937 when James was only six years old, "leaving Mother a widow at fifty with nine children

1 *Fundamentals of Catholicism*, Vol. II (1983), 374.
2 *Heythrop Journal*, June 2009, 603.

and no money." Thankfully, Higgins had a strong character for a mother. He tells her reaction in the face of the situation:

> Twelve words she had obviously had in mind a long time, her challenge to the Lord: not, "What a mess you've got us into...," but not altogether different. It was the *Mandatum*, St. John 13:7, in the Authorized Version, "What I do thou knowest not now but thou shalt know hereafter."[3]

It seems that sober challenge put to the Lord by her was accepted graciously, and when she died forty-three years later in 1980, now ninety-four, she was still lucid. Her son was an Anglican choirboy (and later bell-ringer) at St. Giles', Oxford, just opposite Somerville College, and was godson to Sister Elizabeth at the convent close by, founded by the Tractarian hymnologist J. M. Neale, and the first Anglican convent ever to exist. It is some indication of the nature of those times that the Anglican Higgins was "astonished" to be told one day, at choir practice, that "Roman Catholics" were Christians at all!

James Higgins proceeded in due course to enter Balliol College, Oxford, as an undergraduate. He was there from 1949 to 1952 and graduated in mathematics. In October 1954, just after doing his national service, he became a Catholic at St. Aloysius', Oxford, at the age of twenty-three. Shortly afterwards he tried his vocation for the priesthood by joining the Jesuit order. He became a Jesuit novice in 1957 at Manresa House, Roehampton. From 1959 until 1966 he was a Jesuit scholastic, mostly at Heythrop College, near Chipping Norton, Oxfordshire, the house of studies of the Jesuit order. During this time he spent a term at the Gregorian in Rome starting theology. Eventually, however, he left the order and never became a priest. Instead, he worked for many years at the Ministry of Defense. During this time he published various pieces on mathematics and on violin technique, and made a verse translation of Pushkin's verse novel *Eugene Onegin*. More in line with his main work are three articles written for the *Downside Review* in the 1970s and '80s on questions of nuclear weapons and deterrence. However, his retirement to Wissembourg in France gave him the chance to write in more detail on Catholic and related themes. The great majority of the resulting articles are concerned

3   E-mail to the writer, April 29, 2011.

with St Thomas Aquinas's thought, whether philosophical, or theological, or set in the context of history, politics, morality, or culture. He was finally at leisure to read, in the light of his Jesuit training, his copy of the great *Summa* of St Thomas acquired in 1955, when six months a Catholic.

GROUNDS FOR CONVERSION

Higgins' account of his conversion was little different from that of many others in the established church:

> Nothing interesting to report on why I became a Catholic, except that so many Anglicans do, all different and without strong reasons to deter them. Because my brothers and I were choirboys at Oxford...we sat through innumerable sermons on "the errors of Rome," given largely by Old Etonian parsons, millionaires whose forbears had done very nicely, thank you, out of the loot from the Church, way back (I could go on).[4]

However, he does make a valuable general point by drawing a very important distinction: "what is required of a Catholic believer is his assent to the truth of propositions—and of course the right ones—which he should therefore make an effort to understand, if he wishes to remain a believer." But, and here is the distinction, when it comes to the mental journey that the mind makes (i.e., the argument) from one or more premises to a conclusion, things are rather different. Higgins asks whether the Catholic Church requires its adult members to accept the validity of *arguments* as well as conclusions. His answer is worthy of lengthy quotation:

> Many people seem to think so, believers as well as unbelievers, but carefully considered that surely proves not to be true. How could it be? I believe facts and testimonies: notably, all the things my mother told me about her early life and afterwards—because I knew, then as now, that she was a truthful person and a reliable witness. In much the same way, having come to believe at twenty-three that the teachings of the Catholic Church might well be true I got priests to instruct me and became convinced that they were. But my accepting them ever since, along with my readiness to accept others, is nothing like leaving my

4   Ibid.

thinking to the Church. How could that be expected of anyone, believer or no? Though you might not think so, going by what neo-modernists and other heroic individualists think, over teachings we believers may find hard to accept here and now as articles of faith we Catholics are obliged to convince ourselves, when others have failed to do so, and not to expect others to render the service—and if we can't, not to give up trying.[5]

THE ASSUMPTION OF OUR LADY

James Higgins himself certainly did not give up trying, as his published articles show. But he had to wage a long-standing battle. As an Anglican at the age of twenty-three, he states, he found the dogma of Our Lady's Assumption hard to accept, but at the age of sixty-one he finally realized, as stated earlier, that the idea that the dogma of the Assumption is not to be found in Sacred Scripture is false and that this can be proved. In the context of apologetics and conversion this is an important matter. How did this process happen and what is the proof in question?

The reasoning behind it is treated briefly in the 2009 article mentioned earlier, but in much more detail in a 2013 article entitled "Tracing Our Lady."[6] Higgins states there that anyone concerned to give Our Lady her proper place in the four Gospels can find fourteen passages (one of them in triplicate), comprising the events she took part in or witnessed or appeared in, which, together with Acts 1:14 (her participation in the prayer in the upper room after the Ascension of her Son), contain all the scriptural evidence bearing directly on the question. The very last of these fourteen Gospel passages is John 19:25-27: "Standing by the cross [was]...His mother. When Jesus saw his mother, and the disciple whom he loved, he said to His mother, 'Woman, behold your son!' Then he said to the disciple, 'Behold your mother!' And from that hour the disciple took her to his own home." However, and this is the key, there is also a fifteenth passage, which Higgins points out will be found to gain in meaning if interpreted in the light of the fourteenth passage. His claim is that "the Bodily Assumption is surely implied by this passage." The passage in question is John 21:20-24.

5 "St. Thomas's Pedagogy," 608.
6 *Heythrop Journal*, March 2014, 297.

This is the very last episode in the entire Gospel story, its position being especially appropriate and giving it "a particular poignancy." Here it is: "[Peter asks, what of John?] and Jesus replies, 'If it is my will that he remain until I come, what is that to you?'"

Higgins spells out precisely the significance of all this:

> Christ hints to Peter that he will be coming back for John, though Peter will be dead by then, a martyr. And indeed he was. But come back *when*—and *why*? The belief that the end of time (the Parousia) was meant—and therefore that John would never die—is rejected, despite the commentators: and the hint is meticulously repeated, nine words of Greek, so as to ensure the accuracy of the Gospel record, so transmitted. But then, if not at the end of time (with John still there, only sleeping in his grave, as many came to believe), when? The only alternative is that Christ meant that he would be coming back for his *Mother*, whom he had expressly entrusted to John's care already, just before he died, John 19:27. "And from that hour" they lived at the same address. So it says. No matter what else he may have meant, then, it was clearly a coded message about a family matter, to remain secret until the early Church had matured.[7]

Of course, it cannot be over-emphasized that the false interpretation, about John never dying, is expressly rejected by the evangelist St John himself, and the reply in the Gospel is repeated, as if to stress its importance, though that appears to have been generally overlooked down the ages.

James Higgins makes another important point about the status of the doctrine of the Assumption that flows from Christ's words to St John:

> The timing of those words, no matter what they meant . . . nevertheless puts the message well within the deposit of faith, which was completely fixed only when St John himself died, years later. No matter what Christ's words meant at the time, His intention was manifestly that they *and therefore their true meaning* should be treasured by the Church as part of the Catholic faith.[8]

7   "St. Thomas's Pedagogy," 608.
8   "Tracing Our Lady," 302.

It would seem, then, to be, as Higgins puts it, "the simple truth that the purpose of Christ's mooted return could only have been to fetch His mother, rather than just to leave her to die, without him taking any notice; which would have been strange behavior for a son. Why otherwise come back at all, if not simply to attend her in her last moments on earth?"[9]

Higgins' writings deserved to be more widely recognized. Much valuable knowledge is to be gained on a whole host of topics, including the arguments for the existence of God; many questions relating to cosmology; the nature of moral argument; and specific matters, such as the Gunpowder Plot, the role of Pope Pius XII during World War II, and the thought of Dorothy L. Sayers. At the very least read the 2009 article and renew your appreciation of the genius of St Thomas Aquinas, the Angelic Doctor, and marvel at the skill of his modern interpreter.

9   Ibid., 301.

CHAPTER THIRTY-FIVE

Harriet Brewer Churchill

FROM PURITANISM TO THE PAPACY

IT SEEMS PERFECTLY NATURAL TO INQUIRE whether Catholic converts emerged out of the time of the Pilgrim Fathers. A search was made by asking the computer to find references to Catholics during that period. This resulted sadly in little response. However, the request to locate "pilgrim" proved much more positive. Of course, the bulk of the responses related either to specific pilgrimages or to specific modern pilgrims. Curiously, under both headings, a large result was obtained in the entry for Ernest Hemingway, not exactly a pilgrim father and someone about whom the notion of Catholic or pilgrimage would not figure very highly in some minds. However, as I think I have proved earlier in this book, almost everything written about Hemingway's Catholicism, with the exception of the work of the redoubtable H. R. Stoneback, is very poor indeed.[1]

1   But see also the wide-ranging survey of Hemingway's life and work in Matthew Nickel, *Hemingway's Dark Night* (2013).

Despite these initial setbacks, there are two notable references to converts, which did bring into play at least some reference to the Pilgrim Fathers. One was the long-lived William Stetson Merrill (1866–1969), a librarian, editor, and author. He claimed descent on his mother's side from one of the Mayflower pilgrims, Stephen Hopkins, the only Mayflower passenger with previous New World experience. Expanding upon the work of his predecessor Melvil Dewey, Merrill conducted his own original work that contributed to the library classification system now known as the Dewey Decimal System; and became well known as the editor of several journals on Catholic issues, librarianship, history, archaeology, and literature, and the author of many articles. Much could be said about Merrill and his conversion to the Catholic faith, but perhaps here it would be better to write about someone much less well known, as being more representative of the vast majority of pilgrims to the United States.

The second reference was to Harriet Brewer Churchill. She appeared no doubt because of an essay by her contained in that fascinating collection of American convert stories compiled by Georgina Pell Curtis, published in 1909 under the title *Some Roads to Rome in America: Being Personal Records of Conversions to the Catholic Church.*[2] Harriet was born on January 7, 1855, in Boston. Her father was of Pilgrim descent, some of his ancestors having come on the Mayflower. His wife, her stepmother, was an "advanced Unitarian" or "Parkerite." She had ancestors who took a leading part in the War of Independence and were officers in the army of George Washington. Harriet's father was an agnostic ("admirer of Voltaire [whose works filled whole shelves in our library], of Buckle, Parker, Darwin, Huxley and the rest"[3]). As a result she was given little religious instruction ("I was taught to tell the truth, and not to steal, etc., more as a matter of social polity than because lies and thieving were sins against the law of God"[4]).

Harriet was educated in private schools in Massachusetts and Switzerland. While in Europe she spent several weeks in Rome. A year or so after her return to the United States she converted

2   This is Georgina Pell Curtis's first volume on converts, which was followed in 1914 by *Beyond the Road to Rome*, referred to several times earlier in this book.
3   *Some Roads to Rome in America*, 86.
4   Ibid.

to the Catholic Church. Why? Well, she was mainly influenced by her belief in the papacy and authority. We can examine something of her reasoning, but first something must be noted that hints at some considerable difficulties she encountered and overcame, which may be reminiscent of those the earlier pilgrims to the Church had to face. This is that in his will, her father gave a part of his estate in trust for her use during her life with the express understanding that neither of the trustees (her two brothers) nor she "shall expend any part of such income for the use or benefit of the Roman Catholic Church, its priests or clergy, charities, nuns, saints, or rites, its ceremonies or exhibitions, its images or masses, its lectures or preaching, its cemeteries or processions, or in aid or encouragement or support of anything connected with or pertaining to that church or sect."[5] Well, that's certainly telling her what for!

Of course, this still happens. A friend of the present writer, who had become a Catholic during the lifetime of her mother, was going through the papers of the mother, who had just died. She discovered a document setting up a trust fund making a particular university the beneficiary. One of the terms of the trust read that "my trustees shall hold the . . . fund on trust to pay the income thereof to my daughter during her life or until she takes up residence in a Roman Catholic convent or any similar Roman Catholic institution irrespective of the capacity in which she shall so reside and whether or not she shall take any vows or undergo any instruction." Not a very friendly gesture, and something of a shock for the daughter, but in many cases perfectly legal.

To return to Harriet Churchill—she saw very clearly the contrast between the fate of the Puritans and that of the papacy:

> The peculiar tenets of the Puritans for which my fore-fathers braved the perils of the wilderness are dead and buried like themselves: while the Papacy which saw them come has seen them go—into oblivion, while the Holy Father from the banks of the Tiber still rules a Church greater in numbers and more perfect in organization than at any time in the history of the world.[6]

5 Ibid., 85.
6 Ibid.

In order to illustrate the longevity of the papacy and of the Church that it serves, Harriet then turned to a passage mentioned by many converts. It is the statement by the English historian and Whig politician Thomas Babington Macaulay, 1st Baron Macaulay (1800–1859), who never converted himself. Macaulay was writing at a time of fervent anti-Catholicism, but to his credit he recognized the historical significance of the Church. The passage in question is contained in a book review. Here is the passage in full:

> There is not, and there never was on this earth, a work of human policy so well deserving of examination as the Roman Catholic Church. The history of that Church joins together the two great ages of human civilization. No other institution is left standing which carries the mind back to the times when the smoke of sacrifice rose from the Pantheon, and when camelopards and tigers bounded in the Flavian amphitheatre. The proudest royal houses are but of yesterday, when compared with the line of the Supreme Pontiffs. That line we trace back in an unbroken series, from the Pope who crowned Napoleon in the nineteenth century to the Pope who crowned Pepin in the eighth; and far beyond the time of Pepin the august dynasty extends, till it is lost in the twilight of fable. The republic of Venice came next in antiquity. But the republic of Venice was modern when compared with the Papacy; and the republic of Venice is gone, and the Papacy remains. The Papacy remains, not in decay, not a mere antique, but full of life and youthful vigor. The Catholic Church is still sending forth to the farthest ends of the world missionaries as zealous as those who landed in Kent with Augustine, and still confronting hostile kings with the same spirit with which she confronted Attila. The number of her children is greater than in any former age. Her acquisitions in the New World have more than compensated for what she has lost in the Old. Her spiritual ascendancy extends over the vast countries which lie between the plains of the Missouri and Cape Horn, countries which a century hence may not improbably contain a population as large as that which now inhabits Europe. The members of her communion are certainly not fewer than a hundred and fifty millions; and it will be difficult to show that all other Christian sects united amount to a hundred and twenty millions. Nor do we see

any sign which indicates that the term of her long domin-
ion is approaching. She saw the commencement of all the
governments and of all the ecclesiastical establishments
that now exist in the world; and we feel no assurance
that she is not destined to see the end of them all. She
was great and respected before the Saxon had set foot
on Britain, before the Frank had passed the Rhine, when
Grecian eloquence still flourished at Antioch, when idols
were still worshipped in the temple of Mecca. And she
may still exist in undiminished vigor when some traveler
from New Zealand shall, in the midst of a vast solitude,
take his stand on a broken arch of London Bridge to
sketch the ruins of St. Paul's.[7]

This is indeed a remarkable passage. The Catholic writer Karl
Keating states that it is "one of those passages that should be
memorized by Catholic school children, much as school children in
general once memorized the Gettysburg Address."[8] I am inclined
to agree, but we live in an era when sadly rote learning is not
encouraged. However, Harriet Churchill is the first person that I
have come across who wants to add to the text above. She says, "I
often think I should like to add to Lord Macaulay's famous passage
and to say that when the New Zealander himself shall have passed
away and his land be but a desert; when the inevitable catastrophe
shall have occurred and this old earth drifts a derelict in space,
then and not till then will the Church militant have failed to exist.
Then and not till then will the Sacraments cease to be administered
and the Pope be no more."[9] Powerful words indeed.

In addition to the authority of the Church and the papacy, Harriet also drew inspiration from a consideration of the authority of
Scripture. She recalled hearing her stepmother read aloud to her
the famous chapter of St Paul on charity, and recalled wondering
at the time why she should attach any importance to it unless
she believed that the Bible was an inspired work and the Word
of God. Her stepmother seemed to think that it was "a beautiful
chapter," but no more so than something from Marcus Aurelius.

7   "An Essay on Von Ranke's 'History of the Popes,'" published in *Critical
and Historical Essays Contributed to the Edinburgh Review* (1870), 548.
8   "The Unbroken Rule," March 1, 2007, www.catholic.com/magazine/
print-edition/the-unbroken-rule.
9   *Some Roads to Rome in America*, 85–86.

Harriet's reaction was much closer to orthodoxy of Christian belief when she said to her stepmother that if that was all there was to it, there were other things more interesting!

What is also impressive in Harriet Churchill's process of thought is the way that she focuses in on practical and pastoral activities as well as doctrine. There are at least three examples of this. Firstly, there is her emphasis early in life on an example of the fitness of things, namely her remark to her family who were astonished to hear that "I could not understand, if a person wished to lead a really good life, why it was not a good idea to go to confession as Catholics did."[10]

A second practical influence on her conversion was that before returning home from Europe she spent several weeks in Rome, and "hours and hours were passed in the churches in the presence of the Blessed Sacrament."[11] She was able to appreciate, despite her lack of much care for any religion at that time, that it was from this that her conversion began.

Thirdly, after she had been at home about a year she went to New York, where for the first time she came into contact with the everyday workings of the Catholic Church:

> I saw the doctrines of the Church applied alike to rich and poor, gentle and simple, learned and unlearned. I witnessed the atmosphere of devotion, the unanimity of worship, the daily succession of Masses, the coming and going of one congregation after another, the devout genuflections, and all this in the most commercial and latter-day city in the world.[12]

She was much impressed, and even more so by a succession of providential occurrences. A Protestant friend lent her a copy of *The Imitation of Christ*, of which she had never heard before. Then she came across the writings of Cardinal Newman and recognized that "in the matter of a conversion, his is a name to conjure with."[13]

Although she had never been strictly speaking a Protestant, she felt that she could not openly denounce the opinions under the influence of which she had been educated, which were closer to

10   *Some Roads to Rome in America*, 87.
11   Ibid.
12   Ibid., 88.
13   Ibid.

Unitarianism than to any other form of belief, until she had heard what a Unitarian minister should have to say for that particular sect. She called on the Reverend James Freeman Clarke, secretary of the Unitarian Association and Professor of Natural Religion and Christian Doctrine at Harvard University, who offered to pray with her. Her resulting conclusions mirrored the objective approach to things that she followed, resulting in her rejecting the subjectivism that she found being offered to her:

> I never could divest myself of the idea that all he said
> was merely the sum of his own reflections and opinions
> and being such was no more worthy of credence than the
> sum of my own. I felt that he had no more authority for
> anything he chose to put forward than that "he, James
> Freeman Clarke, thought so" and I think I can with truth
> say that just on this hinge turned the door through which
> I entered the Church.[14]

Finally, Harriet applied to the Reverend Phillips Brooks, a well-known Episcopalian clergyman and lyricist of the Christmas hymn "O Little Town of Bethlehem." The conclusion of his frank advice was that if there were any church on earth which seemed to her to have been founded by Christ it was her duty to join it.

All the strands of evidence, then, establish that the root of Harriet Churchill's conversion was her belief in authority generally and specifically in the Papacy, the principle of authority: "Its very existence carried along and protected through the ages is a perpetual miracle."[15] Soon afterwards, Fr Edward Holker Welch, SJ, himself a convert from Protestantism and a trustee and teacher at Boston College, received her into that one Church. The date of reception and the subsequent death of Harriet have thus far eluded the present writer.

14   Ibid., 88–89.
15   Ibid., 90.

CHAPTER THIRTY-SIX

Georgiana Chatterton, Baddesley Clinton, and Trials in the Church

THESE ARE BAD TIMES FOR THE CATHOLIC
Church. For many years we have had reports of terrible cases of
clerical abuse in many areas of the world. In addition, there are
seeming ambiguities and uncertainties as to what the Church
teaches in certain areas of the moral realm, in particular the

question of communion for divorced Catholics. All these problems have been added to by the Covid pandemic, resulting in Catholics being excluded in many cases from their own churches and their own liturgy.

Perhaps what is needed is a two-fold response. Firstly, words from one of the Catholic masters to restore our confidence in the Church, which, after all, we are told is the Body of Christ. In addition, something relating to romance and affection would also be helpful. The life of writer, traveler, and convert Lady Georgiana Chatterton supplies both. Let us start with this.

Henrietta Georgiana Marcia Lascelles Iremonger, to give her full birth name, was born on November 11, 1806, in Piccadilly, London. She was the daughter of Lascelles Iremonger, Anglican Prebendary of Winchester. Her mother was Harriet Gambier, daughter of John Gambier, Lieutenant Governor of the Bahamas. At the age of eighteen Georgiana married Sir William Abraham Chatterton, baronet of Castle Mahon, County Cork. As years went on she became known by the name of Lady Chatterton as a popular writer, publishing extensively in fiction, biography, travel, and devotional works. After the death of her husband, she occupied a house with her niece and ward Miss Rebecca Dulcibella Orpen, a prolific artist, working in both oil paints and watercolor.

Shortly after her husband's death Lady Chatterton was visited by a friend, author Edward Dering, whose father was chaplain to Queen Victoria. It is this meeting that creates an element of romance, but also humor perhaps. The story is best told by a newspaper obituary of Rebecca Orpen:

> At the time of [Lady Chatterton's] second marriage [she] was fifty-three and Dering was twenty-two years her junior. Indeed there is good authority for the statement that it was for the hand of the young Miss Orpen, the ward, that Dering had really asked of Georgiana Lady Chatterton, and when the latter, in the mistaken belief that it was she who was being wooed, extended her own, Dering was too well-bred to explain.[1]

In consequence Georgiana and Dering were married. She remained known as Lady Chatterton. She was a member of the Church of England, but on September 20, 1865, she was received

1   The *Times of London*, September 13, 1923, 13.

by Cardinal Newman into the Catholic Church, together with her second husband and Rebecca Orpen. The remainder of the story is taken up by the same obituary, slightly annotated by the present writer:

> Soon after her reception into the Roman Catholic Church, Miss Orpen married Marmion Edward Ferrers, of [the old Catholic family at] Baddesley Clinton, [Warwickshire].... Ferrers and Dering had been old friends.... On the invitation of Ferrers, Dering and Georgiana Lady Chatterton went to live at Baddesley Clinton, and there the two married couples lived together for the remainder of their lives.[2]

It is interesting to note that there is yet another Catholic link to this of a literary kind. It is that in Maurice Baring's novel *Cat's Cradle* (1925), there is an important scene based on the above mistaken proposal. In addition, there was a further and final twist in the real story. Lady Chatterton herself died on February 6, 1876, at Baddesley Clinton. After the subsequent death of Edward Ferrers in 1884, Rebecca Ferrers became Edward Dering's wife and lived at Baddesley Clinton until her death several years after that of her husband. Happily ever after it would seem! It is a touching story and is certainly accentuated greatly by the house in which most of it took place. Baddesley Clinton is an exquisite property, a moated house in idyllic surroundings. It is now looked after by the National Trust and open to visitors for most of the year.

Now, let us turn back to the crucial question of confidence in the Church. Well, Baddesley Clinton itself supplies this in part, most importantly by its role as a witness to the heroic faith shown by Catholics during Reformation times, when its three priest-holes often provided a hiding place for Jesuit priests from their pursuers. In his classic account of the old Catholic houses, *Forgotten Shrines* (1910), Dom Bede Camm, whose own story is told in the next chapter, stated that of all these places Baddesley was to him "the most familiar and the most dear."[3]

> The dark winding corridors, broken by unexpected flights of slippery oaken steps, lead here to a priests' hiding place, there to a banqueting hall, here again to a ghostly room,

2   Ibid.
3   *Forgotten Shrines*, 319.

where the blood of a murdered priest sill stains the floor. But the heart of the house is the old chapel where the Master of the house deigns to dwell in His tabernacle, and the haunting legend is inscribed above the door: *Transit gloria mundi: fides Catholica manet.*

Here at Baddesley that Faith has ever had a stronghold; never did this beautiful old house belong to any but a Catholic. Through the dark days of persecution, hidden chaplains ... ministered to the faithful, hidden away in the recesses of the great Forest of Arden. Here for thirteen generations of unbroken line, the Ferrers of Baddesley have worshipped God in the old Catholic manner during nigh four centuries, three of which were ages when no Catholic was suffered to serve his God in peace.[4]

Dom Bede Camm tells the story of the martyr Blessed John Sugar (1558–1604), who said Mass at Baddesley towards the end of the reign of Elizabeth I. It was on the high road, somewhere in the neighborhood of Baddesley, that the priest was apprehended. On the morning that he was going to die at Warwick (July 16, 1604) the priest said to his weeping friends, "Be ye all merry, for we have not occasion of sorrow but of joy; for although I shall have a sharp dinner, yet I trust in Jesus Christ I shall have a most sweet supper."[5] Dom Bede Camm sums up the significance of it all for us:

This is the story that we dream of at Baddesley as we sit under the cedars and gaze at the old grey house, with its black oak gables, sleeping in the sunshine. It is all so tranquil now, the swans in the moat seem to be the only sign of life; and it seems difficult to associate this "haunt of ancient peace" with memories of strife and blood. Yet across the moat we can still discern the narrow loopholes which light the subterranean passage by which the hunted priest escaped and in which one famous Jesuit hid for three days, knee-deep in water. Even now we can visit the strong-room at the foot of the well-staircase in the tower, where the massive door can be barricaded from within, and a pulley lifts a great stone which gives access to the moat.[6]

4 Ibid.
5 Ibid., 324.
6 Ibid., 325.

This other aspect of the question of the Church brings in once again Cardinal Newman. Before her conversion Lady Chatterton wrote in June 1863 to Newman, stating that she possessed "a firm conviction of the truth of the Christian Revelation."[7] However, one difficulty remained for her, best expressed by Newman himself in his reply to her: "Why the present Catholic Church should be in many respects so unlike what she should expect and wish it to be?"[8]

How does Newman respond to the challenge put to him by Lady Chatterton? Certainly not by a refusal to face uncomfortable facts. There has on occasion been a tendency among Catholic apologists to attempt to argue that it was all a bit of a mistake, that many of these uncomfortable things in the life of the Church simply did not take place or, if they did, they were grossly exaggerated. It has even been known for writers to attempt to argue that figures like Pope Alexander VI (1431-1503) in reality led lives of some sanctity and that all the stories against them were malicious falsehoods and some kind of Judeo-Masonic plot. Not only is this kind of approach shortsighted, it also sins against the truth.

All of this Newman fully appreciated, as becomes immediately apparent in his reply to Lady Chatterton's inquiry. Newman does not deny that what she is saying is true. In fact, in his reply he himself asserts as a fact that the face of the visible Church is very often disappointing and, in a certain sense, a scandal:

> I do not believe that there was ever a time when the gravest scandals did not exist in the Church, and act as impediments to the success of its mission. Those scandals have been the occasion of momentous secessions and schisms; in the earlier times, of the Novatian, the Donatist, the Luciferian; in latter of Protestantism and Jansenism.[9]

If one just concentrates on clerics, and leaves out the words and deeds of lay people, many appalling things have been said and done. At the Council of Constance (1414-1418), John Hus (who had presented himself after having been assured of safe conduct) was ceremonially condemned by the bishops and then burned alive, his body, after his death, being pushed further into the flames to ensure its complete reduction to ashes! I think that will stand as

7   *Letters and Diaries,* Vol. XX, 464, n. 4.
8   Ibid., 465.
9   Ibid.

a fair example of bad behavior. As far as doctrine is concerned, priests have often said quite ludicrous things. Perhaps it is true that some of their statements are even sillier today than they have sometimes been in the past. All that this probably means is that, as they inevitably imbibe the spirit of the age (none of us is immune from this), they suffer more than in the past, since we live in an age wedded to trivialities. But, bad though it is, our time does not have a monopoly on such activities.

The point is, as Newman went on to explain in his letter to Lady Chatterton, that in spite of these scandals, much can be said in support of the Church. He highlights three points:

> [1] It is also a fact that, in spite of them still, the Church has ever got on and made way, to the surprise of the world; as an army may fight a series of bloody battles, and lose men, and yet go forward from victory to victory. On the other hand the seceding bodies have sooner or later come to nought.[10]

> [2] Our Lord distinctly predicted these scandals as inevitable; nay further, He spoke of His Church as in its very constitution made up of good and bad, of wheat and weeds, of the precious and the vile. One out of His twelve Apostles fell, and one of the original seven deacons. Thus a Church, such as we behold, is bound up with the very idea of Christianity.[11]

> [3] At least from St. Augustine's day, the fact has been so fully recognized in the Church, as to become a doctrine, and almost a dogma, admitted by all; and never considered in consequence at all to interfere with that Sanctity which is one of her four Notes.[12]

What Newman said at that time is just as relevant now. I'm afraid that Our Lord made no promises that the apostolic succession would not include hireling shepherds, who would promote grossly unchristian attitudes, modes of behavior, and even beliefs. As Professor Michael Dummett acknowledged, "It was not promised that the leaders of the Church will always give guidance in the face of evil, or that they would have either physical or moral

10   Ibid.
11   Ibid. See also *Letters and Diaries*, Vol. XXVIII, 128, 223.
12   Ibid.

courage. One promise was made, however: that, if we kept the bond of unity, we should be able to place entire confidence in the Church's solemn pronouncements on the content of our faith. If such confidence is misplaced, the Catholic Church is a fraud; for the Church has reiterated throughout the centuries that that promise is from God. If the Church is a fraud there can be no justification for belonging to it: no justification for complicity with fraud."[13]

All that is being stated here is, of course, what Catholic tradition says. The saints also testify in exactly the same way. Not a few of them were very badly treated by the Church at different times. Their response was always to remain within the Church and, in particular, to remain in communion with the Vicar of Christ. The idea that just when the barque of Peter is tossed by the roughest seas we should abandon ship and leave her would have been unthinkable for them.

In further correspondence with Lady Chatterton, Newman takes up another issue, which he analyzes in more detail in his more formal writings, namely the way in which inevitably a divine system (the Church) becomes mixed up with human weakness and corruption.

> Christianity was intended for whole populations; now a popular religion is necessarily deformed by the errors and bad taste of the multitude. As the religion of barbarous times will ever be fierce and superstitious, as the religion of the schools will ever tend to be subtle and pedantic, so the religion of a nation will ever partake of the peculiar faults of the national character. The most sublime truths take a vulgar shape and bear a forbidding aspect, when reflected back by the masses of human society—nay, often cannot be made intelligible to them, or at least cannot be made to reach them, till thrown into words or actions which are offensive to educated minds. The Church cannot countenance any such misstatement of the truth, much less any degradation or depravation of it—yet, when it has actually taken place, she may find it quite impossible to root out the tares without rooting out the wheat with them—and is obliged to let them grow together till the harvest. At least,

---

13 "A Remarkable Consensus," *New Blackfriars* (1987), 427.

she is obliged to be patient, and waits her time—hoping
that an evil will at length die of itself—or again that some
favorable opportunity may occur, when she may be able to
do what she has no means of doing at present.[14]

The point which Newman wishes to emphasize is that a people's
religion is always by its very nature a corrupt religion in spite of
the efforts of the Church. The treasury of the truth, which the
Church possesses, is in the hands of corrupt human nature and
therefore is often used in a sacrilegious way. As St Paul says, the
treasure is in earthen vessels (2 Cor. 4:7).

As Fr Ian Ker, Newman's biographer, has expressed it, this is
an example of the old principle that the corruption of the best
is the worst.[15] From this it also follows, given the claims which
the Catholic Church makes, that one should not be surprised to
find the worst of scandals in high places in the Church. Newman
himself expresses this in relation to the papacy, when in a letter
to another enquirer he says, "Where you have power, you will have
the abuse of power—and the more absolute, the stronger, the more
sacred the power, the greater and more certain will be its abuse."[16]

To return to Lady Chatterton, Newman's letters were clearly very
important in her becoming a Catholic, and Newman would try to
help her deal as well with later setbacks. Between 1865 and 1870,
latterly because of the contention that arose over the definition
of papal infallibility, Lady Chatterton developed doubts. These
also seem to have related to Our Lady, to the Real Presence, and
to Purgatory. During this time she was counseled by Newman on
many matters. On some he had success, placing much emphasis on
the words of St Paul, and stressing that the Church was above all
the infallible representative of Christ on earth: "St. Paul says that
the Church is the pillar and ground of the Truth. He says that
there is *One* Body as there is *One* Faith. Our Lord has built His
Church on Peter. These are great facts—they keep their ground
against small objections, however many the latter may be."[17]

Later on Newman turned again in letters to Lady Chatterton
to the question of papal infallibility. As on other occasions, his

14   *Letters and Diaries*, Vol. XX, 470–71.
15   *Newman on Being a Christian* (1990), 80.
16   *Letters and Diaries*, Vol. XXV, 204.
17   *Letters and Diaries*, Vol. XXII, 195.

approach was somewhat ambiguous, expressing it as follows: "I have ever held the infallibility of the Pope myself, since I have been a Catholic—but I have ever felt also that others had a right, if they pleased, to deny it—and I will not believe, till the event takes place, that a Council will make that belief obligatory."[18] Such a statement was not exactly guaranteed to resolve Lady Chatterton's concerns, although it must be noted that once the definition of infallibility was made Newman accepted it. Also, in a later letter to Lady Chatterton Newman did state this:

> My own reading before I was a Catholic strongly impressed me with the belief that as early as the 5th century St. Leo acted as no Pope could have acted unless he was infallible. Long before that, in the 3rd century, Pope Dionysius claimed to act and was obeyed, in matters in which he could not have acted unless he had been generally considered infallible.[19]

Despite these efforts, by 1873 Lady Chatterton again was attending Anglican services. Thankfully, however, in 1875 she returned to the Catholic Church. Once more Newman played a role in this, but it would seem that a more significant figure at this point was Bishop Ullathorne, to whom Lady Chatterton had turned. The Bishop seems to have diagnosed correctly her state of mind when he said: "In the depths of your soul I believe there is a conviction that our God has not left us without His certain truth and certain guidance what we are to do to be saved."[20] That guidance was of course union with the Catholic Church. He emphasized that if that Church truly came from God, it had to be One, Holy, Catholic, and Apostolic. He went on to stress the oneness of the Church by bringing into focus the multiplicity of voices generated by Protestantism. It was almost certainly as a result of this that in 1875 Lady Chatterton returned to the Catholic Church and died the following year in that communion.

The house at Baddesley Clinton, its occupants, and the events that took place there are a valuable witness to the Catholic faith. Much more could be said, in particular about the Jesuit contribution to the house's history. Lady Chatterton's own conversion

---

18   *Letters and Diaries,* Vol. XXV, 23.
19   *Letters and Diaries,* Vol. XXVI, 33.
20   See Jaki, *Newman to Converts,* 293.

issues also teach us a great deal; and looking back much further, one should not forget the history of the Ferrers family, especially the diary of Henry Ferrers, who lived more than eighty years at Baddesley Clinton, from 1549 to 1633. This diary is still preserved in the Bodleian library at Oxford. As Dom Bede Camm states, "In it are to be found minute and vivid details of the life of a typical Catholic country squire during the fiercest period of the persecution."[21] In addition, Rebecca Orpen was an artist of considerable talent. Lastly, Edward Dering is also notable in that he wrote novels on Catholic conversion themes and, more importantly perhaps, a very well-argued article on apologetics in the Jesuit periodical *The Month*. The article is entitled "Given a First Cause—What Then?" His thesis is that "we must affirm the existence of a First Cause; for otherwise we should have to suppose either an infinite succession of causes and effects, or a time when nothing was, and a first something created by itself before it was."[22] All in all, then, Baddesley Clinton and its affairs show us the authentic Catholic way.

21 *Forgotten Shrines*, 319.
22 *The Month*, March 1889, 388. See the extract in the present writer's *Roads to Rome* (2010), 113-14.

CHAPTER THIRTY-SEVEN
Dom Bede Camm

CONVERT AND GREAT
PROMOTER OF MARTYRS

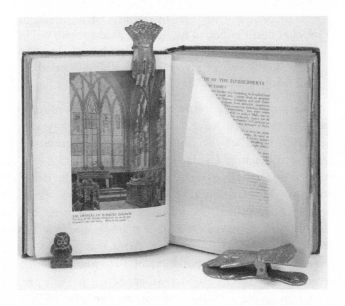

THE PREVIOUS CHAPTER DEALT WITH BADDE-
sley Clinton, the moated recusant house that played a major role
in Catholic history in England: the romantic history of the family
there in the nineteenth century, but inevitably also the heroic witness to the faith of the martyrs who were sheltered within its walls.
In the course of this I cited a book that gives an account of many
of the "Forgotten Shrines" (the title of the book) in my country
that sheltered martyrs. The author of that book was Dom Bede
Camm, whose own life witnessed to the history of the martyrs in
an unsurpassable way. Perhaps it is time to investigate that life in
more detail, especially the route he too took on the road to Rome.

Reginald Percy John Camm, as he was christened, was born on
December 26, 1864, at Sunbury Park in the county of Middlesex. He

was the son of John Brooks Maher Camm, sometime of the Twelfth Lancers, and his wife Caroline, and brought up as a High Anglican. As a schoolboy at Westminster School, he was a keen ritualist. He was educated at Keble College, Oxford, from 1883 to 1887, and graduated in theology. In describing his early years, one incident should be mentioned: during his time at Oxford he was shipwrecked in the Bay of Biscay. In hindsight his reaction to this is significant:

> I have always looked upon this shipwreck as one of the greatest graces of my life. In the first place, it taught me that death is not to be feared if God be with us. In the second place, it filled me with a consuming desire to consecrate to God the life which he had thus wonderfully given back to me.[1]

He then completed his studies for the Anglican ministry, and served as a curate until 1890, but on June 19 of that year he was received into the Catholic Church at the Benedictine Abbey of Maredsous in Belgium. His father was received in 1891 and other members of his family converted later. He entered the Benedictine novitiate at Maredsous in 1890, taking Bede (whose *Ecclesiastical History* he had studied at Oxford) as his religious name. He made his simple profession on December 8, 1891, and was ordained priest on March 9, 1895, in Rome. After that he was based at Erdington Priory, on the outskirts of Birmingham, until 1912. After going back briefly to Maredsous, he spent 1913 preparing the Anglican monks of Caldey Island and the nuns of St Bride's, Milford Haven, for their reception into the Catholic Church. In the same year he was also affiliated to the Downside Abbey community. During World War I he was a military chaplain in Egypt and Palestine from 1915 to 1919. Afterwards he served as Master of Benet House, Cambridge, from 1919 to 1931. He then returned to Downside. Dom Bede Camm died in 1942 in a nursing home at Clifton, Bristol. He is buried at Downside Abbey.

DOM BEDE'S CONVERSION

Let us look at Camm's conversion to the Catholic Church. He identifies the major influences upon him as Newman's *Development of Christian Doctrine*, Manning's *Temporal Mission of the Holy Ghost*,

---

1   *Anglican Memories* (1935), 13–14.

Faber's *Life and Letters*, and the writings of the Church Fathers. He gave an account of his conversion in an essay published in *Roads to Rome* (1901), edited by J. G. F. Raupert. This was followed up by "Memories of a Benedictine Monk," in *The City of Peace by Those Who Have Entered It* (1909), edited by Fr Henry Browne, SJ. The account there was then reprinted as a separate book under the title *Anglican Memories* (1935).

As an Anglican Camm came to realize relatively quickly that the want of heroic sanctity in the Church of England since the Reformation was a major difficulty. Why were there no Anglican *saints?* He gives the reader a picture of Anglicanism at the end of the nineteenth century, which shows its poor state as early as that time:

> The whole [Church of England] system was such a miserable *fiasco*. Here was a Church that had had, for three hundred years and more, full power, enormous influence, over the whole land. She claimed to be Catholic, a branch of the Church of God. Yet the people knew nothing of this, nothing of the faith—were practically pagans, in fact. They had lost all idea of sin (the Church had practically abolished the Sacrament of Penance); they did not know how to make an act of contrition; the commonest Catholic duties, such as the obligation to hear Mass on Sundays, to receive Holy Communion at Easter, were utterly unknown. Next door to us was a Church of the extreme Protestant type, where all we held most sacred was denounced unsparingly every Sunday. There was no unity of belief anywhere, because there was no unity of teaching.[2]

It is interesting to read the informed opinion of someone in his position then, and it reminds one of similar comments made by Dorothy L. Sayers, who as early as 1937, after receiving reactions to her play *The Zeal of Thy House*, was complaining of many people that, "however often they had heard or recited the Creeds, it had obviously never sunk into their minds that Christ was supposed to be God in any real sense of the word."[3] She bewailed also the fact that other people, supposedly Christian, were "astonished to hear that the Church considered pride to be a sin at all."[4] This mirrors an

2   Raupert (ed.), *Roads to Rome* (1901), 29.
3   Barbara Reynolds (ed.), *The Letters of Dorothy L. Sayers*, Vol. 2 (1997), 43.
4   Ibid., 68.

experience of the present writer recently when three "well-educated" friends could recall only two of the deadly sins and were amazed to hear that pride was one of these sins, and the most serious of them. They clearly believed this sin to be one of the virtues!

Camm was also influenced by the words of Herbert Mackay, a notable Anglican canon, who "informed me one day that there were only two positions logically possible. Either Rome's claims were true and all were bound to submit to them, or they were false and were therefore anti-Christian. In a word, Rome was either the one Church of Christ, or she was anti-Christ. I rebelled against being thrust into this dilemma, but I was none the less impaled upon its horns."[5]

Confronted by this dilemma, Camm began to see that communion with the See of Peter was of old the essential test of orthodoxy, the *signum stantis vel cadentis ecclesiae* (the sign by which the Church stands or falls); and if so, why should it not be so still?[6]

In truth he had come to recognize the authentic Catholic tradition, expressed, as it was, by one of the greatest of saints:

> St. Augustine's words haunted me: "*Extra Ecclesiam Catholicam totum potest praeter salutem*" (Outside the Catholic Church anything is possible except salvation). And when I turned to Rome, and saw her so firm, so invincible, so serene, so unfaltering in her teaching, so uncompromising with heretics, so sure of her own rights, so immovable through the ages, I fancied that to her, and to her alone, could apply those other words of the Saint: "*Ipsa est Ecclesia sancta, Ecclesia una, Ecclesia catholica, contra omnes haereses, pugnans; pugnare potest, expugnari tamen non potest*" (This is the Holy Church, the One Church, the Catholic Church, which, contending against all heresies, may herself be assailed, but cannot be overcome).[7]

This firmness so evident to Camm has not appeared so clearly in the last few decades, but we know that the Church is indefectible and so we must not worry. It is interesting to note that for him, despite the power of St. Augustine's words, he was, like many before him, still "tormented with fears and anxieties; still I did not see clearly."[8]

5   *Anglican Memories*, 32–33
6   See Raupert (ed.), *Roads to Rome*, 29.
7   Ibid.
8   Ibid.

What moved him further on was the simple fact of going abroad for a holiday and there, kneeling one day in a monastic church, hearing the brethren chanting those words of the Credo: "*Et unam sanctam Catholicam et Apostolicam Ecclesiam.*" All became clear. As he puts it: "As they sang them the clouds rolled away from off my soul and the light of faith shone on it once for all. I saw them, in a way which I cannot describe, but, like the blind man of old, '*One thing I know, that whereas I was blind, now I see.*' I saw that all this time I had *not* been believing in *One* Church. I saw what the unity of the Church really was, and seeing, I rejoiced and thanked God."[9]

THE "MONASTIC MARTYROLOGIST"

Now, some general reflections on his work promoting the martyrs. Dom Bede Camm has been given the title of a "monastic martyrologist" in view of the immensity of his efforts in this task. One of his favorite schemes was to establish a pilgrimage center for the English martyrs as near as possible to the most famous place of martyrdom, Tyburn, near the present Marble Arch in London. He successfully promoted the shrine and pilgrimages to it with his lectures and preaching, and it was his idea that inspired the Martyrs' Chapel there with its specially designed altar. He obtained relics and stained glass windows, and also designed a re-creation of the "Tyburn Tree," which was a triple gallows in triangular form, as a baldachin over the altar.

The cause of the English and Welsh martyrs was undoubtedly Dom Bede Camm's apostolate and the work of his life. Soon after his conversion he began to gather material on the martyrs and published books and articles on the subject. He wrote some popular texts, for example *In the Brave Days of Old*, published in 1900. These were designed to present clearly the lives of the martyrs and their message to the English public, and especially to English Catholics. In addition, there were more scholarly works, for example the two-volume *Lives of the English Martyrs Declared Blessed by Pope Leo XIII*, published in 1886 and 1895. The most celebrated and influential work of all is *Forgotten Shrines*, published in 1910. This concentrated on Catholic strongholds and consists of some 411 pages dealing with the martyrs known to have been there, but also the houses themselves, together with their priest-holes and the relics contained

9   Ibid.

within them. Notable among these houses are Baddesley Clinton, Harvington Hall, Stonor Park, Wardley Hall, and many others. The history of certain notable families is recounted, for example the tragic story of the Fitzherberts. It is a fascinating book.

Dom Bede Camm set out the purpose behind *Forgotten Shrines* as follows:

> I have attempted in this book to tell the story of some of those ancient manor houses which became the last refuges of the ancient faith, when it was proscribed and persecuted throughout the land. The air of mystery and romance which seems to exhale from the crumbling walls of these old houses irresistibly moves those who come across them to curiosity if not to reverence. And this is an attempt to satisfy such legitimate curiosity.[10]

Dom Bede Camm traveled far and wide investigating the martyrs and was the major promoter of the cause of many English and Welsh martyrs. On the topic of pilgrimages, he went further and also wrote a fine study covering a more extensive area, *Pilgrim Paths in Latin Lands* (1923). This is sometimes referred to as a continental version of *Forgotten Shrines*. In the light of his "getting around," one of his other books was the source of some humor among his fellow monks. This was *A Day in the Cloister*, published in 1900, the title of which led some of them to say that this was about all the time he spent in the monastery!

There can be no denying the importance of his work overall. Making the martyrs known was at the center of his work, and he sought especially to publicize and celebrate their lives and deaths. As a convert to Catholicism himself, he saw the great apologetic value in increasing knowledge of the martyrs and their wonderful stories. Dom Bede Camm has been accused of triumphalism, and certainly there is a gulf between his direct evangelization and the often tame false ecumenism seen in the last fifty years. But his approach is surely something to be applauded. Like one of his heroes, Saint John Henry Newman, he is not afraid to emphasize the need to join the one true Church and the importance of the martyrs in conveying that truth. To Don Bede Camm there was "nothing which refutes so simply and irresistibly the sophisms of modern Anglican theories of

10 *Forgotten Shrines*, vii.

'continuity' and the like as the simple, unvarnished history of those who died in England for the Pope and for the Mass."

To conclude, the importance of the Mass to Dom Bede Camm cannot be over-emphasized. As in the case of all Catholic issues, it must be said that, in the words of Augustine Birrell (a person who ironically never became a Catholic), "It's the Mass that matters."[11] It is therefore valuable to cite some very moving words on the Mass from Dom Bede Camm in a conference entitled "The Martyrs, Witnesses to the Holy Mass." In this conference, given at Tyburn itself during a solemn triduum in honor of the English martyrs in 1904, he emphasizes the great witness of the martyrs to the holy sacrifice of the Mass:

> Let us consider for a moment what the sacrifice of the Mass really is. It is to the Church of God what the sun in the heavens is to this earth of ours. What would be the effect on this globe could that mighty orb be suddenly extinguished? Would not the world be plunged into darkness, frozen with cold? The beautiful flowers would droop and die, the trees lose their leaves, the birds and beasts would perish, and we ourselves could not long survive them. So would the Church on earth be deprived of heavenly light and heat, could the most divine sacrifice be abolished from her midst. It is by this adorable sacrifice that the presence of Jesus is ever ensured to her, and it is in this most pure oblation that his all-prevailing merits are constantly pleaded with God on behalf of sinful man. We sometimes wonder how it is that God can be so patient; how it is that he does not strike the earth with the lightnings of his wrath, and destroy once more a race whose iniquities are constantly crying out to heaven for vengeance. The answer to this mystery is to be found in the sacrifice of the Mass. If God remains silent when men deny him to the face, if he bears so long with their rebellion, their ingratitude, their impurity; it is because there is never a moment of time when from some point of this globe the immaculate Lamb of God is not lifted up between heaven and earth in the hands of some humble priest; and the Father, looking upon the face of his beloved Son in whom he is ever well pleased, for his

11 "What, Then, Did Happen at the Reformation?," *The Nineteenth Century*, April 1896, 655.

dear sake and for his blood outpoured and for his open
wounds has pity on the race that dear Son died to save.[12]

If, as is the case, the "forgotten shrines" are not forgotten today,
and the heroes who are associated with them are lauded, this is
due in so many ways to Dom Bede Camm.

ADDENDUM

It is important to advertise Dom Bede Camm's writings, of
which several have already been mentioned. He wrote a great
deal, all of it well worth exploring today. *Forgotten Shrines* is a
wonderful piece of work and stands as a memorial to him. Copies
of the original 1910 text can still be found online, but thankfully
there is also now a reprint nicely produced in paperback. Of his
other writings not mentioned earlier, here is a selective list: *A
Benedictine Martyr in England: Being the Life and Times of Dom John
Roberts* (1897); *Father Dominic and the Conversion of England* (1899);
The Church and Abbey of Erdington: A Record of Fifty Years, 1850–1900
(1900); *A North-Country Martyr (John Ducket)* (1900); *Courtier, Monk,
and Martyr: A Sketch of the Life and Sufferings of Blessed Sebastian Newdigate of the London Charterhouse* (1901); *The Voyage of the "Pax": An
Allegory* (1906); *A Birthday Book of the English Martyrs* (1908); *William
Cardinal Allen, Founder of the Seminaries* (1908); *Heroes of the Faith*
(1909); *Roodscreens and Roodlofts* (2 volumes) (1909) (with Frederick Bligh Bond); *Sister Mary of St. Francis, SND: Hon. Laura Petre,
Stafford-Jernigham* (1913); *At the Feet of the King of Martyrs* (1916);
Ven. Dominic Barberi and the Conversion of England (1922); *The Story
of Blessed Thomas More* (1926); *The Martyrs of Tyburn* (1928); *The
English Martyrs and Anglican Orders* (1929); *The Good Fruit of Tyburn
Tree* (1929); *The Martyr Monk of Manchester, Blessed Ambrose Barlow*
(1930); *Nine Martyr Monks* (1931); *The Life of Blessed John Wall, OFM,
the Martyr of Harvington Hall* (1932); *The Foundress of Tyburn Convent*
(1935); *The Call of Caldey: The Story of the Conversion of Two Communities*
(1940). In addition, there is an appreciation of Dom Bede Camm
by Dominic Aidan Bellenger, "Dom Bede Camm (1864-1942),
Monastic Martyrologist," *Studies in Church History* (1993), 371. An
obituary can be found in the *Downside Review*, 1942, 333.

12 *Tyburn and the English Martyrs* (3rd edition, revised and enlarged, 1924),
46–48.

CHAPTER THIRTY-EIGHT

The Enigma of Oscar Wilde

CONVERT, REVERT, OR NEITHER?

THE TRADITIONAL ACCOUNT OF THE LIFE OF Oscar Wilde has it that he converted to the Catholic faith on his deathbed in Paris on November 29, 1900, the day before he died. But there are, and always have been, other opinions, as Jeffrey A. Tucker explains:

> It is often dismissed as either fiction or the aberrant action of a very sick man in a moment of grave weakness. Richard Ellmann's 1988 biography of Wilde, which incorrectly speculates that syphilis was the cause of his early demise at age 46 [it was probably cerebral meningitis], treats the conversion as a minor detail, perhaps further evidence of the broken man that Wilde had become after his two years in prison for sodomy. In a particularly uncomprehending passage, Ellmann compares the application of sacred oils to Wilde's hands and feet during the last rites to "putting a

green carnation in his buttonhole." Thus, Ellmann encourages us to overlook Wilde's conversion and not let it spoil our image of him as an icon of the gay lifestyle.[1]

So was this how Wilde ended his life? What is the truth? Let us start at the beginning. There seems no doubt that Wilde, as an infant, born in Dublin on October 16, 1854, to a Protestant Anglo-Irish family, was baptized at St Mark's church, Dublin, the local Church of Ireland (Anglican) church. However, he was later, probably at the age of between four and five, baptized in the Catholic Church at the instance of his mother, who was not a Catholic or even a genuine believer. Fr John Hogan takes up the story:

> Oscar always said he had a faint memory of being baptized a Catholic when a child. Many years later, a Fr. Laurence Fox would confirm this in his recollections, recounting a visit from Lady Wilde in which she asked him to baptize her sons, Willie and Oscar. After a few weeks' preparation the young priest obliged. Lady Wilde was having a flirtation with Catholicism at the time and soon moved on to something else, but Oscar did not forget.[2]

Does this early baptism mean that he had no need to convert later on in his life and that if he did convert later in life, then he was a "revert"? Well, as Fr Hogan goes on to say, "Curiosity [about the Catholic Church] remained and it would emerge most forcefully when he began his studies at university. Entering Trinity College, Dublin, he soon found himself in Catholic circles befriending a number of priests."[3] If the word "curiosity" is taken precisely, then it would seem that Wilde considered at that time that he was not a believing Catholic. Certainly, however, even this stage in Wilde's thought-process concerned his father, a non-practicing Protestant and a Freemason, when news of it reached him. His response, in addition to threatening to disinherit his son, was to send him off to Oxford University to continue his studies at Magdalen College. But, once he got there, the evidence is that Wilde was socializing in Catholic circles in Oxford, attending Mass, and deliberating upon a possible embrace of Catholicism. His main influence at

1 "Oscar Wilde, Roman Catholic," www.catholiceducation.org/en/culture/art/oscar-wilde-roman-catholic.html.
2 "The Conversion of Oscar Wilde," www.faitharts.ie/wilde.html.
3 Ibid.

this time was probably the novelist and critic Walter Pater, one of his tutors, who engendered in him an aesthetic fascination with the mystery of the Catholic ritual. In addition, his dormitory room is said to have had in it photos of Pope Pius IX and Cardinal Manning. His intensive reading was Catholic literature, in particular John Henry Newman and Thomas à Kempis.

One of Wilde's friends at Oxford was the later-to-be Catholic priest Oliver Vassall-Phillips, the subject of an earlier chapter, who wrote about Wilde quite movingly many years afterwards in his autobiography:

> Poor Oscar Wilde, who was a friend of mine during his last year at Magdalen, used to quote in those days a Platonic phrase which he said expressed his ideal of human happiness and indeed achievement—"to sit down and admire the beautiful." Unhappily, this maxim did not save him from catastrophe in later life—a catastrophe which he said himself would have been averted had he been given the right values when he was young, and permitted to carry out the wish to become a Catholic which had persisted through his school days in Ireland and the earlier years of his undergraduate life. He used regularly to collect alms from his Oxford friends for the Mater Misericordiae Hospital in Dublin.[4]

Even in those early days there were times when Wilde came very close to converting. Perhaps the most famous occurred in 1877 and 1878, when he spoke often to Fr Henry Sebastian Bowden of London's most fashionable Catholic church, the Brompton Oratory. During several meetings Wilde poured out his heart to the priest, referring to his sinful life. Fr Bowden's letter to Wilde, written in April 1878, is a model of good advice. He notes that Wilde's nature had been corrupted by "bad influences mental and moral, and by positive sin.... God in his mercy has not let you remain contented in this state.... He allows you to feel the sting of conscience and the yearnings for a holy, pure and earnest life.... He is bound, remember, to give you the means to obey the call."[5] Fr Bowden urged Wilde to convert, telling him that "as a Catholic you would find yourself a new man in the order of nature

4   *After Fifty Years* (1928), 58, footnote.
5   Quoted by Richard Ellmann, *Oscar Wilde* (1988), 94.

as of grace."[6] Ellmann narrates what happened next, an account that coincides with the popular image of Oscar Wilde: "On the Thursday when Wilde was to be received into the Church, there arrived at the Brompton Oratory, instead of Wilde, a large package. On being opened this proved to contain a bunch of lilies. It was Wilde's polite way of flowering over his renunciation."[7]

Wilde's career went on and his literary achievements left him for the most part influenced more by a decadent style of life than by a pious one. What is certainly true is that paganism and Catholicism were always warring attractions for him. If we take Wilde's instruction that in order to understand him, we need to look at his art rather than his public image, then two very different pictures emerge. These are dealt with very well by Fr Hogan, who contrasts the view given by Wilde in the essay "The Critic as Artist" ("Sin is to be exalted and there is far more to be learned from the sinner than the saint. Indeed, it is those who are evil in the world who will, in the end, be the ones who rejoice, not the good"[8]) with that portrayed in *The Picture of Dorian Gray* ("A tale in which the degenerate lifestyle of the protagonist finally claims not only his life, but his soul. It is a moral parable in which the wages of sin are clearly seen and what appears to be beautiful is in fact hideous and morally distorted"[9]).

During this period in Wilde's life there was no definite decision taken by him between these two very different approaches to life. The literary and aesthetic aspects, together with the decadent side, can be seen in detail in many texts. The culmination was Wilde's failed libel action against the Marquess of Queensbury in 1895, and the prosecution in the same year of Wilde himself for gross indecency, resulting in his conviction and sentence to two years' penal servitude with hard labor. The other aspect, Wilde's relationship with the Catholic Church and whether he converted to the Catholic faith, is not so widely attested and so will now be examined in some detail.

Wilde clearly remained fascinated by the Catholic Church even in his period of high decadence. As his libel and gross indecency trials began, he told Lord Alfred Douglas: "If I win this case, as

6   Ibid.
7   Ibid.
8   "The Conversion of Oscar Wilde."
9   Ibid.

of course I shall, I think we must both be received into the dear Catholic Church."[10] Sadly for him, things did not turn out alright. But his reading during his imprisonment did include works by St Augustine, Dante, and Newman, a life of St Francis of Assisi, and the Bible. After his release on May 18, 1897, his very first act was to write to the Jesuits of Farm Street, London. The letter has not survived, and two theories have grown up as to its contents. One account is that he requested to be allowed to make a six-month retreat. The other states that he simply asked for a priest to visit him so that he might "take part in a religious discussion"—presumably to make his confession. Either way, the letter was quickly answered, and the Jesuits refused his request. We have independent evidence that at this Wilde completely broke down and wept bitterly in front of friends. His later attempt to renew his contact with Fr Bowden at the Brompton Oratory also failed, as the priest was away and Wilde felt unable to deal with such matters with a stranger. He left England for Paris a few days later.

Wilde spent much of the last three years of his life in Paris and also from time to time in Rome. Jeffrey A. Tucker describes the nature of his life during this time: "In these years of exile, he attended Mass often, made pilgrimages, and prayed, but these periods of piety were punctuated by...lapses into his old homosexual lifestyle."[11] During this time Wilde made several trips to the Vatican and reported to friends that he had had a private audience with and been blessed "many times" by Pope Leo XIII, about whom he had a very high opinion, speculating that on one occasion the pope's blessing healed him from the effects of food poisoning. Wilde opined that Pope Leo "is no longer of flesh and blood: he has no taint of mortality.... My position is curious: I am not a Catholic: I am simply a violent Papist."[12]

In an article about the relationship between Wilde and the Catholic Church at this time, Gary H. Paterson brings out a significant detail:

> Wilde went to Rome in Passion Week of 1900. There he
> was more than ever before impressed by the outward

10 Tucker, "Oscar Wilde, Roman Catholic"; https://www.catholiceducation.org/en/culture/literature/oscar-wilde-roman-catholic.html.
11 Ibid.
12 Ibid.

splendor of the Easter celebrations. Particularly, he was struck by the figure of the Pope whom he thought was wonderful "as he was carried past me on his throne, not of flesh and blood, but a white soul robed in white, and an artist as well as a saint." It would seem that Wilde's attraction to the Papacy was a form of hero-worship, the same kind of admiration that he felt toward royalty.... Wilde, in being drawn toward the ancient institution of the Church, with all its pageantry and tradition, was quite naturally impressed by the successor of St. Peter and Vicar of Christ. [13]

There is very little in the record that gives directly and exactly the journey of Wilde's mind on its supposed progress at the very last into the Catholic Church, but the *Dictionary of National Biography* does give an indication of what this process amounted to in its examination of his last two works:

De Profundis is . . . an extraordinary record of a man hurled from the pinnacle of literary success to the uttermost public degradation, and of the spiritual means by which he turned away from despair. Wilde fixed his mind on Christ, first as a person, then (in *The Ballad of Reading Gaol*) as a redeeming god.

And so to the last days of Wilde's life. The standard account is that Fr Cuthbert Dunne, CP, an Irish priest, conditionally baptized him, and gave him extreme unction and absolution, being satisfied that Wilde, although now speechless, understood and approved. Is this true? There have been attempts made to deny it, even shortly after Wilde's death. For example, when *De Profundis* was published in 1905 an article appeared in the *St James's Gazette* stating as follows:

He did not become a Roman Catholic before he died. He was, at the instance of a great friend of his, himself a devout Catholic, "received into the Church" a few hours before he died; but he had then been unconscious for many hours, and he died without ever having had any idea of the liberty which had been taken with his unconscious body. [14]

13 "Oscar and the Scarlet Woman," *Antigonish Review*, Spring/Summer 1991.
14 *St. James's Gazette*, February 23, 1905.

The "great friend" was surely the most constant and loyal friend of Wilde, namely Robert Ross, a writer, critic, and art dealer, known always as "Robbie." The article itself was signed "A" and is taken to have been written or inspired by Lord Alfred Douglas, known to all as "Bosie," Wilde's "amour fatale." *De Profundis* itself contained in part Wilde's angry and remorseful account of how he had been ruined by Douglas and their shared lifestyle.

So, what can one say in response to the claims contained in the *St James's Gazette*? Well, a partial response is to refer again to Wilde's strong inclination towards the Catholic Church even from his Oxford days. This is further substantiated and supplemented by his friend and contemporary W. W. Ward in *An Oxford Reminiscence* (appended to Vyvyan Holland, *Son of Oscar Wilde* [1954]). There Ward makes reference to a collection of old letters written to him by Wilde, which Ward says "show him as he lives in my memory, radiant and humorous, affectionate and natural."[15] More importantly he adds: "They show, too, that his final decision to find refuge in the Roman Church was not the sudden clutch of the drowning man at the plank in the shipwreck, but a return to a first love, a love rejected, it is true, or at least rejected in the tragic progress of his self-realization, yet one that had haunted him from early days with a persistent spell."[16]

In August 1900, Wilde confessed to John Clifford Millage, the Paris correspondent of the *Daily Chronicle,* his own Catholic sympathies, which had stretched back, as we have seen, to his time as an undergraduate at Trinity College, Dublin. "He turned to religious subjects," said Millage, "and muttered most savagely: 'Much of my moral obliquity is due to the fact that my father would not allow me to become a Catholic. The artistic side of the Church would have cured my degeneracies. I intend to be received before long.'"[17] At the conclusion of his report, which was written a few days after Wilde's death, Millage observed that Wilde "tried to articulate the prayers which accompany Extreme Unction and his death-bed was one of repentance."[18] More on this later.

15 *Son of Oscar Wilde*, 219.
16 Ibid.
17 See Rev Edmund Burke, C. P., "Oscar Wilde: The Final Scene," *The London Magazine*, May 1951, 37–43; also available at poetrymagazines.org.uk/magazine/record51af.html?id=9404.
18 Ibid.

In addition, the statement above, often attributed to Lord Alfred Douglas, is unsupported by any evidence, and so must in any case be taken with some considerable reserve. We must look at the two eyewitnesses. The first is Robert Ross himself, who had received a telegram from the hotel requesting his immediate presence with "Mr Melmoth," who was dangerously ill. He took the next train back to Paris and hurried to the hotel and from there he came at once to find a priest. Here is Ross's account:

> When I went for the priest to come to his death-bed he was quite conscious and raised his hand in response to questions and satisfied the priest, Father Cuthbert Dunne of the Passionists. It was the morning before he died and for about three hours he understood what was going on (and knew I had come from the South in response to a telegram) that he was given the last sacrament.[19]

The other is, of course, the most important witness, Fr Cuthbert Dunne himself, then aged thirty-one and attached to St Joseph's Church, Paris, who ministered to Wilde in his last hours. And what we have in respect of Fr Dunne is a remarkably detailed account published in May 1961 in an article in *The London Magazine*. The article was written by Fr Edmund Burke of the same religious order as Fr Dunne.

For many years Fr Burke was a companion of Fr Dunne, who himself continued to remain silent about Wilde's death, stating that what took place at the bedside of a dying man was a sacred trust and not to be disclosed. Fr Burke tried to persuade Fr Dunne to speak out, on the basis that the matter was one of historical importance. He met with no success until eventually a "particularly vicious reference to Wilde's death" (based upon a statement in Frank Harris's biography of Wilde) caused Fr Dunne to change his mind. Fortunately Fr Dunne had kept all the evidence, classifying in an orderly fashion the original sick-call and many letters from different sources about both the death and the funeral. During the summer of 1945, five years before his death, Fr Dunne wrote a very detailed remembrance of Wilde's final hours. He also wrote a lengthy memoir of Oscar Wilde, giving the history of his various approaches to the Catholic Church throughout the years. All of

19   Ibid.

this he entrusted to Fr Burke, expressing his wish that it not be published until after his death.

It is worth recounting in some detail the moving description given by Fr Burke of Fr Dunne's encounter with Oscar Wilde, then living in room 16 of the Hotel d'Alsace, 13 Rue des Beaux-Arts [now L'Hotel Paris] under the name "Sebastian Melmoth":

> Having been informed of the patient's condition, Fr Cuthbert Dunne made the requisite preparations. His own account states: "Having been told the necessary details, I went with him, prepared to administer Baptism as well as Extreme Unction, with Holy Communion if possible."
>
> The Archives of the Passionist Church at Avenue Hoche contain an accurate note of the time of the sick-call. The entry reads:
>
> "On Thursday, November 29th, 1900, towards 4 in the evening, Father Cuthbert was called to the bedside of the once famous Oscar Wilde to receive him into the Catholic Church and administer the sacraments of the dying. He was unable to articulate but endeavored to recite the acts of Faith, etc, suggested and showed signs of a sincere conversion. The following day he passed away peacefully."
>
> That is a record of simple fact, but in the priest's personal narrative the scene springs suddenly to life: "As the 'voiture' [carriage] rolled through the dark streets that wintry night, the sad story of Oscar Wilde was in part repeated to me. When we reached the little bedroom of the hotel, the attendants were requested to leave. Robert Ross knelt by the bedside, assisting me as best he could while I administered conditional Baptism, and afterwards answering the responses while I gave Extreme Unction to the prostrate man and recited the prayers for the dying."[20]

However, the key question still remained: what was the precise condition of Oscar Wilde at that moment of supreme spiritual crisis? Fr Burke continues his account of Fr Dunne's ministrations as follows:

> Father Cuthbert Dunne was not unaware of the importance of this point. His is not only an eye-witness account; it is the narrative of one who played the leading part in that last scene. "As the man was in a semi-comatose

20   Ibid.

condition," states Fr Cuthbert Dunne, "I did not venture to administer Holy Viaticum; still, I must add that he could be roused and was roused from this state in my presence. When roused, he gave signs of being inwardly conscious. He made brave efforts to speak, and would even continue for a time trying to talk, though he could not utter articulate words. Indeed, I was fully satisfied that he understood me when told that I was about to receive him into the Catholic Church and give him the Last Sacraments. From the signs he gave, as well as from his attempted words, I was satisfied as to his full consent. And when I repeated close to his ear the Holy Names, the Acts of Contrition, Faith, Hope and Charity, with acts of humble resignation to the Will of God, he tried all through to say the words after me." [21]

Fr Burke makes reference to the fact that Fr Dunne visited Wilde several more times, "[continuing] to observe him closely, and what he saw confirmed his first impression that, although the power of speech had failed, Oscar Wilde still retained a large measure of consciousness and coherence." [22] Fr Dunne himself also stated: "At these subsequent visits, he repeated the prayers with me again and each time received Absolution."

Fr Burke sets out several more interesting facts relating to the death and burial of Wilde. The authorities quoted above, particularly Fr Dunne, would seem to establish beyond reasonable doubt the fact of Oscar Wilde's conversion, confirming in a direct way Wilde's oft-cited statement that "Catholicism is the only religion to die in." The closing words may be left to Fr Dunne, who wrote movingly of the great injustice "done to a dead man who can say no word in self-defense, and who, whatever his sins may have been, expiated them by suffering severe penalties: imprisonment, ostracism from the great world in which he had been an idol, loss of all that the cultivation of his brilliant talents had brought him, poverty in which he was left dependent on others for his sustenance. After all this, he turned to God for pardon and for the healing grace of the Sacraments in the end, and died a child of the Catholic Church." [23]

21 Ibid.
22 Ibid.
23 Ibid.

CHAPTER THIRTY-NINE
Androcles and Newman

THE CONVERSION OF
JOHN ROTHENSTEIN

IT IS AN INTERESTING FACT THAT NOT A FEW converts to the Catholic Church arrive there as the result of the effect on them of non-Catholic Christians. The most obvious example of this exists in the great number of persons who have converted, at least in a significant respect, through the direct influence of C.S. Lewis. I have written about this phenomenon on a number of occasions.[1]

1   See "C. S. Lewis, Conversion, and the 'Mad, Bad, or God Argument,'" *Saint Austin Review*, May/June 2013, 27; and "C. S. Lewis and the Mad, Bad, or God Argument: An Addendum," *Saint Austin Review*, November/December 2013, 30.

In addition, there are many who came to the Catholic Church at least indirectly through imbibing first of all Lewis's powerful arguments for the existence of God, for the historicity of the Gospels, and for the divinity of Christ. These arguments may be found in Lewis's *Mere Christianity* (revised and amplified version, 1952) and in several articles of his in two books edited by Walter Hooper, *Fern-Seed and Elephants and Other Essays on Christianity* (1975) and *God in the Dock* (1979).

Much rarer, however, are cases where an important influence on a person, who proceeds to become Catholic, originated from someone not even Christian at all, in this case George Bernard Shaw, himself never a Christian of any kind. This process may be claimed in the case of art historian and administrator Sir John Rothenstein. It must be admitted that the original influence was moving him away from Christianity, but this led through providence towards another important figure, this time St John Henry Newman, from whom the Catholic truth was gained. We can certainly learn from this case.

John Knewstub Maurice Rothenstein was born in 1901 in London. He was the son of the artist Sir William Rothenstein and the brother of the printmaker Sir Michael Rothenstein. He read modern history at Oxford and then contributed articles on art to newspapers and periodicals and taught fine art at American universities. His administrative work included being director of the Leeds, and then Sheffield, art galleries in England. This work culminated in the directorship of the Tate Gallery in London from 1938 to 1964, in which post he was a great supporter of contemporary British art, writing several books on this topic.[2] He was knighted in 1952 and died in 1992 in Oxfordshire.

Rothenstein gives an excellent account of his own conversion in an article,[3] published almost verbatim sixteen years later in *Summer's Lease* (1965), the first volume of his three-volume autobiography.[4] He starts by recounting a scripture class at his school,

2 *Augustus John* (1944); *Walter Richard Sickert* (1961); *British Art Since 1900: An Anthology* (1962); *Turner* (1964; with Martin Butlin). Later on came *An Introduction to English Painting* (1965); *Paul Nash* (1967); *John Nash* (1983); and *Modern English Painters* (3-volume revised edition) (1984).

3 "Androcles and Mr. Newman: A Fragment of Autobiography for V.T," *The Month*, January 1949, 37.

4 The other two are *Brave Day, Hideous Night* (1966) and *Time's Thievish*

Bedales, taught by the headmaster, John Haden Badley, "a spare, upright, black-bearded figure who put me in mind of an Old Testament prophet."[5] The class was taken through St Luke's Gospel and the Acts of the Apostles, verse by verse. Rothenstein's interest was so roused that he went on to read the other Gospels, in particular that of St John. What attracted his attention was "the frequency and distinctness with which Jesus claimed to be, in a quite special sense, the Son of God and a sharer in his Divinity."[6]

At this point, however, into the action comes George Bernard Shaw, or at least his writings, since Rothenstein was persuaded by the arguments in Shaw's preface to *Androcles and the Lion* (1912) that Jesus's conviction of his divinity was a delusion. Rothenstein states that his interest in religion up to this time was "casual and intermittent, and vitiated by a suspicion that it was an unexciting subject."[7] In truth, and ironically, that suspicion was killed by a "single flashing stroke"[8] from Shaw:

> Before I had read more than a few pages I knew that the relation of man to his Creator—supposing there to be a Creator—ought to be man's ultimate preoccupation. Although its immediate effect was to cause me to reject the notion of the divinity of Christ, this essay brought his personality before me with thrilling vividness. After reading Shaw, Christ was never again for me an archaic or a legendary figure, still less the Pale Galilean: but a complex, enigmatic, an overwhelming, endlessly surprising personality.[9]

Rothenstein attended the Headmaster's Scripture class with enhanced attention. The next step in his development came, albeit indirectly, from another literary giant, this time William Shakespeare. Rothenstein was confronted with something of a surprise:

> The same term we happened to be taking *Hamlet* and I fell to comparing Shakespeare with the Four Evangelists. Shakespeare's utterance is so god-like that there are times

Progress (1970).
5 "Androcles and Mr. Newman," 40; a description not repeated in *Summer's Lease*.
6 *Summer's Lease*, 32.
7 Ibid.
8 Ibid.
9 Ibid.

when it is difficult to remember that he was a man. The
Four Evangelists in comparison with Shakespeare were
quite ordinary men. Only one of them could be said to have
possessed unusual literary talent. Yet the supreme creation
of a unique poetic genius does not compare, in subtlety,
in consistency, in majesty, even in poetic quality, with the
figure which emerges from the attempts at biography of
an imaginative fisherman with a sense of metaphysics, of a
cultured and sympathetic doctor, of a publican and a terse
and competent reporter. The same transcendency marks
the central figure in all four Gospels, widely though the
authors of these differ in outlook and in literary attainment.
Him I therefore began to regard with a new reverence; and
presently with something more than reverence.[10]

The time soon came when Rothenstein was no longer able,
Shaw's persuasive arguments notwithstanding, "to believe that a
Being of such transcendent wisdom could be subject to a delusion,
or that a Being of such transcendent moral force could mislead his
disciples and, through them, a great part of mankind."[11] What he
had come to appreciate, as did such as Chesterton and many more,
was that "Jesus's claim to be God is stated in terms so specific
that they must be rejected or accepted: it cannot be ignored."[12]
At this point he cites four classic New Testament passages, all
containing this direct claim:

"And Simon Peter answered and said, 'Thou art the Christ—
the son of the living God.' And Jesus answered and said
unto him, 'Blessed art thou Simon Bar-Jonah: for flesh
and blood hath not revealed it unto thee, but my Father
which is in heaven'" (Matthew xvi, 16).

"Have I been so long time with you, and yet hast thou not
known me, Philip? He that hath seen me hath seen the
Father, and how sayest thou then, Show us the Father?"
(John xiv, 9).

"And now, O Father, glorify thou me, with thine own self,
with the glory which I had with thee before the world
was" (John xvii, 5).

10 Ibid., 33.
11 Ibid.
12 Ibid.

"Verily, verily, I say unto you, Before Abraham was, I am"
(John viii, 38).[13]

Rothenstein does not spell out the full implications here, namely
the traditional argument, pioneered in modern times by both
Lewis and Chesterton, the "Bad, Mad, or God Argument" examined in my own articles cited above, but the reasoning involved
is implicitly here as well. From this moment on, Rothenstein
accepted the divinity of Christ.

But where was he to go from here? It was plain to him that
Christ had ordained the establishment of a Church, and nobody
has ever questioned the justice of an affirmative answer to this
question. Rothenstein, however, although baptized into the Church
of England, was now a member of none. The only thing to do
was to look around in order to discover which of those bodies
claiming to be part of the Christian Church was the Church of the
Apostles. In relation to the Catholic Church, Rothenstein seems
to have imbibed from an early age the not uncommon notion
held by Anglicans that ever since the Reformation the Catholic
Church "seemed to have acted the part not only of the enemy of
England, but (what would be worse) the enemy of human liberty.
I had often heard it denounced as mercenary and corrupt and
avid of power."[14]

Open now to a possibly different perspective, he turned to further reading and, as a result, "two notions began to take hold of
my imagination; namely that [the Catholic Church] was (whatever
its imperfections) identical with the Church established by the
Apostles; and that it was animated by some vital principle which
I could not detect as being consistently present in other religious
bodies, a principle that lent a note of urgency to its exhortations,
a note of authority to its pronouncements and a note of passionate
zeal to its servants."[15]

One further step remained, and this came from another notable
figure important in the development of many converts. While
rummaging through some books in a cellar at home, Rothenstein
discovered a volume bound in red paper. It was Newman's *Apologia
Pro Vita Sua*. Casually turning the pages, "suddenly I was aware that

13   Ibid.
14   Ibid., 34–35.
15   Ibid., 35.

I was reading words which I had longed to hear, and I lay down on the floor and read on, oblivious of the hours. It was as though, having followed hitherto an erratic path across fields, scrambling through hedges and over walls, I had come out upon a broad and frequented pilgrims' way, upon which I had as a companion a tall delicate-looking young Oxford don."[16]

Rothenstein is gracious in his acknowledgment that he found certain of the subtle and far-ranging arguments set out in the *Apologia* difficult to follow, but he understood the gist of the text and the depth and integrity of the mind that expressed it. But more than this was the vision of the Catholic Church itself which, through Newman, was revealed to him:

> I was chilled by the crimes and the perfidies and above all the complacent hardness of heart of which certain of the officials for the time being of the Church were guilty, but I began to discern, far transcending these, the sublime form of the Great Society itself, embracing both the living and the dead, to which Christ had entrusted the salvation of the world, and I began to understand something of the Faith which it taught—a Faith revealed by Him, and, for nearly two thousand years, the subject of continuous elucidation, under grace, by an unending succession of wise and learned minds, by Councils and by Popes; an immense yet minutely articulated structure, as luminous and tough as burnished bronze....
>
> Once I was convinced that Christ, in claiming to be the Son of God, was neither deceived nor deceiving, the rest followed. The Church of Rome—whatever the shortcomings of many of its servants—was manifestly the Church of the Apostles, and all others in schism, in disregard of Christ's prayer that those who believed in him should be of one fold.[17]

Rothenstein confesses, in his honest way, that there were times when the Incarnation seemed to him to be "an event strange to the point of incredibility."[18] Many converts will appreciate his later reaction to this: "there was at last a time when I found it less incredible than the only alternative of which I was able to

16   Ibid.
17   Ibid., 36–37.
18   Ibid., 37.

conceive: a world empty of meaning."[19] He acknowledges that there were other elements in his conversion, notably his confusion and eventual repulsion by "the vague, well-intentioned Liberalism in which I grew up, in which all was flux and without substance; which offered no hard answers to hard questions."[20] There came for him, therefore, the day in 1926 when "on my knees before a Catholic priest, in the crypt of Westminster Cathedral, I abjured my errors and entered what with Newman I had come to believe to be the One Fold of the Redeemer."[21] In due course, this step was also taken by his wife, Elizabeth, and his daughter, Lucy.

Rothenstein maintains his altogether realistic approach to the Catholic Church, seen in the quotation above, in the conclusion with which he follows this account of his conversion, one which is understandable in these days when there are so many problems in the Church:

> I had indeed come to believe that Christ was God; I believed that, in spite of the knavery and folly of many of its servants throughout the ages, the Roman Catholic Church, as a matter of simple fact—in so far, that is, as a historical fact is ever simple—was the Church established by Christ.[22]

In these troubled and difficult times, it may be asked, "Where do we find the Catholic Church today?" The answer is in the nearest parish church, under the jurisdiction of a bishop in communion with the reigning pope. This continues to be the case in all times, irrespective of the existence at certain times of the crimes and the perfidies and hardness of heart of which certain officials for the time being of the Church may be guilty.

19 Ibid.
20 Ibid., 38.
21 Ibid., 37.
22 Ibid., 38.

CHAPTER FORTY

Does the Catholic Church Still Want to Make Converts?

THE CLASSIC VIEW AMONG CATHOLICS OF CON-version to the Catholic Church, as can be seen in the previous chapters of this book, is that it is a vital matter, one of great seriousness and one focused on the need to join the one true Church and to put the case to inquirers for taking that step. To take just one example, that of Saint John Henry Newman, we can see the stress put on the fact that the Church is the "one true fold of Christ," "the one fold of the Redeemer," and similar powerful phrases. As the great priest-physicist Fr Stanley Jaki, author of ten books on Newman, explains it, "Implied in [those phrases] was the message that joining the Catholic Church as that very Fold was not a luxury or a choice, but a duty, the supreme duty available for man on this earth."[1]

---

1 Introduction to John Beaumont, *Converts to Rome: A Guide to Notable Converts from Britain and Ireland during the Twentieth Century* (2006), ii.

As Fr Jaki emphasized, Newman "kept telling prospective converts that it made more than good sense to sacrifice everything for the one great valuable pearl."[2] In the same vein is another favorite expression of his, that conversion to the Catholic Church is "the only safe way to salvation."[3] There is no fudge to be found there. The thing is crystal-clear.

It is also intensely practical. The teaching of the Church, as well expressed by Fr Jaki, is that "for each individual there is in store the fearsome alternative, the one between eternal salvation [and] eternal damnation. The view of that alternative is the triggering force in each true conversion, notable or not."[4] Cited in support by Fr Jaki is Newman himself, who was faced with the specter of that alternative. One need only refer to the letters he wrote at that time to his sister Jemima. As Fr Jaki puts it, "There he spoke of the possibility that eternal damnation might be his lot were he not to convert and hide thereby in his bosom the fact that there were compelling reasons for joining the Church of Rome, the One True Fold of salvation."[5]

This narrow way is very often not a comfortable one. As Jaki says, "it takes time and again special courage as well as resolve to face various forms of backlash."[6] The backlash in Newman's day often consisted of well-nigh complete ostracism by family and friends, something that Newman knew well from his own experience. Today the position is as yet not so uncomfortable for those joining the Catholic Church, but the terrible scourge of the clerical sexual abuse crisis, a matter in most cases (80%) not of pedophilia but of homosexuality with adolescent and adult males, has left Catholics under fire from the secular world to an extent that has not been seen for a long time. Catholics in my country are not yet required to make the ultimate sacrifice as my descendants had to do at the time of that looting and piracy exercise known as the English Reformation. But signs are there that things are getting worse and worse quickly.

2   Introduction to John Beaumont, *Converts from Britain and Ireland in the Nineteenth Century* (2007), vii.
3   Ibid.
4   Ibid., iii.
5   Ibid., iv.
6   Introduction to Beaumont, *Converts to Rome*, ii.

A DIFFERENT APPROACH?

Is the classic approach to conversion correct? It would seem so and, as we have seen, this approach was adopted by a figure now named a Saint. However, at this point one must hesitate, since recently there have been developments that cause some disquiet. One is referring here to certain recent statements made by high ranking figures in the Church, including Pope Francis.

Before examining all this, it is important to put it in context. That we are living in difficult times in the Church is surely undeniable. It is perhaps best summed up by Richard Rex, Professor of Reformation History in the University of Cambridge and Polkinghorne Fellow in Theology and Religious Studies at Queens' College, Cambridge. An expert in the history of the Tudors and of the Reformation, Rex is the author of several specialist books, including *The Theology of John Fisher* (1991) and *The Tudors* (2006). His most recent book is *The Making of Martin Luther* (2017). Here is what Richard Rex states in "A Faith in Doubt," his review of Ross Douthat's *To Change the Church: Pope Francis and the Future of Catholicism* (2018):

> It is beyond question that the Roman Catholic Church is currently in the throes of one of the greatest crises in its two-millennium history. In human terms, its future might be said to be in doubt for the first time since the Reformation. The broad contours of the present crisis are the onward march of secularization in Europe and North America, the purging of Christians from the ancient heartlands of the Middle East, and the erosion of South American Catholicism by the missions of the Protestant and prosperity gospels. More specifically, the horrific and continuing revelations of the sexual and physical abuse of the vulnerable by the clergy, and of the failure of the institutional Church to identify and address the issue, have in some places turned a Catholic retreat into a rout. The dramatic and utterly unforeseen collapse of Catholicism in Ireland in little more than a generation, for example, harks back to the tectonic religious shifts of the early sixteenth century. Only in Africa is there much by way of good news, and it is not always clear how good that news is.[7]

7 *First Things*, April 2018, 47; https://www.firstthings.com/article/2018/04/a-church-in-doubt.

Now, not a few Catholic theologians and philosophers have expressed a certain degree of perplexity about some statements made by or associated with the pope. These have included such notables as Germain Grisez, John Finnis, Thomas Weinandy, Aidan Nichols, John Rist, Robert Spaemann, Josef Seifert, Peter Kwasniewski, and John Lamont. There have also been the allegations made by Archbishop Viganò over Pope Francis's involvement in the case of Cardinal McCarrick, where he is alleged to have removed sanctions imposed by his predecessor on McCarrick and then to have made the now disgraced ex-Cardinal an advisor on the appointment of "gay-friendly" bishops in the United States. On a more formal level, *dubia* were issued under the names of Cardinals Meissner, Burke, Caffarra, and Brandmüller, to which Pope Francis has never replied. These complaints have most obviously concerned the post-synodal apostolic exhortation *Amoris Laetitia*, issued by Pope Francis in 2016, following the Synods on the Family held in 2014 and 2015, and stating that divorced and remarried Catholics might be able to receive Holy Communion without an ecclesiastical annulment process. This implies a rejection of the direct words of Christ and flatly contradicts the statements of the Holy Scriptures about marriage, divorce, and the reception of the Holy Eucharist.

There have been other statements made by Pope Francis in the public arena that have caused concern, notably the "Who am I to judge?" statement regarding homosexual people seeking God, which garnered Francis an LGBT magazine's "Person of the Year" award. Then there are the cases where the Pope has publicly praised or raised to influential positions prelates and lay people who openly dissent from Catholic doctrine and morals, or replaced orthodox Catholic members of the Pontifical Academy for Life with heterodox ones.

In reaction to all this, in 2015 thirteen cardinals wrote about the abuse of the Synod. In 2016 there were the dubia of the four cardinals. Other statements have included the following: in 2016 a critical analysis of *Amoris Laetitia* was sent to Cardinal Sodano, then Dean of the College of Cardinals. In 2017 there was a letter from John Finnis and Germain Grisez to the same effect, and, more notably, a "Filial Correction" that went directly to the pope the same year before being published. In 2019 there was an Open Letter signed eventually by about seventy figures. An Open Letter issued Easter week of 2019 was signed by several eminent theologians, both clerical and lay, accusing the pope of heresy. Finally, there is another Open Letter dated September 16, 2022 with forty-six signatures, consisting of four bishops, several priests, and numerous Catholic scholars. All of those communications sent so far have been ignored.

The situation outlined in the previous paragraph sets things in perspective. This chapter makes no attempt to answer the various questions raised, and the present writer has no authority to do so. However, it is important to note that the overall uncertainty caused has given rise to perplexity in other important areas as well. All these issues do have a significance for the question of conversion for the simple reason that they all may have a negative effect on someone considering whether to join the Catholic Church. The example I want to cite does relate to the question of converts. This is that on the one hand the Holy Father speaks frequently about the imperative of evangelization and spreading the faith; on the other hand, he rarely misses an opportunity to condemn proselytizing on behalf of the Church. Does this mean, then, that there has been a change on this point in the Church? This is a very important question and must be examined here.

What, then, to start with the basics, does this word "proselytism" mean? Well, it is defined in the *Oxford English Dictionary* as an act of attempting to convert people to another religion or opinion. The word *proselytize* is derived from the Greek prefix προσ- (*pros-*, "toward") and the verb ἔρχομαι (*érchomai*, "to come") in the form of προσήλυτος (*prosélytos*, "newcomer").

Now, in 2013 Pope Francis referred to proselytism as "solemn nonsense" (this was in an interview with an atheist journalist, Eugenio Scalfari, the text of which was unfortunately not reviewed by the pope before publication—wise or not?!). Later on, during an ecumenical service of Vespers at St Paul's Outside the Walls he urged the rejection of proselytism and competition in all their forms. Furthermore, in 2016 he made the following statement: "Proselytism among Christians is a sin. The Church never grows through proselytism. Proselytism among Christians is therefore in itself a serious sin because it contradicts the very dynamics of becoming and remaining Christians. The Church is not a football team in search of fans." The present pope is nothing if not persistent, and similar statements have been made by him on many occasions. For example, in March 2019 in Rabat, Morocco, he told the tiny Catholic community there that "the Church grows not through proselytism but by attraction." Yes, we all know that in many cases what converts a person is more what we do than what we say, but as stated earlier, it has always been recognized by the Church that reasoned arguments put forward for the Faith can be very effective indeed. However, in Rabat Pope Francis told his audience that their mission was not to convert their neighbors but to live in brotherhood with other faiths.

In December 2019 Pope Francis had occasion to speak to a group of high school students at Rome's Pilo Albertelli classical secondary school. During the course of his remarks, he told them that speech should never be used in order to convince a non-believer of the truths of the Catholic Faith. As was stated by commentators, this does seem, even allowing for the various nuances in connotation of the word "proselytism," an apparent repudiation of the Great Commission to baptize and teach all nations (Mt 28:16-20). The pope went on to say:

> I have to live in accordance with my faith. And it will be my testimony that will awaken the curiosity of the other who says: "But why do you do this?" And that's where I can talk. But listen, never, ever advance the Gospel through proselytism. If someone says he is a disciple of Jesus and comes to you with proselytism, he is not a disciple of Jesus. We shouldn't proselytize, the Church does not grow from proselytizing.

As we have seen, Pope Francis has often mentioned his hostility to "proselytism," but on this occasion, he seems to have clarified that for him proselytism consists in any kind of communication of the Gospel using speech. As stated above, this leaves this whole issue in a condition of great uncertainty. That cannot be good and may deter Catholics who naturally seek the conversion of friends and acquaintances, conversion to what they see, following Church teaching, as the one true Church of Christ.

If we leave this whole matter at that, then all one can say is that it looks as if the present writer may be in big trouble. In both of my books on converts I try to bring out the reasons that people have for becoming Catholics, drawing attention to the most powerful arguments in order to bring as many people as possible to Holy Mother Church. It would seem that according to Pope Francis I ought to be castigated as a sinner and put in a place of confinement, especially since the two books combined are 1,606 pages long. Thank goodness that the Mamertine Prison in Rome is no longer used for its original purpose! The other possibility, of course, at which I shrink, is being hurled down from the Tarpeian rock.

What can one say in response? Surely that proselytism, or the urging of conversion, should be an action highly encouraged among Catholics. After all, didn't Our Blessed Lord say in no uncertain terms, "All authority in heaven and on earth has been given to me. Go therefore and make disciples of all nations, baptizing them in the name of the Father and of the Son and of the Holy Spirit, teaching them to observe all that I have commanded you; and lo, I am with you always, to the close of the age" (Mt 28, 19-20)?

So which is it? Are Catholics supposed to be trying to convert people and bring them into the Church or not? There is clearly a certain amount of uncertainty and ambiguity here. In the Christian context, the term proselytism was often used as a synonym for missionary activity. More recently, however, as was explained by the Congregation for the Doctrine of the Faith in 2007, the term has taken on a negative connotation, to mean the promotion of a religion by using means, and for motives, contrary to the spirit of the Gospel; that is, which do not safeguard the freedom and dignity of the human person. There is, then, a distinction to be made between proposing the faith—understood to be a good thing, indeed obligatory—and imposing it through aggressive or coercive techniques, which is seen as wrong. Of course, it is probably true that the majority of converts are not primarily impelled by the words of reasoned argument, helpful though they may be, but by the witness of those living an authentically Catholic life. As has often been said, and moreover by both Pope Benedict XVI and by Pope Francis himself, the Church grows by attracting others. And what attracts is our witness. But we must not throw out the baby with the bath water. The reasons cited by converts are surely themselves often a very powerful witness, as is shown by the correspondence of Newman with potential converts set out in Fr Jaki's book *Newman to Converts* (2001). The problem arises when, as has often been the case recently, we speak of proselytism and not evangelization. And also, the present writer has witnessed Catholics, even priests, telling, for example, a Baptist not to convert to the Catholic Church, but to remain a good Baptist. This is surely not true Catholic evangelization.

As far as the question of proselytism is concerned, it is not necessarily the case, then, that the distinction between proselytism and evangelization is to the point. However, in relation to evangelization, there is another issue. During an inter-religious meeting in Abu Dhabi the Pope said in a joint statement with the Grand Imam of al-Azhar (an important Sunni Muslim) that "the pluralism and diversity of religions are willed by God." This came as a considerable shock to many. For example, Dr John Lamont commented as follows:

> Taken in its normal meaning, the statement that the pluralism and diversity of religions is willed by God in his wisdom is directly contrary to the Catholic faith. The pluralism and diversity of religions is an evil, and as such cannot be willed by God. These religions contradict each other on doctrinal and moral issues. It must therefore be the case that at least some of these religions are in error where they disagree; and it is a grave evil to hold false dogmatic and moral beliefs. Moreover, the Christian teaching is that there is only one true religion, the religion that worships the Most Holy Trinity. Religions that do not worship the Holy Trinity are false religions, that in themselves cause harm to their worshipers. As such, they are evils.[8]

Now, it is the case that various explanations have been proposed for the pope's statement, for example that one must draw a distinction between God's "active or positive will," which concerns that which is good, true and beautiful, and his "permissive will," by which He allows that things will take place that are not in accord with the order He established, arguing that the official statement refers only to the latter case. However, it is surely the case that the Church teaches that God's wisdom and goodness

8 "Francis and the Joint Declaration on Human Fraternity: A Public Repudiation of the Catholic Faith," rorate-caeli.blogspot.com/2019/02.

mean that He will only will to permit an evil if the evil that is permitted will lead to a greater good, and this seems not to be the case here. If the Abu Dhabi statement is correct and diversity of religions is willed by God, why on earth should anyone bother to convert to the Catholic Church?

The whole issue here was taken up by Fr Thomas Weinandy, OFM Cap, a member of the International Theological Commission and author of many books:

> Pope Francis is noted for his ambiguous statements, but I find the indeterminate meaning contained in the Abu Dhabi statement the most egregious. By implication, it not only devalues the person of Jesus, but it also, and more so, strikes at the very heart of God the Father's eternal will. Thus, such studied ambiguity undermines the very Gospel itself. Such implicit doctrinal subversion of so foundational a mystery of the faith on the part of Peter's successor is for me and for many in the Church, particularly the laity, not simply inexcusable, but it most of all evokes profound sadness, for it imperils the supreme love that Jesus rightly deserves and merits.[9]

Fr Weinandy concluded his article as follows:

> Regardless, no one, not even a pontiff, can undo or override the will of God the Father concerning Jesus his Son. It is God the Father who "has highly exalted him and bestowed upon him the name which is above every name." The Father has eternally decreed that at the name of Jesus, and not at the name of Buddha, Mohammed, or the name of any other past, present, or future religious founder, "every knee should bow, in heaven and on earth and under the earth, and every tongue confess that Jesus Christ is Lord." To do so is not simply to glorify Jesus, but also "to the glory of God the Father" (Phil 2:9-11). In his love the Father has given the world Jesus his Son (Jn 3:16), and "there is no other name under heaven given among men by which we must be saved" (Acts 4:12). In this supreme truth we are to rejoice in gratitude and praise.[10]

9 "Pope Francis, the Uniqueness of Christ, and the Will of the Father," *Catholic World Report*, June 2019.
10 Ibid.

Such concerns have not been limited to statements of the Holy Father. We have already seen that Bishop Robert Barron told Ben Shapiro that Christ is merely the privileged route to salvation and that an atheist of good will can be saved by following his conscience; not a word about the obligation to believe in the Lord Jesus, to be baptized, and to join the Catholic Church. Is Christ merely the privileged route for some? That is not the Catholic position. Much authority could be cited on this point, and has been since the statement was made. It is best, however, simply to refer to the Vatican II document *Lumen Gentium*, which states as follows:

> Basing itself upon Sacred Scripture and Tradition, it teaches that the Church, now sojourning on earth as an exile, is necessary for salvation. Christ, present to us in His Body, which is the Church, is the one Mediator and the unique way of salvation. In explicit terms He Himself affirmed the *necessity of faith and baptism* and thereby affirmed also the *necessity of the Church*, for through baptism as through a door men enter the Church. Whosoever, therefore, knowing that the Catholic Church was made necessary by Christ, *would refuse to enter or to remain in it, could not be saved.*[11]

Bishop Barron refers to Newman's oft-cited description of conscience as the "aboriginal vicar of Christ," but Newman is referring to an informed conscience, and Bishop Barron says nothing about this. Once again, the question that arises is as follows: if Bishop Barron's approach is correct, why should anyone in the situation of Ben Shapiro convert?

CONCLUDING THOUGHTS

So where do we stand? Is Saint John Henry Newman an outdated relic of the past and to be passed over? This is clearly not the case. In reality, the answer is quite simple and straightforward. First of all, the statements I have just referred to will be sorted out. That is what we have a Church for. So there is no need for fear. What we must do, in any case, is to hang on to the traditional and classic teaching in respect of conversion to the Catholic Church, the One True Fold, the One Ark of Salvation, as Newman so often expressed it.

11   Chapter II, n. 14.

This tradition is restated forcefully in the Vatican II Decree on Ecumenism (*Unitatis Redintegratio*), where the Council Fathers referred to the Church as "God's only flock, like a standard lifted on high for the nations to see it."[12] They also stated as follows:

> It was to the apostolic college alone, of which Peter is the head, that we believe that Our Lord entrusted all the blessings of the New Covenant, in order to establish on earth the one Body of Christ into which all those should be fully incorporated who belong in any way to the people of God.[13]

Fr Stanley Jaki's response expresses it also, and in a powerful and most compelling way:

> These eternal truths are not a matter of interpretations and reinterpretations, let alone a matter of the whims, fads, and fancies of ever gullible times, but a matter of truths guaranteed by Almighty God who cared so much for such truths as to have His own Son to die on the cross in order to communicate them to us, failing men and women.[14]

The classic and traditional approach to conversion is as strong as ever it was. One may come full circle here. As was stated by the anonymous proofreader referred to in the foreword to this book, when we look at the challenges and in many cases physical and mental hardships so many converts had to face on their journey, their witness and writings afford us such a great opportunity for intercessory prayer and self-denial.

12 Chapter 1, n. 2.
13 Chapter 1, n. 3.
14 Introduction to Beaumont, *Converts to Rome* (2006), v–vi.

Made in the USA
Las Vegas, NV
14 January 2023

65592260R00215